LIFE EMBODIED

McGILL-QUEEN'S STUDIES IN THE HISTORY OF IDEAS
Series Editor: Philip J. Cercone

1 Problems of Cartesianism
Edited by Thomas M. Lennon, John M. Nicholas, and John W. Davis

2 The Development of the Idea of History in Antiquity
Gerald A. Press

3 Claude Buffier and Thomas Reid: Two Common-Sense Philosophers
Louise Marcil-Lacoste

4 Schiller, Hegel, and Marx: State, Society, and the Aesthetic Ideal of Ancient Greece
Philip J. Kain

5 John Case and Aristotelianism in Renaissance England
Charles B. Schmitt

6 Beyond Liberty and Property: The Process of Self-Recognition in Eighteenth-Century Political Thought
J.A.W. Gunn

7 John Toland: His Methods, Manners, and Mind
Stephen H. Daniel

8 Coleridge and the Inspired Word
Anthony John Harding

9 The Jena System, 1804–5: Logic and Metaphysics
G.W.F. Hegel
Translation edited by John W. Burbidge and George di Giovanni
Introduction and notes by H.S. Harris

10 Consent, Coercion, and Limit: The Medieval Origins of Parliamentary Democracy
Arthur P. Monahan

11 Scottish Common Sense in Germany, 1768–1800: A Contribution to the History of Critical Philosophy
Manfred Kuehn

12 Paine and Cobbett: The Transatlantic Connection
David A. Wilson

13 Descartes and the Enlightenment
Peter A. Schouls

14 Greek Scepticism: Anti-Realist Trends in Ancient Thought
Leo Groarke

15 The Irony of Theology and the Nature of Religious Thought
Donald Wiebe

16 Form and Transformation: A Study in the Philosophy of Plotinus
Frederic M. Schroeder

17 From Personal Duties towards Personal Rights: Late Medieval and Early Modern Political Thought, c. 1300–c. 1650
Arthur P. Monahan

18 The Main Philosophical Writings and the Novel *Allwill*
Friedrich Heinrich Jacobi
Translated and edited by George di Giovanni

37 The Subaltern Appeal to Experience: Self-Identity, Late Modernity, and the Politics of Immediacy
Craig Ireland

38 The Invention of Journalism Ethics: The Path to Objectivity and Beyond, Second Edition
Stephen J.A. Ward

39 The Recovery of Wonder: The New Freedom and the Asceticism of Power
Kenneth L. Schmitz

40 Reason and Self-Enactment in History and Politics: Themes and Voices of Modernity
F.M. Barnard

41 The More Moderate Side of Joseph de Maistre: Views on Political Liberty and Political Economy
Cara Camcastle

42 Democratic Society and Human Needs
Jeff Noonan

43 The Circle of Rights Expands: Modern Political Thought after the Reformation, 1521 (Luther) to 1762 (Rousseau)
Arthur P. Monahan

44 The Canadian Founding: John Locke and Parliament
Janet Ajzenstat

45 Finding Freedom: Hegel's Philosophy and the Emancipation of Women
Sara MacDonald

46 When the French Tried to Be British: Party, Opposition, and the Quest for Civil Disagreement, 1814–1848
J.A.W. Gunn

47 Under Conrad's Eyes: The Novel as Criticism
Michael John DiSanto

48 Media, Memory, and the First World War
David Williams

49 An Aristotelian Account of Induction: Creating Something from Nothing
Louis Groarke

50 Social and Political Bonds: A Mosaic of Contrast and Convergence
F.M. Barnard

51 Archives and the Event of God: The Impact of Michel Foucault on Philosophical Theology
David Galston

52 Between the Queen and the Cabby: Olympe de Gouges's Rights of Women
John R. Cole

53 Nature and Nurture in French Social Sciences, 1859–1914 and Beyond
Martin S. Staum

54 Public Passion: Rethinking the Grounds for Political Justice
Rebecca Kingston

55 Rethinking the Political:
The Sacred, Aesthetic Politics, and the Collège de Sociologie
Simonetta Falasca-Zamponi

56 Materialist Ethics and Life-Value
Jeff Noonan

57 Hegel's *Phenomenology*:
The Dialectical Justification of Philosophy's First Principles
Ardis B. Collins

58 The Social History of Ideas in Quebec, 1760–1896
Yvan Lamonde
Translated by Phyllis Aronoff and Howard Scott

59 Ideas, Concepts, and Reality
John W. Burbidge

60 The Enigma of Perception
D.L.C. Maclachlan

61 Nietzsche's Justice:
Naturalism in Search of an Ethics
Peter R. Sedgwick

62 The Idea of Liberty in Canada during the Age of Atlantic Revolutions, 1776–1838
Michel Ducharme
Translated by Peter Feldstein

63 From White to Yellow:
The Japanese in European Racial Thought, 1300–1735
Rotem Kowner

64 The Crisis of Modernity
Augusto Del Noce
Edited and translated by Carlo Lancellotti

65 Imprinting Britain:
Newspapers, Sociability, and the Shaping of British North America
Michael Eamon

66 The Form of Politics:
Aristotle and Plato on Friendship
John von Heyking

67 War as Paradox:
Clausewitz and Hegel on Fighting Doctrines and Ethics
Youri Cormier

68 Network Democracy:
Conservative Politics and the Violence of the Liberal Age
Jared Giesbrecht

69 A Singular Case:
Debating China's Political Economy in the European Enlightenment
Ashley Eva Millar

70 Not Even a God Can Save Us Now:
Reading Machiavelli after Heidegger
Brian Harding

71 Before Copernicus:
The Cultures and Contexts of Scientific Learning in the Fifteenth Century
Edited by Rivka Feldhay and F. Jamil Ragep

72 The Culturalist Challenge to Liberal Republicanism
Michael Lusztig

73 God and Government: Martin Luther's Political Thought
Jarrett A. Carty

74 The Age of Secularization
Augusto Del Noce
Edited and Translated by Carlo Lancellotti

75 Emancipatory Thinking: Simone de Beauvoir and Contemporary Political Thought
Elaine Stavro

76 Life Embodied: The Promise of Vital Force in Spanish Modernity
Nicolás Fernández-Medina

LIFE EMBODIED

The Promise of Vital Force in Spanish Modernity

Nicolás Fernández-Medina

McGill-Queen's University Press
Montreal & Kingston • London • Chicago

ISBN 978-0-7735-5336-1 (cloth)
ISBN 978-0-7735-5337-8 (paper)
ISBN 978-0-7735-5407-8 (ePDF)
ISBN 978-0-7735-5408-5 (ePUB)

Legal deposit second quarter 2018
Bibliothèque nationale du Québec

Printed in Canada on acid-free paper that is 100% ancient forest free (100% post-consumer recycled), processed chlorine free

Funded by the Government of Canada | Financé par le gouvernement du Canada | Canada | Canada Council for the Arts | Conseil des arts du Canada

We acknowledge the support of the Canada Council for the Arts, which last year invested $153 million to bring the arts to Canadians throughout the country.

Nous remercions le Conseil des arts du Canada de son soutien. L'an dernier, le Conseil a investi 153 millions de dollars pour mettre de l'art dans la vie des Canadiennes et des Canadiens de tout le pays.

Library and Archives Canada Cataloguing in Publication

Fernández-Medina, Nicolás, author
Life embodied: the promise of vital force in Spanish modernity / Nicolás Fernández-Medina.

(McGill-Queen's studies in the history of ideas; 76)
Includes bibliographical references and index.
Issued in print and electronic formats.
ISBN 978-0-7735-5336-1 (cloth). – ISBN 978-0-7735-5337-8 (paper). – ISBN 978-0-7735-5407-8 (ePDF). – ISBN 978-0-7735-5408-5 (ePUB)

1. Spanish literature – History and criticism. 2. Modernism (Literature) – Spain. 3. Life in literature. 4. Vital force. I. Title. II. Series: McGill-Queen's studies in the history of ideas; 76

PQ6041.F47 2018 | 860.9'354 | C2018-900039-2
C2018-900040-6

This book was typeset by Marquis Interscript in 10/12 New Baskerville.

Contents

Figures

Preface

Vital force, or the immanent energy that promotes the processes of life and growth in the body and in nature, has always proved a source of endless fascination and controversy. Early pre-Socratic philosophers gazed into the splendours of the firmament and pondered what animated the infinite, living universe of multitude and change. Plato and Aristotle were equally absorbed with the wonders of vital force. In Plato's estimation, life was a crude reflection of a superlative world to which our spirit essence ascended when we died, and he firmly introduced into philosophical discourse the concept of an animating soul. Aristotle, for his part, determined that the soul, conceived as a type of entelechy, not only imbued the living body with its qualities and functions, but also served as the true principle of vitality. "Life is in the soul," he averred in his *Metaphysics*, "and hence happiness is there, too."[1] The question of what vitalizes the human body and differentiates it from lifeless matter, or what channels organic energy into a transformative flux of supreme creation and renewal apparent in all living beings, has always haunted our collective consciousness, whether it be through primitive creation myths, the philosophical controversies of the soul's immortality, neo-vitalist organicism, or modern-day quantum mechanics. And if history is any judge, we have never felt quite satisfied with the answers offered to explain the vital force we sense so profoundly within our bodies. The debates presently under way on machine-regulated life, abortion, cloning, dietetics, homeopathy, assisted suicide, reproductive technologies, alternative medicine, bioenergetic therapy, and gene manipulation, to name only a few, suffice to tell us that the enigma of

1 Aristotle, *The Philosophy of Aristotle*, 109.

what breathes life into our bodies and minds is still very much a part of our ongoing cultural dialogue.[2]

This book deals with the narratives of vital force informing Spanish modernity. These narratives reflected, as I argue, much more than the scientific or philosophical theorizing about body functioning. I contend that they served as formidable vehicles for reimagining the linkages between body and world, and thus proved to be very effective mediums through which to mount critiques of authority in Spain and its claims to religious, scientific, philosophical, and literary legitimacy. By attending to particular figures who were fundamental in elaborating these narratives at key historical junctures between the late-seventeenth and early-twentieth centuries, I have discovered that the concept of vital force was tirelessly deployed in innovative ways and across various knowledge domains to unpack the increasingly complex dynamics between interiority and exteriority. For a range of Spanish trailblazers in the arts and sciences, it also provided not only a unique critical space for unveiling the epistemological practices that articulated the ground of bodily existence, but also a broad platform from which to affirm that the determinants of power, no matter how dispersed or discriminating, required constant redefinition, particularly as they pertained to the body and its potentialities. Viewed from this perspective, this book maintains that the various attempts over time to grasp the mystery of vital force in Spain and establish its exact material locus – the blood, heart, brain, lungs, viscera, nerves, fibres, cells, protoplasm, bodily self, or the vast realm of nature extending into the farthest reaches of the cosmos – reveal new and important aspects of how Spanish culture came to terms with the ever-changing corporeal and sensory relations of existence and the embodiment of life. Despite the diversity of figures, texts, and periods analyzed throughout this book, it revolves around four core points of coincidence that structure its main argument: the unstable category of the body, the anxiety over the nature of the soul, the complex epistemologies of resistance, and the necessity of reform.

As I explore theories of vital force in Spain in various periods and regional and local contexts, I will also refer to the related term "vitalism," which encompasses a constellation of doctrines premised on the assumption that vital force, and the life functions of living organisms, cannot be explained solely through physical and chemical laws, nor, as attempted

2 In *After Life*, Eugene Thacker remarks: "Today, in an era of biopolitics it seems that life is everywhere at stake and yet it is nowhere the same. The question of how and whether to value life is at the core of contemporary debates over bare life and the state of exception" (ix).

in many cases, through theological revelations. Likewise, the term vitalism – a term the French physician Charles-Louis Dumas popularized in 1800 to develop Paul-Joseph Barthez's pioneering theories on the properties of living bodies – serves a heuristic purpose, in that it will allow me not only to string together various theories of vital force within a transnational landscape, but also distinguish particular nodes of vitalist theory, as it were, such as Enlightenment vitalism, Montpellier vitalism, neo-Hippocratic vitalism, and so on. Ultimately, my use of the concept "vital force" in the Spanish frame is purposively comprehensive, as it brings into view the rich indeterminacy that was the hallmark of competing theories about living phenomena.

The difficulty in determining what generative energy constitutes and promotes life, and from where it originates exactly, has always complicated the idea of vital force in Spain in intriguing ways. To begin with, such difficulty stimulated a plethora of innovative research efforts, beginning in the seventeenth century, that were responsible for the general commonality of focus with respect to new methods of articulating life philosophies, whether it be in medicine, literature, or other disciplines. However, it also produced substantial interference on a more fundamental level when it came to erecting coherent frameworks (basic assumptions, bridging principles, etc.) that could extend lines of convergence across rapidly expanding fields of inquiry. All the same, to inquire into vital force has always meant rendering *visible*, through dissection, microscopy, experimentation, performance, writing, criticism, and theory, concrete living bodies and the strange and remarkable workings of the larger organic realm in which they thrive. It becomes readily apparent that no matter how diligently we have endeavoured to discover what vital force is exactly, no matter how microscopically we have scrutinized it and subjected it to all types of cutting-edge instruments and technological analyses to pinpoint its genesis, it has eluded our ability to fully comprehend it. Josef Seifert said it well: "the essence of life is irreducible to physical systems of any sort."[3] This complex and admittedly paradoxical epistemological enterprise of striving to grasp the unknowable has never ceased, never abated. In fact, to this day it has only spurred us on to probe more deeply into who and what we are, as is evident in the criticism and philosophy of Georges Canguilhem, Michel Foucault, Giorgio Agamben, Gilles Deleuze, Félix Guattari, Antonio Negri, and Rosi Braidotti, to name just a handful of scholars who in the past few decades have set the tone of the contemporary discussion on life, including

3 Seifert, *What Is Life?* 75.

animal life, organic life, intelligent life, technological life, posthuman life, biopower, biopolitics, biophilia, biocentrism. The list goes on.

It is with this alluring idea of unknowability in mind that we can properly frame the censure of positivist materialism made by the American naturalist John Burroughs in *The Breath of Life* of 1915. It is worth pausing on Burroughs's attack on positivism during the immense annihilation of life that was the First World War, since it underscores a fundamental point I wish to make in this book concerning epistemology and vital force in the Spanish context: the unknowable, particularly as inflected through the vast complexities of bodily functioning, is an integral part of the contradictory, double-edged movement of possibility and disintegration, emancipation and subjection, that is modernity. With poise and eloquence, Burroughs cannot but acknowledge in *The Breath of Life* the great triumphs of science and technique across the generations, yet he beseeches the prophets of the modern age to re-engage vitalist theory and liberate thought from the straitjacket of dogmatic authority, whatever its guise. As Burroughs laments, it was the height of hubris to dismiss, as countless scientists and philosophers had done in the name of progress since René Descartes, the study of vital force as impractical – or, worse yet, as unscientific and irrelevant. We must recall that Jacques Loeb's *The Mechanistic Conception of Life: Biological Essays*, published three years before *The Breath of Life*, had sharply discounted the epistemological validity of a vital force and proposed in no uncertain terms that "the problem of the beginning and end of individual life is physico-chemically clear."[4] Loeb was responding in part to advances in biology undertaken at the turn of the century by the likes of Hans Driesch, who claimed to have proven the existence of a vital force in nature – what he called entelechy, with a nod to Aristotle – during experiments on sea-urchin embryos. What Burroughs lays out with a prescient clarity during this period of carnage and war is that imposing limits on the enduring discovery of life in all its wondrous forms and infinite complexity is a type of authoritarian control that forecloses possibilities of new knowledge about our bodies, ourselves, and what we can become as individuals and as a community. It is this future-oriented perspective, as Burroughs advises, that dwells at the heart of the modern. The question of vital force – a phrase I will use throughout this book to designate these types of complexities in approaching the organic and living in terms of a fundamental life principle – thus provides a potent way to further define modernity's constitutive dynamics and its

4 Loeb, *The Mechanistic*, 14.

epistemological legacies. As Burroughs notes, a commanding and disconcerting fact has stared us boldly in the face since the beginning:

> When we regard all the phenomena of life and the spell it seems to put on inert matter, so that it behaves so differently from the same matter before it is drawn into the life circuit, when we see how it lifts up a world of dead particles out of the soil against gravity into trees and animals; how it changes the face of the earth; how it comes and goes while matter stays; how it defies chemistry and physics to evoke it from the non-living; how its departure, or cessation, lets matter fall back to the inorganic – when we consider these and others like them, we seem compelled to think of life as something, some force or principle in itself.[5]

The significance of theories of vital force in Spain has passed practically unnoticed, and no single study to date has systematically addressed the topic.[6] Much of the research on vital force in Spain centres on the neo-vitalist movement between the 1890s and the 1930s (including Friedrich Nietzsche, Henri Bergson, José Ortega y Gasset, etc.) and its influence on the cultural revolution known as modernism. In recent years, however, significant attention has been paid to the subject of vital force – and vitalism more generally – in various fields, as I demonstrate in the Introduction. Simply put, the question of vital force is of more than antiquarian interest. Certainly, it adds depth and dimension not

5 Burroughs, *The Breath of Life*, 33.

6 Rafael Amo Usanos's *El principio vital del ser humano en Ireneo, Orígenes, Agustín, Tomás de Aquino y la antropología teológica española reciente* (2007) is the book-length study that has come closest to tackling the topic, yet it is strictly confined to elucidating the rapport between theology and the philosophy of biology. Usanos's guiding aim is "to know what philosophical models the theologians in question have used to explain the vital principle in the human being" (11). See also Laín Entralgo's "Mecanismo, vitalismo, empirismo (siglos XV–XVIII)," 245–386; and Juan Riera Palmero's "El vitalismo y enfermedad," 245–53. Also relevant is Francesc Bujosa Homar's study of J.M. Guardia's vitalism in *Filosofía e historiografía médica en España*, 117–26; also see Josep Lluís Barona Vilar's *Fisiología* for a brief overview of Montpellier vitalism in Spain, 38–9. Álvaro Cardona dedicates a few pages to "vitalist schools" in eighteenth-century Spain in *La salud pública en España durante el Trienio Liberal (1820–1823)*, 214–25. For the influence of Montpellier vitalism in Spain, particularly on the physician Juan Vicente Carrasco, see also Josep Lluís Barona Vilar, *La doctrina y el laboratorio*, 73–80. An introductory study of vitalism in seventeenth-century Spain, focused on the work of José Severo López, can be found in Da Costa Carballo's "El vitalismo en la enseñanza de la medicina del setecientos madrileño." Juan Riera Palmero has also examined Vicente Requeno's theology and philosophy and its ties to Haller's and Stahl's vitalism in "Los médicos y la medicina." Luis Jiménez Moreno's work on late-nineteenth-century vitalism and Friedrich Nietzsche's philosophy is also important. See, for example, "El vitalismo científico y filosófico en el siglo XIX"; "Vitalismo estético"; "Azorín, pequeño filósofo vitalista"; *Hombre, historia y cultura*; and *Nietzsche: Antropología y nihilismo.*

only to the controversies that defined modernity's complex cultural practices and the modern self, but also to the forms of social and institutional authority that were mobilized to regulate our numerous narratives about the body. On this point, Terry Eagleton is right to point out that the emergence of what is generally understood as modern subjectivity in the late-seventeenth century – the period where my book begins with Juan de Cabriada's landmark *Philosophical Medico-Chemical Letter* of 1687 – is characterized by a momentous and irrevocable power shift from "centralized institutions to the silent, invisible depths of the subject itself."[7] The arguments for and against theories of vital force that have been raised in Spain and that I will explore in this book beg the questions: how did the question of vital force alter perceptions of body, mind, and soul in a society so thoroughly grounded in religious authority? How could the assumption that life defies rational analysis expose the underlying anxieties of an age with the modern project? How did an understanding of vital force alter, moreover, the concept of an animated nature and the individual's ability to connect with it? Why was it that "real science," as Auguste Comte liked to refer to it, never succeeded in demolishing the so-called occult fantasies of vitalist theory? And, of course, what role did theories of vital force play in the construction of modern subjectivity?

It must be stated from the outset that the subject of this book is vast, and what I offer here is a first step toward an understanding of theories of vital force and their complexity in Spain. Instead of tackling one period, which would have made for a very interesting book in itself, I have chosen to trace the continuity and evolution of the question of vital force by homing in on particular figures in various fields who attended to it in their work between the late-seventeenth and early-twentieth centuries, a period when concepts of life phenomena were greatly expanding and shaping cultural debates like never before. The emphasis on the body and its interiority that guides the present study is filtered through my own interests, experiences, and tastes, which include concerns ranging from anatomy, iatrochemistry, pathology, and physiology to organicism, autonomy, subjectivity, and embodiment. My approach is, not surprisingly, interdisciplinary, and draws on research in philosophy, the history of medicine, literary studies, and theories on subjectivity and subject formation. It goes without saying that this book provides but one story, so to speak, about vital force in Spain among many possible (and still untold) stories that intersect numerous fields in the arts and sciences and various

7 Eagleton, *The Ideology of the Aesthetic*, 27.

social, cultural, and geographical realities not covered herein. Thus, it does not intend to be comprehensive in breadth or depth, but rather show what I have found to be illuminating on the topic and why (a point I will return to in a moment). At the same time, I have attempted to do justice to a number of key insights related to how theories of vital force informed perceptions and ideas in Spain about the body and its astonishing architecture and potential, and to indicate important questions for further research. Ultimately, I believe that tracing how and why the question of vital force was addressed over time in various fields provides us with another framing of this fascinating subject.

A diachronic and interdisciplinary approach such as the one I offer in this book naturally comes with its freedoms and its constraints. To begin with, it has provided me with the necessary perspective to trace a rich, transnational dialogue on vital force as it was elaborated and interpreted in the Spanish context. As I contend throughout this book, the fact that the question of vital force was consistently formulated in a range of fields and remained integrally interwoven with seminal debates over science, culture, and modernization reveals the complex dynamic between body and world that propelled modernity. Availing myself of Michel Foucault's notion of practical critique, I also argue that taking up this question in the face of authority, particularly religious authority and its preoccupation with the soul's animating properties (the age-old dogmas that stipulated that only the perfect soul vivified the imperfect body) provides further discernment into what was at stake in interrogating and redefining the relationship between body and world in Spain. Interestingly, the same can be said of the authority of science and its expanding "religion" of rationality and empiricism when it came to regarding the spark of life solely through the practices of measurement and instrumentation.

In terms of constraints, I have limited my analysis to peninsular Spain and some of the major debates in the arts and sciences that were triggered by the changing socio-economic and cultural circumstances in the country. While there is no doubt that my analysis would have been enriched by the more explicit inclusion of the scientific and cultural realities of the Spanish American Empire (realities that were deeply influential in reconfiguring how nature's awe-inspiring and living diversity defied the epistemological assumptions underpinning early modern thought, as I suggest in Chapter 4), I have chosen for reasons of scholarly interest, field of focus, and limitations of space to study peninsular Spain. Furthermore, including the Spanish American Empire more overtly would have meant penning a different book with different emphases. I do maintain, especially in light of the excellent scholarship produced in recent years on Spain's colonial enterprise, that the conclusions I draw in terms of the epistemological shifts away from Galenic cosmology, Aristotelianism, and the obscurities of the Scholastic tradition that opened paths to revised notions of life and nature between the seventeenth and nineteenth centuries can also apply to the Spanish American Empire.[8]

Each chapter in this book centres on a significant moment in the chronology of the vital-force question, a moment in which key figures – among them healers, physicians, philosophers, religious apologists, scientists, researchers, statesmen, polemicists, and writers – recollect and reconsider prior observations on the topic as they add their own hypotheses and corrections. These moments are reflected predominantly in the work and thought of Juan de Cabriada, Miguel Marcelino Boix y Moliner, Martín Martínez, Diego de Torres Villarroel, Sebastián Miguel Guerrero Herreros, Ignacio María Ruiz de Luzuriaga, Gaspar Melchor de Jovellanos, Pedro Mata y Fontanet, Ángela Grassi, Julián Sanz del Río, Miguel de Unamuno, Pío Baroja, and Ramón Gómez de la Serna. I have chosen to explore the work of these diverse figures for three primary reasons. But before I get to this, I would like to clarify briefly that I am not blind to the underrepresentation of women in this book, nor am I unaware that concepts of the living human body in the arts and sciences between the late-seventeenth century and the early years of the twentieth century were clearly constituted and interpreted through the dominant male culture of patriarchy. Nancy Tuana's opening words in the preface to *Feminism and Science* say it all when considering scientific matters from this purview: "The politics of science have included women within the gaze of science but have excluded her from the practice of science."[9] I have made every effort to locate relevant materials during this period that meaningfully raised the question of vital force in Spain from the perspective of women's experience, and while I discovered a number of remarkable texts about medicine women, women healers, nursing,

8 I am referring to the line of research exemplified in works such as: Jorge Cañizares-Esguerra's *How to Write the History of the New World*, and *Nature, Empire, and Nation: Explorations of the History of Science in the Iberian World*; Daniela Bleichmar et al.'s *Science in the Spanish and Portuguese Empires (1500–1800)*; and Antonio Barrera-Osorio's *Experiencing Nature: The Spanish American Empire and the Early Scientific Revolution*, to name just a few examples.

9 Tuana, *Feminism and Science*, vii. López Terrada also raises the crucial point here concerning how early-modern science and medicine were regulated to exclude women from medical practice: "Women were during this time period excluded from the regulated exercise of medicine; this was due not only to prohibitions against their attending medical school, but also because they were not admitted to the guilds of surgeons and apothecaries. Because of this, they had to practice in unregulated occupations, as was the case with midwives (matronas)" ("The Control," 286).

midwifery, and women's prominent role in folk medicine and homeopathy, I did not find extensive materials that would have addressed a bodily life principle, given the critical parameters I have set for this book.[10] In Chapter 6, when dealing with Baroja's fiction, I do broach the extensive literature that blossomed with the rise of positivist science, evolutionism, eugenics, and degeneration theory in the mid- to late-nineteenth century, in which the basic issues of women's so-called innate physical and intellectual debility (the notion that women were by nature passive and lacked the constitutive vitality of men) was debated.[11] In Ángela Grassi's fiction, I also glean valuable insights into how the literature of domesticity in nineteenth-century Spain addressed materialism and its sustained assault on vitalism. I have included these insights in Chapter 5.

The first reason why I chose to study these particular figures is that they tackled the question of vital force in their work with clarity and originality and believed it was of great significance in the advancement of their respective pursuits, especially as it pertained to the body. By simply perusing the list of names above, one might immediately object that it is simply inconceivable to pen a book of this nature about Spain without dedicating detailed studies to luminaries such as Matías García, Crisóstomo Martínez, Juan Bautista Corachán, Benito Jerónimo Feijóo y Montenegro, Agustín Cortiñas, Benito Pérez Galdós, Ramón Turró, José de Echegaray, Santiago Ramón y Cajal, and many others. Yet, it is imperative to keep in mind that several prominent Spanish physicians, scientists, philosophers, authors, and intellectuals were not especially concerned with vital force and did not believe its specific analysis to be of any great relevance to their work. Surely, they were aware of it, but not as a problem to be studied and mapped. Such is the case with every figure named in the preceding list. With figures like Gaspar Bravo de

10 The following scholarship was helpful in guiding my understanding of women's role in Spanish science in the early-modern period and the nineteenth century: Julia Osca Lluch's, *La aportación de la mujer a la historia de la ciencia y de la técnica de España*; Montserrat Cabré i Pairet and Teresa Ortiz-Gómez's *Sanadoras, matronas y médicas en Europa. Siglos XII–XX*, and "Mujer y salud: prácticas y saberes"; Teresa Ortiz-Gómez and Gloria Becerra's *Mujeres de ciencia*; and Teresa Ortiz-Gómez's "Protomedicato y matronas: una relación al servicio de la cirugías," and "Las matronas y la transmisión de saberes científicos sobre el parto en la España del siglo XIX."

11 The following works provide a broad outline of this discussion in late-nineteenth-century Spain: Juan Pérez y García's *¿Cuál es la educación físico y moral de la mujer, más conforme a los grandes destinos la ha confiado el destino?* (1859), González Encinas's *La mujer comparada con el hombre: Apuntes filosófico-médicos* (1875), María Concepción Gimeno's *La mujer española: estudios acerca de su educación* (1877), Francisco de Asis Pacheco's *La misión de la mujer en la sociedad y la familia* (1881), María del Pilar Sinués's *El ángel del hogar: estudio* (1881), and Concepción Arenal's *La mujer de la casa* (1883).

Sobremonte, Juan Bautista Juanini, José Casalete, Diego Mateo Zapata, Gabriel Álvarez de Toledo, Andrés Piquer, Vicente Requeno y Vives, José Ponce de León, José Severo López, Tomás García Suelto, Manuel Hurtado de Mendoza, Juan Vicente Carrasco, Tomás Santero y Moreno, Enrique Serrano y Fatigati, Salvador Calderón y Arana, Augusto González de Linares, Francisco Giner de los Ríos, José de Letamendi, Juan Ramón Jiménez, and countless others who were conversant with theories of vital force and drew on them to develop their work, the limitations of space (and for the reasons that follow) have made it impossible to dedicate entire chapters or sections to their inspiring work. Needless to say, every one of these figures appears in this book in some form, and I invite scholars and researchers to continue the discussion.[12]

I would like to address briefly why Ortega y Gasset was not included in this study, given his deep appreciation for theories of vital force and his extensive philosophical work on Being known as ratiovitalism, which blended neo-Kantianism and neo-vitalism. The reason for not dedicating more space to Ortega y Gasset is rather straightforward and has to do with the fact that there have been a number of admirable monographs dealing with ratiovitalism that have explored its vitalist connections in more depth than I could accomplish in this book. The studies I am referring to include J.M. García Mauriño's and J.M. Fernández-Revuelta's *Ortega y Gasset: Ratiovitalism* (1988), John T. Graham's *A Pragmatist Philosophy of Life in Ortega y Gasset* (1994), Antonio Gutiérrez Pozo's *The Dawn of Vital Reason: Phenomenology and Vitalism as the Origin of Ortega y Gasset's Philosophy* (2003), and Antonio Pérez Quintana's *Ratiovitalism: Culture as a Function of Life. Commentary on Chapter V of The Theme of Our Time by Ortega y Gasset* (2005).[13] Obviously, there is still much to learn about ratiovitalism and its place in Spanish and European culture, but for the purposes of this book (and keeping in mind, once again, the limitations of space), I have focused on figures whose engagement with the question of vital force is far less understood within the cultural frameworks of Spanish modernity.

12 A few notable Spanish scholars and researchers who studied vital force in the late-nineteenth and early-twentieth centuries, but who do not appear in this book, include Emilio Ribera Gómez, Emilio Reus y Bahamonde, José Rodríguez Carracido, and Joaquín María de Castellarnau.

13 There are also two unpublished dissertations on the topic, which I have not consulted but are worth mentioning: Elizabeth Mercedes López Tamayo's *El raciovitalismo de Ortega y Gasset* (Universidad del Claustro de Sor Juana, 1990), and Jeferson dos Santos Assumção's *A Ilustração Vital: O Raciovitalismo de Ortega y Gasset como via para o Desenvolvimento de uma Sociedade Leitora* (Universidad de León, 2008).

The second reason I have chosen to study these figures is that they belonged to a myriad of intellectual traditions and harnessed a wealth of resources, both foreign and domestic, both ancient and modern, to investigate vital force. One of my key aims in this book is to demonstrate how and why the question of vital force infiltrated various disciplines – and emerging disciplines – and was developed in disparate, wide-ranging discourses in Spain. Moreover, I am interested in analyzing not only what the materials dealing with vital force revealed about the cultural and scientific contexts and practices that produced them, but also how they created meaning as texts. My priority is to contextualize these materials, historically situate them, and examine their arguments, structure, language, and reception to disclose the larger topics they were addressing, particularly as they pertained to the body and life. More than simply determining influences, I seek to understand how and why long-standing ideas about life were reassessed and applied to new circumstances in Spain, and how innovative ideas, discoveries, and breakthroughs traversed frontiers – both real and ideological – and were transformed in the country, given a host of socio-political agendas and infrastructures. Thus, I have sought to consult numerous sources to complement the primary texts that anchor this book. These primary texts include: four philosophical treatises (Martínez, Mata y Fontanet, Sanz del Río, and Unamuno), a medical treatise (Martínez), a stoichiological treatise (Guerrero Herreros), an epistolary case study of tertian fever (Cabriada), a defence of Hippocratic teachings (Boix y Moliner), a fictional travel journal (Torres), a dissertation and laboratory studies dealing with blood and respiration (Ruiz de Luzuriaga), a number of travelogues, diaries, and poems (Jovellanos), an oration on the magnificence of nature (Jovellanos), an inaugural address to the medical school at the University of Madrid (Mata y Fontanet), a domestic novel (Grassi), essays on gymnastics and national identity (Unamuno), short stories and a modernist novel (Baroja), and avant-garde experimental life-writing, theatre, and manifestos (Gómez de la Serna).

Some scholars may lament the interdisciplinary range of the texts I examine and argue that it hinders a sufficiently robust appreciation of a discrete area of study. This book, they might object, would be better served if it remained within the disciplinary confines of the history of medicine, sociology of the body, philosophy, or literary criticism. I show that this interdisciplinary range is a strength, for it not only allows for a better triangulation of the topic, but it also builds a more variegated picture of the new and imaginative relations between knowledge and body that concepts of vital force in fact forged across disciplines. What is documented throughout this book, and what was especially revealing to me as I expanded my bibliography, is that theories of vital force and the broader socio-cultural landscapes they thrived in underwent constant redefinition and reinvention and touched practically every field of knowledge. The question that I kept asking as I advanced in this project was: how and why did *fuerza vital* remain such a highly malleable concept of resistance in Spain, so that it cut across all types of boundaries and appears over time and with countless shades of meaning in everything from philosophical treatises and specialized medical journals to novels and avant-garde literary experimentation? My hope is that my efforts to trace the question of vital force illustrate its wonderfully fluid character and draw attention to the revealing critical implications that it raises in the Spanish context concerning the body and modernity.

When it comes to the benefits of interdisciplinarity, I also agree with Víctor Navarro-Brotóns and William Eamon's argument that "an interdisciplinary mode, one that weds traditional intellectual history with the methodologies of art history, literature, philosophy, and social analysis," provides one of the most effective means of interrogating the conditions that shaped scientific and cultural practices in Spain.[14] It is worth repeating the truism, particularly when speaking of "relations" and "practices" within the historical context of Spanish modernity, that the strict disciplinary divisions we know today were unheard of prior to the early- to mid-nineteenth century. The line dividing science and literature, for instance – always keeping present the overwhelming complexity of the terms and the wealth of meanings they have conveyed – was blurred well into the nineteenth century, given that these disciplines shared a common language of perception and storytelling. That is to say, "science share[d] with literature the same metaphorical spaces and in doing so therefore also share[d] the same imaginative ground."[15] This imaginative ground takes clear form in seventeenth-century Spain as the rhetoric of science began to migrate into greater spheres of social life and cultural production. So much so, as John Slater proposes, that "if we want to measure the diffusion and popularity of modern scientific ideas in [Golden Age] Spain, scientific publications are frequently not the best place to start."[16] José Pardo Tomás makes an analogous argument concerning the productive rapport between medicine and philosophy in early modern Spain.[17] As it will

14 Navarro-Brotóns and Eamon, *Beyond the Black Legend*, 12.

15 Willis, *Science and Literature*, 72.

16 Slater, "Fables," 220.

17 Pardo Tomás tells us: "[W]e have a presentist idea of the disciplinary divisions of knowledge and, in our present, philosophy and medicine find themselves at quite some distance from each other. In very few cases do we see them converge in common territory

become apparent, several of the figures covered in this book were remarkably adept at synthesizing ideas from various knowledge streams, and it was part and parcel of how they carried out their work.

The third reason behind my choice of figures is that they stood at the forefront of new developments in their respective fields and, as I see it, were representative of key stages in the evolution of the question of vital force in Spain. From the late-seventeenth-century medical pioneer Juan de Cabriada to the early-twentieth-century avant-gardist Ramón Gómez de la Serna, each of the figures I consider opened new avenues for examining established paradigms of thought about the body and world through the prism of vital force. What is more, they challenged and very often transgressed the limits of authority and tradition. With two figures in particular – the polymath Torres and the materialist Mata y Fontanet – I demonstrate that this testing of limits cut both ways. For Torres, the scientific narratives of life in the early-eighteenth century were themselves dogmatic and unyielding (a point that calls to mind Walter Wilmshurst's telling words: "Science is as dogmatic as Theology, and Theology as theoretical as Science").[18] In his fictional travel journal *Anatomy of the Visible and Invisible: Universal Compendium of Both Spheres* of 1738, Torres laboured to discredit modern theories of vital force and their increasing authority over matters dealing with that most sacred and delicate of subjects: the body-soul nexus. What is so illuminating about Torres's *Anatomy* – a work so sympathetic to religious orthodoxy when it came to the soul's supremacy over the flesh – is that, in its critical deployment of modern science and in its ironic retreat from delivering on its promise of locating the seat of the soul within the human body, it provides us with a unique window into how new scientific approaches to vital force were directly colouring anatomical studies in early-eighteenth-century Spain. For Mata y Fontanet, the expansion of neo-Hippocratism in nineteenth-century Spain and its dogged adherence to vitalist theories jeopardized the nation's scientific enterprise. With the discoveries of positivist science and its quantitative methods in mind, he argued that there was absolutely no good reason to advocate for the chimerical fantasy of vital force in the modern age of industrialization and technological discovery. If anything, neo-Hippocratism and its vitalism did nothing if not expose how the concept of vital force had

... But this is not how it was at the beginning or end of the eighteenth century, nor even during the better part of the early nineteenth century in the majority of medical spheres in Europe" (*El médico en la palestra*, 211).

18 Wilmshurst, *Christianity and Science*, 26.

become an organizing idea for the archaic, status-quo policies that were leading Spain into ruin.

I have divided the book into an Introduction and three parts consisting of six chapters. The Introduction, which is composed of three sections, is extensive, for it provides the reader with an organized overview of the topic. My aim in the Introduction is to plainly synthesize the complex contextual, transnational, and critico-theoretical factors that intertwine in narratives of vital force in Spain, always keeping in view modernity's historical dynamics. The Introduction also provides a preliminary account of the key concepts concerning the body and life that the book raises throughout.

Part I, titled "Blood, Circulation, and the Soul," consists of two chapters and examines the *novator* period that runs from roughly the 1680s to the 1740s. The first chapter examines Cabriada's *Philosophical Medico-Chemical Letter* and its contribution in posing the question of vital force within modern theories of blood circulation and fermentation. Cabriada's *Letter* serves as my starting point, since it is by far one of the most groundbreaking texts in addressing vital force in seventeenth-century Spain and synthesizes a wealth of modern scholarship on the topic that would prove decisive for theorizing the medical body in the early Enlightenment. In the second chapter, I analyze the influence of Descartes' philosophy in early-eighteenth-century Spain in terms of body functioning and the operations of the soul as seen through Boix y Moliner's *Hippocrates Defended from the Calumnies that Some Careless Physicians Have Imputed to Him* (1711) and Martín Martínez's *Skeptical Medicine and Modern Surgery* (1722) and *Skeptical Philosophy* (1730). The second part of this chapter deals with an analysis of Torres's imaginative defence of the soul's governance of the body in the fictional travel journal *Anatomy of the Visible and Invisible: Universal Compendium of Both Spheres*.

Part II, titled "Political Reform and the Order of Nature," tackles vital force in Enlightenment and pre-Romantic Spain in two chapters covering the period from the 1740s to the 1810s. Chapter 3 explores the Spanish medical revolution and the role Herman Boerhaave's and Albrecht von Haller's theories played in generating new perspectives in Spain on the wonders of the body's fabric. This chapter also demonstrates how theories of vital force informed the stoichiology and anatomical investigations of Sebastián Miguel Guerrero Herreros and Ignacio María Ruiz de Luzuriaga, two leading figures in the Royal Society of Medicine and Other Sciences of Seville and the Royal Academy of Medicine in Madrid, whose influence was instrumental in modernizing Spanish medicine in the mid- to late-eighteenth century. In Chapter 4, I focus on how the question of vital force inspired artists, scientists, and intellectuals to renew conceptions of nature in Europe during the pre-Romantic period. More specifically, in Jovellanos's travel diaries, poetry, and particularly in his *Oration Pronounced in the Asturian Institute on the Study of the Natural Sciences* of 1799, inspired by the Comte de Buffon's vitalist arguments, I show to what extent the mystery of nature's vital force profoundly shaped his organicist view of the natural realm and its sublimity.

Part III, titled "From Neo-Hippocratism to the Avant-garde," is composed of the fifth and sixth chapters. In Part III, my aim is to trace the manner in which the concept of vital force evolved and deeply influenced Spanish philosophy and literature between the 1810s and 1910s. My starting point in Chapter 5 is the French physiological vitalism that inspired Spanish scholars during the difficult period between 1808 and 1840, which was marked by the Spanish War of Independence, French occupation, Ferdinand VII's oppressive regime, loss of Spanish colonies, and the First Carlist War. From here, I move on to evaluate neo-Hippocratic vitalism – the modernization of Hippocratic doctrines on life and nature that punctuated medicine and philosophy beginning in the mid-seventeenth century – and its dialogue with positivism in the physician, toxicologist, writer, and poet Pedro Mata y Fontanet. In what came to be known as the Great Debate on Hippocrates, Mata y Fontanet set forth a highly polemical agenda of reform in the name of Positive Science that promised to modernize Spanish culture. This agenda was perceived to be such a threat to Spain's moral and religious fabric that it was even maligned in domestic novels such as Ángela Grassi's *The Snowflake.* I continue on to Krausist philosophy and its vitalist undercurrent. Spanish Krausists offered a framework for building a harmonic society whose supreme rationality and vigour depended largely upon the beautiful, healthy, and energetic bodies of its citizens. On the margins of positivist and Krausist socio-corporeal analyses leading into the twentieth century, the question repeatedly raised was this: what intrinsic vital force urges the individual to be artistic, creative, social, and rational, as well as non-conformist, rebellious, and nihilistic? Nietzsche, whose influence was pronounced in modernist Spain leading up to the First World War, took up this important question and brought to the fore of contemporary debates the perceived degeneration of modern life, in which the body was conceived of as the site of struggle, corruption, deviance, and decadence. In Unamuno's, Baroja's, and Gómez de la Serna's philosophical and literary works, which I explore in Chapter 6, I demonstrate in what ways the tangled ties of vital force and cultural renewal (*regeneracionismo*) played out in the redefinition of concepts of embodiment and subjectivity in the early years of twentieth-century Spain. I bring the book to a close in the period around 1914, with Gómez de la Serna, given that various forms of neo-vitalism and the optimism they inspired throughout Europe were irrevocably shattered by the terrible realities of the First World War and its mechanized warfare. Although theories of vital force had a notable impact in Spain and Europe in the 1920s and 1930s, they would never again enjoy the significance or broad-based popularity they had prior to 1914.

As a final note to this Preface, I would like to dedicate a few words to the old debate that kept cropping up in my research concerning to what extent Spain participated in the Scientific Revolution, or whether it could even be considered modern within the context of European modernity. With the rise of the Black Legend in the sixteenth century, Spain was denigrated for centuries as the land of ignorance, brutality, and fanaticism. Madame d'Aulnoy's travel diary *Relation du voyage d'Espagne* of 1691 represented one of those quintessential early-modern texts which propagated the myth of a decadent Spain, reinforcing a sclerotic image of the country that would endure through Montesquieu, Voltaire, Nicolas Masson de Morvilliers, Immanuel Kant, and Napoleon Bonaparte, all the way up to Jacob Burckhardt, Theodore Roosevelt, and Oliverio Girondo.[19] As more recent scholarship on Spanish early-modern history, Enlightenment culture, nineteenth-century studies, and modernism attests, Spain's place within modernity is no myth. There is no denying, for example, that these fields have evolved and transcended the critical myopia that was common even in Spanish historiography with the likes of Marcelino Menéndez y Pelayo, Américo Castro, and Ortega y Gasset, who found it difficult (at times impossible) to utter the words Spanish and Enlightenment, or Spanish and Romanticism, in the same breath.[20] It is well documented that Francisco Franco's dictatorship did everything in its power to paint key phases of Spanish modernity (those associated

19 Interestingly, the popularity of Madame d'Aulnoy's *Relation* continued well into the late-nineteenth century, when an anonymous reviewer commends Madame Carey's new edition of d'Aulnoy's text in *The Atlantic Monthly*, noting: "It is true that time has had considerable effect in softening the ways and manners of the Spanish people, but Spain still remains, as it then was, the least civilized of the old countries of Europe" (631).

20 "The more one reflects on our history," Ortega y Gasset lamented as he pondered Spain's place within the European Enlightenment, "the more one discerns the disastrous absence of our eighteenth century" ("El siglo," 600). For Américo Castro, "in the eighteenth century ... Spain, steadfast in its faith, refuses to acknowledge the political, philosophical, and religious transformations that characterized the modern period" (38). Menéndez Pelayo contended that the Spanish eighteenth century was "a period of transition lacking any character" (quoted in Subirats, 25). He also referred to it as "that unfortunate century" (*Historia* 2, 1108).

primarily with liberalism and scientific rationalism) as sterile and unpatriotic, which only perpetuated the belief within transnational historiography that Spain was, and always had been, insular and unmodern. It is from this perspective, for instance, that we can better frame fascist historian Joaquín de Entrambasaguas's infamous assessment of the Spanish monk and scholar Feijóo as "the prototype and origin of Spanish liberalism – with the full miserable and sordid meaning that this word conveys."[21] Thanks to a number of contemporary studies, we can appreciate Spain's transnational *modernidad* in science, philosophy, and literature as a reality, a reality whose complexity and character undoubtedly still requires more definition.[22]

The point of this book is not to debate how historiographical criticism has valued Spain's place in narratives of scientific progress and modernization. Yet it bears saying that, when one spends time analyzing Spanish science and history, it becomes clear that we can oftentimes read the discourses on Spain's lack of modernity and its "otherness" as formidable political constructions that reveal not only the anxieties of the individuals, authorities, and states that sanctioned them, but also the complex

21 Quoted in Zavala, "Hacia un mejor conocimiento del siglo XVIII español," 342. A few emblematic examples in more recent scholarship of the reductionist assessment of Spain's modernity comes by way of Octavio Paz and Anthony Pagden. "Spain did not have a modern age," Paz declares conclusively in *Children of the Mire*, "she had neither critical reason nor bourgeois revolution, neither Kant nor Robespierre ... [Spain] remained on the fringe of capitalist development and did not share in the Enlightenment" (82). For Pagden, "Spain never experienced a 'scientific revolution' or ... anything which could possibly be accommodated under such a description. The only 'modern' science to achieve any degree of intellectual uptake (and that only at the very end of the eighteenth century) was political economy" (139).

22 A representative snapshot of this scholarship – much of which appears in this book – includes José López Piñero, *Ciencia y técnica*, and *Historia y sociología de la ciencia española* (with González Blanco and Jiménez Blanco); Josep Lluís Barona Vilar, *La doctrina y el laboratorio, Sobre medicina y filosofía natural en el renacimiento*, and "Las tercianas de su excelencia"; Enrique Fernández, *Anxieties of Interiority and Dissection in Early Modern Spain*; David C. Goodman, *Power and Penury: Government, Technology, and Science in Philip II's Spain*; Enrique García Santo-Tomás, *La musa refractada: Literatura y óptica en la España del Barroco*; David T. Gies, *The Cambridge Companion to Modern Spanish Culture*; Àlvar Martínez-Vidal and Pardo Tomás, "Un siglo de controversias"; Rebecca Haidt, *Embodying Enlightenment: Knowing the Body in Eighteenth-Century Spanish Literature and Culture*; Michael P. Iarocci, *Properties of Modernity: Romantic Spain, Modern Europe, and the Legacies of Empire*; Jesús Pérez-Magallón, *Construyendo la modernidad: La cultura española en el tiempo de los novatores (1675–1725)*; Dale J. Pratt, *Signs of Science: Literature, Science, and Spanish Modernity Since 1868*; Eduardo Subirats, *La ilustración insuficiente*; José Pardo Tomás, *Ciencia y censura: La Inquisición Española y los libros científicos en los siglos XVI y XVII*; John Slater, Maríaluz López-Terrada, and José Pardo Tomás, *Medical Cultures of the Early Modern Spanish Empire*; Russell P. Sebold, *The Trajectory of Spanish Romanticism: From the Enlightenment to Bécquer.*

and ever-changing shifts in national and geographic power structures that have shaped modernity since the Renaissance. In their aptly titled volume *Beyond the Black Legend: Spain and the Scientific Revolution*, Navarro-Brotóns and Eamon call much-needed attention to the ways in which the current master narrative of the Scientific Revolution is "so biased … that Spain's absence from the narrative reflects a prejudice whose origins go back to the Black Legend … [T]he Black Legend looms as a prejudice that invites misunderstanding and distortion."[23] The title of Jorge Cañizares-Esguerra's 2004 article in *Perspective on Science* could not be any clearer in this respect: "Iberian Science in the Renaissance: Ignored How Much Longer?"[24] The old, time-worn stereotypes, these critics claim rightly, must be addressed and ultimately overcome to thereby open fertile ground for a more-balanced assessment of Spain in historical accounts of scientific and cultural development. This book participates in this revisionary spirit.

Unless otherwise noted, the translations in this book are mine, and I am responsible for any and all errors. The titles of articles, books, treatises, periodicals, pamphlets, and ephemera, as well as the names of institutions, organizations, and societies, are also given in English. The titles as they appear in the original language, along with all relevant bibliographical information, can be found in the bibliography. All quotations from Spanish sources have also been translated into English. In an effort to save space, first and foremost, and secondly, to improve the reading experience, I have not included the original source materials after the translation, except when I believed it was useful to further clarify the meaning of a particular word or phrase. None of the primary Spanish texts I analyze in this book, except for Karl C.F. Krause's *The Ideal of Humanity and Universal Federation*, Unamuno's *The Tragic Sense of Life* (as well as a handful of his articles and a portion of his diary), and Baroja's *The Tree of Knowledge*, have been translated into English. It should be noted that I did not use William Hastie's English translation of Krause's

23 Navarro-Brotóns and Eamon, *Beyond the Black Legend*, 9–10.

24 Cañizares-Esguerra is likewise drawing much-needed attention to Portuguese science and technology, which is similarly excluded from narratives of the Scientific Revolution. For Cañizares-Esguerra, "[t]he roots fo this exclusion, to be sure, hark back to the Protestant Reformation and the Enlightenment. The oversight is unfortunate for it has blinded scholars to the fact that the Iberians first created a culture of empirical, experimental, and utilitarian knowledge-gathering of massive proportions that did not get its cues from the classics of the learned, but from merchants, enterprising settlers, and bureaucrats" ("Iberian Science," 86). Cañizares-Esguerra expanded somewhat on this essay in "The Colonial Iberian Roots of the Scientific Revolution," which appeared in *Nature, Empire, and Nation*, 14–45.

The Ideal of Humanity and Universal Federation and instead translated parts of it directly from Sanz del Río's translation, *Ideal de la humanidad para la vida, con introducción y comentarios* (the Spanish translation that circulated throughout late-nineteenth- and early-twentieth-century Spain). I have used Anthony Kerrigan's translation of Unamuno's *The Tragic Sense of Life* and other related articles, and Aubrey F.G. Bell's translation of Baroja's *The Tree of Knowledge*, but I have made adjustments to Bell's translation and indicated when I have done so.

A condensed version of Chapter 1 appeared as "The Body of the Letter: Vital Force and the Practice of Spanish Medicine in Juan de Cabriada's *Carta Filosofica, Medico-Chymica* (1687)," *Revista Hispánica Moderna* 68, no. 2 (2015): 109–25. A few paragraphs in Chapter 5 dealing with Ángela Grassi and Mata y Fontanet were taken from "Atomism and the Feminine Ideal in Ángela Grassi's *El copo de nieve*," *Revista de Estudios Hispánicos* 45, no. 1 (2011): 133–54. Portions of the section on Gómez de la Serna in Chapter 6 were taken from two separate articles: "Autobiography and the Task of the Writer: The Case of the Young Ramón Gómez de la Serna," *Anales de la Literatura Española Contemporánea* 39, no. 1 (2014): 61–83; and "Writing the Self: What Gómez de la Serna Learned from Nietzsche," *Revista Hispánica Moderna* 62, no. 1 (2009): 25–39. I would like to thank *Revista Hispánica Moderna, Revista de Estudios Hispánicos,* and *Anales de la Literatura Española Contemporánea* for allowing me to reprint from these articles.

Acknowledgments

The idea of this book emerged in the summer of 2010, when I spent a month conducting research on pragmatism at the Instituto Franklin at the Universidad de Alcalá, Spain. With the generous support of a Richard Rorty Scholarship from the Instituto Franklin, I discovered several fascinating documents about the influence of William James and John Dewey on Spanish intellectuals throughout the modernist period. Yet I also learned how intensely the question of vital force had resonated in Spain's cultural imaginary. I extend my best wishes to Iulia Marcela Vescan, Cristina Crespo, Serafín Vegas, and the staff at the Instituto Franklin and the Biblioteca de la Universidad de Alcalá for their generous help and hospitality during my stay.

I would like to thank the National Endowment for the Humanities for supporting my research throughout the years. I am also grateful to the Department of Spanish, Italian and Portuguese at Pennsylvania State University for its support and consideration of my work, as well as the Spanish and Italian Modernist Studies Forum (SIMSF), which I cofounded in 2013 with my colleague Maria Truglio. I am indebted to the Resident Scholars and Artists program at Penn State, which is jointly sponsored by the Institute of the Arts and Humanities, the College of Arts and Architecture, the College of the Liberal Arts, and the Commonwealth campuses of the Penn State system for providing me with a one-semester release from teaching in 2013 to make significant progress on the manuscript. Thanks to the Resident Scholars and Artists program, I presented an early version of Chapter 1 on Juan de Cabriada's *Carta Filosofica, Medico-Chymica* at Penn State and received helpful feedback from numerous colleagues, friends, and students. Likewise, the Penn State Libraries, and in particular Manuel Ostos, the Humanities Liaison Librarian, have been very supportive of this book and assisted me with locating research materials. In collaboration with Manuel Ostos and the Penn State Libraries, I co-organized a lecture series in 2013, titled *Embodying the Avant-garde: Corporeal Visions in Spain and Italy*, that allowed me to sound out some of my ideas on body and modernity with invited speakers Lucia Re, Shirley Mangini, and Luca Somigli. The lecture series culminated with the publication of the volume *Modernism and the Avant-garde Body in Spain and Italy* (Routledge, 2016), which included contributions by Susan Larson, John McCulloch, Keala Jewell, Ara H. Merjian, Luca Somigli, Shirley Mangini, Lucia Re, Rebecca Bender, and Enrico Cesaretti. I am indebted to all the contributors for their support and efforts on the volume, and for their comments on my research into Ramón Gómez de la Serna's avant-gardism (Chapter 6).

In September of 2015, SIMSF organized a second lecture series, *Refiguring Gender and Youth in Spanish and Italian Modernisms.* I would like to thank Gayle Rogers, Leslie Harkema, and Elena Coda for participating in these lectures and for their stimulating conversation on modernity, corporeality, and science. I owe special gratitude to Leslie Harkema for her friendship and support. In November of 2016, Leslie and I organized the colloquium *The Aesthetics of Youth in Modernist Spain* at Yale University, a colloquium generously sponsored by SIMSF (Penn State), the Department of Spanish, Italian and Portuguese (Penn State), the MacMillan Center (Yale), the Council on Latin American and Iberian Studies (Yale), The European Studies Council (Yale), and the Department of Spanish and Portuguese (Yale). The colloquium brought together Christopher Soufas, Alberto Medina, Nil Santiáñez, Juan Herrero-Senés, and Susan Larson to reconsider Spanish art, literature, and culture of the early-twentieth century in light of its representation and thematization of youth. I want to recognize all the participants for their insightful feedback, comments, and suggestions on my presentation of Pío Baroja's concepts of corporeality and action (Chapter 6).

I am especially grateful to John Slater and Enrique García Santo-Tomás for reading portions of the manuscript in its early form and for offering me valuable comments and suggestions. It was a pleasure to present a paper on Juan de Cabriada with John and Enrique, as well as Alice Brooke, on the MLA panel "Science (and) Fiction in Early Modern Spain" in Chicago in 2014. I owe warm thanks to María Portuondo, José Pardo Tomás, Juan Pimentel Igea, Ricardo Padrón, and Pablo F. Gómez for their stimulating conversation and suggestions on this project during the 46th Annual Meeting of the Association for Spanish and Portuguese Historical Studies at Johns Hopkins University in March 2015, where I presented a portion of Chapter 2 that deals with Diego de Torres Villarroel's *Anatomia de todo lo visible, e invisible: compendio universal de ambos mundos.* I want to thank the organizers of the 18th Annual Conference of the Southern Association for the History of Medicine and Science at the

University of Nevada, Las Vegas, in 2016 for allowing me to present my work on the great Hippocratic debate in nineteenth-century Spain (Chapter 5) via Skype, when last-minute transportation difficulties made it impossible for me to attend the conference in person. At the 89th American Association for the History of Medicine Annual Meeting in Minnesota in 2016, I had the pleasure of discussing my views on Ignacio María Ruiz de Luzuriaga's vitalism (Chapter 5) with Dr Walton O. Schalick III, Department of Orthopedics and Rehabilitation and Department of History, University of Wisconsin, Madison, whose expertise in medieval medical philosophy made me reconsider the figures of Galen and Hippocrates in early-modern Spain. I also profited from my conversations on concepts of corporeality and vital force in ancient Greek philosophy with Sergio Gallegos, Metropolitan State University of Denver, during the 2016 Annual Meeting of the Canadian Society for the History and Philosophy of Science, University of Calgary. In 2017, I was fortunate to present my work on Gaspar Melchor de Jovellanos's vision of nature (Chapter 4) on the panel "Reclaiming Romanticism in Spain," organized by David T. Gies at the MLA Convention in Philadelphia. My sincere and grateful thanks to David for organizing the panel and for running it with intensity and good humour, and to my fellow panelists Hazel Gold, Bécquer Seguín, and Jeffrey Bersett, whose comments and questions provoked me to further thinking about Jovellanos's concept of nature.

I am indebted to the following institutions for granting me access to research materials and for their contributions to this book: Real Academia Nacional de Medicina, Colegio Oficial de Médicos de Barcelona, Galeria de Metges Catalans, Consejo Superior de Investigaciónes, Científicas, Instituto Cajal, Fundación Foro Jovellanos, Biblioteca Nacional de España, and Wellcome Library.

Finally, I express my gratitude to Loretta Zehngut for reviewing my translations of Jovellanos's poetry, as well as Bob Blue for reading parts of my manuscript and for his unwavering and generous support over the years. I would also like to acknowledge Gonzalo Rubio, whose advice on a variety of topics has been greatly appreciated. And many, many thanks to Maria Truglio for her invaluable friendship and encouragement. Special acknowledgment is due to the professional staff at McGill-Queen's University Press and to the anonymous readers of this manuscript. Kyla Madden in particular has been an outstanding editor, who from day one shared my vision and enthusiasm for this book. Lastly, I am deeply grateful to Patricia Kennedy for her outstanding work editing the manuscript.

I extend my deepest appreciation and gratitude to my wife, Kelli, and daughter, Beatriz, for their love and support.

LIFE EMBODIED

Introduction

Life, Critique, Modernity: Vital Force and the (Un)certainty of Science

All science rests upon shifting sand.
Karl Popper, *Conjectures and Refutations*[1]

IN ONE OF HIS NUMEROUS PHILOSOPHICAL FRAGMENTS, Nietzsche turns his mind to ancient Greece, as he often liked to do, and quips: "[F]or the Greeks everything became *life*!"[2] As Nietzsche recognized, a great many of the core assumptions concerning the origins and determinants of vital force in the body and nature derived from the rich wells of ancient Greek philosophy. In varying ways, to engage the daunting question of vital force – also known as vital principle, life force, animating force, life energy, entelechy, and *vis vitalis*, among other terms – has always meant conjuring up the arcane processes of life and whether they are, as the neo-vitalist Hans Driesch referred to them in his landmark *The History and Theory of Vitalism* of 1914, "the result of an *autonomy* peculiar to the processes themselves."[3] In conjecturing about vital force, artists and healers, poets and philosophers, physicians and scientists alike have sought to gain unique insight across the ages into the self-activated, non-mechanical energies that fill our bodies and the world with that most precious gift of life. The seventeenth century, which serves as the point of departure for this book, saw a marked expansion of theories of vital force that not only were notoriously inconsistent, but also amalgamated various strains of ancient and modern thought. As the eclectic reform of philosophy expanded, these theories did a masterful job of repeatedly transgressing scientific and religious frontiers, while, quite ironically, controverting each other and laying bare their own fundamental

1 Popper, *Conjectures and Refutations*, 34.
2 Nietzsche, *Unpublished Writings*, 17.
3 Driesch, *History and Theory of Vitalism*, 1.

inconsistencies. Certainly, theorists of vital force both safeguarded and upended the prerogatives of rationality and religious authority to advance all sorts of claims to suit their agendas. "There was great explanatory diversity [within vitalist thinking]," Ernst Mayr clarifies, "but no cohesive theory."[4] Yet, it was precisely this productive diversity, coupled with the far-reaching implications of reinterpreting vital force, that transformed these theories into effective tools of critique and resistance. On this point, Mayr observes further: "Vitalism, from its emergence in the seventeenth century, was decidedly an antimovement. It was a rebellion against the mechanistic philosophy of the Scientific Revolution and against physicalism from Galileo to Newton."[5] When speaking of this crucial point of resistance, however, we must clarify from the outset that the question of vital force in Spain encompassed more, much more, than a rebellion against mechanism. The truth is that it delved into the very ideological fabric that undergirded not only prevailing body-world theories and their interpretation in various spheres of inquiry, but also the meaning of life itself.

BODIES, DISEASE, AND AUTHORITY

Until fairly recently, it has been a mainstay in European historiography to regard Spain throughout the early-modern period as the great defender of Catholicism, an intolerant country bogged down in religious conservatism and ignorant, for the most part, of advances in science that were taking place in Europe. The scholarship produced in the last few decades on Spanish science and culture reveals a sharper and much more compelling picture of Spain's modernization, in which the assimilation of scientific knowledge and the resistance to authority not only manifested themselves in numerous forms, but were many times mutually dependent. By and large, the notion that Habsburg Spain was little more than a dark and ignorant backwater on the European scene, in which the dreaded Inquisition stifled any meaningful scientific development, has been debunked.[6] García Santo-Tomás said it well: "the notion that [Habsburg] Spain was closed to foreign influences is completely false … Baroque ingenuity was neither as dogmatic nor reactionary as has often been supposed."[7] Likewise, we have come to more fully comprehend

4 Mayr, "What Is the Meaning of 'Life'?" 92.

5 Ibid., 92.

6 See David Goodman's *Power and Penury,* which addresses science and technology in Philip II's Spain.

7 Santo-Tomás, *La musa refractada,* 15.

that the "insufficiency" of the Bourbon Enlightenment, as Eduardo Subirats referred to it in his classic study, requires a more nuanced appraisal of the geopolitics that has punctuated Spain's exclusion from the cultural narratives of modernity.[8] The same can be said of much of post-Fernandine Spain leading into the twentieth century, including the Bourbon Restoration.[9]

It will become apparent throughout this book that the Church and religious apologists exercised powerful authority in Spain when it came to regulating discourses about the body in the service of tradition and order. This is not a new idea. What remains little known, however, is how and why individuals wielded this authority to ridicule, undercut, and even denounce the idea of an inherent vital force that regulated the body's sundry biological processes. The question that immediately arises is: what was so menacing, even sinister, about claiming the existence of a constituitive vital force within the body? Let us recall that, in Scholastic doctrine, the body was believed to be a corruptible, earthly husk given form by the soul, and it was the incorruptible soul that inhabited this husk to generate the composite whole of existence. Only the ensouled body was a living body as such, although the soul certainly did not require a lowly body to be a soul. There was no equivocation on this point: the perfect soul imbued the imperfect body with its vital force and granted it its remarkable abilities to move, grow, and think. The body, therefore, could not be what it was, much less fulfill its potential in any capacity, without the vital properties of the soul. The Jesuit Agustín de Castejón counsels his readers in 1739 to never lose sight of the body's inferior state, and he analogizes it to a sack of excrement, of all things. Only the soul, and not the frail body, was allied to the lofty sphere of the divine and could illuminate a path to otherworldly bliss in the end: "Miserable body: without your soul, you are a sack of excrement … [W]ithout your soul, not even dogs will want to glance at you. With your soul, the angels in heaven will be your friends."[10] For mystics, the body was a source of temptation and torment, and its vital force – associated with everything from avarice to lust – had to be suitably disciplined. The flesh itself was the ground of the sacred, and consequently, as Petra Hendry points out, "[t]he discipline of the body is seen as synonymous with and essential to the discipline of the mind and full devotion to Christ. Taming the body is necessary to resist temptation of all kinds."[11]

8 Subirats, *La ilustración insuficiente*, 24.

9 See note 11 of the Preface for the scholarship I am referring to here.

10 Agustín de Castejón, *Voces del alma*, 78.

11 Hendry, *Engendering Curriculum History*, 88.

To suggest, as many men of learning did through the methods of science and artistic expression, that the somatic itself produced its own vital agency, to advocate that it functioned irrespective of the soul, or that it was, at the very least, on equal footing with it, transgressed the canons of Scripture and challenged the prevailing divine cosmology erected upon the fragilities of the flesh. In short, these men of learning studied the body, they produced empirical knowledge of its inner biochemical workings and structures, and they increasingly elevated it over the soul with forceful and convincing counter-critiques. In so doing, they subverted what Foucault called pastoral power and its disciplining authority grounded in the spiritual welfare of the individual and his salvation (what he labels "the government of souls"), which opened a door to reconceptualizing the crucial bonds that linked the individual to nature and the divine.[12]

In his foundational study on science in sixteenth- and seventeenth-century Spanish society, López Piñero is right to emphasize that the Church and Inquisition in Spain did not make it a practice to openly persecute progressive thinkers, as has often been claimed.[13] Part of the reason for this, as López Piñero has shown, is that new ideas could scarcely penetrate those archaic institutions such as the university that made it their mission to uphold traditional doctrines and the status quo they relied upon. The Inquisition's impact on science, Henry Kamen proposes further, was "minimal, and largely indirect."[14] François Lopez echoes these assessments with his eye on this decisive period between the 1660s and the 1730s that saw the rise of the *novatores*, or the reform-minded intellectuals in various fields of study, who engaged, as Jesús Pérez-Magallón documents in his compelling study on the topic, the innovative and modernizing trends throughout Europe.[15] For Lopez, "it behooves us to discard the idea that to refuse the doctrines of established schools of thought for the opinions of Gassendi, Descartes, Maignan, and other moderns implied exposing oneself to inquisitorial persecution."[16] Patricia Manning has examined the inconsistencies and

12 Foucault, *Security, Territory, Population*, 88.

13 López Piñero, *Ciencia y técnica*, 393.

14 Kamen, *The Spanish Inquisition*, 152.

15 Pérez-Magallón's *Construyendo la modernidad: La cultura española en el tiempo de los novatores (1675–1725)* is an invaluable reference book on the Spain of the *novatores*. The term *novator*, as Pérez-Magallón clarifies, came into circulation sometime around 1714, and was used to refer to those scientists or intellectuals who broke with Aristotelianism and Galenism. With time, however, it became more widespread and referred to those individuals whose work or intellectual outlook was considered subversive (35).

16 Lopez, "Los novatores," 110.

loopholes that obstructed the government of the Spanish monarchy and the Inquisition – keeping in mind the network of laws and regulations within the different reigns – in effectively policing scientific culture on the peninsula. Shortcomings in the process of approving books, coupled with problems related to unclear standards for assessing texts, selective censorship, internal disorganization, and an over-issuance of permissions to read prohibited works all contributed to undermine their authority.[17] In Pardo Tomás's rigorous analysis of scientific censorship and inquisitorial policies in Habsburg Spain, it becomes clear that the Inquisition, although powerful, entered its period of decline as early as 1640.[18]

What further complicates this picture is that a number of prominent intellectuals in seventeenth- and eighteenth-century Spain took holy orders. Juan Caramuel y Lobkowitz, one of the luminaries of the Spanish Baroque, was a Cistercian whose vocation as a preacher, vicar, abbot, and bishop deeply influenced his ample oeuvre on astronomy and mathematics. The satirist and philosopher Baltasar Gracián y Morales belonged to the Society of Jesus, and Benito Jerónimo Feijóo y Montenegro, the indefatigable spokesman for the Enlightenment, was a Benedictine father, whose faith directly informed his application and interpretation of science (he was also one of the most formidable critics of the Inquisition during his time). Before their expulsion from Spain in 1767, the Jesuits, as is well documented, contributed greatly to fostering modern science on the peninsula, particularly in the fields of mathematics and physics.[19] And, as López Silvestre has argued, a crucial group of moderate priests and theologians during the Spanish Enlightenment significantly expanded the project of natural theology when they decided to adhere to the dictates of science and empirical observation rather than the revelations of Scripture.[20] More broadly, Sánchez Granjel has demonstrated that men of the cloth played a pivotal role in the scientific project of reform throughout eighteenth- and nineteenth-century Spain.[21]

We may safely say, then, that the relationship between religion and scientific discovery in Spain, particularly as it pertains to the study of the body and nature, is by no means uniform and clear cut, a point that speaks to the highly fluid religion-versus-science debate at the heart of

17 Manning, *Voicing Dissent*, 1–108.
18 Pardo Tomás, *Ciencia y censura*, 307–10.
19 Navarro-Brotóns, "Science and Enlightenment," 390–404.
20 López Silvestre, "Dios y la naturaleza," 440–1.
21 Sánchez Granjel, "Panorama de la ciencia de la ilustración," 108–9.

modernity.[22] The struggle against scientific innovation and discovery in Spain took on a range of guises through the complex mechanisms of tradition and religious and institutional control that are not always straightforwardly clear. At root, this struggle involved what we could call systems of authority based on a range of discursive practices and administrative and disciplinary procedures of power that not only linked institutions like the Inquisition, Church, university, and local governing bodies through a set of common interests and deep-seated fears, but also sought to destabilize those epistemic networks that posed a threat to their very legitimacy.[23] As a rule, the central strategy of these systems was to disrupt these networks, to impede their expansion and influence within given regional contexts or local spheres of influence (the court in Madrid, for instance, as we will see with Juan de Cabriada in Chapter 1), though not necessarily to eliminate them. Indeed, to eliminate them would have required more administration and resources precisely from institutions like the Inquisition, Church, university, and local governing bodies that were many times burdened under the weight of their own inefficiencies. This strategy of disruption, which was flexible and inevitably adjusted to the many social and legal environments that flourished on the peninsula before the consolidation of the modern state, included slandering progressive scientists in open forums, publishing criticisms of works deemed heretical, excluding reformist physicians from medical *juntas* and governing bodies, regulating medical and scientific practices through guilds and tribunals, exiling or imprisoning individuals considered threats to the status quo, and prohibiting the teaching and dissemination of new science in university classrooms, among other things. Yet, this strategy of disruption would often prove to be ineffective. With the establishment of academies and societies of learning in the late-seventeenth century, as we shall see, progressive scientists carved out a productive space in which to challenge established paradigms of knowledge and engage the ruling elite.

With the emergence of the *novator* movement in late-seventeenth-century Spain, the body and its wondrous vital capacities were beginning

22 John H. Brooke makes the case that "to portray the relations between science and religion as a continuous retreat of theological dogma before a cumulative and infallible science is to overlook the fine structure of scientific controversy, in which religious interests certainly intruded, but often in subtle rather than overtly obstructive ways" (*Science and Religion*, 7).

23 For more on this topic during the reign of the Habsburgs, see López Terrada's short but informative article "The Control of Medical Practice under the Spanish Monarchy during Sixteenth and Seventeenth Centuries."

to be imagined beyond the constraints of ancient semiotics and religion. The sacred cows of medical and scientific dogma, most notably Aristotle and Galen, whose principles on anatomy and pathology had been definitive in appreciating body functioning for centuries, were showing their age. After Vesalius published his landmark *De Humani Corporis Fabrica* of 1543, which challenged aspects of Galenic theory and changed how anatomy was regarded and practised, Descartes' series of innovative models of animation in *Treatise of Man* (written before 1637, but published posthumously in 1662) fundamentally altered concepts of body and vital force throughout Europe. When Descartes divided the world into *res cogitans* (the realm of mind) and *res extensa* (the realm of substance), he conceived the *res extensa* as wholly devoid of any underlying teleological principle or vitalistic agent. What is more, he perfected a new language, a mechanistic language, with which to measure and adequately quantify the organic and living. Beyond the *cogito* there opened up for Descartes a universe of corpuscles driven by simple necessity. The great miracle of nature and its bounteous life and diversity was no more than matter in motion, but a motion emptied of intrinsic drives and theorized relationally between agent and object, cause and effect. To use A.N. Whitehead's phrasing, nature, as seen through the lens of Cartesian mechanism, was "senseless, valueless, purposeless. It just does what it does do, following a fixed routine imposed by external relations which do not spring from the nature of its being."[24] In the end, nature was simply matter.

The influence of Descartes' bodily mechanics on the question of vital force in early eighteenth-century Spain and Europe more broadly cannot be overstated. It would not only undercut Aristotelian principles of extension and motion that sustained the Scholastic tradition and its cosmological framework, but also alter the soul's very qualities and actions, as I demonstrate in Chapters 1 and 2. Although the physician and *novator* Martín Martínez – a man of sharp intellect and not one to shy away from controversy – was critical of Descartes' approach to vital force, he nevertheless lauded him for his bold stance against the tyranny of tradition: "the most famous René Descartes fabricated an entire philosophical system … [and] shook off, once and for all, the peripatetic yoke and restituted reason to its rightful place."[25] It comes as no surprise that Descartes' works, particularly associated as they were to a reassessment of the body-soul nexus, were listed on the Roman Index of forbidden

24 Whitehead, *Science and the Modern World*, 18.
25 Martínez, *Philosophia sceptica*, 3.

books and banned in most Spanish universities (although, interestingly, they were never included on the Spanish Inquisition's index of forbidden books). It is worth keeping in mind, likewise, that the consequences of Philip II's strict measures to insulate his kingdom from Protestant heresy in the sixteenth century endured well into the seventeenth century, which had a lasting effect on what was considered acceptable reading for university students. Geoffrey Woodward put it succinctly: "Philip knew it was his duty as a Christian and as the Most Catholic King to extirpate all brands of heterodoxy from his dominions."[26] It was after Charles II's accession to the throne in 1665 that Spain would make significant headway in publicly modernizing its scientific frameworks, yet the roots of this modernization date back much earlier.[27]

The early 1680s marked one of Spain's most acute periods of administrative instability and economic hardship during the seventeenth century, yet it had been suffering a prolonged crisis on various socio-political fronts for decades, which had allowed the peripheral regions of the country a certain degree of autonomy to develop culturally and organize economically.[28] A larger socio-economic perspective reveals, however, that by the late 1680s – earlier by some estimates – various regions in Spain had already begun a slow and halting process of recovery.[29] The socio-economic and doctrinal obstructions present in Spain notwithstanding, one of the key obstacles to the development of any scientific

26 Woodward, *Philip II*, 51.

27 See Pérez-Magallón, *Construyendo la modernidad*, 18–32. The Peace of Westphalia in 1648, and the Treaty of the Pyrenees in 1659, placed several European powers – France in particular – in an advantageous socio-economic position over Spain. The scientific research undertaken abroad, particularly the New Science of Cartesian rationalism, was beginning to have a broader appeal in Spanish intellectual circles. The Treaties of Nijmegen of 1678–79 gave France even more cultural and political power over Spain. Despite institutional censorship, indices of Prohibited Books, the Inquisition, and the rigid control over education and questions of pedagogy, this influence from Europe was significantly reinforced with the War of Succession between 1701 and 1714 and the defeat of King Philip V's forces in the War of the Quadruple Alliance between 1718 and 1720.

28 There is some debate concerning what exactly constituted Spain's "decline" during this period and how it should be conceived and measured. I have relied on the following sources to buttress my argument: Elliott, *Imperial Spain – 1469–1716*, 361–6; Elliott, *The Count-Duke of Olivares*, 86–101; Payne, *Spanish Catholocism*, 52–60; Israel, *The Dutch Republic*, 28–39; Israel, "The Decline of Spain," 170–80; Molas Ribalta, "El primer," 3–39.

29 Molas Ribalta argues that "between 1680 and 1700, a series of mercantilist initiatives begin to take form in Spain's centre and periphery … [T]hus, the factors that contributed to economic recovery and that are observed around 1680, should be analysed in all of Spain's coastal regions … Recent studies have shown that northern and northeastern Spain, from Galicia to the Basque Country, did not suffer as much [economically speaking] as the Crown of Castile throughout the seventeenth century" ("El primer," 16). Elsewhere,

discipline were imposed in part by what López Piñero describes as the lack of institutionalization of modern scientific practice, or the lack of institutional networks capable of cohesively integrating new scientific paradigms and linking Spanish intellectuals with the rest of Europe.[30] The absence of institutional networks of this kind in Castile so provoked the physician and *novator* Juan de Cabriada in 1687 that he laments in his *Philosophical Medico-Chemical Letter*:

> Why is a Royal Academy not founded in the court of the King of Spain, just like the academies in the court of the King of France and England [?] … Given the worthy, beneficial, and valuable purpose of advancing knowledge of natural things (we only advance in knowledge through physico-chemical experiments), why wouldn't our gentlemen and nobility contribute [to such an enterprise] since it concerns us all [?] … In a court like this one, why is there no chemistry bureau staffed with the leading experts of Europe [?][31]

Cabriada's *Letter*, which I will examine in Chapter 1, represents one of the most significant medical treatises on vital force published in late-seventeenth-century Spain. Through a case study on the treatment of tertian fever, the *Letter* boldly announced "modern medicine" in the court of Madrid and challenged the long-standing authority of Galenic doctrine and the epistemological foundations upon which body functioning and health had been grounded for centuries.[32] By exploiting the rhetorical conventions of an epistolary treatise, Cabriada's *Letter* strategically combined a wealth of domestic and foreign theories on vital force, using the workings of the cardiovascular system and the properties of the blood to propose a radical idea: the soul does not vitalize the body. What was so revolutionary about his assessment of vital force is that he convincingly raised hard questions through a modernized anatomopathological framework about precisely how, and from where, the body derived its life energy. Furthermore, he offered a new hybrid paradigm of body functioning that effectively undermined the Galenic cosmological hierarchy of the humoral body and its animating soul. Ultimately, he challenged medical practitioners in Spain to revisit inquiries such as: Where is the seat of life if not in the soul? How does the motion of the heart and the

---

Molas Ribalta reiterates that "the economic recovery [in Spain] is visible by 1680, even earlier in 1660; however, a more generalized economic growth did not come about until 1730" (*La transición*, 13).

30 López Piñero, *Historia y sociología*, 39.

31 Cabriada, *Carta*, 217.

32 Ibid., 16.

properties of the blood vitalize the body? What are the origins of bodily movement and change? And, how is it possible to sustain a state of bodily well-being?

The increasing relevance of vital force in seventeenth-century Spain had a great deal to do with epidemics and the lucrative economy of healing. In *The Pythagorean Century and the Life of Don Gregorio Guadaña* (1644), the poet and playwright Antonio Enríquez Gómez provides us with a satirical portrait that gives witness not only to the great prevalence of diseases in Europe during the period, but also to the highly profitable business of healing and medical practice. Blending humour, irony, and all sorts of imaginative wordplays, Enríquez Gómez reveals the frivolousness of seventeenth-century barber-surgeons and physicians in bilking their patients for phlebotomy procedures for everything from migraines to gastroenteritis that many times proved fatal. Yet, it is Francisco de Quevedo's numerous satirical portraits of physicians that provide the most illuminating and humorous insights into the economy of healing. In *The Book of All Things* (1631), he describes with his typical wit and flourish what it takes to become a renowned and wealthy physician in early seventeenth-century Spain: "If you want to be a famous physician the first things you will need are a fine mule, a large emerald ring on your thumb, a pair of folded gloves, and a long doublet; and in summer you must wear an imposing taffeta hat; and with all of this, even though you have never cracked open a [medical] book, you cure people and are considered a physician."[33]

Juan Bautista Juanini, the Milanese physician to Juan de Austria and resident in the court of Madrid from 1667, wrote his famous *Political and Physical Treatise that Demonstrates the Movements and Effects Produced by Fermentation and Nitrous Substances* in 1679 to tackle the specific problem of urban epidemics. Juanini's *Treatise* is but one of dozens of texts appearing during the period that laid bare the epistemological anxieties of an age over the unknown sources of disease. As cities expanded, he noted, they produced ever more lacerated, scarred, fevered, phlegmatic, infected, and fetid bodies in their thoroughfares. With some alarm he stated: "Any treatise can be effortlessly filled with the horrors that our eyes stumble upon in the centre and confines of Madrid."[34] We must recall that the plague had decimated a number of Spanish cities as late as 1649, the year sixty thousand inhabitants in Seville perished, or roughly half of the city's population.[35] All types of dreaded *calenturas*

33 Quevedo, *Book of All Things*, 127.

34 Juanini, *Political and Physical Treatise*, 4.

35 Elliott, *Imperial Spain – 1469–1716*, 361.

(fevers) were afflicting swaths of young and old alike, draining their bodies of vital force with alarming rapidity and for unknown reasons. For Juanini, it all came down to air quality: Madrid's air was tainted with noxious exhalations and nitrous vapours that were emanating from piles of biotic detritus that accumulated everywhere in the city.[36] The healthy body, Juanini conjectured, required unadulterated air to properly purify the blood, and it was the inhalation of fouled city air that instigated a series of chemical imbalances in the body and affected its vital force. Thus, diseases like the plague, Juanini submitted, are really caused by foul vapours emanating from detritus in urban centres, particularly the animal corpses that were regularly left to rot in ditches and alleyways.

What was innovative about Juanini's epidemiological model was not, obviously, its reliance on the bad-air theory that can be traced back to Hippocrates, but rather its iatrochemical argument – or the chemical understanding of human physiology and disease – in terms of how noxious air trapped in Madrid's urban network interacted with the body and fundamentally altered its vital force.[37] It is from this vantage point that we can more aptly address not only the evolving rapport between precepts of hygiene and bodily well-being that begin to appear in medical discourses throughout the seventeenth and early eighteenth centuries, but also in more specialized treatises like José Alonso de Arce's *Difficulties Conquered and the Natural Plan in Which Speculative and Practical Rules Are Given for the Cleansing and Sanitation of the Streets of This Court* (1735) on urban sanitation. What the engineer and architect de Arce proposed was a modernized waste-management program for Madrid, and his unease with the infirm appearance of the Spanish court in comparison to those of northern-European powers articulated a fascinating aesthetics of decay, in which fevered bodies drained of their vital force found along Madrid's thoroughfares served as metaphors of national decline.

Within the milieu of halting economic recovery and political instability that extended from roughly 1680 to 1714 – a period also marked by

36 The theory that explained poisonous air as the origin of diseases had by this time a long history stretching back to the Hippocratic treatise *On Breaths* of the fifth century BC, which cites miasmas as contributing to disease. In the early-modern period, it was believed that "corrupted, 'miasmic' air arising from dirty stinking environments" was the most common cause of pox and plague, and in Enlightenment Spain Diego de Torres Villarroel instructed his readers on how to manufacture an odiferous candle, capable of keeping airborne poisons at bay (Healy, 24).

37 For López Piñero, Juanini's *Discurso* is the first fully "modern" medical work published in Spain (*Ciencia y técnica*, 408). Indeed, Juanini's treatise was one of a select few during this period in Spain that had a repercussion abroad (it was translated into French in Montpellier in 1685).

the War of Spanish Succession and its political fallout – Spain experienced a series of social and demographic transformations that presented a group of scholars like Cabriada and Juanini with the opportunity to interact with a transnational scientific community.[38] With a few notable exceptions, the university environment in Spain during this prelude to the Enlightenment was steeped in the most intransigent scholasticism and closely regulated critical debate, especially as it pertained to advances in medicine and science that resulted in new knowledge associated with the body and its vital potentialities.[39] For J.H. Elliott, "there were still isolated groups of devoted scholars [in Castile beginning in 1680], but educational standards had slumped, as the universities fell back on the most arid Thomism and showed themselves hostile to any sign of change."[40] José Andrés Gallego also underscores the general scientific decline in Spanish universities in the seventeenth century, particularly in the fields of surgery, mathematics, and astronomy. The discipline of natural philosophy, he points out further, and several of the more important disciplines within the medical field, were governed by the "worst scholasticism."[41] Scholars open to reform had little choice but to seek out the emerging *tertulias*, or salons, which not only functioned as forums for the exchange of ideas, but also established discursive spheres for the development of an emergent and learned social class (the so-called "bourgeois without bourgeoisie" that prefigure what would become Spain's emerging and enlightened class).[42] As the physician Diego Mateo Zapata noted upon entering the court in Madrid in 1687: "beginning in the year 87 when I came to Court there always existed the public and celebrated *tertulias* that were enriched and adorned by the men of most dignity, authority, and erudition."[43] The *tertulias*, which laid the groundwork for what would become the Enlightenment *academias*, or academies, furnished a welcoming atmosphere in which the *novatores*

38 As López Piñero argues, the country's periphery began to benefit from an increase in population growth and emigration in the seventeenth century, which improved lines of communication between Madrid and cities like Barcelona. He clarifies that the economic recovery of 1680 directly affected the "scientific renewal" in Spain ("Juan," 13–14). See also López Piñero's *Ciencia y técnica*, in which he analyzes these socioeconomic shifts in more detail, 387–401. Iris Zavala reiterates this assessment, emphasizing an "economic expansion," particularly in the periphery of Spain, during the final decades of the seventeenth century, 27–8 and 65–6.

39 The University of Valencia, for instance, remained a crucial hub of modern scientific learning in Spain throughout the Renaissance. See López Piñero's "The Faculty of Medicine of Valencia."

40 Elliott, *Imperial Spain – 1469–1716*, 367.

41 Gallego, *La crisis*, 50.

42 Zavala, *Clandestinidad y libertinaje*, 17.

43 Quoted in López Piñero, *Ciencia y técnica*, 391.

could develop their scientific experiments and learn of innovations from abroad, including the latest theories dealing with vital force and the origins of disease.

Beyond the court in Madrid, *tertulias* flourished in Barcelona, Seville, and Valencia in the 1680s and 1690s, and it was, after all, the intellectual stimulus of Seville's Venerated Tertulia that cleared the way for the founding in 1700 of one of the most influential centres of medical and scientific learning on the peninsula: Seville's Royal Society of Medicine and Other Sciences. Similarly, the humble Literary and Medico-Physico-Chemical Tertulia in Madrid, founded in 1733, planted the seed for the Royal Medical Academy of 1734, which would then flourish into Spain's renowned Royal Academy of Medicine some decades later. With the establishment of the Patriotic Society of the Friends of the Nation in 1783, Madrid Athenaeum in 1835, The Free Institution of Learning in 1876, and the Student Residence in 1910, to name just a few key institutions that introduced science and philosophy into Spanish culture, intellectuals and scientists were able to establish crucial spaces across the generations in which to undertake research, foster critical dialogue, forge channels of communication with scholars abroad, and implement new pedagogical practices with which to interrogate the status quo and the sanctity of tradition.[44] These institutions were of paramount importance in the formation of modern science, for they operated independently from the university system and often entered into direct conflict with its ideological ambitions.[45] Needless to say, they were pivotal in introducing theories of vital force in Spain, as I will demonstrate in Chapters 2 and 3. Antonio Lafuente and Nuria Valverde rightly consider them as new types of institutions in Spain that fostered research through scholarly awards and competitions and developed crucial points of contact with those intellectual spheres thriving in European cities such as London and Paris.[46] It must be said that these institutions were themselves embedded in various structures of authority at the local and regional levels (almost all of them operated under the patronage of nobility, politicians, philanthropists, wealthy merchants, and government administrators), and thus they not only had a hand in influencing public policy within given

44 See Jean-Pierre Clement's *Las instituciones científicas y la difusión de la ciencia durante la ilustración*, 30–40. Clement focuses on the Enlightenment *academias*, specifically showing that they also played a significant role in publishing and circulating a number of texts in Spain.

45 For more on this topic see the "Prólogo" to Antonio Hermosilla Molina's *One Hundred Years of Sevillian Medicine (The Royal Society of Medicine and Other Sciences in the Eighteenth Century)*, xxi–xxxiii. Also Peset, "Academies and Sciences in Enlightened Europe."

46 Lafuente and Valverde, *Los mundos*, 8.

territorial contexts, but also operated increasingly in a grey area between convention and heterodoxy. Miguel A. Pereyra describes this process, referencing Daniel Roche's scholarship on the French *academies*, which provided administrative models for the Spanish *academias* and *sociedades* during the Enlightenment:

> Life in the academies [in Spain] acted to fuse the different strata of the elite given that, although there were differences in birth and class [among individuals], this elite socialized and interacted and at all times privileged the ideal of meritocratic advancement … The result of all of this – although we should really speak of results – can be seen in the expansion of the Enlightenment in a type of "management" thinking that favoured autonomy when it came to the administration of science and cultural goods, which it controlled and put in the service of power.[47]

Unsurprisingly, the status of the men of medicine and science rose significantly in early eighteenth-century Spain with the emergence of the *academias*. The elite came to view physicians and scientists as a unique group of learned individuals who could apply reason, logic, calculation, cool-headedness, and their distinct objectivity (the Foucauldian speaking eye) to a wide range of bodily disorders. The eighteenth century more generally saw the rise of "the specialist in scientific knowledge who demonstrated his worth in his usefulness and power," a figure who was sometimes mocked (*el petimetre*, or the middle-class fop) for his snobbery and affected scientific speech.[48] While Feijóo expressed consternation at the stature of apothecaries and barber-surgeons in Spain – the great majority of them were, in his opinion, quacks who did little to advance bodily knowledge and simply exploited the unlettered masses – he nevertheless had to concede that there existed such a thing as a wise physician, a true modern man of medical learning, capable of reading the body and rendering an authoritative judgment as to the sources and workings of its vital force.[49]

47 Pereyra, "Hubo una vez unos maestros ignorantes," 792.

48 Peset, "Academies and Sciences in Enlightened Europe," 399. For an excellent study on the figure of the *petimetre*, see Chapter 3, "Reading the Body: Petimetres, Physiognomic and Gendered Otherness" in Rebecca Haidt's *Embodying Enlightenment*, 107–50.

49 Ironically, the true modern man of medicine for Feijóo was radically skeptical about the healing powers of medicine ("Al doctor," *Teatro*, vol. 2, 373–4). It is important to note that physicians during this period, unlike artists, did not have access to a national *academia* that regulated instructional practices and provided a recognized structure of social support and advancement. See Vega, *Ciencia, arte e ilusión*, 35–6.

A.1 An eighteenth-century frontispiece, featuring the emblem of the *Regia Sociedad de Medicina y demás Ciencias de Sevilla.*

The understanding of body functioning – its physiology and sources of vitality – promised to supply rigorous answers to age-old epidemiological quandaries. It also opened new avenues of investigation leading into the Enlightenment in far-reaching social, philosophical, and scientific contexts. To grasp, for instance, how the body generated its vital force to ward off disease promised further insights into the universe's fundamental mechanics. "Because in the constant economy of our body," writes Martín Martínez in his foundational *Complete Anatomy of Man* of 1728, "we see reduced to compendium all the indisputable laws of nature in general."[50] The belief that it was possible to achieve such a macroscopic comprehension of the universe through the body's microscopic life functions (and, likewise, through their corruption and degeneration) derived from Platonic and neo-Platonic sources, and it was sustained in Renaissance hermeticism, among other fields, throughout the better part of the seventeenth century. Even as the body's interior was subjected to greater scrutiny on dissection slabs in anatomical theatres and under the microscope throughout the eighteenth century, the material origin of vital force continually eluded reason and scientific analysis. Indeed, the fascination with the human interior and the desire to comprehend what animated the body's intricate and individual parts had powerfully conditioned the science of anatomy and the broader culture of dissection. As Jonathan Sawday has it, "the 'culture of dissection' is, then, the culture of enquiry: an incisive recomposition of the human body, which entailed an equivalent refashioning of the means by which people made sense of the world around them."[51] The question of vital force certainly raised new challenges for Enlightenment science when it came to advancing empirical knowledge of the body and its life energy. Medical practitioners and philosophers soon learned that the obscurities surrounding vital force could be effectively employed to theorize the body (its autonomy, integrity, self-regulation, and so on) beyond the confines of theological dogma, and even the so-called certainties of empirical reason. Put another way, instead of conceiving of the body as simply subject to external agency and established authority, medical practitioners and philosophers began to apprehend it as an agent and producer in its *relation* with the world, which in turn provided them the occasion to begin not only connecting various fields of knowledge (the emergence of anatomy, chemistry, physiology, theology, etc.), but also generating new practices for reading and writing the living body.

For the astrologist, writer, satirist, and non-practising physician Diego de Torres Villarroel, as I will show in Chapter 2, the soul, and only the soul, regulated the body. Scripture recognized this fact, and to suggest otherwise, as many learned men of science were doing, was sacrilegious.

50 Martínez, *Anatomía completa del hombre*, 1.

51 Sawday, *The Body Emblazoned*, ix.

In his *Anatomy of the Visible and Invisible: Universal Compendium of Both Spheres* of 1738, he set out to clarify the body-soul nexus with an eye toward discrediting once and for all the increasingly popular notion that a vital force inherent in the body might very well be the source of all its motion. What remains "unspoken" in Torres's defence of the soul's authority over the body reveals to what extent his *Anatomy* points ironically to the great gains of vitalist science in early eighteenth-century Spain. With this conjunction of science and theology serving as a backdrop, the work of the eminent anatomist Sebastián Miguel Guerrero Herreros and physician Ignacio María Ruiz de Luzuriaga in Chapter 3 illustrates in what ways theories of vital force continued to inform the Spanish medical revolution of the mid- to late-eighteenth century. As honourable faculty and senior members of the Royal Society of Medicine and Other Sciences in Seville and the Royal Academy of Medicine in Madrid respectively, Guerrero Herreros and Luzuriaga advanced remarkable studies on vital force that directly challenged therapeutic custom and tradition regarding the animating properties of the soul. Through the progressive assimilation of Boerhaavian and Hallerian fibril theory (a set of principles that explained the composition of the body in terms of miniscule fibres and cellular tissues) and the latest French, Scottish, and English vitalist physiology, their innovative theories of vital force paint a compelling picture of the complex cultural shifts within Enlightenment Spain that fostered scientific discourses in which the body's unique materiality and autonomy were privileged.

In a world increasingly secularized in the late-eighteenth and early-nineteenth centuries, there emerges, predominantly with the pre-Romantics of the 1790s, a renewed understanding of nature as a beckoning and vitalized sphere. Marquis de Condorcet, David Hume, John Locke, Jean-Jacques Rousseau, and Adam Smith, as Nathaniel Wolloch points out, "often understand by this word [nature] specifically human emotions, whether this be natural law, or the 'state of nature' as signifying human forms of social organization and natural surroundings."[52] What Rousseau called the pure state of nature, the state of man existing in harmony with the living environment before the impositions of morality and the socio-political conventions of urban life, represented a quasi-utopian yearning for a more unmediated experience with nature's vitality. Nature, and its cognate *naturaleza,* was thus a highly evocative term, pressed into service for a myriad claims about social and bodily forces and boundaries. In Spain, Feijóo had expanded the meaning of

52 Wolloch, *History and Nature in the Enlightenment,* x.

naturaleza early on in his *Universal Critical Theatre.* In his 1734 entry "The Wonders of Nature," nature did not simply reflect the intricate architecture of the divine, but it also comprised the arcane wonders of pervasive force that continually altered and improved this most marvellous structure. For Feijóo, nature's animating pulse was apparent everywhere in the individual's day-to-day life, and he advised that the *ilustrado* – the enlightened individual – would do well to ponder upon such astonishing phenomena as gravity, germination, magnetism, tides, and cloud formation in order to attain a more edifying comprehension of the world. Standing face-to-face with nature's dynamic system, Feijóo argued, the individual was hard pressed not to find himself transported into a state of "ecstatic awe."[53]

A few years later, in 1737, the physician Manuel Gutiérrez de los Ríos penned his *Language of Nature with Which the Physician Is Instructed How to Properly Cure Acute Diseases*, arguing that to comprehend man, anatomically and otherwise, is to understand him directly through the generative forces of nature and their phenomena. For Gutiérrez de los Ríos, nature was a sweeping term for the complex energies that governed everything from the motion of heavenly bodies to the most microscopic and unfathomable dimensions of man's interior economy. To invoke *naturaleza,* then, was to strive to make sense of nature's language, as it was codified in and through the living body. The physician had no choice but to become an interpreter of the visible grammar of vitality and disease, life and decay, movement and stagnation that connected body and nature. The larger implication of Gutiérrez de los Ríos's argument was that, in reading the body's vital force, it was possible to discern the interrelationships that immanently bonded man and world. Although this idea was not new per se, and found its antecedents in portions of Hippocrates' precepts on nature, Gutiérrez de los Ríos made evident how science re-engaged in earnest the body's direct bond with nature and its bounteous life: "Opinionated physicians do not study in Nature nor observe its constant and simple way of working, but rather study school books filled with charitable ideas, fantastic theories, and sham syllogisms that are only good for the splendors of the medical *juntas* and not for curing the infirmed ... Our ideas should adjust to Nature, and not the other way around. Only Nature acts in the living; heed it and you will not err in your healing."[54]

53 Feijóo, *Teatro crítico universal,* 245.

54 Gutiérrez de los Ríos, *Idioma de la naturaleza,* 9–16.

The profound sense of awe concerning the body's vital bond with nature can be traced in Spain throughout the Enlightenment and leading into the early-nineteenth century. During this period, men of learning aspired to observe and catalogue nature and its diversity as accurately as possible, and one of the more ambitious enterprises on the peninsula worth mentioning in this respect was physician and botanist Joseph Quer y Martínez's multivolume *Spanish Flora*, begun in 1762, which aimed to showcase the beauty, utility, and variety of Spain's abundant plant life. In the literary arena, authors like Francisco Gregorio de Salas, Nicasio Álvarez de Cienfuegos, and particularly Juan Meléndez Valdés, likewise elevated nature's glories. In poems like "Order of the Universe and Admirable Chain of Its Beings: Dedicated to Jovellanos," and "Immensity of Nature and the Ineffable Goodness of its Author," Meléndez Valdés envisaged the body and nature participating in the same vital unity. In "Immensity of Nature and the Ineffable Goodness of its Author" the speaker praises the Almighty for the remarkable harmony that governs living nature on earth: "Forms, movements, lives, / species, climates, seasons, terrain, / everything is connected in the loftiest and most joyous consonances. Oh, beneficent God!" For Gaspar Melchor de Jovellanos, as I argue in Chapter 4, the body's vital bond with nature is articulated at its most inspiring level of complexity when it lends itself to an organicist rendering of the universe and foreshadows Romantic notions of the Absolute, or the infinite, active, and living becoming. In his extensive travel journals, poems, diaries, and *Oration Pronounced in the Asturian Institute on the Study of the Natural Sciences* of 1799, which condensed his outlook on nature's divine splendours, we can grasp to what degree the question of vital force in Spain not only played a role in the expression of a subjective self, but also challenged the authority of reason in revealing how the ineffable wonders of an animated nature could open a path to a new type of epistemology about life. This reading of Jovellanos indeed problematizes and expands our current understanding of the radius of his thinking and adds to the complexity of his views on the limits of reason when confronted with living nature.

By the close of the eighteenth century, the Scottish surgeon John Hunter, one of the most representative vitalists at the time, known for his *Observations on Certain Parts of the Animal Oeconomy* and an important influence on Spanish *ilustrados* like Ruiz de Luzuriaga, as we shall see in Chapter 3, concluded simply that "[l]ife is a property we do not understand."[55] A few decades later, Antonio Ballano's widely used

55 Hunter, *Observations*, 117.

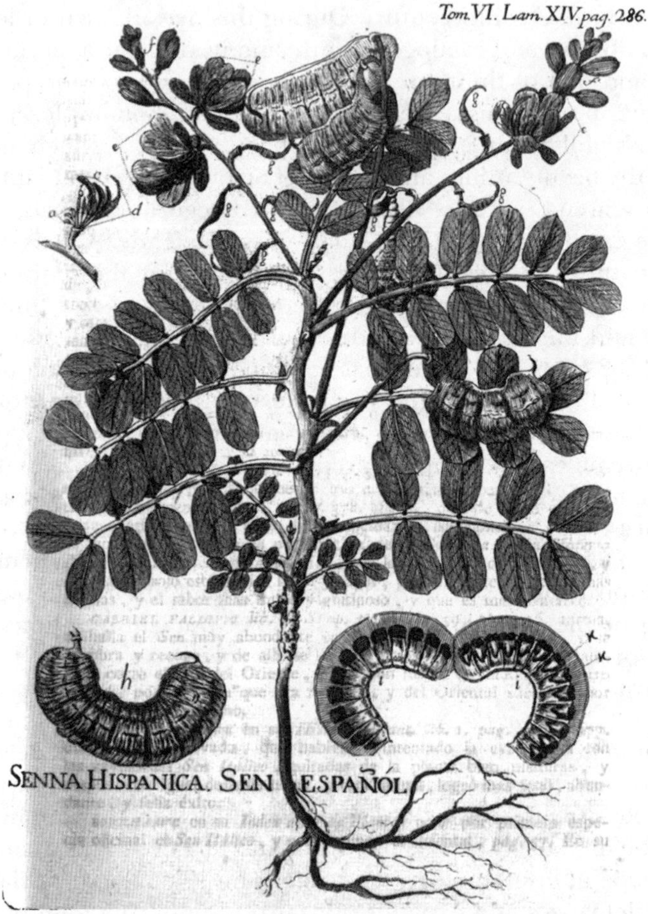

A.2 Plate XIV, "Senna Hispánica," from Joseph Quer y Martínez's *Flora española, o historia de las plantas de España, Tomo VI*, 1784.

reference work *Dictionary of Medicine and Surgery, or Medico-Surgical Manual* of 1805 made a similar claim and defined life as an "imponderable agent" lurking everywhere throughout the body.[56] Conjuring up

56 Ballano, *Diccionario de medicina y cirugía*, 880.

the shifting notions of the organic that characterized advances in physiological science, which I will discuss in more detail in Chapter 5, he described life as if arising out of a dizzyingly elaborate network of vital relations and interdependencies that constituted the body's system. He finally concluded: "It is impossible to discover the primary origin of vital force."[57] For the Romantics in Spain and across Europe, what came to be known as "vitalism" opened new possibilities of thinking the body, and likewise elicited a new corporeal semiotics and innovative, if at times unorthodox, metaphysical beliefs about self and world. There was perhaps no question of greater consequence for the Romantics than discovering what exactly produced, directed, and sustained the miraculous spark of life throughout the diversity of living organisms in nature. Wary of materialist progress and sensing humanity's estrangement from the natural world, they aspired to unravel nature's "divine vitality," to use William Wordsworth's well-known phrase, and comprehend, even if only intuitively, the unifying vigour that connected the individual with the infinite web of the Absolute.[58]

For Mata y Fontanet, one of Spain's leading and most erudite materialists, covered in Chapter 5, vitalism in early- to mid-nineteenth-century Spain made evident the country's stagnation in science in the great age of modernization. In his opinion, vitalism was not science, but pure fantasy; it was an obscure religion of sorts that theorized inscrutable bodily forces to sidestep the difficult and thoroughly modern task of utilizing empirical principles to discover life's processes. He challenged the Spanish medical establishment when, during the inaugural lecture for the 1859 academic year at the Royal Academy of Medicine in Madrid, he argued for "the modern method": a positive science of experimentation that could make empirical sense of the body's energies once and for all.[59] Matías Nieto y Serrano, the renowned physician and Royal Medical Academy member, celebrated for his *Outline of the Living Science* of 1867, employed Calderón de la Barca's famed *Life Is a Dream* as a fitting backdrop to censure materialists like Mata y Fontanet and drive home a key point of vitalist theory reminiscent of Hunter and Ballano's conclusions. In Nieto y Serrano's words: "Life is at the same time exceedingly common … and what has been least understood and known."[60] Certainly, materialists like Mata y Fontanet were not alone in calling for a renewed approach to vital force in Spain during the nineteenth century. The Krausist movement, which was decisive in advancing body culture

57 Ibid., 888.
58 Wordsworth, *The Collected Poems*, 277.
59 Mata y Fontanet, *Hipócrates y las escuelas hipocráticas*, 15.
60 Nieto y Serrano, "Discurso sobre Calderón de la Barca," 214.

through a belief in health regimens and calisthenics, addressed the issue and understood the need for a constructive focus on the individual in a modernizing world. For Krausists like Sanz del Río, the question of vital force served as the underlying principle upon which to begin building the perfectible and rational society that the German Romantic philosopher Karl C.F. Krause had envisioned in *Ideal of Humanity for Life.* Only healthy, vigorous, and beautiful bodies, whose vital force harmonized with nature, Krause maintained, were properly suited to contribute to the teleological project of transforming society into a fully constituted "human family."[61]

In the modern era of mass culture and commoditization, capitalist forms of social organization were thought to impoverish life, which, as Max Weber and Georg Simmel proposed, had the tendency to engender alienation and foster a sense of powerlessness in society.[62] Miguel de Unamuno, as I will argue in Chapter 6, directly challenged capitalism in his socialist writings during the 1890s. For Unamuno, the question of vital force was critical in comprehending the individual's potential to overcome the burdens of modern life, yet it had been brushed aside with the triumph of capitalist modes of production throughout the nineteenth century. In *On Casticism* of 1895, and later in his landmark *The Tragic Sense of Life* of 1912, he argued that there was no regenerating the nation without first regenerating the individual, a process that entailed reconnecting the individual with the vital essence of life. Yet, he went

61 Krause, *Ideal de la humanidad,* 182.

62 As Max Weber conceived it, scientific development was an integral part of a broader disenchantment with the world that came about as a result of the expansion of reason and progress. He asked: "Does [this process of intellectualization] mean that we, today, for instance ... have a greater knowledge of the conditions of life under which we exist than has the American Indian or a Hottentot? Hardly" ("Science," 14). In Weber's view, alienation and powerlessness were the fundamental consequences of the modern capitalist economy, or what he termed "the technical and economic conditions of machine production, which today determine the lives of all the individuals who are born into this mechanism, not only those directly concerned with economic acquisition, with irresistible force" (*The Protestant,* 180–1). The bureaucratic structures of the modern capitalist economy (the rationalization of society) reproduced the morality of efficiency, discipline, and quantification that further organized social relations in which individuals were severed from traditional spheres of communal signification and belonging. Simmel makes a somewhat similar case, approaching the issue in *The Philosophy of Money* from the exchange relations developed in modern capitalist societies. There was a subjective aspect to all exchange relations for Simmel, and thus, "exchange takes place not for the sake of an object previously possessed by another person, but rather for the sake of one's own feeling about an object ... The meaning of exchange, moreover, is that the sum of values is greater afterward than it was before, and this implies that each party gives the other more than he had himself possessed" (44).

further, and argued that the lived body and its obscure sources of protoplasmic life-energy could in fact hold the answers to a number of sociophilosophical problems. By this time, the body was interpreted through reference to personality types and the genetic factors postulated in evolutionary theory to explain everything from anomie and deviancy to secularism and sociability. Evolutionism maintained that man's relationship with nature had fundamentally changed with the Industrial Revolution, and it increasingly reduced life's complexity to physiological functions, necessity, instinct, and genetic variations. "Darwinism reduces the dogma of creation to nothing," writes the theologian and philosopher Zeferino González in 1892, with a mix of trepidation and resentment, "and here remains its principal merit: it has opened a door where the supernatural and miraculous, and creation itself, will be tossed out for ever."[63]

The early-twentieth century provided fertile ground in Spain in which theories of vital force could take root and grow into various fields of inquiry like never before. Philosophers such as Nietzsche offered Spanish intellectuals solutions to problems concerning the regulatory order of science championed by the likes of Mata y Fontanet. In *Human, All Too Human,* Nietzsche pointed out that, if "science provides us with less and less pleasure ... and [casts] suspicion on the consolations of metaphysics, religion and art, then that mightiest source of joy to which mankind owes almost all its humanity will become impoverished."[64] One of Nietzsche's major philosophical contributions was to pursue the question of vital force in the context of contemporary debates on religion, morality, power, and social class, and he theorized an inner force within the individual, a fundamental will to power through which he could overcome the deadening uniformity of life to realize his ambitions. In *On the Genealogy of Morals,* he argued that "the essence of life, its *will to power* ... [is the] essential priority of the spontaneous, aggressive, expansive, form-giving forces that give new interpretation and directions."[65] For Pío Baroja and avant-gardists like Ramón Gómez de la Serna, whom I also examine in Chapter 6, Nietzsche's philosophy on vital force brazenly set out the framework for a theory of action in which the individual's vital force provided crucial insight into a world that was believed to be suffering through a stage of degeneration. This insight, however, involved more than a passive scrutiny of the world from the comforts of the philosopher's armchair. It was through bodily action and movement that

63 González, *La Biblia y la ciencia,* 545.

64 Nietzsche, *Human, All Too Human,* 119.

65 Nietzsche, *On the Genealogy of Morals,* 79.

one could reveal what was true about the world – and thus, what was meaningful and possible.

Baroja and Gómez de la Serna borrowed from Nietzsche the central idea that the *lived body* served as the inviolable source of truth. In my close reading of Baroja's foundational novel *The Tree of Knowledge*, I explore the complexity of the lived body in relation to the various discourses of social hygiene, degeneration, pathology, and eugenics that were embedded in the larger narratives of vital force in the *fin de siècle* and early-twentieth century. As I argue, Baroja's novel turns to the Nietzschean ideal of "supreme health" to draw out the larger social implications associated with the lived body in Spain at the time. In surveying Gómez de la Serna's texts, including his first autobiography, *Morbidities*, his manifesto, "The Concept of a New Literature," and other writings, such as his celebrated *greguerías*, it becomes clear that the modern aesthetics of the future did not depend on the ossified norms of tradition and convention, but rather on the contingent actions of individuals brimming with vitality as they wrestled with the contradictions of modernity and its fragmented time and space. He stated it clearly in his manifesto: "The new literature does away with the commonplace and unearths the true concept of life."[66]

MODERNITY AND THE LURE OF VITAL FORCE: A TRANSNATIONAL PERSPECTIVE

To further illuminate the complexities that surrounded the question of vital force in Spain that I traced in the previous section, we must step back and address more generally the larger transnational perspective in which it gained its relevance. Since the pre-Enlightenment period, when the likes of Cabriada and Juanini were advancing knowledge of the body and disease, the question of vital force increasingly challenged medico-philosophical theory and began to permeate numerous branches of cultural activity in Europe. With a more revisionist reinterpretation of ancient Greek philosophy and mechanistic reasoning, and with the advancement of science in new arenas of intellectual exchange (the political field, for instance), the great disputes over vital force radically oriented scientific production and interpretation. Catherine Packham, Peter H. Reill, Barbara Stafford, and Elizabeth A. Williams all point to the crucial period between 1690 and 1800 as a profoundly revolutionary

66 Gómez de la Serna, *Obras*, vol. 1, 151.

epoch in theorizing the body as a site of knowledge and resistance.[67] The flourishing sciences of anatomy, microscopy, and physiology revealed how little understood the body truly was, a point Spanish physicians and philosophers such as Cabriada, Martínez, Guerrero Herreros, and Luzuriaga repeatedly emphasized. These disciplines likewise established new correspondences between bodily life and nature, thereby providing more encompassing frameworks for the discovery of the body's well-spring of vital force. Yet, as the aforementioned critics have pointed out, the epistemological field within which these discoveries were made was more fluid and less rigidly demarcated than has often been supposed. Major concepts, such as science, nature, reason, and life, were systematically problematized and refined. In the German tradition, Wilhelm and Alexander von Humboldt's theories on nature in the late-eighteenth and early-nineteenth centuries are illuminating in this respect:

> [Wilhelm and Alexander] attempted to formulate a way in which nature could be comprehended and explained without relying on reductive systems founded upon discursive logic. For this reason, they eschewed clear-cut analytical categories. Their language of nature is shot through with ambiguity and paradox, just as their analysis shifts abruptly from one realm to another to describe their conception of harmonic mediation that cannot be couched in mechanistic terms.[68]

Wilhelm's and Alexander's antisystematic thought and their strategic use of ambiguity and paradox was a hallmark of early Romantic scientists, who discerned the germ of life in the immensity of nature's vital workings. For a Romantic like Novalis, nature's flux and seemingly boundless generative energy was best understood in totalizing terms as a ubiquitous life force that not only implicated the individual subject in its awe-inspiring mysteries at the most intrinsic level of Spirit, but also destabilized further the very notions of objectivity and truth given the aporias that beset society. The sciences of sensation that developed from anatomical discoveries during this period would have profound consequences for the arts, as they opened the way to revised forms of corporeality that allowed the Romantics to "derive a basis for self-conscious

67 I am referring to Catherine Packham's *Eighteenth-century Vitalism: Bodies, Culture, Politics*; Peter H. Reill's *Vitalizaing Nature in the Enlightenment*; Barbara M. Stafford's *Body Criticism: Imaging the Unseen in Enlightenment Art and Medicine*; and Elizabeth A. Williams's *The Physical and the Moral: Anthropology, Physiology, and Philosophical Medicine in France, 1750–1850*. I will refer to these texts throughout.

68 Reill, *Vitalizing Nature*, 26.

reflection on the social and political claims of imaginative work."[69] Put another way, the self-reflective and creative experience, particularly as it related to the body-nature dynamic, could guide the individual to a more profound understanding of life than could reason alone. This was Jovellanos's telling conclusion in his *Oration*, a conclusion he reached after studying nature from numerous viewpoints. As he came to see it, the active life-bearing force of nature defied reason on several fronts, yet simultaneously opened the individual to a new organicist epistemology that was not only thoroughly edifying, but could also provide revolutionary glimpses into the workings of the universe. For Jovellanos, as with the pre-Romantics and Romantics, the experience of sublimity was key in this respect, for nature's grandeur often elicited profound emotional states from the contemplative individual, particularly those that defied verbal description and welled up from the depths of what he called "secret astonishment."[70] The phenomena that were most conducive to producing these types of emotional states included the immensity of the firmament, prodigious expanses of sea, volcanic eruptions, earthquakes, violent tempests, and immense and verdant landscapes bursting with life.

The sciences expanded greatly in the period that ran from 1770 to 1830, and the enigma of vital force disclosed new relations between the creative and the analytical. In his work on Romantic vitalism, Robert Mitchell demonstrates to what extent artists and poets sought to cultivate organicist ideals of vital force that could transcend the divide between organic and inorganic, interior and exterior, and, ultimately, science and art. In Mitchell's words: "experimental vitalism confuses the categories 'scientist' and 'artist' in part because it is a project of tracing, and thereby encouraging, the self-reflexivity of life, producing new possibilities *for* individual and social life through new sensations and perception *of* life."[71] The question of vital force thus pointed to a sprawling realm of subjective self-definition and, in the end, of possibility and transcendence. It is little wonder that vital force had evolved by this period into its own discrete category of analysis, a fact owing not only to the changing idea of matter itself, thanks in large measure to Cartesianism and its critics, as Deutsch and Terrall point out in *Vital Matters*, but also to the great influence that Montpellier vitalism (the vitalism developed at the renowned Montpellier medical school in France) exerted throughout

69 Jackson, *Science and Sensation*, 4.
70 Jovellanos, *Obras*, vol. 4, 280.
71 Mitchell, *Experimental Life*, 3.

Europe.[72] In his studies on how electricity mixed with oxygen to generate a primary vital agent within the body, the Spanish physician José Ponce de León proposed in 1804: "Three things that united form the nature of man: body, vital force, and rational soul."[73]

Frederick Burwick and Paul Douglas's edited collection, *The Crisis in Modernism: Bergson and the Vitalist Controversy*, argues convincingly that theories of vital force, from the early Enlightenment all the way through to the paragons of modernist vitalism like Bergson and Driesch, served as formidable frameworks of socio-political and cultural criticism – frameworks that similarly revealed the fundamental aporias and contradictions inherent in modernity's relationship with nature.[74] Sebastian Normandin's and Charles T. Wolfe's edited collection elaborates on this point concerning modernity and nature, noting that "vitalism again comes to the fore, as it does whenever the question of boundaries arises ... Vitalism is thus always on the borderland of thought."[75] That is to say, the question of vital force points repeatedly to the paradoxical nature of modernity itself, to that part of its critical project that is powerless to make sense of its own claims about organic life. The bewildering forms of vitalism that brought several fields of inquiry into closer alignment throughout Europe during this period speak to the fundamental *limits* of science and philosophy in decreeing what exactly vitalized the body. With materialists like Mata y Fontanet, who believed that if the murky notion of vital force could be banished from scientific discussion altogether then modern medical research would progress by leaps and bounds, we gain a clearer picture of how positivism attempted to respond to growing skepticism about science and its rationality in the nineteenth century through the development of new discourses of authority. Invoking the positivist mantra of Order and Progress against the ideal of

72 Deutsch and Terrall, *Vital Matters*, 5–9. See also Elizabeth A. Williams, *A Cultural History of Medical Vitalism in Enlightenment Montpellier* concerning the role of the Montpellier medical school in popularizing the "empirical" aspects of neo-Hippocratic vitalism in Europe as opposed to mechanistic science, 80–146. Also relevant is Chapter 1 of Williams, *The Physical and the Moral*, 20–66.

73 Ponce de León, *Phisiología chimica*, 106.

74 Frederick Burwick and Paul Douglas put it succinctly: "So wide was the net of vitalism then cast that it embraced even diametrically opposed sets of doctrines and winds of philosophical belief ... [T]he essential issue in any divide (Bergsonian or other) between Enlightenment and modern sensibilities, or between rational and irrational mentalities, rests on conception of nature and the ways in which nature is codified into science" (17–19).

75 Normandin and Wolfe, "Vitalism and the Scientific Image," 2.

vital force, Mata y Fontanet repeatedly declared that "progress ... is the aspiration of the nineteenth century, even though ephemeral and bastardly reactions of all types furiously attempt to drown it."[76]

With the development and diversity of vitalist discourses in the early-twentieth century, the question of vital force shifted to the centre of cultural dialogues and underscored that special "something" of life beyond the domain of scientific proof that Burroughs had alluded to in *The Breath of Life.*[77] For modernists and avant-gardists like Unamuno, Baroja, and Gómez de la Serna, who grew disillusioned with progress and its claims to truth, addressing this special "something" of life powerfully illuminated the relevance of intuition, imagination, self-reflection, personal liberty, and irrationality in day-to-day existence.[78] For Mikhail Bakhtin, this new critical vitalism sweeping across Europe only perverted scientific objectivity in order to privilege – to the detriment of modernity's ivory tower of science – all manner of "subjectivist, valuative definitions."[79] Ortega y Gasset's influential ratiovitalism in Spain, for instance, derived naturally from this milieu and maintained a somewhat intermediary view in which reason and life were complementary and indissoluble: reason was rooted in the vital flow of our existence and was thus continually moulded by the experiential here-and-now; and yet, our existence was dependent on the powers of reason for its practical, moral, and ethical concerns. Clearly, the issue was not so cut-and-dried during this period, as Donna V. Jones has convincingly argued, since although the promise of vital force was instrumental in emphasizing corporeality, bodily capabilities, the will, and the logic of self-realization in the pursuit

76 Mata y Fontanet, *Doctrina médico-filosófica española*, 7.

77 See the Preface.

78 Richard A. Lofthouse demonstrates how vitalist theories influenced the way German and British artists like Otto Dix, Stanley Spencer, Max Beckmann, and Jacob Epstein approached the self-world divide. For Lofthouse, "there is a more basic sense in which [Dix, Spencer, Beckmann, and Epstein] can be named vitalists. First, they foreshadowed fidelity to the life-force as a concept, and secondly and more visibly, the values symbolized by that fidelity had repercussions when it came to aesthetic debate and the practical business of painting. Centrally ... they objected to the subordination of art to the formal elements of its creation, or what is commonly referred to as formalism and broadly associated with abstraction ... [Their objection] amounted to far more than a particular style of artistic expression, embracing much deeper issues concerning the nature of reality and the importance of art portraying it truthfully" (*Vitalism in Modern Art, c. 1900–1950*, 29).

79 Bakhtin, "Contemporary Vitalism," 96.

of truth, it also opened new paths in Europe to develop and shape powerful racial and anti-Semitic discourses.[80]

In the immediate aftermath of the Second World War – a period not covered in this book, but sketched here briefly to show the continuity of the discussion – when vitalism descended into the shadows of cultural debates for its linkages to "bad" science, occultism, decadentism, irrationalism, and totalitarian politics (fascism's emphasis, for instance, on youth and body culture), various of its tenets were partly incorporated into existential philosophy.[81] This is the period when Erwin Schrödinger's *What Is Life? The Physical Aspect of the Living Cell* of 1944 resonated far and wide within the scientific community and opened new avenues of investigation into the emerging field of genetics. As countless scientists before him, Schrödinger was more than optimistic that the physical and chemical sciences, with more-rigorously defined concepts and improved technical methodologies and instrumentation, would one day be able to pinpoint the fundamental origin of life in the cell.[82] The physician and scientist Georges Canguilhem is one of the key figures who came full

80 Donna Jones sums up this double articulation as follows: "One cannot understand twentieth-century vitalism separately from its implications in racial and anti-Semitic discourses … we cannot understand some of the dominant models of emancipation within black thought except through recourse to the vitalist tradition … In the end, I argue that *Négritude*'s grounding of black oppositional culture in vitalism needs to be handled much more critically than it has been by the critics who have noted the connection. At the least, I hope to show that some of the dominant models of emancipation within black thought cannot be understood except through recourse to the vitalist tradition" (*The Radical Discourses of Life Philosophy*, 5–6).

81 In terms of the vitalism-fascism connection, Stanley Payne notes that "the essential divergence of fascist ideas from certain aspects of modern culture lay more precisely in the fascist rejection of rationalism, materialism, and egalitarianism – replaced by philosophical vitalism and idealism and the metaphysics of the will, all of which are intrinsically modern. Fascists aspired to recover what they considered the true sense of the natural and of human nature … in opposition to the reductionist culture of modern materialism and prudent egotism" (*A History of Fascism, 1914–1945*, 8). For the vitalism-existentialism connection, see Jacques Salvan's *The Scandalous Ghost: Sartre's Existentialism as Related to Vitalism, Humanism, Mysticism, and Marxism.*

82 Schrödinger states this point clearly in the introduction: "How can the events *in space and time* which take place within the spatial boundary of a living organism be accounted for by physics and chemistry? … The obvious inability of present-day physics and chemistry to account for such events is no reason at all for doubting that they can be accounted for by those sciences … Organic chemistry, indeed, in investigating more and more complicated molecules, has come very much nearer to that 'aperiodic crystal' which, in my opinion, is the material carrier of life" (*What Is Life?*, 3–4). Schrödinger's concept of aperiodic crystals, or stable, non-repeating structures of genes, was highly influential in the development of DNA research. See Watson and Berry's *DNA: The Secret to Life*, 35–7.

circle with vitalist inquiry in the 1960s and pondered the same questions about vital force that had been raised by the likes of Guerrero Herreros and Luzuriaga at the end of the eighteenth century. Unlike Schrödinger, Canguilhem attempted to understand organisms through their relationship to their environment, and asserted that reducing biology to purely a physical science obviated the complexities of life. According to Canguilhem, Giuseppe Bianco notes, "life consists in the plastic power, proper to all organisms, of creating qualitatively new norms; if life is essentially a potentiality, then this means that the living being is not simply a machine, an assembly of pieces reacting to the environment, but is what modifies and creates it."[83] While Canguilhem understood the limits of classical vitalism and the fallacy of precluding physical and chemical laws in appreciating the resoluteness of life, the question he asked frequently, and which condensed his thinking on the specificity of vital force, was this: "Yet would it nevertheless be possible, without rendering biology suspect, to ask of it an occasion, if not permission, to rethink and rectify fundamental philosophical concepts, such as that of life?"[84]

Foucault, whose work I will turn to in more detail in the following section, likewise revisited vital force, and he himself was a great admirer of his mentor Canguilhem. Through a type of Nietzschean genealogical critique, Foucault examined vital force as it was interpreted through the intersecting discourses of sexuality, medicine, disease, criminality, and insanity, and traced its various permutations, beginning in the early Enlightenment. In his landmark *The History of Sexuality*, he articulated with clarity one of the core arguments that subtended his critical method and which I believe to be of crucial importance when tackling the historical trajectory of vitalist thinking in Spain: "deployments of power are directly connected to the body – to bodies, functions, physiological processes, sensations, and pleasures."[85] The slippery concept of bio-power that marked his later work theorized the security mechanisms through which institutions invested in "taking control of life and the biological processes of man-as-species and of ensuring that they are ... regularized."[86] These security mechanisms, which can be traced back to the early-modern period, have sought to frame the question of vital force – or, at the very least, to supervise and restrict the spheres in which it can be discussed – by pronouncing what justifies the right to take life, for instance, or what justifies the right to foster and improve it. Gilles Deleuze

83 Bianco, "The Origins of of Georges Canguilhem's 'Vitalism,'" 243.

84 Canguilhem, *Knowledge of Life*, 59.

85 Foucault, *The History of Sexuality*, 151.

86 Foucault, *Society Must Be Defended*, 246–7.

was one of the critics who championed Foucault's strategic fascination with vital force, and he discerned rightly that Foucault's later oeuvre on bio-power was essentially vitalist in its outlook. The later Foucault, according to Deleuze, did nothing if not interrogate how resistance transforms into the formidable power of life, "a vital power that cannot be confined within species, environment or the paths of a particular diagram."[87]

The revisionist interplay of looking back to look forward informs Mariam Fraser, Sarah Kember, and Celia Lury's edited collection that addresses not only why vitalism has haunted our cultural imaginary since antiquity, but also why it matters now, given the social transformations that characterize our present information age of digitalization, computing, cyberspace, virtual reality, and technological dependency. Critics such as Antonio Negri, Félix Guattari, Elizabeth Grosz, and Rosi Braidotti have also expanded the theoretical application of vitalist critique, yet it was Deleuze who most consistently returned to the question of vital force and placed it at the centre of his critical practice. With Deleuze, vital force as a concept and as a potential anchor for philosophical inquiry is not simply revisited in contemporary theory, but palpably extended, reconfigured. The rhizome, or the complex network of life, much in the sense of Bergson's *élan vital*, is traversed with a continual flow of vital becomings and events that connect people and things. The embodied self must contend with the rhizome; it must navigate its space of interconnectivity and discover new territories of vital meaning in hopes of resisting the "apparatus of capture" (the means by which the singular is reduced to the common and quantifiable) encoded in present-day capitalist production. One of Deleuze's lasting contributions is to take up the torch for a cause that is integrally embedded in the modern itself and that becomes readily discernible with the question of vital force: reorient philosophy to the somatic and expand life's *possibilities* by rethinking the task of ontology. It is from this restorative outlook that he declares: "It's organisms that die, not life."[88] Vital force thus becomes with Deleuze, much as it did with the Spanish philosophers, physicians, scientists, and authors I examine in this book, one of the most pressing issues facing contemporary society.

87 Deleuze, *Foucault*, 77.

88 Deleuze, *Negotiations*, 143. In his article "Immanence: A Life…," Deleuze elaborates on this point through the notion of "virtuality," which alludes to the continuous and unpredictable becoming of life: "A life contains only virtuals. It is made up of virtualities, events, singularities. What we call virtual is not something that lacks reality but something that is engaged in a process of actualization following the plane that gives it its particular reality" (31).

VITAL FORCE AND THE MODERN SUBJECT

There are few concepts as elusive and compelling as modernity. Marshall Berman's classic definition of modernity as a "maelstrom" of continual disintegration and renewal, of conflict and contradiction, of uncertainty and anguish, brings into view the dialectical tensions inherent in the processes of rationalization and self-constitution that have marked the advancement of Western culture and which various critics have explored at length.[89] My aim in this section is not to undertake the daunting task of elaborating a theory of (Spanish) modernity through the lens of vital force. Rather, I wish to specify one of the inquiries that frames this book and that I briefly contextualized in the previous sections: to what extent can the question of vital force in Spain beginning in the seventeenth century shed new light on the practices of self-constitution that were part and parcel of modernity? The question of vital force itself sprang from the ideologies of body normativity and discipline that shaped Western culture, and thus they influenced, and were influenced by, the larger development of rationalization, or the organization of society based on scientific reason, the systematization of knowledge practices, the progressive secularization of attitudes and values, the regularization of new forms of bureaucratic administration and authority, and the rise of the nation state. What I wish to suggest is that the question of vital force in Spain, while it was often shot through with inconsistencies and occupied an ambiguous space between the scientific and the metaphysical, not only challenged at key junctures the truth claims upon which this larger development of rationalization and subject formation depended, but also served as a powerful resource in the politics of reform.

When speaking of subject formation, we would do well to recall what Foucault tells us about the origins of modernity: "modernity begins when the human being begins to exist within his organism, inside the shell of his head, inside the armature of his limbs, and in the whole structure of his physiology."[90] What Foucault suggests is that modernity takes form the moment the individual comes into awareness of his body and its

89 Berman, *All That Is Solid*, 15. A very brief sample of this scholarship, some of which undergirds this book, includes Zygmunt Bauman, *Modernity and Ambivalence*; Slavoj Žižek, *Less Than Nothing: Hegel and the Shadow of Dialectical Materialism*; Anthony J. Cascardi, *The Subject of Modernity*; Terry Eagleton, *The Ideology of the Aesthetic*; Anthony Giddens, *The Consequences of Modernity*, and *Modernity and Self-Identity* and *Self and Society in the Later Modern Age*; Jürgen Habermas, *The Theory of Communicative Action*; Harvie Ferguson, *Modernity and Subjectivity: Body, Soul, Spirit.*

90 Foucault, *The Order of Things*, 346.

complex rapport with social and institutional frameworks and the domain of nature, and thus begins to ponder the power relations that inform how the corporeal is conceived, interpreted, and, ultimately, governed. Foucault is likewise referring to the various methods by which we apprehend and actualize our bodies as subjects in response to various modes of authority and their disciplinary practices. As he understood it, the underlying crisis of modernity is given clear form the moment Descartes advocated for the fundamental division between mind and body, yet he was also addressing something much more essential, more far-reaching, with the conjunction of "human being" and "organism" that is crucially important: modernity signalled the paradoxical emergence of the vital bodily-self as both problem and solution, as both locus of subjugation and liberation.

It is worth taking a moment to follow through on this paradoxical tension and see how it frames the question of vital force in relation to the emergence of the modern subject. Judith Butler has been one of the most vocal critics of Foucault's concepts of body and subject, arguing that, if the concept "body" is discursively produced and culturally bound, how then can it ostensibly elude ever being subjected to the disciplinary practices of power?[91] The central question Butler raises is: what forms of resistance can feasibly disrupt or transform the structures of domination and serve as instruments of change? Elizabeth Grosz elaborates on this point, tracing the manner in which Nietzsche's genealogical method both informs and encumbers Foucault's approach to the body as cultural signifier, particularly as it concerns the modes of social inscription of bodies. Echoing Butler's argument, Grosz proposes that "[t]he body is not outside of history, for it is produced through and in history," and thus, its meanings are always already enmeshed in the politics of power and authority.[92] She notes further that Foucault's concept of body is excessively abstract: it is a body capable of being conceptualized before the impositions of power, and yet also puzzlingly gendered since, "implicitly, or without adequately acknowledging it, Foucault talks only about the male body."[93] While Foucault's notion of body *in* history has raised as many questions as it has answered, particularly in relation to gender and sexuality, he readily admits that signifying bodies cannot escape being sites of cultural inscription and resistance. Quite simply, the body cannot elude being subjected in some form to the disciplinary practices of power (while a type of fundamental anarchism, or "originary freedom,"

91 Butler, "Foucault and the Paradox of Bodily Inscriptions," 601–7.

92 Grosz, *Volatile Bodies*, 148.

93 Ibid., 157.

is possible, Foucault admits, it remains ever elusive).[94] While this deceptively simple point of subjection has fuelled a substantial debate that goes well beyond the scope of subject formation and identity politics, the force of Foucault's core argument still stands: the determinants of power (discourses, fields of interactions, forms of knowledge, etc.) cannot be fathomed except through the tangible realities of resistance (living physical bodies and their vital energies and activities). More important still, it is precisely in spheres of resistance where these determinants of power are rendered most visible and reveal to what extent the subject is by no means a constant and fixed essence:

> [T]here are no relations of power without resistances; the latter are all the more real and effective because they are formed right at the point where relations of power are exercised; resistance to power does not have to come from elsewhere to be real, nor is it inexorably frustrated through being the compatriot of power. It exists all the more by being in the same place as power; hence, like power, resistance is multiple and can be integrated in global strategies.[95]

Any attempt to situate ourselves as subjects beyond our discursive traditions and practices – what Foucault defined as the gesture to transcend the inside/outside logic of critique to thereby gain a sharper view of how discourses are constituted and perpetuated – is itself an act of resistance within the so-called regime of power. Indeed, a wealth of contemporary criticism, from posthumanism to biocentrism to social-systems theory to network studies, has focused on drawing out the implications of this crucial movement of reflecting upon constraints, of coming into an awareness of how the body and its subjectivity is discursively produced and culturally bound. Rosi Braidotti, in her seminal work on posthumanism, argues that even contemporary technologized subjectivity blurs the division between human and machine, organic and inorganic, yet it is precisely the problematics of blurring and its fast-paced dynamic nature that defines the posthuman subject as a subject that exceeds boundaries, a subject that is mediated, refigured, and redesigned virtually and symbolically.[96] The posthuman body, which Foucault prefigures in his later period by emphasizing biopower and its relation to disciplinary technologies on the body, projects itself then as a fusion of heterogeneous components that are both real and virtual and whose boundaries

94 Foucault, "What Is Critique?" 75.
95 Foucault, *Power/Knowledge*, 142.
96 See Chapters 2 and 3 of Braidotti's *Nomadic Theory*.

undergo constant redefinition.[97] This fundamental awareness of boundaries, which clearly remains very much a part of our postmodern distrust for everything from metaphysics to cyberculture, is precisely what makes it possible to undertake, as Foucault proposes, a practical critique into "the events that have led us to constitute ourselves and to recognize ourselves as subjects of what we are doing, thinking, and saying."[98] Inspired by Kant's foundational critique, Foucault's notion of *practical critique* attempts to identify and signal the forms of power that determine and restrict the ways we think – the very history of rationality and subjecthood, as it were – and our given modes of embodied existence:

> A critique is not a matter of saying that things are not right as they are. It is a matter of pointing out on what kinds of assumptions, what kinds of familiar, unchallenged, unconsidered modes of thought, the practices that we accept rest … Criticism is a matter of flushing out that thought and trying to change it: to show that things are not as self-evident as we believed, to see that what is accepted as self-evident will no longer be accepted as such.[99]

A practical critique of this nature can very well take the form of a transgression that can instigate shifts in knowledge, or at the very least illuminate paths to further instances of transgression. The concept of transgression, however, needs to be clarified here. For Foucault, it should not be regarded only in relation to "the limit as black to white, the prohibited to the lawful," or as those social and institutional mechanisms that interpellate subjects and impose rules, laws, prohibitions, issue warnings, and likewise deliver punishments if limits are exceeded. Transgression should also be understood as that which "forces the limit to face the fact of its imminent disappearance, to find itself in what it excludes."[100] In other words, the limit points beyond its own conditions of existence to unstable and empowering possibilities, to a space that philosopher James Tully calls "critical freedom."[101] Clearly, Foucault is envisioning a practice of critique situated in the here and now, an engagement founded upon a type of historical investigation (the deployment of archaeological and genealogical methods to properly trace the critical attitude that takes hold in the sixteenth century onwards with a more secularized approach to governmentalization) capable of

97 Hayles, *How We Become Posthuman*, 3.
98 Foucault, *The Foucault Reader*, 46.
99 Foucault, *Politics, Philosophy, Culture*, 154.
100 Foucault, *Religion and Culture*, 60.
101 Tully, *Strange Multiplicity*, 198–202.

determining the conditions underlying the complex relation between subjectivity and knowledge within the frame of modernity. Yet, the point I want to underscore in this book is that the bedrock of any practical critique, as Foucault recognized, is always contestation itself, the impulse and, indeed, the inherent reflexivity of modernity to identify and interrogate apparatuses of control and systems of normativity with relation to the embodied self and its life-world: "I will say that critique is the movement by which the subject gives himself the right to question truth on its effects of power and question power on its discourses of truth. Well then!: critique will be the art of voluntary insubordination, that of reflected intractability. Critique would essentially insure the desubjugation of the subject in the context of what we could call, in a word, the politics of truth."[102]

If we consider Cabriada's *Letter* (Chapter 1) within this purview, we find that his interpretation of vital force in the late-seventeenth century was certainly transgressive in this respect. From his readings of William Harvey's model of circulation (the continuous flow and regeneration of quickening blood through the heart and body) and Franciscus Sylvius's theories of blood pH (the balance of acidity and alkalinity levels that produce properly vitalized blood), he devised a theoretical framework that served as a blueprint for a novel approach to comprehending body functioning. By challenging the notion that vital force hinged on the hierarchies of Galen's humoralism, in which bodily interiority mirrored the cosmic order (the four humours of blood, phlegm, black bile, and yellow bile corresponded to the universe's four qualities, and thus transformed the body into a miniature cosmos of sorts), and by advocating for a more systemic understanding of human anatomy grounded at its most intrinsic level in relentless movement and renewal, Cabriada provided Spanish physicians with a crucial set of conceptual tools to theorize the body beyond the confines of Galenic cosmology and its legislative and doctrinal authority. Doubtless, the space for critique within Spanish culture (or the crucial moment of contestation and reflexivity) expanded greatly thanks to Cabriada's *Letter*, yet we must not lose sight of the following point: the concept of body-self was similarly adumbrated with a revised notion of vital force that came about in the decisive shift away from Galenism. If the body's energies originated from its own unique, anatomic-biological specificity and the socio-environmental contexts that act upon it at any given time, then the nature of the critique itself when conceiving the corporeal and the use to which it is put must be of

102 Foucault, "What Is Critique?" 47.

a very different sort. This is a fundamental point that connects all the figures analyzed in this book from Cabriada to Gómez de la Serna. How might the body's unique, anatomic-biological specificity open up new critical horizons of health and bodily well-being? How might this specificity cast the established or traditional procedures of therapeutic treatment and body disciplining in a new light? How might it wedge open and broaden the definition of agency, autonomy, desire, self-determination, and the will within a given hierarchized epistemology?

Imagining the locus of vital force in the body, whether it be through Cabriada's anatomical findings or Gómez de la Serna's avant-gardism, becomes both instigator and arbitrator for notions of embodiment and subjectivity – a type of subjectivity, however, that is self-reflexive, even analytical, and enmeshed in a series of increasingly unstable definitions of life and world. This unavoidable instability brings into view the extent to which the modern subject has remained, as Cascardi points out, "at the intersection of a series of discourses or cultural spheres, each of which is essential for an understanding of modern culture and none of which can define modernity as a whole."[103] The problem rests in that we have all too often misjudged the historical implications of subject formation and downplayed the fundamental premise that reason carries within *itself* its own limitations and constraints. The subjective experience as cognized through the enigmas of the living, material body can be said to be founded upon the promise of wholeness (locating the true origin of embodied life, for instance), and the reality of rupture, or, more aptly, convergent ruptures along various strata of value and meaning.[104]

The foregoing observations help us identify the intersection between Foucault's notion of practical critique and the question of vital force in Spain on the larger issue of transgression and modernity. Foucault observes that modernity begins with a particular awareness of the body, a moment not without irony when reason attempts to disentangle itself from (living) substance. While modernity expands the boundaries of reason, then, it inevitably destabilizes them and renders them porous in its demand for relentless critique. Zygmunt Bauman's understanding

103 Cascardi, *The Subject of Modernity*, 2.

104 Anthony Giddens fleshes out this point, stating: "Modernity is constituted in and through reflexively applied knowledge, but the equation of knowledge with certitude has turned out to be misconceived. We are abroad in a world which is thoroughly constituted through reflexively applied knowledge, but where at the same time we can never be sure that any given element of that knowledge will not be revised … No knowledge under conditions of modernity is knowledge in the 'old' sense, where 'to know' is to be certain" (39–40).

of this ironic stance clarifies further: "modernity makes itself possible through setting itself an impossible task … The impossible task is set by the *foci imaginarii* of absolute truth, pure art, humanity as such, order, certainty, harmony, the end of history. Like all horizons, they can never be reached."[105] What I argue is that plumbing the horizon of vital force in Spain proved to be a most formidable mode of critique in that it forced reason to reflect upon itself, upon its own very nature and constraints, and thus afforded momentary, yet profound, glimpses of the concrete, living body that transgressed the normative margins of authority and power. As I suggest throughout the book, beginning with Cabriada's call for "modern science" in 1687, it is imperative not to overlook that in this same procedure the question of vital force also played a hand in resetting, so to speak, the focus of the critique concerning the living, material body. This crucial shift in turn spurred further debate on the acceptability of mechanisms of authority and discipline that inscribed, or could inscribe, meaning upon embodied life. Considered from this vantage point, it becomes evident that the question of vital force not only negotiated, but also became an integral part of, modernity's inexorable reflexivity, and it thus opened what I show is ideal ground in which to undertake the practical critique Foucault outlines above. Ultimately, the impossibility of truth encoded and often concealed at the core of modernity is brought continually to the fore when we raise the daunting question: what is this vital force within our bodies that makes us who we are?

105 Bauman, *Modernity and Ambivalence*, 10.

PART ONE

Blood, Circulation, and the Soul

1

The Heart of the Matter: Remapping the Body Economy in Juan de Cabriada's Philosophical Medico-Chemical Letter

> I consider modern authors like a young lad who sits on a giant's shoulder and can see the same world as the giant, and even more.
>
> Juan de Cabriada, *Carta filosofica, medico-chymica*[1]

JUAN DE CABRIADA WAS A YOUNG PHYSICIAN of twenty-two when he published *Philosophical Medico-Chemical Letter* in 1687. On the face of it, the *Letter* provided a case study on the proper course of treatment for tertian fever, a malarial malady that produces recurring febrile paroxysms in roughly forty-eight-hour cycles and brings about debilitating vomiting, headaches, exhaustion, chills, and anemia. What prompted the publication of the *Letter* was Cabriada's involvement in the treatment of the Duke of Osuna, who had taken ill with the fever on 23 May 1686. Throughout the ensuing sixteen-day ordeal, Cabriada fell in with the *junta* (or council) of court physicians who convened daily to deliberate on the duke's medical condition. Besides Cabriada, the *junta* was composed of three physicians, all of whom were fervent Galenists. To Cabriada's dismay, during the duke's illness the *junta* was not only dismissive of his revisionist understanding of medicine, but it refused to follow any course of primary treatment other than phlebotomy.

In the tangled skein of medical publications that polarized the intellectual atmosphere in Spain in the concluding decades of the seventeenth century, Cabriada's "epoch-making" *Letter,* as Jonathan Israel refers to it, provides one of the most illuminating texts on how the body's

1 Cabriada, *Carta,* 152.

vital force was beginning to be reinterpreted during the period.[2] To be sure, Cabriada's *Letter* was bold, derisive, and inspired, and it set a precedent for a new understanding of modern medicine in Spain. One of the key aspects of Cabriada's *Letter* that has never been addressed when it comes to its modernity is its strategic use of theories of vital force, especially as concerns its polemical claims about the circulatory system and the blood's chemical composition. As with many treatises in Spain that sought to examine what Cabriada called *medicina moderna,* the *Letter* dialogues with a wide range of theories concerning circulation and blood properties. It must be pointed out that the cardiovascular system, and the spirit-laden blood that nourished the body, exercised a profound fascination on the medico-philosophical mind of the period. From the earliest speculations of ancient Greek philosophers, the heart had always been considered an organ of immeasurable wonder, and was recognized as one of the primary wellsprings of the body's energies. In the sixteenth century, anatomists like Andreas Vesalius extolled the heart and its vascular network with equal enthusiasm as the ancients. In exquisitely detailed drawings collected in the sixth book of his pioneering *De Humani Corporis Fabrica* of 1543, he recorded how the cardiac system generated and replenished the body's vital spirit.[3] Yet, it was the publication of William Harvey's *De Motu Cordis* of 1628 that constituted a fundamental leap forward in the understanding of cardiac functioning. In *De Motu Cordis,* Harvey not only revolutionized the mechanics of the heart and circulatory system, but he also dealt a decisive blow to the prevailing Galenic doctrine on human physiology. Against this backdrop, López Piñero reminds us that "[the] doctrine on the circulation of the blood was one of the central themes around which the battle between medical traditionalists and the partisans of new ideas was waged in seventeenth-century Spain."[4] As we shall see, Cabriada's *Letter* offered revised methods of conceiving of vital force that were grounded not only in Harvey's

2 Israel, *Radical Enlightenment,* 531.

3 Several of Vesalius's observations on the cardiovascular system defied prevailing Galenic theory concerning the heart's vital functions (he confessed, for instance, that he never could detect the supposed grooves that Galen observed in the heart's septum, which permitted blood to drain from the right ventricle into the left). Vesalius's disagreements with established paradigms of body composition and mechanics would facilitate the fundamental reorientation of how anatomical analysis was conducted, not only in Spain, but also throughout Europe. As López Piñero tells us: "Vesalian anatomy … played a central role in the establishment of the anatomical school at the University of Valencia … The influence of this Valencian school was … decisive in divulging the new anatomy to other universities [in Spain]" (*Historia y sociologías,* 32–3).

4 López Piñero, "Harvey's Doctrine," 231.

circulation, but also in other key scientific discoveries in the fields of anatomy and iatrochemistry.

Cabriada's seminal letter is often referenced as a touchstone for the new spirit of medical and scientific inquiry that swept across Europe at the end of the seventeenth century. Rarely, however, is it analyzed in terms of its core medical arguments, much less read in dialogue with other scientific texts of the period. In Jesús Pérez-Magallón's view, what was innovative about Cabriada's *Letter* was not its medical claims per se, but rather its condemnation of Spain's scientific backwardness and its influence on the debates over scientific reform. From this vantage point, as Pérez-Magallón explains, "Cabriada's critical vision and recommendations hold enormous symbolic value in deepening our understanding of [Spain's] modernization."[5] For her part, Adelina Sarrión Mora writes: "Cabriada's *Letter* can be considered the first complete exposition of the doctrines and ambitions of the learned men who concerned themselves with scientific renewal in Spain."[6] Sarrión Mora likewise underscores that the most enduring aspects of Cabriada's *Letter* are its criticisms of established medical doctrines and its championing of the empirical method. Other critics, like Allen G. Debus and José Andrés Gallego, echo these assessments, emphasizing Cabriada's bold call for modernization on several scientific and intellectual fronts.[7] Àlvar Martínez-Vidal and José Pardo Tomás observe that, while Cabriada's *Letter* is undeniably a singular text of scientific reform, it also demonstrates that he was "entrenched in a line of continuity and progress in which the 'original scholars' were not renounced, but rather put in their place."[8] For Martínez-Vidal and Pardo Tomás, the *Letter*'s approach to the circulatory system and its functions, particularly in relation to health and disease, was clearly innovative for the period. López Piñero, the critic who has attempted the most comprehensive appraisal of Cabriada's oeuvre, has argued that the *Letter* represents "the manifesto of renewal in Spain in terms of medicine and the biological and chemical knowledge associated with it."[9] While López Piñero has documented the text's historical reception and the manner in which it conditioned the medical polemics at the turn of the eighteenth century (he advances the now well-established argument that the modernization of Spanish science takes root in the mid- to

5 Pérez-Magallón, *Construyendo la modernidad*, 115.

6 Sarrión Mora, *Médicos e Inquisición en el siglo XVII*, 62.

7 Debus, *Chemistry and Medical Debate*, 167–8; Gallego, *La crisis de la hegemonía española*, 61–2.

8 Martínez-Vidal and Pardo Tomás, "Un siglo de controversias," 116.

9 López Piñero, "Juan de Cabriada," 4.

late-seventeenth century with figures like Cabriada), his analysis of the *Letter* never quite manages to address the finer points of Cabriada's theoretical assimilation of anatomical and iatrochemical science. To maintain, as he does, that "in Cabriada's work … there is no original contribution of any kind" is to overlook Cabriada's fundamental role as a *bricoleur* of sorts, who resourcefully assembled, integrated, articulated, and disseminated a vast array of traditional and modern learning to offer a solution to Spain's outdated medical profession.[10]

With the *Letter* and the vigorous polemics that ensued, we must be cautious not to speak of a vitalist philosophy properly understood. With the term "vital force," I refer to the complex workings of bodily life as they were discerned through a close analysis of the body's biochemical processes and concreteness. Insisting on observation, experience, and modern advancements in anatomy and iatrochemistry, Cabriada circumvents Galenic humoralism for the most part and challenges ancient systems of thought and traditional notions concerning the actions of the soul in the body. He likewise sidesteps questions concerning purity of blood – the complex socio-political distinctions in Spain having to do with ancestry, lineage, race, miscegenation, and family legitimacy – and their role in Galenic humoralism, which had a tendency to consider blood as either "clean" or "unclean" and thus associated with a range of behaviours and diseases. This manoeuvring, of course, does not imply that he outright neglected the tried-and-true wisdom of the ancients or challenged the validity of religion, but it does illustrate the manner in which his medical thinking was bound to the empirical body first and foremost. For Cabriada, any consideration of disease had to go hand in hand with an appreciation of the body's interiority and the environmental circumstances that acted upon it.

As I dialogue with the *Letter* and its referents, then, I will define how the *Letter* takes up the question of vital force, a topic Cabriada believed was paramount to the modernization of science in Spain. To properly frame my analysis, I will also refer at key junctures to Cabriada's complementary treatise, *Triumphant Truth, Apologetic Response Penned by Filiatro in Defence of the Philosophical Medico-Chemical Letter by the Doctor Juan de Cabriada*, published in the same year of 1687, which illuminates and extends some of the arguments presented in his *Letter*.[11] Ultimately, I argue

10 López Piñero, "Primeras etapas," 129.

11 The author of *Triumphant Truth* is listed only as "Filiatro." Given how swiftly it appeared after the publication of the *Letter*, and given the author's thorough knowledge of the sources and arguments presented in the *Letter*, there is little doubt that Cabriada was the author. Also relevant in this respect is what appears in the Medical Tribunal and

that the *Letter* provides, at least from a practical therapeutic standpoint and for a specific readership, a type of heuristic for a reassessment of the body that is capable of guiding Spanish medicine out from under the spell of Galen. This reassessment, moreover, was rooted in the concepts of iatrochemistry and the mechanico-vitalist discoveries of William Harvey, Franciscus Sylvius, Thomas Willis, and Jan Baptist van Helmont, and its epistemological implications were far more subversive to established modes of therapeutic thinking than has previously been acknowledged.

ON EPISTOLARITY AND PARATEXTS: CABRIADA'S PERSONA

Born in Valencia in 1665, Cabriada was familiar from childhood with science and medicine. His father, also named Juan de Cabriada, was a staunch Galenist physician and professor at the University of Valencia, who exerted a considerable influence on his schooling. After graduating from the University of Valencia, the young Cabriada completed a degree in medicine ("bachiller en medicina") in 1681. He relocated to Madrid in the mid-1680s, where he served as the physician to Juan Domingo Méndez de Haro, the Count of Monterrey, a prominent political figure who, throughout the years leading up to the eighteenth century, had served as Capitan General of Aragón, Viceroy of Catalonia, and member of the Council of State, among other posts.[12] During his years in Madrid, Cabriada participated actively in its burgeoning network of scholarly *tertulias*, and through various publications, prefaces, notes, and ephemera spanning the better part of the 1690s, he defended his iatrochemical approach to medicine. His famous *Letter* alone elicited extensive

Licensing Board's report of the 1690s included in Doctor Cabriada's Personal File (Box 55, Document 1) in the General Archive of the Palace of Madrid. Said document states that Cabriada published two books shortly after treating the Duke of Osuna for tertian fever. We can surmise that the two books were the *Letter* and *Triumphant Truth*, both of which appeared in 1687. Finally, López Piñero points out that "in the copy [of *Triumphant Truth*] that exists in the National Library in Madrid you can find an annotation, apparently fairly recent, that states: '... it's author, Filiatro ... Juan de Cabriada'" ("Primeras etapas," 141).

12 In terms of Cabriada's medical training, López Piñero adds: "As was expected, [Cabriada's] father sent him to the University of Valencia for his education, where he obtained the degree of 'bachiller de artes' [bachelor of arts] before entering medical school sometime in 1675. It would be logical that he would enter medical school at the same university, but his name appears nowhere in the university's registration nor grade records ... We know that he received his doctorate in 1680 or 81, but we do not know from which university" ("Juan," 28).

criticisms in book form, as we shall see, from the traditionalist Andrés Dávila y Heredia, also known as "el Aduanero," who in *Response That Dogmatic and Rational Medicine Delivers to the Book Published by Dr. Juan de Cabriada* of 1687 condemned practically every aspect of it.[13] And, in 1688, the Catalan physician Cristóbal Tixedas published an almost five-hundred-page reply to Cabriada's *Letter* titled *Truth Defended, and Response to Filiatro on the Philosophical, Medico-Chemical Letter That the Physician-Chemist Juan de Cabriada Penned Against the Medical Council of the Court and Against Galenists,* which marshaled the most intractable scholasticism to demonstrate the utter poverty of Cabriada's "pernicious innovations."[14] Despite the critics, Cabriada's erudition and eloquence transformed him into a veritable spokesman for the *novator* movement and won him the favour of the highest ranks of the nobility when he helped found the Royal Chemical Laboratory in 1694. In the final years of the seventeenth century, he was graced with the honour of Royal Physician and worked diligently with like-minded reformists, such as Miguel Marcelino Boix y Moliner and Diego Mateo Zapata, to establish Seville's Royal Society of Medicine and Other Sciences, which became an institutional reality in 1700. With the socio-political turmoil brought on by the Spanish War of Succession, he relocated to Bilbao in 1705, where he continued his medical practice until his death in 1714.

To properly assess the *Letter*'s engagement with the question of vital force, it is best to begin by considering its epistolary frame. John Slater has tackled the *Letter*'s rhetorical dimension, remarking that, while it was indeed an effective treatise of polemic, as a scientific text it was "more conventional than has been understood ... textually, its features are more familiar than revolutionary."[15] Undeniably, the conventions of the period inform Cabriada's method of scientific exposition, but we must keep in mind that the *Letter*'s content is bound to its epistolary form. What is most intriguing about the *Letter*'s epistolarity is how it prefigures the indeterminacy, imaginativeness, and resistance to closure that Elizabeth MacArthur identifies in eighteenth-century epistolary narratives preoccupied with "the actual process of creating meanings

13 *Response That Dogmatic and Rational Medicine Delivers to the Book Published by Dr. Juan de Cabriada* was published anonymously. I follow López-Piñero's recommendation here in terms of authorship: "The attacks against Cabriada began with a pamphlet expressively titled *Response That Dogmatic and Rational Medicine Delivers to the Book Published by Dr. Juan de Cabriada.* It was signed 'El Aduanero,' undoubtedly a pseudonym for Andrés Dávila y Heredia, an intransigent traditionalist" ("Juan," 36). Dávila y Heredia had also previously published "The Faction of Impostors in Medicine."

14 Tixedas, *Truth Defended,* n.p.

15 Slater, "Rereading Cabriada's *Carta,*" 68.

and a desire to put into question the moral and political status quo."[16] The epistolary form, with its fluid structure of inquiry and truth (how questions of intimacy, identity, and authenticity are articulated), becomes an integral part of the *Letter*'s scientific framework itself, as it manipulates and defies the reader's expectations on various levels. Benito Jerónimo Feijóo y Montenegro's later *Erudite and Curious Letters* immediately springs to mind when reading the epistolary form in this light. In Spain, there were notable antecedents to Cabriada's *Letter* that experimented with this form, such as Francisco Cascales's *Philological Letters* (1634).[17] Abroad, the hugely popular *Lettres Portugaises* (1669) attributed to Gabriel de Guilleragues had made waves in literary circles across Europe and established the stylistic foundation for later epistolary novels, including Montesquieu's *Lettres persanes* (1721) and Jean-Jacques Rousseau's *Julie, ou la nouvelle Héloïse* (1761).

Cabriada's *Letter* is conceived as a lengthy response to Filiatro, an apocryphal court physician, confidant, and master. Filiatro had inquired into the health of their common benefactor, whose identity remains a mystery (although we know from official court records that he was referring to the Duke of Osuna).[18] Of note is that Filiatro will reappear

16 MacArthur, *Extravagant Narratives*, 18.

17 Juan de Segura's *Process Having to Do with Love Letters* of 1548 is often cited as the first epistolary novel in Spain. Other epistolary manuals and guidebooks included Gaspar de Tejada's *With This Style You Can Write Messenger Letters* (1548); Juan de Iciar's *New Style to Write Messenger Letters* (1552); Juan de Leras's *The Style to Write Letters* (1549); Jerónimo Paulo de Manzanares's *Style and Forms of Family Letters* (1600); and Juan Vicente Peliger's *Style and Method to Write Missive Letters* (1617).

18 There is some speculation concerning who exactly Cabriada was treating for tertian fever. It has long been stated that Cabriada was tending to the Count of Monterrey (see López Piñero's "Juan de Cabriada," 29, and John Slater's "Rereading Cabriada's *Carta*," 70). Yet, as it appears in the Medical Tribunal and Licensing Board's report of the 1690s, included in Doctor Cabriada's Personal File (Box 55, Document 1) in the General Archive of the Palace of Madrid, there is no doubt that Cabriada's *Letter* was inspired by his treatment of the Duke of Osuna: "Doctor Juan de Cabriada states that, having submitted to His Majesty (may God keep him) and to Your Excellency as Chamberlain [Sumiller de Corps] an official record … he was honoured with a title from the royal House, for at the time he had twenty years of experience in medicine and was determined (impelled by his natural genius), and at great personal expense, to discover the nature of natural things through chemical means, which is the only method to obtain knowledge of nature and knowledge of the causes and cures for disease. And believing that in making this knowledge known would be of great utility to public health [salud pública], he did so taking advantage of certain controversies that arose relating to the cure of tertian fever that the Honourable Duke of Osuna had suffered in the year eighty-six. In said year, he published two books that have had the good fortune of receiving the applause of learned men in Spain and abroad" (Muñoz Utrilla, "D. Juan de Cabriada y Borrás," 30). The books mentioned here are the

transformed as Cabriada's commanding alter ego in *Triumphant Truth*, an apologetic defence of the *Letter*.[19] The persona Cabriada cultivates in the *Letter*'s opening pages is that of a lettered man of science hunched over at his bureau with pen in hand, presumably from the auratic locus of Madrid's court. This image of the solitary Cabriada at his bureau, which accompanies the reader throughout the letter, announces the intimacy and rhetorical self-reflexivity of the medical insights that lay ahead. To be sure, Cabriada inscribes himself into the *Letter* with a great degree of sophistication, not only as the physician-expert, which was the norm in medical texts of this nature, but also as the redactor of a medical case involving a nobleman:

> My *memory*, oh Filiatro, tends to the past; and my quill reminds me of those who are no longer here. With my memory, I acknowledge my obligations; with my quill, I speak to them. You have asked me to respond to your letter informing you of the illness of our common patron and benefactor (I will not state his name for reasons you well know). As a friend, I owe you obedience; as a courtier, I owe you consideration. I also owe you respect for in all areas of knowledge, and principally in medical science, I recognize you as my master. To write you these lines, I have sharpened my judgements … You asked me to write you at length on this matter, and I will do so.[20]

The *Letter*'s overall epistolary effect and the obligation Cabriada is under to reply to his master play a hand in generating the tone of sincerity in his excursus against doctrinal tyranny in the court of Madrid, against intellectual mediocrity, against the deadening influence of the obsequious physicians of the court, and against the unreflective and impoverished science that was being conducted in the universities.[21] It was precisely the

---

Letter and, almost certainly, *Triumphant Truth*, both of which appeared in 1687 and not in 1686 (see note 11 above). Martínez-Vidal and Pardo Tomás reiterate: "In Cabriada's case, what most immediately prompted him to publish his *Letter* was his participation in a medical *junta* that was convened to treat the Duke of Osuna, a fact that is documented in an official report in his handwriting" ("Un siglo," 114).

19 With the name Filiatro, Cabriada could be alluding to Swiss physician, botanist, linguist, and alchemist Evonimus Filiatro (pseudonym of Conrad Gesner), author of significant texts on medicinal substances, healing, and zoology (e.g., his four-volume *Historiae Animalium*). With his *Thesaurus Euonymi Philiatri, de Remediis Secretis* (1552), Filiatro paved the way for "the philosophical development that throughout four centuries would stimulate the introduction of some alchemical concepts in the preparation of medicines. The culminating point of this process corresponds to Paracelsus" (Bueno, "Alchemy," 57).

20 Cabriada, *Carta*, 1–2.

21 Ibid., 152.

professed authenticity of Cabriada's criticisms that most resonated with the *novatores,* who were already committed to the politics of reform. In the *Letter*'s second introductory approbation, for instance, Dionisio de Cardona, surgeon to Charles II and one of Spain's foremost physicians, admonishes the reader on this point, declaring that Cabriada should in no way be faulted for his candour in revolting against Galenic medicine: "the author of this book does not deserve to be maligned for distancing himself, perhaps contrary to reason, from the opinions of Galen."[22]

If we consider the *Letter*'s larger paratextual frame with its epistolarity in mind, it is evident that Cabriada seeks to instruct his readers on the letter's discursive trajectory and how to properly interpret it. Paratexts bring to the fore how texts produce meaning, and, just as importantly, they introduce the text's array of literary and communicative strategies, which expand its horizon of reception and allow for what Gérard Genette called "a more pertinent reading of it (more pertinent, of course, in the eyes of the author and his allies)."[23] Of note is that the *Letter*'s paratext does not acquaint the reader with the finer points of the Duke of Osuna's illness, and in fact, nowhere in the treatise is the duke even named. Cabriada's own exordium to the *Letter,* in which he honours his current patron, the Count of Monterrey, makes no mention of the duke's illness, but instead declaims against the practice of phlebotomy. More directly, Cabriada's exordium introduces the fundamental binarisms that structure his letter: modern/ancient, truth/ignorance, us/them (the reformists versus the *junta*). Moreover, he professes his allegiance to modern iatrochemisty and to "Modern Authors" who seek to understand the natural world using observation, experience, and reason.[24] He submits that the indiscriminate practice of phlebotomy in Spain to treat all types of diseases exposes the barbarous ignorance that hinders the modernization of the Spanish medical profession. While the underlying criticism of Galenic pathology here would certainly not have been lost on any reader of the period, Cabriada is in fact providing his readers and "allies," to use Genette's word, a signpost to one of the core themes that subtends his letter: the role of blood in regulating the body.

Antonio de Ron's and Dionisio de Cardona's ensuing approbations of Cabriada's *Letter* bolster the significance of blood in modern medicine. The presbyter Antonio de Ron refers to Francis Bacon's call for empirical analysis to lend credence to his argument that medical practice in Spain has for too long ignored the facts when it comes to the perils of

22 de Cardona, "Aprobación," n.p.

23 Genette, *Paratexts,* 2.

24 Cabriada, *Carta,* n.p.

phlebotomy. On this point, he adds: "the two most frequent and capital remedies that are applied for almost every ailment are … bloodletting and purges, since they are easy to apply even though they do not carry the same risks and benefits to the patient."[25] Dionisio de Cardona also acquaints the reader with a number of medical advancements, and he applauds the "ocular understanding" that now informs the burgeoning anatomical sciences. He lauds anatomy and underscores the importance of the new interior structures of the body it now renders visible: "Anatomy makes visible [descubre] solid parts of the body and the various fluids contained within it, and it forces Cabriada to examine the nature and causes of disease differently than Galen and others."[26] What is more, de Cardona also provides readers with a succinct genealogy of luminaries in European and Spanish science who have defined what he calls the freedom to philosophize, beginning with Paracelsus and van Helmont and continuing through Pedro García, Rodrigo a Castro, Ponce de Santa Cruz, and Bravo de Sobremonte, among others. One of de Cardona's key points of reference is William Harvey's doctrine of circulation, which in conjunction with developments in understanding blood chemistry (Franciscus Sylvius and Thomas Willis) represent, in his opinion, science's most revolutionary discoveries. Likewise, the renowned physician José Casalete's one-page approbation in Latin also calls the readers' attention to the relevance of *Sanguinis Circulatione* in the study of modern medicine. The one point, then, that the paratext makes abundantly clear is that the blood's significance in modern medical practice grounds Cabriada's *Letter*. Moreover, it not only situates the *Letter* within a larger historical context of medical and scientific debates on disease and therapeutic regimens in the seventeenth century, but also introduces readers to the transnational scientific framework that he uses to analyze blood's vital properties.

HARVEY, SYLVIUS, AND THE BODY'S INTERIORITY

During the seventeenth century, with the rise of the anatomical, mathematical, and chemical sciences, phlebotomy began to fall from favour as a curative treatment. Phlebotomy had been ingrained in Europe's cultural imaginary for centuries, thanks in large measure to Galenic medicine, yet the therapeutic practice can be traced back to antiquity, well before Hippocrates made mention of it in the fifth century BCE. In Spain, it was so pervasive that it inspired a subgenre of poetry in the

25 de Ron, "Aprobación," n.p.
26 de Cardona, "Aprobación," n.p.

sixteenth and seventeenth centuries dedicated to the sensuous experiences associated with handling the extremities of bleeding and swooning female patients during phlebotomy procedures.[27] As María González de Fauve has demonstrated, phlebotomy began to be seriously questioned in the sixteenth century, as it was performed more freely to combat epidemics such as the plague, which had ravaged the country in the particularly deadly year of 1507 and then again in the 1560s, 1580s, and 1590s.[28] Already in 1623, the physician Lorenço Romeo had condemned the abuse of bloodletting in his treatise *Disabuse of Error on the Abuse of Bloodletting and Purgation.* He had witnessed first-hand the rampant use of bloodletting at the hands of inexperienced barber-surgeons, and noted how very often the procedure itself, and not the disease, sent unsuspecting victims to their graves. The court physician Antonio Ponce de Santa Cruz penned *De Impedimentis Magnorum Auxiliorum, in Morborum Curatione* a few years later in 1629 to provide healers and medical practitioners with a nosological index that could be used to determine whether it was appropriate to bleed a patient. José Casalete had also argued against the arbitrary use of phlebotomy in *Duae Controversiae* of 1687, in which he outlined clearly that a patient should be bled only if the venous blood was found to be "inflamed, festering, or corrupted."[29] By the end of the century, opinions like those of Bernardino Ramazzini, professor at Padua and author of the widely popular *De Morbis Artificum Diatriba* of 1700 on occupational diseases, were beginning to exert a wider influence in medical circles throughout Europe. Ramazzini lamented that "it seems as if the phlebotomist grasped the Delphic sword in his hand to exterminate the innocent victims rather than destroy the disease."[30] Diego de Torres Villarroel, himself a trained physician, demonstrates to what extent attitudes were beginning to change towards phlebotomy by the early-eighteenth century in Spain. It is common knowledge, he advises, that "[o]nly in desperate cases should bloodletting and purgation be considered as sound medical treatment, and they should not be accepted without grave need or deliberation."[31] All the same, phlebotomy was still the most practised medical therapy in Europe until the early-nineteenth century.[32]

27 Peraita, "Catalina Clara Ramírez de Guzmán," 171.

28 González de Fauve, "La práctica de la flebotomía en España," 1407–11.

29 Casalete, quoted in Martínez-Vidal and Pardo Tomás's "Un siglo de controversias," 113.

30 Eknoyan, "A History of Diuretics," 8.

31 Torres Villarroel, *Tratado físicos*, 58.

32 Carter, *The Decline of Therapeutic Bloodletting*, 1–2.

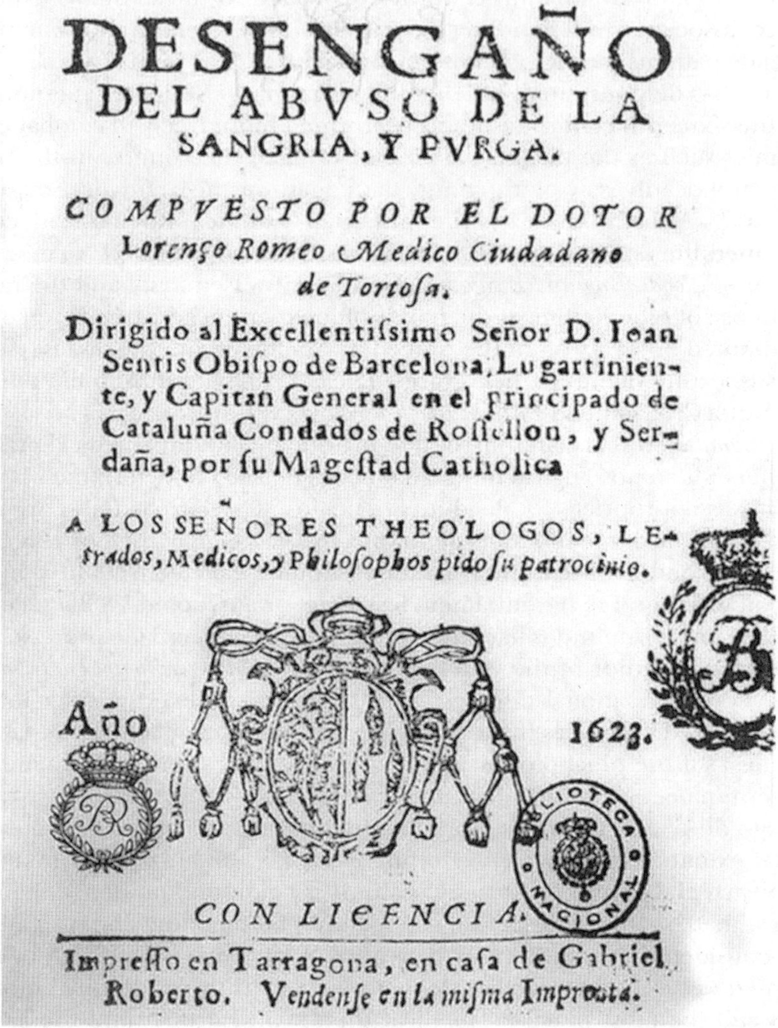

DESENGAÑO
DEL ABVSO DE LA
SANGRIA, Y PVRGA.

COMPVESTO POR EL DOTOR
Lorenço Romeo Medico Ciudadano
de Tortosa.

Dirigido al Excellentissimo Señor D. Ioan Sentis Obispo de Barcelona, Lugartiniente, y Capitan General en el principado de Cataluña Condados de Rossellon, y Serdaña, por su Magestad Catholica

A LOS SEÑORES THEOLOGOS, LEtrados, Medicos, y Philosophos pido su patrocinio.

Año 1623.

CON LICENCIA.

Impresso en Tarragona, en casa de Gabriel Roberto. Vendense en la misma Imprenta.

1.1 Title page of Lorenço Romeo's *Desengaño del abuso de la sangría, y purga,* 1623.

To understand the *Letter*'s subversive elements and appreciate how it reframes the body economy within the Spanish medical field, we must begin charting Cabriada's objections to the phlebotomy procedures administered to the duke. Throughout the duke's illness, he was bled on three occasions spaced three days apart, on day six, day nine (through leeching), and day twelve. Additionally, he was administered four purges during this period. In light of the predisposing external causes that influenced the duke's infirmity – these included his excessive travel, dietary irregularities, courtly obligations, and the humid climate of Madrid in May – Cabriada is confident that the duke's tertian fever originated from crude humours in the first region (in Hippocratic medicine the first region referred to the general area of the abdomen, which comprised the viscera and the cavities of the spleen, pancreas, liver, and so on, where impurities are generated and where blood was thought to flow more slowly). With this diagnosis in mind, Cabriada confides to Filiatro: "I arrived at the definite opinion that his [Excellency's] illness was caused by thick, cold, phlegmy, bilious, and impure humours with some mixture of melancholics; there was no cause other than this with a general acidic and corruptive ailment. Given my opinion, I told his Excellency, especially considering the recurrence of the paroxysms, that what was required was purgation."[33]

Cabriada deploys a wealth of ancient and modern scholarship to explain why phlebotomy was an ill-advised treatment for the duke's tertian fever. From the teachings of Hippocrates and Galen to contemporary physicians like Willis and van Helmont, Cabriada argues that putrid fluids derived from crude humours in the first region had seeped into the duke's bloodstream and produced the fever.[34] With Harvey in mind, he explains in his complementary treatise *Triumphant Truth* why the fever originated in all likelihood in the first region: "Assuming that the blood takes one hour to pass through the heart, it would follow that the fever should return every hour. This truth, which the circular movement of blood in the body brings to light, proves that the origins of tertian fever lie outside the veins and vessels that deliver blood."[35] It comes as no

33 Cabriada, *Carta*, 13.

34 He summarizes his objections to the phlebotomy regimen as follows: "FIRSTLY: That according to HIPPOCRATIC and GALENIC doctrine, bloodletting should not have been performed. SECONDLY: According to classic authors who follow the Galenic school, it should not have been performed. THIRDLY: According to modern Galenic-Chemist authors, it should not have been performed. FOURTHLY: Following sound judgement, it should not have been performed" (42–3). In another section of the *Letter*, we learn that Cabriada, by his own estimation, had cured almost two hundred people of tertian fever: "Two years ago a great Lady of this Court … witnessing the multitude of sick people [in the city] and moved by her great charity, requested thirty beds [for them]. She also requested that their every need be met, and she sent me to visit the sick. Almost two hundred of the sick were cured in two and a half months, and almost all of the cases were tertian fever [tercianas]" (79).

35 Cabriada, *Carta*, 64.

surprise, therefore, that Cabriada believed that, firstly, eliminating these crude humours from the duke's digestive tract with purges constituted the most effective treatment; and secondly, performing phlebotomy therapies was not only ineffective in eliminating these putrid obstructions, but it also impaired the body's ability (in terms of vital force) to do so.[36] While the duke was in fact administered four purges in hopes of eliminating the crude humours, the *junta* of Galenists ignored Cabriada's insistence on a stricter schedule of purgation as the most appropriate treatment.[37] Instead, the duke was bled, which in Cabriada's opinion only aggravated the fever:

> My esteemed colleagues came and voted with their customary ERUDITION and BOOKISHNESS: The indicated remedy was bloodletting, which was applied. And it appeared a crime to my esteemed colleagues that a lad [mozo] like me, and against such learned and venerable elderliness, should speak and defend his opinions ... They belittled my views (they have done so on many occasions) for their novelty and because they differ from the ancients.[38]

The bulk of Cabriada's *Letter* is devoted to offering Filiatro his closely argued rationale for objecting to the phlebotomy regimen as a responsible treatment in this specific case. Needless to say, his ensuing commentaries are more than simple clarifications of the matter, and while

36 Ibid., 88.

37 Cabriada's insistence on the therapeutic value of purgation calls to mind the Antimony Wars between Paracelsians and Galenists that characterized the early-seventeenth century. The Antimony Wars, ultimately won by the Paracelsians, introduced purgatives such as antimony into mainstream medical practice. Cabriada is indeed conversant with Paracelsian chemistry, noting that Paracelsus, like van Helmont, was fond of using "ALCHAEST LIQUOUR, of CORAL ARCANUM and ORO ORIZONTAL [sic], among others" for therapeutic purposes (41). *Alkahest*, also known as *Ignis-aqua*, or Fiery Water, was a so-called dissolvent with purgative properties that aided with liver ailments. Cabriada notes that Galenists do in fact use certain medicaments – including the purgative antimony – popular among Paracelsians (38). Cabriada also recommends Paracelsus's *Elixir Propietatis* (as described by van Helmont) to aid in the cure of various gastro-intestinal diseases involving "crude humours" like those afflicting the duke (37). For more information on the reach and influence of antimony as a curative agent in Spain, see Pardo Tomás (*El médico*, 175–89).

38 Cabriada, *Carta*, 16–17. Martínez-Vidal and Pardo Tomás shed much-needed light on the hierarchy that ruled the medical *juntas*: "the composition of the *juntas* hierarchized physicians publicly and conferred them distinction not only within the medical profession, but more importantly, within the 'public' that constituted their clientele and who provided their essential means of existence, prestige, and ultimately, their economic well-being" ("Las consultas," 305). It is understandable why a young doctor like Cabriada, who publicly challenged the Galenist physicians of the *junta*, became the target of criticism.

they deliver the major lines of thought informing his medical world view, they also reveal a mild inferiority complex that manifests itself in his sensitivity about his age, on the one hand, and his unsparing display of erudition, on the other (or what Pérez-Magallón calls "the rigorous character of the text" and its impressive scholarship).[39] It is clear from Cabriada's diagnosis that he subscribes to humoral theory on some level, and he is sympathetic to some of Galen's therapeutic recommendations. He even advocates for the use of phlebotomies, but only as a last measure to relieve patients of an abundance of blood.[40] Humoral theory is but one component of Cabriada's larger medical philosophy, which in the spirit of the age is marked by eclecticism and ambiguity. For Cabriada, physicians had to be proficient in three classes of observations and experiments: practical, chemical, and anatomical. At the intersection of these three classes of observations and experiments, he tells us, the physician's gaze can be drawn to one of the most fundamental and overlooked aspects of medical science: the manner in which the body is an astonishingly integrated and vitalized system of biological and chemical processes, rather than a hierarchized assemblage in the Galenic sense, with two discrete circulatory systems and a tripartite soul.

It is worth exploring the practical, chemical, and anatomical facets of Cabriada's therapeutic outlook to gauge just how they remap the body's vital force and its complex biological and chemical workings through the circulatory system and the properties of the blood. In referring to practical experiments and observations, Cabriada has in mind a medical praxis mediated by the close examination of the pathological body in its natural environment. Any type of scrutiny of the body and infirmity should yield, as Hippocrates proposed in *The Book of Prognostics*, a *historiae*, a case history of the course of the disease. In the *Letter*, Cabriada puts together a case history that includes a host of symptoms that will allow him to make an accurate diagnosis, and he avails himself of the developing practices of narrativizing disease that came about with a reinterpretation of Hippocratic empiricism. There is a detached and almost clinical air in the way he goes about listing days one through fourteen of the duke's sixteen-day illness (the days of most severe bodily distress) with brief, to-the-point narrative accounts, including dates, times, patient details, treatments provided, and other pertinent commentary:

39 Pérez-Magallón, *Construyendo la modernidad*, 135.

40 Cabriada, *Carta*, 62.

1. Thursday, twenty-third of May, the day the fever manifested itself in His Excellency, the day the illness began. On this day in the morning His Excellency awoke feeling heavy and aggrieved. With this malaise, he ate breakfast and attended the Council of State where his fever increased, which forced him to depart hastily and return to bed. He suffered chills until six in the afternoon. I examined His Excellency at this hour, more or less, and I found him wracked by considerable fever that lasted until midnight.
2. The following day Friday, His Excellency was clean of the fever, although his appetite was poor. On this day, he dressed in the afternoon.
3. On Saturday at eleven in the morning the chills returned, like on Thursday, and would last almost an hour. His Excellency had urges to vomit: there was great turmoil in his stomach, as well as a flatulence with some complaints of the heart, which aggrieved His Excellency considerably. Afterwards came the fever and lasted six hours. His Excellency was not thirsty and detested water, for his stomach could not tolerate it.[41]

For Cabriada, medicine's practical component is rather straightforward, and had to do with properly assessing and diagnosing patient problems. The physician's task, provided he could exercise his profession in a sphere of tolerance and reason, is to interpret the patient's symptoms to improve and prolong life through medical practice, which did not necessarily mean forcing the patient to undergo painful and ongoing phlebotomy treatments. The implicit distinction here between medical *theoria* and *praxis* inspires him to review the practical healing techniques of twenty major schools of medicine. The type of medicine practised on the duke, however, figures in none of them, since it is nothing short of quackery: "And I observe that [this medicine] is founded on the lancet … which is wielded against the blood of poor Spaniards."[42] The practical component, as Cabriada understands it, is grounded in a precise empirical examination of the body and the signs of disease, and only after this examination is complete can the physician begin to offer up a cure. Not surprisingly, of all the physicians who were present at the duke's bedside, only Cabriada perceived something divergent, only he deciphered bodily signs of infirmity that violated the normative humoral paradigm. In the anonymous pamphlet *The Medical Diogenes*, which made the rounds shortly after the publication of the

41 Ibid., 6.
42 Ibid., 34.

Letter, Cabriada is ridiculed and lambasted for his transgressive, almost voyeuristic, observational skills.[43]

Human anatomy was a complex and wondrous realm of mysteries for Cabriada. The sweep of anatomical "inventions," as he referred to new discoveries in anatomy, radically redefined the representation of the body. In his words: "With these new anatomical inventions we have come into knowledge of the function of the parts of the body, which have been unknown until now."[44] A good physician must acquire a thorough knowledge of anatomy, Cabriada declares, since it provides crucial visual evidence on how the body sustains, and is sustained by, a confluence of vital biochemical processes in its organs, tissues, and fluids. He asks Filiatro: "One cannot be a good physician without anatomical experiments. How can one come to ingeniously know the nature of the body and the cause of its functions and operations both in the natural and preternatural states without being well versed in these types of anatomical experiments, and principally, the new ones that have been discovered and of which the ancients knew nothing?"[45] Cabriada's understanding of anatomy, considered more comprehensively, takes root in modern blood theories and their relevance to vital force and body mechanics. These theories, all judiciously selected and interpreted, provide the foundational premises on which he defends his diagnosis and treatment recommendations to Filiatro. Van Helmont's findings on fermentation, Thomas Willis's work on blood chemistry and urine analysis, Jean Pecquet's discovery of the cisterna chyli and sanguification, and Raymond Vieussens's insights into cardiac output are all influential. However, Harvey's doctrine of circulation and Sylvius's theory of the rarefaction of blood – the process through which blood was thinned, fermented, and converted into an effervescent mist to vitalize the body – most clearly map the body's interior for Cabriada. Indeed, Cabriada conflates Harvey's circulation (what he lauds as "the *New Sun of Circulation* in medicine")[46] with Sylvius's theory of rarefaction to imagine the body as a complex circulatory network characterized by a continual state of vital movement and chemical change:

43 "It is notable what first comes into view (unless you are blind), which is that Cabriada publishes a cure, although he did not apply it, nor did he vote [in the medical *junta*]. He reveals what happened in a medical *junta* in which he had no influence, no esteem … in which he only contributed as a gawker [mirón]" (*Diogenes Medico*, 2–3).

44 Cabriada, *Carta*, 25.

45 Ibid., 21.

46 Ibid., 151.

> The CIRCULATION of the blood is, then, a new anatomical invention that Harvey, doctor to the King of England, so much illuminated. What usefulness has this new announcement not brought to medicine? Once one is knowledgeable of the circulation of the blood in the body, the doctrine of pulses becomes clear and patent and is unfettered from the obscure veils that antiquity used to teach it through the pulsatile faculty, which is unintelligible. It is now known, after this new light, that the pulse is caused by the RAREFACTION that the blood acquires through fermentation in the ventricles of the heart, by the FIRE, or vital ferment, that resides in it.[47]

Sylvius's theory of rarefaction is indeed of great importance to Cabriada's understanding of cardiac physiology. Sylvius had synthesized Harvey's doctrine of circulation and Descartes' concept of rarefaction into a more-or-less unified theory. Much like Descartes, he argued that within the heart burned an innate fire. As blood entered the heart's right ventricle, it produced an effervescence with the fire (a type of dilation), and circulated then to the lungs through the pulmonary artery, where it was condensed with air and distributed to the heart's left ventricle to be perfected. Harvey's theory of circulation in *De Motu Cordis,* particularly as it concerns the blood's vital properties, is also critical in Cabriada's assessment of the duke's illness. Harvey differed from Sylvius not only regarding the heart's basic functioning, but also in his ideas concerning the properties of the blood and the origins of metabolic heat. In Harvey's words, the heart was the body's active "prime mover," the "*primum vivens, ultimum moriens* – the first part to live and the last part to die," rather than an organ whose systolic and diastolic action was precipitated by the rarefication of blood.[48] The heart circulated blood throughout the body and its extremities in a "circle" and served, as he phrased it in the famous dedication of *De Motu Cordis* to King Charles I, as the "foundation of … life, the sovereign of everything … that upon which all growth depends, from which all power proceeds."[49] Ultimately, the heart served as the body's sovereign, and from its authority and rule it derived all its life energies. This type of aristocratic metaphorology, to use Barbara Stafford's term, brought into scientific consciousness a series of images that could render visible the body's interior, make known the unknown, and facilitate a new and imaginative hermeneutics of the body and the sovereign power of the heart.[50] Harvey's belief in the heart's sovereignty

47 Ibid., 21–2.
48 Harvey, *The Works,* 29.
49 Ibid., 3.
50 Stafford, *Body Criticism,* 1–24.

would ingrain in the minds of early scientists countless images of the circulatory system as a circuit, loop, or closed course, in which blood nourished the body and generated heat through its own movement. When the blood finally returns to "its sovereign the heart ... it recover[s] its state of excellence. Here it resumes its due fluidity and receives an infusion of natural heat – powerful, fervid, a kind of treasury of life."[51]

In *Circulation of the Blood* of 1649, it should be noted that Harvey revised his earlier theories concerning the heart's supremacy. He meditated upon the properties of the blood more specifically, and concluded that a vital agent existing within it must imbue it with its heat, motion, and spirit. "I do not believe," he clarified, "that the heart is the fashioner of the blood; neither do I imagine that the blood has powers, properties, motion, or heat, as the gift of the heart ... I hold that the innate heat is the first cause of dilation, and that the primary dilation is in the blood itself."[52] For Harvey, therefore, the body's life energy was a product of its own materiality and constitution, and did not originate in something as vague as the immortal soul of theological doctrine. In fact, in *Anatomical Exercises on the Generation of Animals* of 1651, he proposed that "the blood should be viewed as the familiar divinity, as the soul itself of the body."[53] Since the blood directly helped replenish the body's vital force, it stands to reason why he concluded that it must be alive.[54]

It could very well be that Cabriada first learned of Harvey's work through Sylvius, who had acknowledged the English physician as the discoverer of circulation. Yet, there were more immediate Spanish sources from which Cabriada could have discovered circulation theory, although judging from the references in the *Letter*, there is little doubt that he was directly acquainted with *De Motu Cordis*.[55] The distinguished physician

51 Harvey, *The Works*, 46–7.

52 Ibid., 137.

53 Ibid., 381.

54 In Harvey's words: "[And] if the moderns be correct in their views that they say that the seminal fluid of animals emitted in coitu [sic] is alive, wherefore should we not, with like reason, affirm that there is a vital principle in the blood ... Unquestionably the blood is that in which the vegetative and sensitive operations first proclaim themselves; that in which heat, the primary and immediate instrument of life, is innate ... and the vehicle by which life is conveyed into every particle of the organized being" (*The Works*, 381).

55 We know that José Joaquín Izquierdo's assertion that Harvey was virtually unknown in Spain for three centuries after the publication of *De Motu Cordis* is far from accurate ("On Spanish," 105–6). Izquierdo's *Harvey, Initiator of the Experimental Method* (1936) claims that Harvey's theories never really took hold in Spain, partly because the work was never translated into Spanish. In his follow-up study, published in 1948 and titled "On the Spanish Neglect of Harvey's 'De Motu Cordis' for Three Centuries," Izquierdo reiterates that "Harvey's book was not known in Spain during a long period of time" (106).

Gaspar Bravo de Sobremonte had published *De Sanguinis Circulatione et de Arte Sphygmica* in 1662, which not only praised Harvey's doctrine of circulation, but also defended it against critics such as the staunch Galenist James Primerose and the Venetian physician Emilio Parigiano. Other physicians like Matías García, Juan de la Torre y Valcárcel, and Francisco Morelló had likewise published treatises between 1666 and 1678 that dealt with the fundamentals of Harvey's theories. Of note in this respect is that, in 1677, a decade before the publication of the *Letter*, Cabriada's father had written an introductory note to Matías García's *Disputationes Medicinae Selectae*, in which he lauded García's remarkable erudition and refuted Harvey's doctrine of circulation. Juanini and Casalete, two of Spain's most eminent reformists in the seventeenth century, similarly demonstrated capable knowledge of Harvey's work in the 1680s. It should also be noted that not only was the University of Zaragoza's medical school teaching aspects of Harvey's circulation by 1687, but court physicians like the Italian Federico Bottoni were performing public demonstrations of the circulatory system for a wide and learned public in Madrid.[56]

Regardless of the sources, Cabriada melds Harvey's doctrine of circulation and Sylvius's theory of rarefaction to offer a hybrid paradigm of how life-bearing and properly alkalinized blood continually flows from the heart to the extremities and vitalizes the body. What is more, he upholds Harvey's foundational metaphor in *De Motu Cordis* that the heart is the sovereign of all life (the dictum *primum vivens, ultimum moriens* even appears in Cabriada's complementary treatise, *Triumphant Truth*) and the calculation that blood circulates throughout the body in roughly an hour.[57] In binding Harvey's and Sylvius's theories, Cabriada proposes that the heart moves blood and aids to chemically perfect it, or restore its special life-bearing spirits. In Cabriada's words: "arriving at the

Izquierdo's study makes no reference to luminaries of Spanish medicine like Juanini, Casalete, or Cabriada, who clearly adopted Harvey's discoveries to build their own theoretical models of body functioning.

56 Bottoni recalled his demonstrations around 1700 stating: "Not only in large animals and quadrupeds do we observe circulation, as I have demonstrated to many learned men in Spain and Italy an infinite number of times using dogs, deer, monkeys, and the little fish that can be found in Madrid's Manzanares River" (qtd. in Martínez-Vidal, *El nuevo*, 85). Bottoni would later author *Evidence of the Circulation of the Blood* – a treatise prefaced by the eminent polymath Pedro Peralta y Barnuevo – that was published in Lima in 1723 and helped disseminate Harvey's theory of circulation throughout the Spanish-American Empire.

57 Cabriada, *Verdad triunfante*, 150.

HEART, THE BLOOD IS PERFECTED."[58] The trademark lucidity and vigour of Harvey's scientific reasoning is palpable in the *Letter*. In certain passages, it is possible to discern subtle nuances and shifts in tone in Cabriada's prose that elevate the vital properties of blood in a manner reminiscent of *De Motu Cordis*. A few of these passages in the *Letter* include: "the blood filled with this spirit in which life is principally contained"; "That the life of a man is in his blood"; "it is true that life, in as much as it is alive, disappears with the cessation of the circulation of the blood."[59] In some fragments there are explicit intertextual references that connect the *Letter* and *De Motu Cordis* more firmly, such as with Harvey's expression "treasury of life" and the words "balsam" and "noble" (the rich metaphoric language that conjures up the nobility, or ultimate authority, of the sovereign organ), which refer to the manner in which the blood's vital properties are replenished in the heart. In the *Letter*, we read: "Blood is the treasury of life [tesoro de la vida]. In it we find that living, balsamic nectar that Hippocrates referred to as *impetum faciente* and that is ordinarily called vital spirit; through it nature undertakes the noblest operations; it is celebrated by philosophers and poets alike; Aristotle referred to it as the animated and fecund substance … [T]he blood (as the treasury of life) should not be evacuated."[60]

These shifts in tone, intertextual allusions, and metaphoric language bring into relief and extend the margins of Cabriada's concept of body economy, and in so doing, they compel readers to deepen their understanding of vital force and how it is generated. A handful of these intertextual allusions function as subtexts in the Riffaterrean sense. For Michel Riffaterre, a subtext is a specular *mise en abyme* that makes manifest the leitmotifs of the larger narrative and represents "a unit of reading … [and] a hermeneutical model."[61] Subtexts serve as signposts that build up in the text through "successive variants" to provide another level of coherence to its core meanings. Thus, the subtext is not, nor should it be regarded as, an instance of rearticulation, but rather it "always constitutes a second reading of what the text surrounding it is about … The subtext thus actualizes the relationship of referentiality."[62] The following passage, for instance, functions as a subtext, in the sense that not only does it invoke Harvey's and Sylvius's theories on circulation and blood composition, but it also bolsters the *Letter*'s underlying rationale

58 Cabriada, *Carta*, 25.
59 Ibid., 133, 147, 147–8 respectively.
60 Ibid., 66–9.
61 Riffaterre, *Fictional Truth*, 131.
62 Ibid., 28.

concerning the affinity between circulation and disease that is echoed in other variant subtexts throughout the treatise:

> That this VITAL SPIRIT, which is destroyed with bloodletting, constitutes the balsam that preserves the blood and all the parts of the body from putrefaction, I PROVE AS FOLLOWS: if there are any causes that obstruct the transit of this balsamic spirit to one or more parts of the body, these parts become corrupted, just as the blood within them becomes corrupted, which is evident and can be witnessed daily in gangrenes; and when the blood in gumboils turns to matter, which is caused for no other reason than the coagulation of blood, it is clear that this spirit cannot penetrate it or foment it. And thus, stripped of its balsamic virtue (its volatile salt) it degenerates from its state of perfection to the hideous state of corruption, as is recognized in the previous examples of gangrenes and gumboils. For this reason, philosophers have called this spirit by numerous names. Some have called it *universal balsam.* Others, *vital fire.* Others, *philosophers' salt.* And others, *universal ferment.* I beseech you, what good can bloodletting do that nature cannot?[63]

I have included Riffaterre's concept of subtext to draw attention to the *Letter*'s deeper discursive structures. In passages like this one, we see the extent to which Cabriada challenges Galenic anatomy in order to advance a universal circulatory system that animates the body with a vital and renewable agent present in the blood. Even the *Letter*'s language – terms like spirit, vital, balsam, preservation, transit, penetrate, foment, ferment, putrefaction, corruption, and nature – reflects the way in which Cabriada constructs the body as a dynamic system of vital movement and change, which in turn influences his understanding of the causes and development of disease. Admittedly, this language can be found in Galenic medicine, and even Aristotelian philosophy (and physician's like Harvey were certainly sympathetic to Aristotle's theories on vital force), since it had traversed schools of thought and influenced all types of scientific, anatomical, and poetic writings since the early Homeric era. But the *Letter* itself, read against the backdrop of Harvey's vitalist signifiers and metaphoric descriptions, which it builds up beginning with the paratext, leaves little doubt concerning the expectation of meaning.

These subtexts represent a compelling aspect of the *Letter*'s literary dimension as well, especially when considered in relation to Cabriada's complex persona and the larger epistolary frame that invites the reader to peek into a young physician's personal struggles with the court's

63 Cabriada, *Carta*, 131–2.

medical authority. Additionally, they illuminate that vein of Cabriada's medical thinking that transcends the boundaries of iatrochemistry when it comes to vital force. That is to say, while a confluence of iatrochemical functions sustain organs and flesh, Cabriada suggests that, at a more fundamental level of somatic functioning, an unknown vital force lurks in the circulating blood and invests the total body system with life.[64] To be sure, this vitalist undercurrent in Cabriada's *Letter* is allusive, hard to pin down, and evocative of ancient and modern learning, and yet it obliges us to revisit his broader iatrochemical arguments and re-evaluate in a new light what we know of the duke's fevered body.

Before Cabriada outlines the chemical class of observations and experiments, he pauses to confide in his master Filiatro once again: "Oh, how true it is that medicine, as with the objects of nature, cannot be understood without chemical experiments!"[65] He poses the following rhetorical question to Filiatro: "Above all, let us ask: what is this CHEMISTRY, whose name alone inspires such horror?"[66] In various medical and scientific circles in Spain during this period, chemistry (*chymica*) was still eyed with suspicion and often considered a species of alchemy, which had been associated over the centuries with everything from magic to demonology. At the time, alchemy had experienced a notable resurgence through figures like Luis Aldrete y Soto, who boasted in his popular work of 1682, titled *The Purest Truth*, to have distilled a curative water that could restore life to even the most moribund individual (not surprisingly, he was swiftly reprimanded by the Medical Tribunal and Licensing Board, or *Protomedicato*, and his treatise was censored).[67] Mar Rey Bueno has demonstrated that, contrary to what is often assumed, alchemy was not as pervasive in Spain as in the rest of Europe during this

64 Ibid., 107.

65 Ibid., 166.

66 Ibid., 34.

67 Aldrete y Soto, *La verdad acrisolada*, 2. See Josep Lluís Barona's article "His Excellency's Tertian Fever" for a discussion of the condemnation of Aldrete y Soto's "water of life" (52–3). Cabriada was also involved with alchemy during his years in court. Muñoz Utrilla relates one interesting incident worth mentioning: "[I]n his occupation as Court physician Cabriada had to deal with, and even collaborate with, strange people beyond academe who arrived at Charles II's Court offering miracle cure-alls through alchemy and magic that were intended to restore the monarch's delicate health. One of these odd people was Roque García de la Torre, who came with his 'elixir vitae' … Roque García ended up being a swindler and ran off leaving Juan de Cabriada and the more seasoned spagyricist Juan de Bayle in charge of continuing with the alchemical experiment, which required blue stones that Roque García had created and left in a laboratory in Leganitos" ("D. Juan de Cabriada y Borrás," 31). For more information on de la Torre's cure and his laboratory in Leganitos, see Mar Rey Bueno's *El hechizado* (44–6).

period. As she argues, "the great impact the practice of this art had [was with] the most powerful strata of society, particularly the nobility and monarchy ... who attempted to surround themselves with known alchemists to profit from their curative practices."[68] Miguel López Pérez has revealed that the distinction between alchemy and chemistry was blurred during this period, yet the establishment of the progressive Royal Society of Medicine and Other Sciences in Seville in 1700 went a long way in legitimizing chemistry as a discipline, given that "the practice and perfection of chemical and spagyric medicine [in Spain] was to be the main task of the Royal Society."[69] The Royal Society of Medicine and Other Sciences, of which Cabriada was a founding member (he was also instrumental in establishing the Royal Chemical Laboratory in 1694), was, at least in its beginnings, devoted mostly to the study of chemistry. López Pérez demonstrates convincingly that it owed its founding to the sharp disagreements between Galenists (or academic physicians holding doctorate degrees) and independent practitioners of chemical medicine (or independent physicians holding bachelor's degrees in medicine who completed their medical training beyond the academic sphere) concerning the relevance of chemistry to therapeutic practice. The point is that chemistry was by no means well defined as a discipline in the early-eighteenth century, but as Sánchez-Moscoso Hermida also points out in her reading of Félix Palacios's landmark *Pharmaceutical, Chemico-Galenic Forum* of 1706, attitudes toward chemistry in Spain had changed radically thanks in large measure to reformists like Cabriada.[70] In addition, there was a more concerted effort among the younger generation of physicians to openly examine the therapeutic value of chemical processes (many of which are referenced in Cabriada's *Letter*), including those that involved antimony and various salts.[71]

Cabriada labours to convey in his *Letter* that chemistry is more than science: it is a most remarkable art. Without question, chemistry is the true seat of natural philosophy, since it alone empowers the physician to bring to knowledge truths about the concealed vital force that animates all biological organisms in nature: "With this prodigious art it is possible

68 Rey Bueno, *El hechizado,* 41. See also Chapter 1 on occult sciences in Goodman's *Power and Penury.* As Goodman shows, the occult sciences were largely accepted in sixteenth-century Spain, particularly astrology and alchemy.

69 López Pérez, "Novatores or Alchemists?" 335.

70 Sánchez-Moscoso Hermida, "¿Química o alquimia en la medicina de los novatores?" 64–8.

71 In 1711, the novator Miguel Marcelino Boix y Moliner dedicated a number of pages of his treatise *Hippocrates Defended* to highlighting the marvels of chemistry and the many criticisms that were levelled against it at the time (303–7).

1.2 Portrait of Félix Palacios from *Palestra pharmaceutica, chymico-galenica*, 1706.

to penetrate into the most obscure aspects of nature and bring to light that pure substance concealed in the centre of compound bodies, which is the one and only foundation of nature, the true balsamic nectar, the root of all good medicine."[72] What is more, chemistry also offers fundamental concepts that are indispensable in producing life-giving medicines: "Chemistry is thus an art of … creating beneficial, safe, and

72 Cabriada, *Carta*, 36.

agreeable medicaments."[73] Cabriada's musings on the ways chemical experimentation can advance our understanding of the duke's malady take up a substantial portion of the *Letter* and draw on a number of iatrochemical theorists of the period. When it comes to sanguification (the creation of blood), Cabriada cites the Italian anatomist Gaspare Aselli (the discoverer of the lacteal vessels and the lymphatic system) and the French physician Jean Pecquet to condemn the Galenic view that the liver transformed chyle from the intestines into blood and directed it to the venous system. The *Letter* also references Thomas Willis's research on blood chemistry, which centred on specifying and, in a sense, reinterpreting the very chemical nature of life.[74] Cabriada gravitates once again toward the vital properties of blood and the fundamental notion – popularized by Sylvius – that an imbalance of the body's pH was a contributing factor in producing disease.

If we take a closer look at the marginalia in Latin that constitute a type of running bibliography throughout the *Letter* and imbue it with scholarly authority, we find repeated references to Sylvius's works. For Sylvius, bodily well-being demanded a state of acid/alkali balance, and it was the continuity of a series of chemical reactions, through fermentation primarily in the blood and viscera, that vitalized the body. Salt was an integral part of this activity, given that it regulated the fermentation processes and balanced the body's acidity and alkalinity. With Sylvius in mind, we can appreciate why Cabriada insisted that the blood is inherently alkaline and composed of a synthesis of spirits and volatile salts ("sales volátiles") that ferment with acids.[75] "For Sylvius," as Thomas Fuchs explains, "chemical reaction in the forms of (slower) fermentation and (more violent) 'effervescence' becomes the motor of all living processes; the basic model for this is provided by the reaction of acids and alkaline agencies."[76] Cabriada takes a page from Sylvius in accepting that putrid obstructions in the digestive tract, like those he conjectures afflicted the duke, release a foreign *materia* into the blood stream that ferments and instigates a preternatural movement of the blood, in turn elevating the body's temperature (the cause of fever). This explanation of fever challenged Galen's notion that a blend of hot humours overheated the heart and then the body. For those illnesses particular to the digestive system, Sylvius maintained that the body was unable to properly extract the chyle from waste fluids and solids. The chyle then decomposed, affecting the

73 Ibid., 35.

74 Clericuzio, "The Internal Laboratory," 66–9.

75 Cabriada, *Carta*, 201.

76 Fuchs, *The Mechanization of the Heart*, 151.

natural processes of chemical fermentation in the blood, and turned the body's interior more acid or alkali. In adopting Sylvius's chemical approach to digestive illness, Cabriada can effectively weld intestinal obstructions with putrid fevers to bolster his core argument that the most effective course of treatment for the duke was a more thorough purgation regimen.[77]

CABRIADA VERSUS THE MEDICO-SCIENTIFIC ESTABLISHMENT IN MADRID

The Galenists on the *junta* repeatedly condemned Cabriada's recommendations. Within a few months of the publication of the *Letter*, the military engineer and dilettante scientist Andrés Dávila y Heredia, "el Aduanero," published *Response That Dogmatic and Rational Medicine Delivers to the Book Published by Dr. Juan de Cabriada*, in which he refutes almost every single argument that the inexperienced lad Cabriada had set forth in the *Letter*. Of interest is that Dávila y Heredia focuses particular attention on the loathsome theory of circulation, and remarks that this offensive idea imported from abroad only confused the issue of pulsatile force and the tried and proven treatments of disease. In response, Cabriada published *Triumphant Truth*, a treatise in which he defends – via his alter ego, Filiatro, the honoured physician of great learning – the medical theories espoused in his *Letter*.[78] The anonymous and undated pamphlet titled *Caveats Offered by a Friend of the Aduanero* directed criticism of the *Letter* into a more personal and defamatory arena, and it set off a series of polemics that appeared in the medical ephemera of the period. In another anonymous pamphlet titled *The Medical Diogenes*, for example, Cabriada is not only condemned for being a mechanist ("Mecánico") and falling prey to the errors of the growing "empirical sect," but he is also criticized for questioning the efficacy of phlebotomy procedures.[79] Another pamphlet appeared shortly thereafter, titled

77 Casalete's pioneering work on fevers in *Duae Controversiae* foreshadows Cabriada's conclusions here. Barona Vilar argues rightly that "[i]n the early 1680s Casalete began to theorize … that the origins of fevers had nothing to do with humoural flows [fluxión humoral], as the Galenists would have it, but as a consequence of the pathological alteration of the solid parts of the body, which led to the corruption of organic humours" ("Las tercianas," 50). Casalete, a close acquaintance of Cabriada's, could have very well influenced Cabriada in this respect, although there are no explicit references in the *Letter*. In all likelihood, Casalete and Cabriada were employing the same iatrochemical theories to reach their conclusions.

78 Cabriada, *Verdad triunfante*, n.p.

79 *Diogenes Medico*, 6.

Colloquium between Diogenes and Pedro Grullo, which defended not only Cabriada, but also other physicians like Agustín Gonzalo Bustos de Olmedilla, a strong opponent of phlebotomy, whose treatise *Horrible Monster of Greece, Mortal Enemy of Man* of 1669 was aimed at discrediting Galenic medicine. The young Diego Mateo Zapata also bitterly censured Cabriada in *True Apologetic Defence of the Rational and Philosophical Medicine* of 1691, a treatise which also condemned the Veronese physician José Gazola's *Medical, Political, and Astronomical Joys* (1690), since it praised Cabriada's innovative work. Zapata reserved his sharpest and more sarcastic comments of the *Letter* for the objectionable theory of circulation:

> Thank God I considered this portentous anatomical invention of the circulation of the blood that the gang of chemists have so highly extolled and that doctor Cabriada has so ardently celebrated to such a degree as to consider it a *New Sun*. I imagine he believes that it has rid us of the ignorance of the ancients since as far back as the year [16]28, the year William Harvey of the University of London, brought this invention out onto the world stage … I will turn now to the words of the arch-blabbermouth [archisoplón] himself and deny the assumption that we are alive thanks principally to the circular movement of the blood in the body … This movement is impossible, repugnant, and chimerical … and [it is] supposedly connected to our life in a special manner. I deny this assumption, and I will prove my arguments with the use of reason, which is what counts.[80]

The physician and traditionalist Cristóbal Tixedas, associated with the University of Barcelona, wrote the extensive *Truth Defended*, which likewise focused on the special affinity that Cabriada articulates between the circulatory system and the body's vital force. As with Dávila y Heredia and Zapata, Tixedas seeks to safeguard the validity of Galen's doctrines against the falsehoods of modern medicine:

> When philosophers proclaim that life consists in heat, they do not mean that life emanates from heat directly, given that life is in the soul, which animates the organized body. What they mean to convey is that life endures in the heat, inasmuch as the heat is the last disposition that preserves the soul in the body and vivifies the innate heat, or innate spirit. For this reason, it is known as vital fire …

80 Zapata, *Verdadera apología*, 51–2. For more information on the nuances of Zapata's criticisms of Cabriada's *Letter* – for instance, Zapata's need to distinguish himself as a scholar, the late date of publication of his treatise in relation to the *Letter*, the treatise's long introductory excursus by Ponce de León – see Pardo Tomás, *El médico en la palestra*, 149–55.

> Therefore, the theory of circulation does not discredit the ancient doctrine that life endures in the heat, or that the heat is the last disposition of life; nor does it prove that life consists in the circulation of the blood. Thus, there is no obfuscation in saying that life endures in heat; and if there ever was obfuscation on this point, it will remain regardless of the circulation of the blood.[81]

To appreciate why Cabriada's *Letter* sparked such bitter polemics, it is necessary to gain a better understanding of how scientific innovations challenged the institution of medicine in late-seventeenth-century Spain. More than simply a clash between ancients and moderns, the emerging scientific culture in Spain had begun to rely on increasingly complex networks of resistance and collaboration through salons and societies to advance its modernizing agenda with the elite. The number of independent physicians securing their professional accreditation directly with the Medical Tribunal and Licensing Board was on the rise during this period.[82] As the reputation of these physicians began to surge and spread within courtly circles, the academic Galenists – a good number of them university professors and physicians – witnessed the decline of not only their incomes, but just as importantly, their status and political influence. The growing schism between independent physicians and academic physicians brought into sharp focus the shifting terrain of power and authority in Spain's scientific community in the early-eighteenth century.[83] In *Triumphant Truth*, Cabriada's alter ego, Filiatro, repeatedly condemns Galenic medicine for its rootedness in the university system and in particular for its cult of textual erudition over empirical knowledge. The Galenists responded in various ways to these types of assaults. They published criticism of modern science, presented a united front within and across universities, spread fierce rumours concerning the demonic and heretical nature of new scientific theories, and excluded *novatores* whenever possible from medical proceedings and *juntas*. And when one of their own had the audacity to criticize Galen or the university system, as was the case with the professor of medicine at the University of Zaragoza Lucas Casalete in his 1687 treatise *Duae Controversiae*, they would denounce the professor's scholarship and prohibit him from teaching or publishing further on the matter.[84] Clearly, then, what was at stake in the circulation and reception of treatises like Cabriada's *Letter* was not only a significant transformation in the nuanced politics of

81 Tixedas, *Truth Defended*, 64–5.

82 Hermosilla Molina, *Cien años de medicina sevillana*, 3–5.

83 Pardo Tomás, *El médico en la palestra*, 168–70.

84 Peset and Albiñana, *La ciencia en las universidades españolas*, 24.

medical practice, but also the very real possibility of altering how the body could be interpreted and governed within the medical institutional order. Indeed, the ideological basis of Galenists' world view was being publicly challenged like never before. The medical polemics apparent in texts like Cabriada's *Letter* and *Triumphant Truth* were thus more than heated exchanges among factions or cliques within the court's cultural sphere. These polemics, many of which extended over years, effectively circulated new ideas, publicized texts, subverted custom, established imagined communities, reinforced group solidarity, and conferred importance on the free expression of dissent and antagonist views.

There is little doubt that Cabriada's notions of the circulatory system, blood properties, and the workings of the heart flew in the face of Galenic theory. For Galen, there were two different circuits of blood, the venous and arterial, and each retained specific functions and qualities (or spirits) that governed separate parts of the body. The arteries carried the life-giving air throughout the body, while the veins carried only the blood that the body "consumed." The heart for Galen was not responsible for the movement of blood, but rather served as the site where blood mixed with air to produce a vital spirit (*pneuma zotikon*) that nourished the body. In Galenic theory, fevers came about when hot humours overheated the heart and its surrounding tissue, which in turn overheated the body. The core of humoral theory depended on a strictly hierarchized cosmology that linked the human being through the four humours and temperaments with the cosmic energies of balance and change, which in turn revealed to what degree life mirrored the extraordinary architecture of God's universe.[85]

In *Triumphant Truth*, Cabriada presses the question of vital force and ponders, as did Harvey, whether the immortal soul regulates the body. Clearly, this line of inquiry was sacrilegious and challenged the bedrock assumption of Christian theology that the immortal soul vitalized the body. In 415, St Augustine had made it clear in *De origine animae hominis* that "we know nothing of our internal functions in the very central region of the soul itself, where that power is present which imparts life and animation to all else – A mystery this which, I apprehend, no medical man of any kind, whether empirics, or anatomists, or dogmatists, or methodics, or any man living, has any knowledge of."[86] Cabriada skilfully fashions an image of a pulsating, living heart torn from a man's chest – a rather grisly image he borrows from Descartes – and he beseeches his

85 Kemp and Wallace, *Spectacular Bodies*, 42.
86 Quoted in Smith et al., *Animal Spirit Doctrine*, 53.

readers to conjecture from what source the organ's vital force originates if it is no longer appended to the body. If the immortal soul flees from every last particle of flesh upon death, as dictated by theological doctrine, what enigmatic spark, what intrinsic and life-bearing vigour induces the organ to continue its systolic-diastolic action? Furthermore, why does life, once perceivable throughout the entirety of the bodily system, linger now only in this lone disembodied organ?

I ask: what is *this faculty* [that makes the heart pulsate]? We cannot say it is the soul since it is known that, as René Descartes proclaims, in ripping the heart from a man who has just died the heart pulsates violently. Here [in the heart] there is a pulse, but no soul – Thus, we cannot say that the pulsatile faculty is the soul. Furthermore, the soul is not the [body's] *señora*, nor can it dominate the movements of the heart, nor are the movements of the heart dependent on its cogitations ... [I]f the pulse depended on the faculty of the soul, then how could the heart of a recently deceased man beat if he has no soul?[87]

Cabriada brings the image of the Cartesian excised heart to bear upon the constraints of the soul concerning vital force. It is as if all he needs to do to shake the great edifice of theology is to present this anatomical image of a bodiless heart beating in the palm of the hand. In his reasoning, life and death are inexplicably rendered in this image.[88] In the end, he accepts the conclusion that the physical body must produce within its materiality and constitution the source of its vital force. The soul, then, is by no means its "señora," or caretaker. And with the word "señora" in this context, Cabriada might very well be attempting to challenge the age-old Platonic opposition presented in stanza 13 of Jorge Manrique's *Ode on the Death of His Father*, in which the body is conceived as the "cativa," or slave, to the soul, which is described as its "señora."[89]

87 Cabriada, *Verdad triunfante*, 60–4.

88 The disembodied heart also fascinated G.W. Leibniz, and, likewise, brought to the fore the rapport between soul and flesh. As Jacques Roger notes: "One particular instance brought out, for Leibniz, the latent materialism in the doctrine [of animism]: a heart removed from the chest palpitated for several instants. If this movement was due to the soul, as Stahl claimed, this meant that 'the soul of the animal is divided into parts and remains partially in the excised heart.' Moreover, everything was thus immediately clarified: the soul was matter, and we were back with mechanism. But this was clearly not what Stahl intended" (*The Life*, 346).

89 In *Phaedo*, Socrates argues that the body is the cage, or tomb, of the soul, and only when the body dies can the soul be set free. Stanza 13 of *Coplas on the Death of his Father* reads as follows (I leave these verses in Spanish, since I have not found a translation that does justice to the original): "Si fuese en nuestro poder/tornar la cara fermosa corporal,/

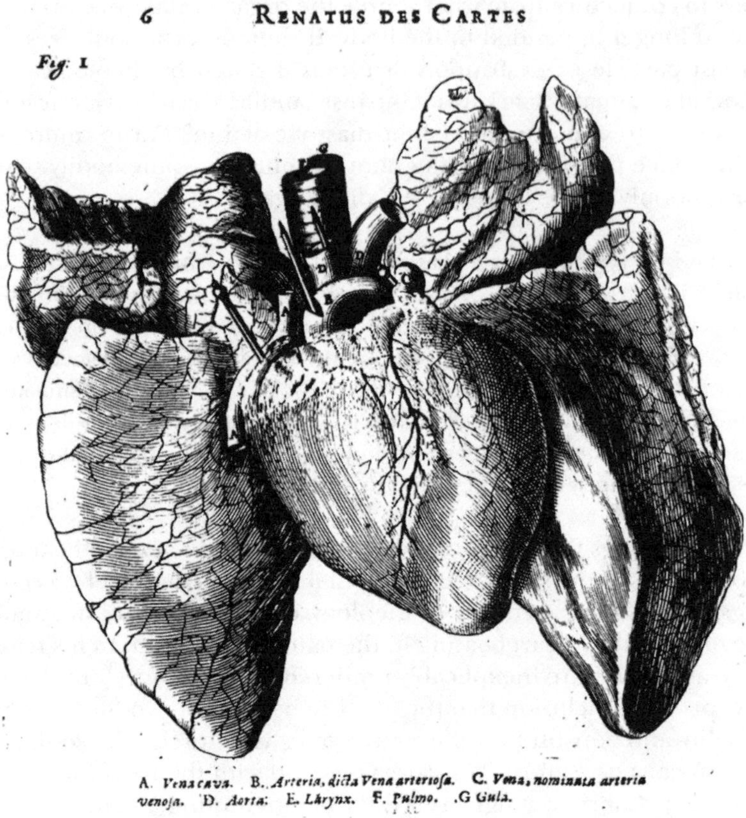

1.3 Figure 1 showing a heart and lungs from René Descartes' *De Homine Figuris et Latinitate Donatus à Florentio Schuyl*, 1662.

A question comes to mind when we take stock of the *Letter*'s staging of disease and its practical, anatomical, and chemical referents: can vitalist and iatrochemical theories, like those of Harvey and Sylvius, be reconciled? In Cabriada's medico-scientific thinking, the iatrochemical framework is in no way impoverished by vitalistic notions. When Cabriada

como podemos fazer/el ánima gloriosa/angelical,/¡qué diligencia tan biva/toviéramos toda hora,/y tan presta,/en componer la cativa,/dexándonos la señora/descompuesta!" (Manrique, 25). See Frank A. Dominguez's "Body and Soul: Jorge Manrique's 'Coplas on the Death of his Father' 13.145–156" for an excellent reading of the body-soul dualism in these verses.

wrote his *Letter*, iatrochemical theories stemming from a revisionist understanding of the circulatory system were still not widely disseminated in Spain, yet the crucial rapport between vital force and iatrochemistry that would resonate in Enlightenment science is already perceptible in his work. The debate that takes shape in the seventeenth century concerning what exactly constitutes life – whether it was mechanically or biochemically derived – established the foundational counterpoint that propelled the line of vitalist inquiry that runs from Georg Ernest Stahl to Johann Friedrich Blumenbach. What brings this all together is how the *Letter*'s vitalist argument buttresses the iatrochemical framework when it runs up against a limit of interpretation. One such moment is specified in the question the *Letter* raises about the body and disease: what is it about the chemical constitution and circulation of blood itself at its most intrinsic level that vitalizes the body and saves it from fever and decay? While Cabriada enlists the science of Sylvius, van Helmont, Willis, and others to answer this question, it remains clear that their theories can take him only so far. My argument is that Cabriada's *Letter* articulates this threshold and makes it visible to the reader: that is, the treatise strings together a cohesive set of iatrochemical arguments through a complex scientific and imaginative framework, but returns repeatedly to an intrinsic vital force contained in circulating blood as the ultimate guarantor of bodily health. By privileging a generative, unknown energy produced through properly circulating blood via the heart, Cabriada offers his readers a body divested of the hierarchies of Galenic humoralism. The truth is that he challenges humoral theory the moment he brings into play a universal circulatory system the purpose of which is to replenish throughout the body "a balsamic spirit, a remedy to all putrefaction."[90] In the *Letter*, the body becomes a destabilizing sign for it defies humoral theory and its cause-and-effect relationships. Said otherwise, the body becomes through the lens of Cabriada's scientific thinking more challenging to interpret and codify, much less discipline. Implicit in Cabriada's *Letter* is the assumption that the body – *every* body – bears within itself, within its very materiality, a vital force that cannot be effectively decoded with Galenic theory. And given the *Letter*'s many foreign referents and its tangled lines of theoretical inquiry, one Galenist physician feared, in an anonymous pamphlet criticizing the *Letter*, that Cabriada sought to "trade a Catholic medicine for a Lutheran one."[91]

90 Cabriada, *Carta*, 166.

91 *Diogenes Medico*, 7.

It has long been noted that Harvey's metaphorical concept of the heart's sovereignty coincides with the establishment of absolute monarchies throughout Europe. In his later treatises *Circulation of the Blood* and *Exercises on the Generation of Animals*, it is possible to discern a shift in his anatomical analogies concerning vital force, in which the heart is dethroned, so to speak, and the properties of the blood take on increasingly more relevance. The implication of such a shift, as Christopher Hill suggests, is that the very idea of authority in Europe had undergone significant changes. The importance Harvey attaches to the blood "can only be described as republican … Harvey's somersault is surely remarkable. So is the coincidence between the change in his way of expressing himself and the political changes of the two decades which followed 1628."[92] Anatomical analogies during the period reflected socio-political structures and the powerful wish to transform them. It is fair to say that Cabriada adopts a similar analogical-metaphorical approach, especially given his belief that the discovery of the circulatory system represented nothing less than a "*New Sun*" for Spanish medicine that could bring decisive change to courtly medical policy.

The circulatory system and its role in the processes of life remained a central point of contention among Spanish physicians, precisely because it displaced, and oftentimes stripped away, the very foundations of Galenic humoralism. "The leitmotif of Spanish *novatores*," writes Martínez-Vidal and Pardo Tomás, "would be the controversial doctrine of circulation … The doctrine of circulation was seen by the most recalcitrant or 'intransigent' Galenists (Matías García, Cristóbal Tixedas) as a real threat that could pervert a number of true medical dogmas."[93] Cabriada's *Letter* is not a rehash of Harvey's theory of circulation or Sylvius's theory of rarefaction. On the contrary, it strategically interprets the circulatory system and the vitalistic aspects of the blood in a dependency relation not only to rethink body functioning, but also to devise new methods for analyzing disease and discovering the bodily sources of vital force. From this perspective, the *Letter* contributes directly to the broader reformist culture in Europe that characterized the push toward making new sense of the body and its life-bearing energies in that complex transitional period between the Renaissance and the Enlightenment. Thus, Cabriada's core argument is as bold as it is categorical: blood should not be evacuated from the body at the first sight of disease, but

92 Hill, "William Harvey and the Idea of Monarchy," 162.

93 Martínez-Vidal and Pardo Tomás, "Un siglo de controversias," 108.

rather examined and analyzed scientifically through its intrinsic and dynamic properties in the circulatory system.

Even when the circulatory system was generally accepted as fact in Spain in the early-eighteenth century, traditionalists maintained that the ancients had been the first to discover it. As López Piñero points out, distinguished Galenists like Luis Enrique de Fonseca, Alonso López Cornejo, and Pedro Aquenza Mossa had acknowledged the existence of the circulatory system at long last, but they argued that Hippocrates and Galen were well aware of it, even though they had never developed it in their work.[94] In 1717, physician and university professor Juan Martín de Lesaca contended that Harvey had in fact reinterpreted Galenic doctrine to develop his theory of circulation. He lamented: "I do not want to dispute whether circulation exists or does not exist ... Yet, I cannot help but notice that I have longed for a number of Galen's doctrines from which the movement of blood can be inferred with equal clarity."[95] Even Feijóo embedded circulatory theory in a displaced past, but he rooted it in a distinctly Spanish past when he argued that the sixteenth-century polymath Miguel Servet had invented it.[96] This so-called nationalization of circulatory theory would persist with Spanish physicians such as Anastasio Chinchilla Piqueras (1801–1876) and Nicasio Mariscal y García (1859–1949). Pedro Laín Entralgo notes rightly that "nearly every country has claimed for itself the honour of having begun to think of the blood circulating in a circle [in the body]."[97]

94 López Piñero, González Blanco, and Jiménez Blanco, *Historia*, 56.

95 Lesaca, *Formas ilustradas*, 10–13.

96 Feijóo refers to a note Leibnitz uncovered in the journal *Mémoires pour l'histoire des sciences et des beaux arts* in which Miguel Servet was credited as the discoverer of circulation: "[T]he true discoverer of the circulation of the blood was that famous antitrinitarian heretic ... Miguel Servet ... Thus, the glory of discovering the circulation of the blood, which up to now fell upon three Italians and an Englishman, rests with a Spaniard" (*Suplemento*, 142). Feijóo would later argue a similar case in favour of the veterinarian Francisco la Reyna. For Feijóo's full consideration of Francisco la Reyna's work on the circulatory system, see *Erudite and Curious Letters*, vol. 3, Letter 28. See also J.J. Keevil and L.M. Payne's *Francisco de la Reyna and the Circulation of the Blood.* In "Marvels of Nature," included in his *Universal Critical Theatre*, Feijóo admits, nevertheless, that the circulation of the blood still remained a mystery, regardless of modern medicine and its discoveries. In the late-eighteenth and early-nineteenth centuries, the physician Ignacio Ruiz de Luzuriaga (covered in Chapter 3) would attempt to prove once again that Spanish physicians were in fact the true discoverers of circulation (Soldevilla, 62–4).

97 Laín Entralgo, "La obra de William Harvey y sus consecuencias," 235.

THE MODERN PROJECT IN SPAIN: SCIENCE AND REFORM

It goes without saying that any science in late-seventeenth- and early-eighteenth-century Spain concerned with interrogating epistemological claims associated with the basic functioning and disciplining of the human body was considered subversive by those apparatuses of power that stood to lose the most in such a manoeuvre. As a popular text penned by a court physician against court physicians and invested with the authority of reformist intellectuals of the stature of Antonio de Ron, José Casalete, and Dionisio de Cardona, Cabriada's *Letter* exposes this schism at the very heart of the court in Madrid. The *Letter*'s most subversive contribution to Spanish modernity is not its championing of Harvey's circulation or Sylvius's theory of rarefaction, nor is it its many criticisms levelled against the court's scientific establishment. At the centre of the *Letter* stands the bold claim that the body, in all its wondrous complexity and mystery, is not vitalized by the soul. The subversive and liberating impact of this claim in the late-seventeenth-century context cannot be overstated. Cabriada's account of life hinges upon the dynamic, life-bearing force produced when properly alkalized blood – itself burgeoning with life – circulates through the heart and nourishes every part of the body. There is no escaping the special emphasis he places on the material genesis of vital force in the body (the reader is drawn repeatedly to the marvels of blood and the circulatory system), and it should come as no surprise that the soul is mentioned only three times in his 234-page-long *Letter*.[98] As Fay Alberti reminds us, the push toward rethinking vital force during this period took place in the larger context of "attempts to redefine and understand the human body and its links to the soul and the divine."[99] Alberti demonstrates that the various competing narratives undergirding the study of the body and its vital force appeared in complex and shifting contexts throughout the seventeenth century, when the functions of the soul came under increased scrutiny and criticism. The numerous theories on anatomy, pathology, physiology, and chemistry that flourished in the Enlightenment provided fertile ground for conjecturing about the body's vital force without having to turn to the soul as the purveyor of movement and vitality.

Cabriada's *Letter* not only challenged the epistemology that sustained Madrid's scientific establishment, but it also confronted the intellectual

98 Harvey likewise avoided mentioning the soul when he explained his theory of circulation and vital force in *De Motu Cordis*.

99 Alberti, *Matters of the Heart*, 4.

community with a series of questions concerning what constitutes vital force. These questions included: How does the motion of the heart and blood vitalize the body? What generates bodily movement and change? What produces disease, and how is it possible to maintain a state of well-being? Where is the seat of life exactly, if not in the soul? All these questions are deployed in some form in the *Letter*, and they are bound up in a complex and imaginative narrative form, in which the young and daring Cabriada confides to his readers that the continued modernization of Spanish science and medicine depends on a new understanding of the body economy. In the eyes of traditionalists, the *Letter* transformed the body into a locus of inquiry and resistance and thus threatened the very bedrock of their time-honoured traditions and beliefs. In the eyes of reformists, the *Letter* opened paths of investigation and revealed the liberating possibilities of new science. There is no doubt that the *Letter* made Cabriada one of the most formidable representatives of the *novator* movement. In the final years of the seventeenth century, he worked with like-minded reformists to found Seville's Royal Society of Medicine and Other Sciences. There is no question that his ideas on vital force were disseminated through Seville's Royal Society and found their way into mainstream scientific practice for a small, but enormously important group of reformist intellectuals who would make it their aim to usher Spain into the Enlightenment.

2

Cartesianism and Its Discontents: Marcelino Boix y Moliner, Martín Martínez, and Diego de Torres Villarroel

The human body is a machine.
Antonio José Rodríguez, *Medicina palpable*[1]

"IT IS NOT A CRIME TO BE INTERESTED IN ANATOMY." When René Descartes wrote these words in 1639, he was evoking his many forays to the butcher shops in Amsterdam almost a decade earlier. During this period, he lived in the Kalverstraat (Calf-Street) quarter known for its butcher shops, and his routine never wavered: he would make the rounds to these establishments every few days, personally witness the slaughtering of animals, and then indicate the precise organs and tissues that he wished to be delivered to his home for private study. In dissecting and scrutinizing animal parts, Descartes extrapolated complex mechanistic models of bodily functioning that would revolutionize anatomical knowledge, particularly as it was understood in relation to the activities of the soul in the human body. Ever since Plato gave extensive philosophical form to the soul's immortality in *Phaedo*, philosophers had speculated about the complexities of the body-soul nexus. Yet the mechanism Descartes devised through his anatomical studies of animals and numerous observations of dissections in the anatomical studios in Amsterdam and Leiden in the 1630s represented a definitive milestone in how the problem was dealt with. Indeed, it established a new point of reference on the topic for decades to come. To use A.R. Hall's words, "the application of mechanistic philosophy to biological problems was not attempted before Descartes."[2] Descartes likewise revolutionized the fields of

1 Rodríguez, *Medicina palpable*, 195.
2 Quoted in Carter, *Descartes' Medical Philosophy*, 20.

geometry and mathematics and employed the new physics he had developed to elucidate the movements of all types of animate and inanimate bodies in space. In the 1751 preface to the *Encyclopédie*, Jean le Rond D'Alembert praised Descartes as a beneficent luminary who had single-handedly deciphered the language of modern science through his anatomical and mathematical learning. "[Descartes] has opened the way for us," D'Alembert declared, adding: "We see his inventive genius shining forth everywhere."[3]

Our understanding of the ascendancy and reception of Cartesianism in the seventeenth and eighteenth centuries has advanced significantly in the past few decades, but there are still lacunae in our account of how it influenced the investigation in anatomy and physiology in Spain.[4] As we saw in the previous chapter, reformist physicians, such as Juan de Cabriada in the late-seventeenth century, were in fact knowledgeable about Descartes' anatomical findings and had benefited from them greatly to interrogate body functioning and the workings of the soul. In this chapter, I will demonstrate how the question of vital force in Spain intersected, and was further facilitated by, the Cartesianism that began to circulate more widely during the early-eighteenth century, a tumultuous period marked by the War of Succession, in which the forces of modernity powerfully shaped the country.[5] Without question, Descartes' theories on anatomy stimulated significant research into vital force during this period. Owing in great part to Cartesian-inspired theories (William Harvey's, Thomas Sydenham's, Pierre Gassendi's, and Emmanuel Maignan's studies on anatomy and atomism were also critically important), the long-standing divisions between interiority and exteriority, visibility and invisibility, and animate and inanimate that informed the study of the body were revisited and shown to be wanting. In truth, in no other period in Spain up to this point did the discussion on body functioning and the soul stir up such bitter controversy and directly

3 D'Alembert, *Preliminary Discourse*, 79.

4 I am referring to Richard Carter's *Descartes' Medical Philosophy* (1983); Daniel Garber's *Descartes' Metaphysical Physics* (1992); Stephen Gaukroger's *Descartes' System of Natural Philosophy* (2002); Peter Schouls's *Descartes and the Enlightenment* (1989); John Sutton's *Philosophy and Memory Traces: Descartes to Connectionism* (1998); and Justin Skirry's *Descartes and the Metaphysics of Human Nature* (2005).

5 The period of the *novatores* extended from roughly 1675 to 1725. It was a period in which a small, but highly influential, group of intellectuals, scientists, philosophers, physicians, and statesmen steered Spain toward modern science. As Pérez-Magallón explains, the *novatores* were interested in developing "a program to secularize thinking … [and] displace scholastic epistemology in favour of a rationalist and sense-based epistemology" (*Construyendo la modernidad*, 14).

involve the Church and government, since what was at stake was determining what vitalized the body and organized its biological, moral, and intellectual activities.

The body's complex internal processes associated with vital force came under sharp scrutiny during this period, thanks in large measure to the questions that were raised in mid- to late-seventeenth-century anatomy and medicine covered in the previous chapter. Two of the most compelling and widely discussed questions included: What generates bodily movement and change (for instance, cardiac motion)? And where is the seat of bodily life if not in the soul? The fact that renowned physicians and philosophers in early-eighteenth-century Spain, such as Miguel Marcelino Boix y Moliner and Martín Martínez, were questioning, and in some cases challenging, fundamental assumptions about how the body functioned through their criticisms of Cartesianism was a cause for deep concern and suspicion among traditionalists and the clergy. Thanks to *tertulias* and scientific salons, the New Science, also known as the New Philosophy, as Cartesianism came to be known in Spain, swept intellectual circles, and it would have a direct impact on the ways in which vital force and the soul were interpreted in the scientific sphere. As will become apparent in my analysis of Diego de Torres Villarroel's creative and often overlooked *Anatomy of the Visible and Invisible: Universal Compendium of Both Spheres* (1738), even physicians who safeguarded religious paradigms of body-soul dualism were strongly influenced by the modern sciences that they vehemently condemned. Through Torres's *Anatomy* we can also see how his examination of vital force, despite itself, illuminates the deep-seated anxiety within the Spanish medico-scientific community about the soul's shifting status with respect to the body.

MECHANISM, NATURE, AND THE ART OF HEALING

It is difficult to conceive of the body politics in Spain in the early-eighteenth century without referring to Descartes' writings on human anatomy and his mechanistic views on life. As adumbrated in Cartesian science, organisms did not possess an inherent vital force or any independent or immaterial property that generated and sustained life. For Descartes, the world beyond the solipsistic *cogito* was an expansive sphere of corpuscles driven by necessity. That is, no teleological principle or vitalistic agent animated the material *res extensa.* It is easy to see how the Cartesian body/mind dualism allowed the subject to adopt a critical distance with respect to the thingness of the world, and, in so doing, it opened the way for what William Barrett argued was "man's self-assertion in the face of nature ... Nature sinks to the level of mere material for exploitation, and man towers as the master over it."[6] Descartes' expansion of mechanistic science was so broad and encompassing that it engulfed the operations of both the body and the soul. Furthermore, he deployed skeptical doubt strategically "to undermine our commitment to sensible qualities by detaching us from our reliance on the senses."[7]

Descartes' mind/body split and his theories on the origins of metabolic heat and what he understood as the body's "inner movements" had a significant impact on how anatomy and physiology were valourized within medical science. Recent scholarship has demonstrated to what degree Descartes examined that most difficult of questions: how is life possible in the human body?[8] Richard Carter's *Descartes' Medical Philosophy* reveals the complexity of Descartes' oeuvre, not only on the question of life, but also on the far-reaching consequences of the dialogue between scientism and anatomy. In Descartes' thinking, as Carter clarifies, there is no one formulation of the concept "body," but several, which obey two complementary spheres: there is the mathematical body (the "body grasped by Cartesian geometrical algebra," which includes problems related to matter, extension, and solidity); and there is the naïve body (the "body as grasped by the senses in everyday experience").[9] For Carter, Descartes is keenly aware of the complexity and ambiguity of the term "body" in his work, and for good reason:

> The primary reason he was so carefully ambiguous [of his use of the term body] is that, on the philosophical side … he saw it possible to achieve freedom from blinding impulses that lead men to assign an "objective" existence to the soul's innate reaction to a very complicated machine's reaction – that is, the human body's reaction … On the other side, by using this same freedom, men also can overcome those blinding prejudices that lead to indiscriminate adherence to authority, to any authority.[10]

6 Barrett, *Illusion of Technique*, 212.

7 Rozemond, *Descartes's Dualism*, 100.

8 See Chapter 1 of Peter Schouls's *Descartes and the Enlightenment*, particularly the discussion on observing life (24–32). In Part III of *Descartes Embodied: Reading Cartesian Philosophy through Cartesian Science*, Daniel Garber analyzes Descartes' famous letter to Elisabeth of 1643 on mind-body and body-body interactions. He argues that Descartes' concepts of mind and body are inconsistent with his earlier theories. He also demonstrates that Descartes' mind-body interaction represents "the ultimate model in terms of which we understand all physical interaction" (8). See also Chapter 5 of Justin Skirry's *Descartes and the Metaphysics of Human Nature*, which discusses the unity of mind and body in relation to the principle of life (121–44).

9 Carter, *Descartes' Medical Philosophy*, 34–5.

10 Ibid., 18.

Descartes' *Treatise of Man* was a revolutionary work on the naïve body, to use Carter's term, and it represented one of the most pioneering studies on human anatomy since Galen's *Anatomical Procedures.* Within a theoretical framework determined by mechanical forces and the actions of corpuscles, it examined the workings of life and advanced a series of innovative models of animation that analogized the body to a richly sophisticated machine. Descartes' anatomical studies in Amsterdam in 1629–30, the period that inspired the *Treatise of Man,* were of great importance in this respect. In a letter to Father Mersenne in 1639, Descartes made no apology for his interest in anatomical study, which was seen as an objectionable field of study at the time: "I spent one winter in Amsterdam during which I used to go almost every day to the butcher's house to see him kill the animals, and I used to take home with me parts that I wanted to dissect with more leisure. I have done the same thing on many occasions in all the places where I lived, and I do not think that any intelligent person could blame me for that."[11] As he scrutinized animal parts for insights into the functioning of the human body, it appeared logical to him that muscles, nerves, vessels, and valves should be correlated to wheels, counterweights, pipes, and doors, since they served the identical mechanical functions. He determined that the soul resided in the pineal gland in the brain and acted "like a turncock," directing the animal spirits that flowed in and out of it to the muscles and nerves like "a very subtle wind, or rather a very lively and pure flame."[12] He believed nerves were hollow tubes that carried various fluids and spirits to the extremities, allowing the body to react to exterior stimuli.[13] When it came to the heart, he described it as an astonishing organ, containing a lightless fire fuelled by drops of blood originating from the vena cava. The heart, moreover, was responsible for motion in the bodily machine, yet it was not a self-generated motion, but one God had instigated. How drops of blood flowed to the heart through the vena cava had to do not only with circulation, but also with the spontaneous contraction of the

11 Quoted in Clarke, *Descartes: A Biography,* 104. On Descartes' defence of anatomical study, Thomas Hall adds: "Descartes no doubt earned ridicule and even contempt as a student who thus soiled his hands by direct contact with the structures of animals, and who sought truth in the experiences of direct contact, rather than solely in books and disputations" (*Treatise,* xiv).

12 Descartes, *Treatise of Man,* 19–22.

13 Ibid, 22–3.

vessels, a theory inspired by William Harvey's work on cardiac motion.[14] The profound implication of Descartes' *Treatise of Man* was that, if the idiosyncrasy of life was generated in the gestalt of biological parts, then it was indeed feasible to study these parts – and the forces that animated them – as if they were "the movements of a clock or other automaton."[15]

Víctor Navarro-Brotóns has made the case that Descartes' influence in Spain in the late-seventeenth and early-eighteenth centuries was felt mostly in the disciplines of cosmology, dynamics, mathematics, and optics.[16] The philosopher and mathematician Juan Caramuel's *Mathesis Audax* of 1642, for instance, had examined a number of mathematical principles in Descartes' *Essais.* The Jesuit Sebastián Izquierdo's ambitious *Pharus Scientiarum* of 1659 had also dialogued closely with *Discourse on Method* and several of its core assumptions.[17] Yet, it was Juan Bautista Corachán, professor of mathematics at the University of Valencia and a regular participant in the city's most-popular literary salons, who first translated excerpts of Descartes' *Discourse on Method* into Spanish in 1690. In *News from Parnassus,* Corachán imagines a literary salon (a Parnassus), in which several scientists, including Descartes, make an appearance and speak on the lofty objectives of science and philosophy in present-day society. Corachán praises Descartes in particular, stating: "René Descartes is among the many and great philosophers who convene at the Parnassus and who Apollo greatly esteems not only for his excellent judgment and profound way of reasoning in the natural and moral, but also for all the truths he has brought to light."[18] The Jesuit and mathematician Pedro de Ulloa penned *Mathematical Elements* in 1706, which introduced important aspects of Descartes' analytical geometry into Spain.[19] Ramón Ceñal's study on Cartesianism demonstrates

14 Ibid., 10–11. As early as the *Discourse on Method* of 1637, Descartes states: "Harvey also proves very soundly what he says about circulation of the blood by pointing to certain small membranes which are arranged in various places along the veins in such a way that they do not permit the blood to pass from the middle of the body towards the extremities but only let it return from the extremities towards the heart. He proves his theory, moreover, by an experiment which shows that all the blood in the body can flow out of it in a very short time through a single artery" (137). In *Description of the Human Body,* which appears in 1664, he praises Harvey further, although he explains why he disagrees with him on the movement of the heart.

15 Descartes, *Treatise of Man,* 113.

16 Navarro-Brotóns, "Descartes," 225–52.

17 Fuertes Herreros, "La influencia de la metodología cartesiana," 383–405.

18 Quoted in Rodríguez Sánchez, *La introducción de la medicina moderna,* 203.

19 Ausejo, *Las matemáticas en el siglo XVII,* 41.

that the broader inquiry concerning the composition and extension of matter – a subject that was influential in how compound bodies were appraised in the emerging sciences of anatomy and physiology – was the "battle-horse" of Cartesianism in Spain.[20] Yet, as Ceñal and Navarro-Brotóns point out, Descartes' theories spread into Spain through various means in the seventeenth and early-eighteenth centuries, and thus Cartesianism was understood as an amalgam of concepts that could be adopted in a wide range of contexts extending from metaphysics to mathematics.

Descartes' anatomical discoveries also gained traction in Spain during this period. We know from Cabriada's *Philosophical, Medico-Chemical Letter* of 1687, explored in the previous chapter, that Descartes' theories on circulation and vital force in *Treatise of Man* were being discussed in Spanish scientific circles in the 1680s. Cabriada lauded Descartes as a "modern author" who had perfected a "new philosophizing in medical subjects."[21] He noted in his complementary treatise, *Triumphant Truth*, that Descartes' two volumes of epistles, as well as what he referred to as Descartes' more "erudite works," were readily available and circulating throughout Spain.[22] From what Diego Mateo Zapata noted, the Duke of Montellano's *tertulias* during this period of the 1680s provided the ideal atmosphere in which "the systems of Descartes and Maignan were disseminated."[23] The physician Cristobal Tixedas, one of Cabriada's harshest critics, as we saw previously in Chapter 1, referenced Descartes' "book of man" in his *Truth Defended* of 1688 to identify the sources that had inspired Cabriada's "horrendous" theories on pulsatile force.[24] Several of Descartes' anatomical discoveries – such as his many observations on the baffling and persistent beating of excised animal hearts he observed in the butcher shops in Amsterdam (crucial observations that likewise appeared in Cabriada's *Letter* and *Triumphant Truth*) – were also circulating throughout Europe by this time and had found a home in the more progressive spheres of the Spanish medical establishment. Ruth Hill confirms the influence of Cartesian anatomy on figures like the historian, poet, and theologian Gabriel Álvarez de Toledo, whose theories on the circulatory system and brain functioning owed a great deal to Descartes' *Treatise of Man*. As Hill explains, "Álvarez resorts to the activity of animal spirits in order to explain the processes of taste, smell and

20 Ceñal, "El cartesianismo en España," 16.
21 Cabriada, *Carta,* 115.
22 Cabriada, *Verdad triunfante,* 56.
23 Quoted in Pardo Tomás, *El médico en la palestra,* 133.
24 Tixedas, *Verdad defendida,* 16.

touch, and he appears to translate theories and hypotheses of Gassendists and Cartesians."[25] Álvarez de Toledo's *History of the Church and the World* of 1713 provides further evidence of how New Science influenced the way the soul and vital force were being interpreted. In chapters titled "On the Body of Man" and "On the Soul and its Qualities," Álvarez de Toledo openly recognized the ingenuity of modern science in explaining the material origins of vital force: "There are authors who with sound foundations deny that animal spirits are the ministers of sensation and movement [in the body], and with ingenious efforts they explain one thing and another only with the mechanical movement of the fibres."[26] For her part, María Victoria Cruz del Pozo's demonstrates the relevance of Cartesian science in Spanish medicine through the *novator* physician and philosopher Martín Martínez, whom I will deal with in this chapter.

Miguel Marcelino Boix y Moliner's 1711 critique of Cartesianism in *Hippocrates Defended from the Calumnies That Some Careless Physicians Have Imputed to Him* provides an eloquent example of how Descartes' mechanism spurred further inquiry into the mysteries of anatomy and vital force in early-eighteenth-century Spain. Boix y Moliner, a noted *novator*, court physician, surgeon, and co-founder of Seville's Royal Society of Medicine and Other Sciences, had grown skeptical of Cartesian philosophy and its dogmatic mechanism. *Hippocrates Defended* censures a slew of ancient and modern medical doctrines in favour of a simplified system of therapeutic reasoning based on a reinterpretation of Hippocratic teachings. The overarching ambition of Boix y Moliner's treatise is to demonstrate that, when it comes to pathology and the body's processes of vitality and healing, "it is not easy to find in all of medicine a doctrine or system in which human understanding can find some stability or solidity."[27] Hippocratism, however, is presented as the superior foundation upon which to modernize anatomy and pathology in comparison to Cartesianism, for the simple reason that it accounts for the body-nature dynamic, particularly in examining the inherent bodily forces involved in healing. One of the key premises of Boix y Moliner's treatise is that to be a true physician, as Hippocrates proposed, one must have knowledge of the natural workings of the cosmos and the *natura medicatrix* principle that emphasized the body's vital connection to nature in the curative process.

In a lengthy section of his treatise, Boix y Moliner envisions a *junta* of physicians in which each major school of medicine throughout the ages is duly represented. The physicians are invited to step forward and offer

25 Hill, *Sceptres and Sciences in the Spains*, 118.

26 Álvarez de Toledo, *Historia de la Iglesia del mundo*, 49–50.

27 Boix y Moliner, *Hipócrates defendido*, n.p.

their judgments on how they would go about curing a diseased patient. As the title *Hippocrates Defended* suggests, Hippocrates evaluates the tenability of any and all judgments. Likewise, he serves as the authoritative mouthpiece for Boix y Moliner's anti-Galenism, since the *novator* contends that Galen, the great medical authority, had in fact misconstrued Hippocratic doctrine in order to sanction the gruesome practice of phlebotomy. In an earlier section of *Hippocrates Defended,* Boix y Moliner states: "It is evident that we cannot infer from the aphorisms of the first and third books in *Of the Epidemics* that Hippocrates bled sick patients ... Read these aphorisms with care and you will be disabused of your error ... You will see that Galen, in his commentary, lacks evidence to support his doctrine ... Galen drags the poor old [Hippocrates] by his nose so that he says what he wishes."[28] The first to speak in the *junta* is Galen, naturally, who argues that phlebotomy is the only reasonable treatment for the patient, and he is promptly dismissed. Next up is a Paracelsian and a Helmontian, who recommend the use of iatrochemistry for its restorative benefits, and they are also excused. Several other physicians appear and recommend a number of therapeutic techniques, before a Cartesian physician ("médico Cartesiano") comes forward to render his opinion. Hippocrates asks: "And René Descartes, was he a physician or a philosopher?" The Cartesian physician replies: "He was a philosopher, and one of the greatest ... To be a good physician, it suffices to have good philosophical principles, just like René Descartes."[29] Upon further discussion, Hippocrates arrives at the conclusion that Descartes' anatomical investigations are little more than a rehash of Democritus's philosophy of atoms.

As Hippocrates see it, Descartes, like Democritus, had formulated rather abstract theories about matter in which mechanical laws alone could explain life and movement in bodies, which are conceived as nothing more than complex assemblages of corpuscles. Hippocrates throws up his hands in frustration and responds: "What did I tell you? After such haughtiness and pretense we end up with philosophy ... Is this the philosophy that you, sir, and the rest of the Cartesian physicians and philosophers, have sold throughout the world as new? Fools are those who have believed it."[30] One of the more illuminating passages in *Hippocrates Defended,* and one which reveals how Cartesianism was perceived in progressive circles in Spain by the early-eighteenth century, comes after Hippocrates levels a number of criticisms against Descartes'

28 Ibid., 39–40.
29 Ibid., 366.
30 Ibid., 367.

mechanism. The Cartesian physician replies: "We are satisfied with René Descartes without having ever felt the pulse of anyone, because he has such sound philosophical principles."[31] Cartesianism, as Boix y Moliner sees it, had no place in medicine. To begin with, it absurdly dispensed with the patient in medical practice; that is, it did not require a careful examination of the pathological body or a thorough understanding of its relationship with nature's forces to prescribe a cure. All that was needed in this respect was a handful of facts related to the body's present condition and a general sense of disease progression. "Your master [Descartes]," Hippocrates tells the Cartesian physician, "does not know medicine."[32]

Boix y Moliner's treatise, which demonstrates a familiarity with Descartes' *Meditations on First Philosophy* and its commentary by Gassendi, exemplifies to what degree iatromechanism was beginning to fray in Spain with some of the more progressive medical practitioners. Similarly, it reflected how Hippocratic theory, renewed and reinvigorated, was being deployed to engage not only the reformist empiricism of medical science (a type of clinical observation that advocated knowing the body and its vital workings through direct examination), but also the age-old belief that mind and body were indissolubly harmonized with nature's forces. Wesley D. Smith's analysis of the Hippocratic tradition raises here the valid argument that, in terms of the neo-Hippocratism that emerged in the mid- to late-seventeenth century and extended well into the early-nineteenth century as we shall see in Chapter 5, medical practitioners studied Hippocrates' teachings directly, without Galen or other Galenist scholars serving as intermediaries or interpreters. As Smith explains, "medical men led the way, generating medical 'history' out of their own current interests instead of out of historical study … The crucial first step in the process was dissociation of Hippocrates from Galen in 'spirit' and doctrine."[33] The direct reading of Hippocrates' therapeutic principles, particularly on vital force, greatly expanded the scope of Hippocratism and likewise modernized its concepts on anatomy and pathology. David Cantor also draws attention to how the figure of Hippocrates was powerfully transformed throughout this period into "a malleable cultural artifact, constantly moulded and remoulded according to need … The Hippocratic tradition is, therefore, an 'invented tradition,' constantly reinvented over time."[34] Ultimately, *neo*-Hippocratism offered a set of familiar theories and a practical framework for observing nature and the

31 Ibid., 367.
32 Ibid., 368.
33 Smith, *The Hippocratic Tradition*, 14.
34 Cantor, "Introduction: The Uses and Meanings of Hippocrates," 3.

2.1 Image of Hippocrates from Marcelino Boix y Moliner's *Hippocrates defendido*, 1711.

body that both complemented and refined the empirical approach of forward-thinking science (the same empirical approach, it should be noted, that marked Cabriada's ideal of modern medical practice in the 1680s). For Thomas Rütten, neo-Hippocratism was synonymous with progress in medical circles throughout Europe, beginning in the late Renaissance:

> Hippocrates was a forerunner who had set medicine on a certain course – a course which had to be followed through into the future; Hippocrates became the ultimate yardstick of technological, moral and social advance and a timeless

figure predestined to serve as a contemporary companion to any physician … Ultimately, Hippocrates and his writings served not only as both origin and ultimate goal for highly divergent concepts of "progress," but also as the benchmark against which any kind of "progress" could be measured.[35]

From this vantage point we can better appreciate Boix y Moliner's strategy of reinterpreting Hippocrates to denounce not only Galenism, but also Cartesianism. These criticisms include the following: firstly, Cartesianism is derivative (the notion that, behind the smoke and mirrors, Descartes' corpuscular theory smacks of Democritean atomism that conceived the cosmos as lifeless matter obeying natural laws); secondly, Cartesianism is blind to the role nature plays in bodily health (the body's vital force, or "native heat," is directly bound to forces in nature, according to Hippocrates); and thirdly, Cartesianism is needlessly abstract, if not outright impractical, in pathological medicine, since it overlooks the most critical aspect in the treatment of any disease: a comprehensive examination of the *living* body. Deductive reasoning alone, or what Boix y Moliner terms "philosophizing," is insufficient in discerning the why and how of health and vital force, given that the answers to these questions quite obviously lurk in the body itself. That is to say, within medicine, mechanistic reason is based purely on "philosophizing" rather than on an empirical study of the body and its life energy. In an earlier section of the treatise, Boix y Moliner even expresses his displeasure with William Harvey, who, although admittedly a brilliant anatomist, was a poor "practical physician," incapable of properly observing the medical body.[36] However, Thomas Sydenham, the great advocate of Hippocratic medicine and known for his careful clinical observations and methodical studies of diseased bodies, is presented as the model of a true practical physician.[37]

What Boix y Moliner is indicating is that medical practice, while clearly benefiting from anatomy and philosophy, must be based upon a comprehensive understanding of the living body, which had to be observed and auscultated (the Cartesian, we must recall, had boasted of having "never felt the pulse of anyone"). The physician had to not only read, but also sense through physical contact, the bodily signs of vitality and

35 Rütten, "Hippocrates and the Construction of 'Progress,'" 45.

36 Boix y Moliner, *Hipócrates defendido,* 277–88.

37 Boix y Moliner declares: "Thomas Sydenham did not waste as much time in discovering the fabric of man and other animals through anatomy, as with Bartholin and Willis. And perhaps for this reason he was better in [medical] practice, since he occupied himself with what was important" (Ibid., 290).

disease and determine the best course of treatment, even if it meant violating the dictates of tradition. Boix y Moliner is referring here to what he saw as Galen's misreading of Hippocrates when it came to removing life-bearing blood from the body with phlebotomy procedures. Antonio Díaz del Castillo, a professor of medicine at the University of Alcalá de Henares, harshly condemned Boix y Moliner's work in *Hippocrates Restored from the Offenses in Hippocrates Defended* (1713) for not only dialoguing with the fantasies of Cartesianism (even if it was to discredit them), but also for its permissive interpretation of Hippocratic doctrine, which he believed distorted several of Hippocrates' core teachings on body functioning and cast the great Galen in a negative light.

What was most illuminating about del Castillo's *Hippocrates Restored*, however, was how it shed light on the epistemic divide that was becoming ever more apparent between university scholarship and the research taking place at independent institutions like Seville's Royal Society of Medicine and Other Sciences, or what Castillo called the "sect of academicians."[38] Indeed, del Castillo's text drew attention to the changing relationship among medicine, politics, and religion in early-eighteenth-century Spain. We must keep in mind that Charles II, during the final days of the illness that took his life on 1 November 1700, requested that he be examined not by a practitioner of Galenic medicine or one of the many healers who frequented the court, but by Tommaso Donzelli, a Neapolitan apothecary and iatrochemist conversant with Cartesianism and the latest anatomical developments in Europe.[39] Many of the leading court physicians – all Galenists – had passed away in the same year of 1699, marking a generational transition in courtly medical policy in Madrid that opened the door to more modern forms of medical practice.[40] In his prefatory address in *Hippocrates Restored* to Don Francisco Ronquillo y Brizeño, the Count of Gramedo, del Castillo urged the count to consider how medical practice in Spain had changed in recent years, since it no longer enjoyed the protections of the church, government, and nobility. Medicine, he lamented, had become entangled in political squabbles and the broader assault on religious authority and its legitimacy. Thus, to openly publish and circulate a treatise like Boix y Moliner's *Hippocrates Defended*, which elucidated Cartesianism and condemned Galen's cherished dogmas through a brazen reinterpretation of Hippocrates' notions of vital force, was akin to a revolt against all that was true and holy, a revolt that had to be quelled:

38 Castillo, *Hipócrates desagraviado*, n.p.

39 For Donzelli's specific treatments of the monarch, see Mar Rey Bueno's *El hechizado*, 125–9.

40 See Valera and López Fernández "Giuseppe Cervi, Guillaume Jacobe," 382.

The sect of the academicians, which Boix's *Hippocrates Defended* seems to uphold, opposes Catholic dogmas, and it opposes the state of the politicians. It would be worth your most serious consideration, Your Excellency, to banish this sect, even from medical disputes, so that [its doctrines] do not advance from the stepping stone of medicine into the political arena, and from the political arena into the religious arena [lo católico] given that the topics are universal, even though they are determined by subject.[41]

One of Boix y Moliner's most enduring legacies in Spanish science is that, with *Hippocrates Defended*, he unleashed a series of polemics on the merits of modern medical theory and practice. Behind the polemics, however, there loomed the larger issue of the increasing authority of modern science to interpret the body and its vital force.[42] As Boix y Moliner's treatise made clear, Cartesianism did in fact raise challenging questions about the body's workings and the bio-mechanical sources from which it derived its life energy, yet it was neo-Hippocratism, and not Galenism or theology, that could address them most effectively. Moreover, Cartesianism had already made abundantly evident the medical limitations associated with conceiving of the body as nothing more than a rationally ordered machine responding to a confluence of cause-and-effect relations.

In the first volume of the landmark *Skeptical Medicine and Modern Surgery* of 1722, Martín Martínez voices similar concerns through the mouthpiece of a Hippocratic physician regarding the implications and shortcomings of Descartes' medical philosophy. Likewise, he also dedicates substantial attention to impugning "the principle proofs of Scholasticism … with the reasons and experiences of the Modern School."[43] For Martínez, Cartesian anatomy had not resolved any of the major difficulties facing the medical profession concerning vital force and the body-soul nexus. In fact, it had generated significantly more confusion. In the dialogue among a Galenist, a chemist-healer [Chimico],

41 Castillo, *Hipócrates desagraviado*, n.p. On this topic, see also Juan Martín de Lesaca's *Scholastic Apology in Defence of the University of Alcalá and All Spanish Universities against the Skeptical Medicine of Doctor Martínez* (1729).

42 After Boix y Moliner published *Hippocrates Defended* in 1711, Antonio Díaz del Castillo replied with *Hippocrates Restored* in 1713. In this same year, the physician Antonio Álvarez del Corral published *Hippocrates Vindicated, and Medical Considerations on Hippocrates Defended* that attacked Boix y Moliner's treatise. In 1716, Boix y Moliner sharpened his criticisms of Galenic medicine in *Hippocrates Clarified and the System of Galen Impugned for Being Founded upon Misreadings of Hippocrates' Aphorisms.* Three years later, Díaz del Castillo replied with *Hippocrates Understood, Demonstrating the Benefits of the Doctrine of Galen, His Faithful Interpreter.*

43 Martínez, *Medicina sceptica*, n.p.

and a Hippocratic physician that structures *Skeptical Medicine*, the Hippocratic physician is by far the most critical of Descartes:

> Did Descartes answer the question: what is thought? Did he discover the locus or instrument of our cogitations? Did he prove that this work is undertaken in the pineal, splenium, or fornix? Did he provide evidence of where, how, and by what means ideas are received? By what fibrous canals or interstices they travel? If by retrogradation [retrogradación] or undulation? And being corporeal, did he explain how they bond with the soul? Or being material, how they are spiritualized? Did he clarify what change occurs in the mind in passing from one idea to another? Or how the workings of the mind are transferred to the organs of movement? You will answer no. Well, look how greatly Descartes fell short.[44]

Cruz del Pozo notes that, while Martínez was conversant with Gassendi's views on the nature of matter and life, he never fully developed them in his work. It could be that, as Cruz del Pozo argues, "the Gassendist position appeared dangerous to Martínez as it pertained to religion ... It stands to reason that Martínez, in attempting to introduce modern thought into Spain against Thomistic Aristotelianism, considered the animal-machine less problematic."[45] In the section entitled "On the Spirits" in *Skeptical Medicine*, Martínez tackles the role of animal spirits in the body, which Descartes had theorized resided in the brain. Unlike Galen, who believed that the animal spirits were contained in a vascular network at the base of the brain, Descartes postulated in *Treatise of Man* that animal spirits were perfected in the pineal gland (the seat of the soul), from which they flowed to the rest of the body through a network of hollow nerves. As the animal spirits passed through the nerves, they opened or closed valves in the muscles via contraction and relaxation, which in turn provided the body with its vital force. Through the Hippocratic physician, Martínez argues that postulating an animal spirit in the body is redundant, given that the function of the nerves alone, as modern medicine had proven, can account for sensation and the body's vital movements. Thus, "[animal] spirits are not necessary and should not be admitted."[46] Ultimately, the life-bearing spirit contained in the blood itself, and not the animal spirits supposedly dwelling in the pineal gland, is responsible for vital force: "I am not speaking of the vital spirits, but of the animal spirits ... It is superfluous to conceive of a spirituous substance separated [from the blood] to understand bodily heat and the

44 Ibid., n.p.

45 Cruz del Pozo, *Gassendismo y cartesianismo en España*, 147.

46 Martínez, *Medicina sceptica*, 151.

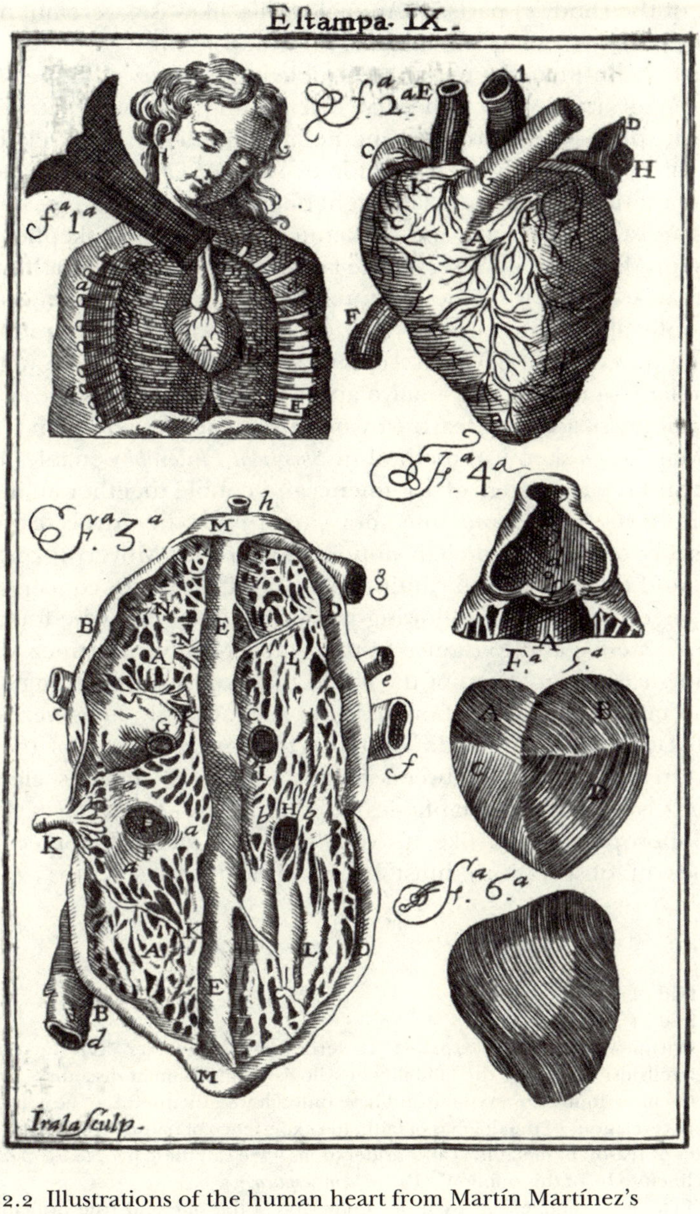

2.2 Illustrations of the human heart from Martín Martínez's *Anatomia completa del hombre*, 1728.

vitality of the [body's] parts."[47] Animal spirits, likewise, were not needed to account for the complex union of body and soul.[48]

Descartes' influence is more discernible in Martínez's treatise *Skeptical Philosophy* of 1730, which aims at discrediting the Aristotelianism of Scholastic philosophy through a methodical inquiry into the relation between matter (the body) and vital force. *Skeptical Philosophy* is structured around a series of imaginary late-night dialogues among an Aristotelian, a Gassendist, a Cartesian, and a Skeptic (or "reformed skeptic"), who speaks for Martínez and reserves the last word on any topic for himself.[49] The treatise opens with the Aristotelian's homecoming after studying philosophy abroad for several years. In his absence, modern modes of thinking have all but eclipsed Aristotle's teachings, and each night the Aristotelian – portrayed as a naïve and ignorant youth – retires with his companions in order to learn why exactly Aristotle had fallen from favour. Martínez's skeptical method in *Skeptical Philosophy* enables him to accept and reject a range of arguments and cobble together an intricate philosophical system, and thus, not surprisingly, he advocates for the practicality of the Aristotelian notion of a Primer Mover in one paragraph, and then sinks into ruminations about Cartesian conceptions of bodily mechanics in the following paragraph.[50] In dialogue four, titled "On the Essence and Existence of the Natural Body," Martínez analyzes metaphysical explanations of the world that confuse something as obvious and tangible as the corporeal, living body. Clearly, Martínez is referring to Descartes' famous doubt about the very existence of the living body. On the relation between body and life, it remains clear that Martínez is critical of metaphysics in general, and he declares that any true philosophy (much like his own skeptical method, rooted in the methods of observation) must begin with "physical truths" that are

47 Ibid., 150.

48 Ibid., 153–4.

49 Martínez, *Philosophia sceptica*, 3. In terms of the moniker "reformed skeptic," Martínez tells us: "In seeing the fallibility of syllogisms and human discourses, there are others who have doubted everything and have only allowed themselves to be convinced by the divine revelations of the dogmas of faith, the experience of natural things, and the first principles of reason in metaphysical considerations – We call these people *reformed skeptics.* I am inclined to be of this opinion" (*Philosophia sceptica*, 3).

50 Take, for example, this excerpt: "Only God is the one and true principle of all movement since He gave the first impulse to all matter … Plato defined nature accurately when he said that it was *The Art of God in Matter*, since all the natural things are no more than machines of the Divine idea" (*Philosophia sceptica*, 15).

empirically determined.[51] While he declares that he is amenable to Descartes' bodily mechanics, it is on this encompassing question of vital force that he is most critical of Cartesianism, particularly in terms of its subordination of the living body to the immaterialities of the mind. The question Martínez asks of the Cartesian is this: What is the essence of the concrete, living body?

> You addressed the physical and natural body and you define a body according to its metaphysical essence with no determined extension, no figure, no form, all its particularities abstracted ... Your definition, sir, is even more intolerable ... What I wish is that, in any given physical body, you could answer me this: What is its essence? I am afraid that not only do we not know the answer to this question, but we are still far from knowing it.[52]

One of the more provocative aspects of *Skeptical Philosophy* is how Martínez's understanding of the body homes in on the existential experience, so to speak, of embodiment itself. Martínez is not thinking only of vital force when he takes up the subject of embodiment, but also the strange fact of existence and the nature of human life. It is by working through the problematics of Cartesian dualism that Martínez is able to raise key questions about bodily life. These questions include: What does it mean to exist, to be alive, and imbued with vital force? Is it not apparent that we are contingent, physical beings who are inextricably bound to other living beings in a concrete experiential here and now? What is death? Is it a mere metaphysical illusion that can be rationalized away as a breakdown in bodily machinery? Does it not surround us at every turn and transform once-living bodies into insensible matter? Although thinly sketched, Martinez's notions of the embodied self and the facticity of vital force add an ontological depth to his work that falls out of step markedly with not only Cartesianism, but also with the Scholastic's metaphysical concept of the soul in early-eighteenth-century Spain. We read further:

> But to seriously doubt if there are living bodies and waste time proving it given the observations of this visible world: namely, that we are born; that we interact and reflect with our friends and colleagues; that they respond to us ... that we feel happiness, anger, sadness; that we die; that cadavers of the dead no longer speak to us; in sum, that all of this is associated with a successive, ordered, and

51 Ibid., 61.
52 Ibid., 60.

consequent experience … Let us be careful with our physical considerations, and let us not drink the mandrake juice and forget the goal of these dialogues. Wanting to reveal the mysteries of nature with metaphysical conjecture is the same as wanting a sparrow to hunt a hare.[53]

Descartes' theories, as one might expect, were harshly censured in Spain, particularly by Thomists, who were vocal in their opposition to Cartesianism and its criticisms of Aristotle's philosophy. In 1714, Francisco Polanco, the bishop of Jaca and a staunch Aristotelian, wrote *Dialogus Physico-Theologicus contra Philosophiae Novatores, sive Thomista contra Atomistas* to rail against the notion of a godless atomism, yet some of his sharpest criticisms were aimed at Descartes. The crux of the matter for Polanco was that the so-called Cartesian body presented various difficulties for theology. As Jonathan Israel explains, the Cartesian body undermined the core belief in transubstantiation "owing to its unsatisfactory account of the union of body and soul, and the rigid duality of substance."[54] What the Thomists in Spain most feared about Cartesianism was how it destabilized the rigidly hierarchical schema of the cosmos, beginning with the radical split between body (matter) and soul (spirit). Ultimately, the theological discourse of the Church, as the Thomists well knew, could be powerfully subverted through a strategic reading of Descartes' definition of matter and spirit, such as those undertaken by Boix y Moliner and Martínez. In 1738, the humanist and theologian Antonio María Herrero, a professed admirer of Descartes, summarized in his treatise *Modern Physics* why Descartes' philosophy had been met with such bitter attacks in Spain: "[I]f philosophers would reflect on what Descartes says, they would see that their criticisms have very little merit when they declare that Cartesian philosophy is opposed … to the Catholic Faith. A clear example is Feijóo, who assumes that, to philosophize properly as Descartes proposes, we must doubt everything, even God's existence."[55]

53 Ibid., 65. In "The Rationality of Beasts," Feijóo tells us the following on mechanism and movement: "Returning to the question on beasts, I say that some philosophers deny them sentiment, and others grant them speech. The leader of the first group is René Descartes, who affirmed that beasts are nothing more than animated statues whose movements depend solely on the figure and organic disposition of their parts … This is a necessary consequence of Descartes' philosophical system. But if Descartes knew of this when he devised his system, or he became aware of it and its dissonance after his system was formed and published, he must have wanted to accept it so as to not ruin that edifice in which his reasoning had laboured so hard" (*Teatro III*, 190–1).

54 Israel, *Radical Enlightenment*, 531.

55 Herrero, *Physica moderna*, 108–9.

Thomistic theology during this period came under assault from reformist physicians and philosophers, thanks in part to the reception of Cartesianism. Needless to say, Descartes' works were included in the Roman Index of Forbidden Books shortly after his death in 1663 and prohibited in a number of Spanish universities, while in France Louis XIV banned the teaching of Cartesian philosophy altogether in 1685. One of the most troubling aspects of Cartesianism for the Church more broadly was that it advanced a powerful individualism that resisted all modes of authority except the authority of the intellect. With his famed dictum *cogito ergo sum*, we cannot lose sight of the fact that Descartes positioned the self-reflexive subject as the ultimate authority on certainty and the complex nature of (bodily) existence itself. Doubtless, Thomists' fears of Cartesianism had much to do with the Church's inability to formulate a counter-discourse with which to challenge anatomical and scientific advancements on vital force and the body's complex workings.

For all the criticism levelled at Descartes, the influence of his anatomical theories in Spain was palpable. The expansion of Cartesianism put into circulation exegetical and theory-constitutive methodologies of vital force that not only increasingly stood independent from theological reason and Galenic medicine, but also transformed the understanding of life and well-being into a fundamental subject of the sciences. In *Discourse on Method*, Descartes had already argued that the true object of the sciences was "the maintenance of health, which is undoubtedly the chief good and the foundation of all other goods in life."[56] With a touch of hubris, and inspired by the age-old obsession with discovering the fountainhead of immortality, he postulated that he could grasp the body's enigmas associated with vital force, since death was no more than an anomaly in the corporeal machinery, an anomaly that could be identified and duly corrected if one understood what he called the body's "principle of … movement."[57] As he studied anatomy more closely, he became "quite certain to be able to render one's life equal to the Patriarchs."[58] A compelling facet of Descartes' anatomical studies was the significance he ascribed to the relationship between matter and life. As one critic has pointed out, his understanding of physiology "require[d] nothing more than inert matter … and an understanding of circulatory systems."[59] While Descartes' concept of nature made no reference to

56 Descartes, *Discourse on Method*, 143.
57 Descartes, *Passions of the Soul*, 330.
58 Quoted in Schouls, *Descartes and the Enlightenment*, 130.
59 Gaukroger, *Descartes' System of Natural Philosophy*, 196.

inherent vital properties, it nevertheless theorized a universe filled with bodies and objects and utterly traversed by all types of forces.

One of Descartes' central contributions to anatomy and physiology has to do with this fundamental examination of matter and life, the same examination that preoccupied Boix y Moliner and Martínez. Descartes resolved that the motion of the body originated from matter – and more concretely, the precise arrangement of the organs – rather than from the faculties of the soul. This conclusion, which both Boix y Moliner and Martínez allude to in their work, carried a radical implication, particularly for the Spanish medical establishment in Madrid still steeped in Galenism. Quite simply, the idea that vital force was generated in the organization of matter implied that the soul no longer governed the body's fundamental actions. For Descartes, the so-called kingdom of the soul was limited in dictating all types of visible and invisible movements in the body, since all movements of the body not dependent directly on the conscious mind were beyond its scope. Even voluntary movements, he conceded, could be regarded as operating without the necessity of a soul since "the movements which we call 'voluntary' occur principally as a result of this disposition of the organs, since, although it is the soul that determines the movements, they cannot be produced without the requisite disposition of the organs."[60] Obviously, the soul still inhabited the body, but it was tethered to the sphere of rationality and its demands: volition, intellection, imagining, denying, and affirming. Thus, in *Description of the Human Body*, the body did not obey the authority of a soul imbued with Aristotelian capacities, such as nutrition, sense-perception, and movement, as outlined in *De Anima*. For Descartes, there was no denying that the "[s]oul is single in man, and withal rational."[61] In *Passions of the Soul*, he acknowledged further that death should not be seen from the theological perspective as the moment when the soul flees the body. On the contrary, the body should be understood teleologically in terms of the organs' aggregate "decay," and ultimately it is the inevitable cessation of inner bodily movement that ushers the soul out of its material husk.[62] These ideas challenged the doctrinal claim, as set forth by the dramatist and moralist Juan de Zabaleta in 1704, that "the soul is created is to vivify the body."[63] Descartes tells us in *Description of the Human Body*:

60 Descartes, *Description of the Human Body*, 315.

61 Descartes, *Treatise of Man*, 114.

62 Descartes, *Passions of the Soul*, 329.

63 Zabaleta, *Obras*, 82.

I believe that we would have been able to find many very reliable rules, both for curing illness and for preventing it, and even for slowing down the ageing process, if only we had spent enough effort on getting to know the nature of our body, instead of attributing to the soul functions which depend solely on the body and on the disposition of the organs ... Our ignorance of anatomy and mechanics has also played a major role here. For in restricting our consideration to the outside of the human body, we have never imagined that it has within it enough organs or mechanisms to move of its own accord ... So I will now try to prove the point, and to give such a full account of the entire bodily machine that we will have no reason to think that it is our soul which produces in it the movements which we know by experience.[64]

Any theory that argued against the soul's supremacy over the body prompted sharp criticisms from Galenists and theologians in Spain, but it also had the contrary effect of inspiring *novatores* to revisit the tantalizing question of vital force. We may say that the critic Francisco Sánchez-Blanco's belief that "Cartesian rationalism ... played absolutely no role in the discussions of the *novatores*" is far from true.[65] What Sánchez-Blanco does demonstrate with clarity is that the Spanish medical establishment in Madrid and numerous reformist physicians and philosophers resisted Cartesian science for all the reasons Boix y Moliner and Martínez put forward. In truth, Boix y Moliner and Martínez, as we have seen, condemned Cartesian anatomy and its mechanist principles, yet in doing so they were obliged to reconsider the origins and meanings of vital force in the body through modern science and the wisdom of the ancients, especially Hippocrates. This reappraisal of vital force had a profound impact on the direction of Spanish medicine in the eighteenth century.

There is no denying that Cartesianism occupied a central place in medical debates throughout eighteenth-century Spain, yet more often than not it served as a whetstone on which to sharpen criticisms of medical and scholarly institutions and practices. As Feijóo later conceived of it in his famed "Causes of the Backwardness Suffered in Spain with Respect to the Natural Sciences" of 1745, a society's knowledge of Cartesianism served as a barometer of its modernity. Feijóo enumerated in his discourse the six causes of Spain's backwardness ("atraso") as compared to other European nations in the realm of the natural sciences. He identified the first cause with the Spanish university system, an institution resistant to New Science and particularly disparaging of Descartes.[66]

64 Descartes, *Description of the Human Body*, 314–15.

65 Sánchez-Blanco, *La ilustración en España*, 21.

66 Feijóo, "Causas del atraso," 215–16.

The remaining causes had to do with a generalized fear of progress and a fundamental lack of understanding of modern science and its aims. The truth was that Feijóo's discourse represented not only a panegyric of Descartes' critical spirit, but also a commentary on the growing irrelevance of the Spanish university system with respect to scientific inquiry. The Inquisition, likewise, entered into the discussion, since Feijóo called attention to how its censorship of science and its methods of suppressing new ideas were becoming increasingly ineffective and outmoded. He lauded Descartes as a scholar of great genius and extraordinary subtlety in reasoning, yet he also pointed out that New Science in Spain, while unthinkable without the French philosopher's contribution, was but one component within a much broader program of renewal. What can be gathered from a nuanced reading of Feijóo's discourse, particularly in light of Boix y Moliner's and Martínez's work, is that there was a part of Spain that was already thoroughly modern by 1745, if by modern we understand a form of critique oriented toward delivering a blow to the burdens of tradition.

LIFE IS THE SOUL: THE VISIBLE, INVISIBLE, AND REPRESSED IN DIEGO DE TORRES VILLARROEL'S ANATOMY

In examining Descartes' reception in Spain, it remains clear that the understanding of the body's vital force underwent a significant re-evaluation in the first half of the eighteenth century. Thanks in large measure to New Science, the question of the soul's relation to the body occupied an important place in medical philosophy and practice, and anatomists, chemists, and physicians, whether critical or not of mechanistic reasoning, began interrogating established notions of vital force and bodily movement. In *Anatomy of the Visible and Invisible: Universal Compendium of Both Spheres,* Torres delivered one of the more intriguing defences of the soul's authority in matters of vital force in early-eighteenth-century Spain, which ironically laid bare the great gains made by New Science during this period.

Remembered mostly as an astrologist, almanac writer, mathematician, and author of extraordinary wit and humour, Torres was, as his first biographer Antonio García Boiza noted, an eccentric innovator when it came to questioning the boundaries of established knowledge in numerous fields.[67] Torres's range of literary and scientific interests and his overall

67 García Boiza, *Don Diego de Torres Villarroel,* 8–9.

breadth of view made him an ingenious "folk-scientist," who "moved mentally in a grey area, somewhere between the ground occupied by empiric specialists and that inhabited by dogmatic theorists."[68] We must keep in mind that Torres was a lifelong student of medicine, who kept abreast of the latest advancements in anatomy and physiology (mostly to criticize and diminish them), and he had practised medicine with minimal training and no formal degree during his first sojourn to Coimbra, Portugal, in 1715. As he declared in his autobiographical *The Life, Ascendancy, Birth, Upbringing and Adventures of Doctor Diego de Torres Villarroel*, the bulk of his formal learning in medicine came some years later, when he befriended the royal physician, Agustín González, in Madrid. González provided him with the instruction and literature to pass the medical qualifying exams.[69]

Although conversant with the theories and writings of Giorgio Baglivi, Franciscus Sylvius, Thomas Willis, and Thomas Sydenham, Torres tended to filter his medical thinking through astrological theory. In *Interment of the Last Judgment and Vivification of Astrology* (1727), he stated that "in medicine it is necessary and needful to keep abreast of the latest advancements in the true astrology [la buena astrología]; the physician who practises without them, is only a physician in name."[70] Invoking Galen's *De ingenio sanitatis*, he proclaimed that physicians unconcerned with astrology were no better than executioners. Surely, no God-fearing physician would dare practise medicine without recourse to astrological revelations, given how the movement and position of heavenly bodies not only influenced the onset of pestilences, but also indicated the appropriate times during which to undertake medical procedures on diseased patients. Torres asked: "How many have died from a purge or a phlebotomy procedure administered at the wrong time? ... Proper timing can only be revealed through astrological precepts."[71] It was a mortal sin, therefore, to practise medicine without astrology's guiding hand. In *Physical, Medical and Moral Treatises, Natural and Catholic Life* (1730) and *The Terminally Ill of the World and of the Glory* (1736), he meditated upon the great prevalence and lethality of mysterious diseases and railed against modern physicians – Martín Martínez in particular, whom he despised – for their disregard of astrology and their skeptical stance with

68 McClelland, *Ideological Hesitancy in Spain*, 58.

69 Torres, *Vida y ascendencia*, 49.

70 Torres, *Entierro del juicio final*, 239.

71 Ibid., 241.

regard to healing practices.[72] Overall, Torres offered a prescriptive guide to the problem of body and disease in these texts and advocated for a wholesome and morally grounded way of life (always paying heed to astrological revelations) as the surest method to stave off disease. In pamphlets like *The Traveling Doctor and Medicine from Hand to Hand* (1730), *The Traveling Doctor, Affordable Medicine* (1735), and *The Pocket Physician, The Traveling Doctor* (1737), he sharpened his criticisms of modern medicine, while offering his readers practical, day-to-day advice on maintaining a healthy body and soul.[73]

In the preamble to *Anatomy*, Torres makes clear that his approach to the epistemological conundrum of coming to know the concrete, living body is grounded in the assumption that science is inadequate in illuminating the divine sphere to which the body's soul ultimately belongs. He attempts to put forth, as one might expect, a transcendentalist argument of the body, an argument not without irony, as we shall see, and grounded in first-hand observation and practical learning he acquired during his medical training. He declares that "we all live in the dark without having discovered other lights than those that were lit by the revelations of God and His Church."[74] We know from Torres's various medical publications that he was disparaging of medicine in general and had a very low opinion of physicians, whom he placed on the same rung as public servants and poets. He tells us: "But if you, Mercurio, drag yourself along and become a student, then become an attorney, physician, or poet … [T]hese professions are easy and make you a lot of money since there is always a need for troublemakers, profiteers, and loafers."[75] In publications like *Treatise on Tremors and Other Movements of the Earth* (1748), his animosity toward philosophers and sages of all stripes comes through clearly in a sharp criticism of their utter worthlessness in epistemological matters. As he explains, "they are pallid, baffled, thin, bearded, and hideous men, who have taken to the nonsense of walking about in a sad, broken, slovenly, and hesitant way, always wanting to persuade the innocent and careless."[76] In terms of the growing question of vital force,

72 Martín Martínez had published *Final Judgment of Astrology, In Defence of the Universal Critical Theatre Divided in Three Discourses* in 1727 to condemn the study and practice of astrology. He stated categorically that "astrology is useless in medicine" (39). This claim inspired Torres to write *Interment of the Last Judgment and Vivification of Astrology*.

73 For a more-thorough account of Torres's medical training and writings see Luis Granjel's *Medicine and Physicians in the Works of Torres Villarroel*. Granjel's work is still the most comprehensive analysis of Torres's medical thinking.

74 Torres, *Anatomía*, n.p.

75 Torres, *Viaje fantástico*, n.p.

76 Torres, *Tratado de los temblores*, 1.

these same philosophers and sages "are determined … to discover the source of life, and the soul, and they do not advance their knowledge in the slightest in this line of questioning."[77] On a more pragmatic level, the sum of all epistemological claims, as Torres proposes in *Anatomy* – the grand compendium, as it were, of pedagogical treatises, scientific theories, philosophical systems, and great books of secular learning stretching back to antiquity that give credence to man's endless pursuit of truth – are incapable of doing justice to the origins of vital force in the human body as profitably as theology. In sum, philosophy, medicine, and particularly the burgeoning science of anatomy and its unwholesome preoccupation with dissecting and scrutinizing cadavers, can never cast light on the mystery of life as it quickens the body.

For Torres, the body's vital force originates in the remarkable material-spirit union, a traditional approach to the topic that rings of what Thomas Aquinas proposed about the human soul necessitating a *determinata materia* in which to dwell, or a distinctive type of material home.[78] Deprived of the soul, the body is nothing more than a hollow shell, a heap of lifeless matter, whose inevitable putrefaction calls to mind the blessings of the afterlife. Certainly, the soulless and decomposing body is no longer a mystery, even if it sweats, vomits blood, bleeds from its orifices, and resists rigor mortis. "These unfortunate occurrences," Torres explains, "that appear preternatural portents … can be chalked up to natural causes."[79] What is needed to truly comprehend the body's vital force, yet is unfeasible as Torres admits in his *Anatomy*, is "an Anatomy of living bodies … to understand the animation, functions, and faculties of vitality."[80] What Torres is referring to here is an anatomical science that could unobtrusively see *into* the living body and examine the extraordinary mingling of bodily fabric and soul essence that generated vital force. There can be no mistake about it: the divine soul vitalizes the body, and it was sacrilegious to infer that vital force originated from the bodily system itself, as many modern physicians were arguing in Spain at the time:

> Some said there was no soul and that bodies moved through their own motion. Others believed that the soul was a very subtle element scattered and sown throughout the material body. To fortify this opinion, others have said that the soul had the qualities of fire, which is what Hipparchus and Eucipio [sic]

77 Ibid., 11.
78 Aquinas, *Summa theologica*, 1062.
79 Torres, *Tratado físicos*, 360.
80 Torres, *Anatomía*, 67.

believed … And lately (leaving aside various other considerations), many say that it is a force that lives in every human body … I believe that it is a divine and spiritual substance, a perfection of the natural, organic body that cares for it throughout and whose perfection provides it the principles of thought, feeling, and movement: it is immortal like God.[81]

Torres's *Anatomy* explores the binary logic of visibility and invisibility, as the title indicates. It examines the larger problem of making known the body's (and universe's) undersurface and vital operations. It is structured around the trope of the journey, and in its paragraph-long title, Torres informs his readers of an impending "fantastical journey."[82] As the treatise opens, Torres rests in his lounge chair one balmy afternoon and, in a moment of sweet languor on the limen between dream and reality, he is transported to a world of "fantasy," where he voyages with a group of companions through the depths of the earth (Day One), the earth's surface and human anatomy (Day Two), the oceans and meteors (Day Three), the atmosphere (Day Four), and the moon, planets, and stars (Day Five).[83] This fantastical journey is one of visual discovery, and at each waypoint along the way, Torres's companions beseech him to share his knowledge regarding the structure of the world and the cosmos that they are witnessing.

The trope of the journey, as is often the case in treatises like *Anatomy* that combine pedagogical and entertainment functions, serves as an extended metaphor for the enlightenment that comes with not only the act of reading itself, but also with being transported to imaginary spatiotemporal landscapes (a voyage akin to what M.H. Abrams called an "educational journey" when referring to a very similar trope in Romantic literature).[84] Before *Anatomy*, Torres had perfected the trope of the journey in several texts, yet it is *Fantastic Journey of the Great Piscator of Salamanca* of 1724, inspired by the observation of an eclipse, that allows us to draw a line of continuity on this topic, since it was *Fantastic Journey* that was re-edited, enlarged, and republished with a new foreword as

81 Ibid., 67–8.

82 The full title reads: *Anatomy of the Visible and Invisible: Universal Compendium of Both Spheres: Fantastical Journey: Days Devoted to Each Sphere: Discovery of their Beings, Substances, Generations, and Productions. News on their Movements, and the Nature of Earthly and Heavenly Bodies, and the Science of the Influence of Solar and Lunar Eclipses, until the End of the World.*

83 Torres, *Anatomía*, 2. After the journey ends, *Anatomy* concludes with a commentary titled "Rest from the Journey," dedicated to the phenomena of eclipses, which fascinated Torres.

84 Abrams, *The Fourth Dimension of a Poem*, 203.

Anatomy in 1738.[85] The trope of the journey also appears repeatedly and in various contexts throughout the more extended *Moral Dreams* of 1736. In the prologue to *Fantastic Journey*, Torres declares that he was inspired to explore the journey motif after reading Athanasius Kircher's *Ecstatic Celestial Journey* (1656), a travel treatise narrated by Theodidactus (Kircher himself), who embarks on extraordinary voyages throughout heaven and earth with the learned angel Cosmiel.[86] What is compelling about Torres's treatise, as with Kircher's treatise, is how the figurative journey unfolds through the complementary practices of visualizing and knowing, of making present to the reader, and thus making fathomable and knowable, the dominion of the unknowable spanning from the mysteries of subterranean caverns to the vital force animating the human body.

Through its own rhetorical play, Torres's journey into the body presents the reader with an anatomical topography that destabilizes the very revelations of God and His Church that it purports to extol. From the outset, Torres's travel companions insist that he explain the wondrous complexities of human anatomy in more depth. While he tells them that everything ever written after Galen adds nothing to anatomical science, he obliges, stating: "I obey Your Majesties in revealing the anatomy of the human body … [B]ut being that you do not yield in your request, I will repeat what I have seen, and what has remained in my memory with the repetition of some of the lessons that I heard in Salamanca's lecture theatres."[87] In this vast anatomical exposition that comes about with bestowing sense and unity to the living body, "know-all" Torres, as his opponents used to refer to him, is driven to geometrize, quantify, itemize, enumerate, categorize, and codify for his travel companions everything he observes (just as Kircher, who was fond of quoting Plato's dictum "nothing is more divine than to know everything," aspired to schematize the entirety of the universe).[88] Consequently, as Torres and his companions journey in and through the body's numerous regions and cavities, bones are classified, organs are labelled, arteries and veins are individualized and described, and fluids, ligaments, membranes, orifices, tendons, tissues, and valves of every class are identified and

85 Martínez Mata, *Los 'sueños,'* 24–5.

86 Torres's "Prologue to the Reader" in *Fantastic Journey* begins by invoking Kircher's travel narratives: "The very learned Atanasio Kiker [sic] wrote at length and with pleasure of this journey in his book, which he later titled *Ecstatic Journey*. In this book, he says he was taken by an angel to search all of the places of the globe" (n.p.).

87 Torres, *Anatomía*, 65–6.

88 McClelland, *Diego de Torres Villarroel*, 131.

enumerated. Torres's explanation of the body, although at times schematic and punctuated with a blend of ordinary descriptions and specialized medical terminology (the more specialized language typically appears in cursive), clearly transgresses the boundaries of Galenic thought. In fact, it attests to the tremendous influence the culture of dissection exerted on his concept of human anatomy. It should come as no surprise, therefore, that when Torres and his companions arrive at the waypoint in the journey dedicated to examining the intricacies of the human heart, it is presented in an anatomical verbiage that leaves no doubt that the travellers have now crossed the boundary into modern science:

> *The heart* is one of the principle organs in our bodies, the source of natural heat and vital spirits. It is located in the middle of the chest between the lungs, and touches the diaphragm. It begins on the right side, and ends at a point on the left side; its magnitude is about five fingers long, and four fingers wide ... Its substance is fleshy, thick, dense, and fibrous, and it is harder on its left side ... On its broadest part the heart is surrounded by fibres, and the most twisted ones appear in the shape of a snail ... and there they form fleshy pyramids that work in the dilation of the heart, and when they relax (when the heart suffers some distress) the blood flows out and is forced to exit the aorta. The heart has other parts that help it with its actions and functions, and these parts include *two auricles, two ventricles, the mid septum, eleven valves, and four veins* ... In the orifice of the aorta there are three valves called *semilunar*: they open adjacent to the minor arteries so that in allowing the blood to flow from the left ventricle it can pour throughout the body ... From this doctrine, gentlemen, you can infer the circulation of the blood ... and this circulation repeats itself until death.[89]

The rational physician in Torres wins out over the dogmatic theologian in this excerpt, and we can appreciate how the more he visualizes and codifies the body throughout the anatomical journey, the more the *Anatomy*'s referents are circumscribed by a modern medical science concerned with vital force. Harvey's theory of circulation, for instance, a theory with strong vitalistic implications and whose merits were still debated at the time, makes a brief appearance in the classic metaphor of a self-sustaining circular motion of life throughout the body. Although Torres reiterates the doctrinal belief that man is a divinely inspired "composite" of flesh and spirit, we begin to intuit, nevertheless, that in the treatise's anatomical journey of discovery through the body's organs

89 Torres, *Anatomía*, 88.

and tissues, the soul is often relegated to a subordinate position in revealing the complexities of bodily functioning that fill each page.[90] These complexities and, just as importantly, the ways Torres substantiates them through scientific discourse, underscore the irony that pervades his *Anatomy*. Indeed, there is a conflict of narratives in his anatomical findings in which the text's rhetorical devices and presentation of the soul, despite themselves, signal the repressed impulse of the text: to explore the pivotal role played by modern science in conceiving the body's vital force. As Pérez López points out, Torres was certainly not blind to the ways in which empiricism negotiated the difficulties of knowing the body, yet he attempted to apply this empiricism strategically and for specific ideological ends, as we shall see.[91]

Admittedly, Torres does offer a few preliminary pages in *Anatomy* to outline the doctrinal tenets of the Church regarding the soul's supremacy over the body when it comes to vital force (the treatise is dedicated, moreover, to the Cardinal Fray Gaspar de Molina y Oviedo, one of Torres's most generous patrons associated with the Council of Castile and the Inquisition). Following Aquinas – and through Aquinas the philosophy of Aristotle – Torres states: "As for the soul that animates, it works with three faculties in the body, which are *nutritive, sensitive, and intellective.*"[92] Yet, page after page, and sojourn after sojourn along the anatomical journey – these sojourns include "On the Head," "On the Eyes and Vision," "On Hearing," "On Smell," "On Taste," "On Touch," etc. – the body's organs, fluids, functions, and tissues multiply, while the revelations of God and His Church are obliquely stated, evaded, and even omitted for lack of space. In the concluding refrains to several of these sections, Torres reminds his travel companions that, regardless of the bewildering complexity of the human anatomy that they have just witnessed, it is the simple truth of the invisible soul that vitalizes the body. At one point, he even grapples with the dogma of the soul's immortality, and he conducts a brief survey of the inaccuracies that atomists, stoics, Aristotle, Averroes, and contemporary thinkers have delivered on the subject. However, just as Torres and his companions come to a break in the journey that lends itself to an explanation of the soul's embodiment – an explanation that promises to deliver a blow against modern theories of vital force – he retreats and deflects the issue, referencing offhandedly the revelations of God and His Church.[93]

90 Ibid., 69.

91 Pérez López, "Para una revisión de Torres Villarroel," 21, 33–5.

92 Torres, *Anatomía*, 70.

93 Ibid., 69.

When it comes to the burden of proof, Torres privileges the authority of anatomists, scientists, and physicians to map the body throughout the journey, the same authority he claimed in the treatise's preface to be all but bankrupt. This inconsistency uncovers something of significance that is worth pausing over: the treatise is never fully one with itself, so to speak, never identical with its proselytizing ambitions, since the constant intervention of science nudges the travellers (and the reader) to reflect upon an array of extra-textual clarifications, erudition, and medical and philosophical sources. We could argue that the anatomical journey itself – its very purpose of demonstrating the soul's supremacy over the body – is imperilled, as the travellers' and readers' attention is drawn repeatedly to the profound revelations of modern science:

> Physicians call it *Cuticula or Epidermis* ... beneath this cuticula the anatomical blade has discovered another cutis, which they call *true*; it is a very dense membrane ... In the cavity of the head there are several hidden parts that physicians called *contained* ... physicians call these *soporal* arteries ... anatomists say *septum lucidum* ... among physicians it is called *Vomer* ... anatomists call some of them *incisors* ... here anatomists add a conduit called aqueduct, two windows, and other cavities, which they do not know their function ... anatomists called true those ribs that are born from the espondiles and are joined to the sternum bone ... Thus, the anatomists have divided the abdomen into three regions.[94]

In her study on *Anatomy*, Rebecca Haidt argues rightly that Torres's text is "directed to a readership far different from that addressed by Martínez or Suárez; his readers are neither doctors nor surgeons." She adds that "Torres eschews precise anatomical terminology in his explanations of what without the soul is an imperfect and imperfectly understood entity."[95] While Torres may direct some of his discoveries to a non-specialized readership, his terminology and anatomical insights are far more precise and encompassing than first meets the eye, and bring into play a number of scientific traditions. As Luis Granjel put it, "what is undeniable about Torres ... is the depth of his knowledge about the different medical doctrines that were the subject of constant polemics during the period."[96] Torres, the physician and scholar of medicine, was well aware of anatomical terminology and its meanings, and he was in fact codifying his own imagined dissection of the living body in *Anatomy* in response to the perceived failings of the medical

94 Ibid., 71–98.
95 Haidt, *Embodying Enlightenment*, 37–9.
96 Granjel, *La Medicina*, 258.

practice of his day. "Medicine is fallible," he admonishes his fellow travellers, "even in the mechanical dissection of the body; when you are staring upon the cadaver I ask you to consider, gentlemen: What can medicine say about the complexity [inteligencia] of the living body where only conjecture is possible?"[97] The point is that his own corrective anatomical study and his syntheses and critiques of medical and scientific doctrines have the unintended effect of estranging the reader from the ensouled human body.

Torres grasps human anatomy as a highly organized structure that requires, if the physician is to ever make heads or tails of it, a specific visual and conceptual decoding (an extraordinarily precise empirical observation, as it were). To understand human anatomy also requires a practice of medical sense-making and interpretation, or a process of constructing meaning through specialized terminology that conforms to sound scientific principles. Yet, we intuit that even these complementary procedures of decoding and sense-making are inadequate to the task of comprehending vital force. Tellingly, it is not the mystery of the soul that presents a problem. Rather, the body itself is at issue here, since no matter how he labours to address what he calls its "marvellous architecture" through empirical observation and anatomical language, its inner, living complexity simply lies beyond comprehension.[98] There is a palpable "anxiety of interiority" at work in *Anatomy*, to use Enrique Fernández's words. While Fernández is referring to sixteenth- and early-seventeenth-century Spain, I believe his concept of "anxiety of interiority" is applicable here. While there is no doubt that the field of anatomy and medicine had changed by the time Torres published his *Anatomy* in 1738, the core problem of "making sense" of the body's interior was just as prevalent. Within the scientific framework of Torres's *Anatomy*, I agree with Fernández that "dissection, also a technology, could be used to express the anxiety of an interiority that was deemed concurrently inscrutable and exposable. While it threatened the subjects with the punitive revelation of their inner secrets, it portrayed an inner body so complex and ambiguous, made up of so many organs, that it defied explanation."[99] Every anatomical term and every scientific clarification, no matter how carefully observed, presented, and reasoned in *Anatomy*, points to a plethora of extra-textual frameworks of knowledge that, in turn, point to more terms and clarifications.

97 Torres, *Anatomía*, 66.

98 Ibid., 72.

99 Fernández, *Anxieties of Interiority*, 5.

It could be said that Torres provides his reader with a type of Foucauldian commentary on the body that attempts to question modern medical discourse and uncover its "essential truth" (that is, the shortcomings of modern medicine in explaining vital force), but in so doing has to restate and recirculate this modern medical discourse, which brings to light new and unexpected meanings.[100] Indeed, the anatomical terminology that fills the text, most of which is informed and precise, is nevertheless lacking, since it is incapable of accounting for the mystery of the body's vital workings. Of note is that Torres even tops off the anatomical journey with a four-page index of additional terms to guide his travellers and readers through the intricacies of human anatomy that were examined along the way. This surplus terminology serves as a supplement, since it intervenes at this specific juncture as an accretion and substitution to the text in order to accomplish what can never possibly be accomplished: a full comprehension of the human body and its vital force.

The logic of supplementarity, as Derrida put it, "insinuates itself *in-the-place-of*; if it fills, it is as if one fills a void … It produces no relief, its place is assigned in the structure by the mark of an emptiness."[101] The tension that is generated between absence and supplementarity in *Anatomy* illuminates the fundamental gap in Torres's epistemological project when it comes to vital force, particularly from the vantage point afforded the travellers at the close of his journey, when he leads them into unfamiliar anatomical territory. At the end of the journey into the living body, Torres laments that he devoted far more time than he had anticipated to the complexities of human anatomy, which inevitably steered them off course. In this moment of closure, Torres, the faithful guide, finds that he has no more "room" to show how the soul vitalizes the body, which is the fundamental question that framed the entire anatomical journey in the first place. He turns to his companions and states: "These are the proper conditions and functions of the animal body; the rest of them belong to the rational [body], and these belong to the soul, which I will ensure to reveal to you gentlemen another day because we have no more room … Let us continue with our journey."[102] The final irony that marks Torres's *Anatomy* is that the marvels of the body are not only privileged over those of the soul, but that the conditions and functions of the soul are left in a liminal space of aporia: the final promise of meaning "another day" that hangs over the conclusion.

100 Foucault, *The Birth of the Clinic*, xvi.
101 Derrida, *Of Grammatology*, 145.
102 Torres, *Anatomía*, 102.

DIFINICIONES DE LAS partes ſolidas, y liquidas del cuerpo.

C*Uticula*, es una membrana denſiſsima ſin ſentido, que no conſta de fibras ſenſibles, y eſte es el primer tegumento de nueſtro cuerpo.

Cutis, es una parte compueſta de fibras nerveas, en las quales eſtà ingerida una ſubſtancia carnea, y es el ſegundo tegumento, ò cobertera de nueſtro cuerpo.

Gordura, ò pinguedo, es una ſubſtácia à modo de aceyte elado, y es el tercer cubierto de nueſtro cuerpo.

La membrana, es una tela compueſta de nervios, venas, y carne.

El hueſſo, es un cuerpo denſo, frio, y ſeco.

Cartilago, es un cuerpo muy parecido al hueſſo, ſolo que es mas blando, mas flexible, y menos frio.

Vena, es un caño hueco, redõdo, compueſto de una tunica, y muchas fibras para llevar la ſangre à todas las partes del cuerpo.

Ligamento, es un cuerpo denſo, flexible, blanco, y frio.

Arteria, es un miembro hueco, largo, compueſto de tunicas por donde paſſa la ſangre, y los eſpiritus vitales à todo el cuerpo.

Tendon, es una eſpecie de ligamento; ſolo ſe diferencia de èl, en que conſta de mas fibras, y eſtas eſtàn tan unidas, que forman un cuerpo denſo.

Fibra, es un cuerpo largo, y ſuave, y una ſubſtancia de inſigne blandura, y agrado en el cuerpo.

Carne, es un cuerpo blãdo, laxo, y rubro, por la ſangre eſparcida que ay en èl.

Nervio, es un cuerpo compueſto de membranas, que proceden de la ſubſtancia medular del celebro.

Glandula, es un cuerpo duro, pequeño, denſo, y comunmente blanco.

Medulla, ò tuetano, es una eſpecie de groſura encerrada en la cavidad de los hueſſos.

Uñas, eſtas ſon una medianìa entre el cutis, y el hueſſo, aunque mas ſe inclinan à ſer hueſſo. Conſtan de fibras paralellas tiradas deſde la raiz de la uña à ſu extremidad.

Na Pes

2.3 First page of the four-page index of anatomical terms from Diego de Torres Villarroel's *Anatomía de todo lo visible, e invisible: compendio universal de ambos mundos*, 1738.

We can raise the following question with respect to Torres's approach in *Anatomy*: namely, what can a figurative journey into the body reveal about vital force in early-eighteenth-century Spain? We know that Torres was a lifelong student of medicine and was conversant with the prevailing anatomical theories of his day, although he did not display the acumen of Feijóo's or Martínez's scientific thinking. What is most illuminating about *Anatomy*, particularly considered against the backdrop of Torres's medical writings and their ideological and religious underpinnings, is its repressed content, or that which on every page remains "silent" and nevertheless exposes the treatise's relation to its historical context. In using the word silent, I am referring to Pierre Macherey's concept of the unspoken, and, more explicitly, to his "symptomatic reading" of works, as his translator Geoffrey Wall referred to it.[103] Macherey admonishes us that we, as readers, must resist the natural fallacy of empiricism and assume that the work before us is there to be passively "received, described, and assimilated through the procedures of criticism."[104] Macherey's concept of *work* relies heavily on the psychoanalytic manifest/latent distinction. The core premise that guides his concept of *work* is that a text may "speak" in a seemingly structured, consistent, and uniform way, but in reality, it is "not what it appears to be," since it acquires its meaning through "the [inner] conflict which impels it and gives it its ordinances."[105] Like his mentor Louis Althusser, Macherey is interested in comprehending the complex rapport between ideology and text, yet, more subtly, he aims to show how a text's inconsistencies, incoherencies, gaps, and omissions must be accounted for in the process of interpretation. Given a text's ideological determinants, Macherey concedes that all works establish "second realities" that disclose to what extent they "never arrive … unaccompanied: [the work] is a figure against a background of other formations, depending on them rather than contrasting with them."[106]

In the case of *Anatomy*, Macherey's concept of the unspoken allows us to appreciate to what extent Torres is torn between contradictory responses to the soul as it concerns vital force. Throughout the anatomical journey, the unspoken can be discerned in the ambitious question that Torres lays out but is incapable of answering by way of the scientific framework he himself constructs. The question is this: how can an unextended substance (soul) be conjoined with a complex and highly

103 Wall, "Translator's preface," viii.
104 Macherey, *A Theory of Literary Production*, 13.
105 Ibid., 20, 36.
106 Ibid., 53.

organized organic entity (body) and supply it with its vital force? In essence, Torres confronts the same problem of the soul's objective existence in *Anatomy* that both inspired and deeply frustrated Descartes. Macherey's concept of the unspoken is especially illuminating when we assess *Anatomy*'s "silence" in relation to this crucial question of how the soul vitalizes the body.

As a guide who unveils an unfamiliar anatomical realm to a band of travellers, it remains clear that Torres is no Virgil, nor is he anything like Kircher's guiding angel, Cosmiel. While he may indicate a terminus of understanding throughout the journey in the splendors of the soul, he provides no real guidance on how to reach it through the vast anatomical landscapes of the human body he has made visible to his companions. In reality, it is the body itself that repeatedly impedes the travellers' progress, for its sheer complexity elicits far too many observations, far too many questions, comments, digressions, and clarifications, which ultimately transforms such a terminus of understanding into an expression of desire. At the journey's end the soul is not rendered any more visible than at the beginning, if by visible we understand, as Torres does, knowable. The truth is that the so-called journey of discovery creates more obscurity than light, more absence than fullness, when it comes to the operations of the soul and vital force. This obscurity and absence stem from the fact that *Anatomy* is a work informed by theology, faith, divine revelations, and the conviction that the soul vitalizes the body, and yet it offers evidence through science and medicine of how the body-soul nexus had become problematic. The resulting dissonance that emerges from this conflict of aims calls to mind what Paul Ilie tells us about the way dreams, much like the one that frames Torres's *Anatomy*, have the strange and disruptive effect of exposing the shortcomings of knowledge systems.[107]

What Torres's *Anatomy* shows is that the body-soul nexus and the question of vital force in Spain were strongly linked to the role of empirical science in elucidating body functioning. If we are to appraise ideology in Torres's work from Macherey's stance that all texts dissimulate a "historically necessary discrepancy between [their] various components," we can identify not only the treatise's gap between its form and content, but also the anxieties that beset religious dogma in Spain concerning the scientific advancements that sought to explain the body's vital force without recourse to the soul. Even from the perspective of the journey itself in *Anatomy* (a fantastic five-day expedition devoted to opening the

107 Ilie, "El conocimiento a través de los sueños," 39–41.

cosmos to the reader's eye), it is worth mentioning that the only day to require a supplement in this extraordinarily vast project is the one devoted to human anatomy. Doubtless, it was in the Church's interest to safeguard at all costs the doctrine of the immortality of the soul and the authority bound up in its belief, and it stands to reason why there was perhaps no age-old dictum reiterated with more zeal in doctrinal treatises throughout this period in Spain than this one: "The soul is of a much better nature than the body."[108]

For men of science and learning in Spain, the body-soul nexus grew to be a topic of great relevance in medical literature throughout the Enlightenment, even among such progressive men of science as Andrés Piquer. For Piquer, "the movement of our arm, tongue, or legs; the movement of our heart, nerves, and all the little muscles [in our body], proceed from the soul."[109] The questions that persistently lurk in the background of several scientific and theological treatises published in the first half of the eighteenth century in Spain include: how would social, political, and institutional structures change if the immaterial soul were shown to be a fantasy? What would happen to the scope of religious authority if science could demonstrate beyond a reasonable doubt the soul's inability to regulate the body? Haidt has shown to what extent the shifting relationship between science and epistemology in early-eighteenth-century Spain affected how academies, universities, and the Church theorized the complexity of the body. "The naming of body parts," she proposes, "was a conflicted issue in Spain at the beginning of the [eighteenth] century because knowledge of the body itself was in dispute."[110] Torres's *Anatomy* reveals that the very act of naming the body, of rendering it intelligible and visible, bore directly upon pinpointing anatomically the exact origins of its vital force in the soul, which ultimately proved impossible. This larger project of what I call anatomizing the soul does not end with Torres, however, but continues into the late-eighteenth century, as we shall see in the following chapter.

108 Nieremberg, *Obras cristianas*, 282.
109 Piquer, *Lógica Moderna*, 2.
110 Haidt, *Embodying Enlightenment*, 24.

PART TWO

Political Reform and the Order of Nature

3

Vitalizing the Medical Revolution in Spain; or, How Sebastián Miguel Guerrero Herreros and Ignacio María Ruiz de Luzuriaga Theorized Life, Death, and Everything in Between

> Within living bodies there exists a series of phenomena that cannot be explained by mechanical laws of movement.
>
> Miguel Barnades, *Instrucción*[1]

WHEN CHARLES III ACCEDED TO THE SPANISH THRONE in 1759 after serving as King of Naples for twenty-five years, he found Madrid to be dull and unappealing, a city of convention mired in the political disputes that had dogged his predecessor Ferdinand VI. Furthermore, it was the filthiest and foulest-smelling city he had ever encountered. Upon assuming the throne, he used his political savvy to surround himself with trusted allies who could carry out a series of reforms across the kingdom to open Spain further to the progressive currents of the Enlightenment. In a few short years, he had succeeded in transforming Madrid into a more cosmopolitan and hygienic city known for its vibrant salon culture, in which modern scientific wonders were regularly showcased and debated.[2] One of the reform challenges that Spain faced at the time was the improvement of its higher education. In 1770, Charles III issued a royal decree to overhaul the university system throughout the kingdom (what was known as the Royal Studies of the Court), which included not only

1 Barnades, *Instrucción*, 103.

2 It became fashionable among the expanding learned class to attend scientific salons, which transformed science into an important aspect of day-to-day life in Madrid. See Vega, *Ciencia, arte e ilusión*, 29.

broadening course offerings across universities in the fields of botany, logic, natural history, philosophy, and physics, but also dismantling the legacies of the Jesuit order (a manoeuvre, fully realized in 1767, that directly affected Spanish science and politics, given the Jesuits' important contributions in mathematics and their extensive missionary work in the Americas).[3] There were also numerous attempts, with varied success, to modernize the procedures for hiring and promoting university professors, elevating the academic standards across universities, and revising the curricula for developing competencies and the conferral of degrees on graduates.[4]

As part of this overhaul, a range of reforms were instituted to improve anatomical and medical studies in particular in order to place Spanish science on a more secure footing with the rest of Europe. In the court's records, we read that "the study of anatomy was strengthened, and the renowned [Herman] Boerhaave and [Friedrich] Hoffmann lectured in the medical schools." With the introduction of Boerhaave's and Hoffmann's theories in Spanish universities, Galenism was finally removed from the curriculum for medical students.[5] In this same period, the Royal Society of Medicine and Other Sciences, the Royal Academy of Medicine, and the San Carlos School of Surgery provided crucial institutional spaces in which to strengthen bonds of co-operation with researchers across Europe. Other institutions, like the Economic Societies of the Friends of the Country that began appearing in major cities across Spain, also played a role in this respect.[6] With the increase in quality medical publications written in Spanish instead of Latin, medical knowledge was

3 For the influence of the Jesuits in Spain, particularly in science and mathematics, see Víctor Navarro-Brotón's "Science and Enlightenment in Eighteenth-Century Spain: The Contribution of the Jesuits before and after the Expulsion," 390–404. For the impact of Jesuit missions, I consulted Chapters 4 and 5 of Julia Sarreal's *The Guaraní and Their Missions: A Socioeconomic History*, which deal with how the expulsion of the Jesuits from Spanish lands in the Americas affected local economies.

4 Martín Domínguez Lázaro tells us that: "[W]ith the arrival of the reformists in power during the reign of Charles III, there are attempts to put into practice several of the desired reforms, above all through the figures of Campomanes and Floridablanca. To this end, the open professorships and the materials the Jesuits left behind with their expulsion are put to good use … The reforms are initiated from above beginning with the institution of the university, and then progressed to tackle professorships, which required royal power for their concession. The problem of degrees is likewise examined, and there are three: baccalaureate, graduate, and doctor. Moreover, various curricula of study are unified" (78–9).

5 *Memorial literario, instructivo y curioso*, 230.

6 José Luis Peset provides a concise summary of how other institutions, such as the University of Valencia, also played an important role in medical science during this overhaul period. See "Enlightenment," 231–9.

also popularized and disseminated to a wide public, particularly in pamphlets and treatises dealing with domestic medicine that combined age-old folk remedies with the latest advancements in anatomy, hygiene, and physiology.[7]

Several leading Spanish physicians during the eighteenth century had debated the merits of various theories of vital force stretching back to the Stoics. The expansion of Cartesianism, as we saw in the previous chapter, was crucial in shifting the debate into new territories of inquiry and kindling renewed interest in neo-Hippocratic empiricism and the direct observation of the body and its vital milieu. Physicians like Boix y Moliner and Martín Martínez both appropriated and critiqued aspects of Descartes' philosophy in the early-eighteenth century, not only to sharpen their medical thinking, but also provide direction for future research concerning body functioning. In Spain, as in the rest of Europe, vital force had become one of the most pressing and perplexing questions to frame modern science. The vital force that animated all living organisms was still bitterly debated, but science was making it increasingly knowable through advances in microscopy and new discoveries in anatomy and the life-giving properties of blood. Thanks to the expanding fields of botany and zoology, science was likewise demonstrating that the individual participated in nature's awe-inspiring system of biological growth, development, and fecundity. What became apparent for the *ilustrados*, or the enlightened thinkers in Spain concerned with the country's modernization, was that while the barbed question of vital force brought forth new and fruitful discoveries, it could also challenge the authority of the rationalist-empiricist project itself and expose the power relations underpinning the task of epistemology. Indeed, the polemics it generated within and across the university system, scientific academies, learned societies, and religious orders made these power relations patently visible and demonstrated that expanding knowledge of the body was a process fraught with conflicts and controversies.

In this chapter, I shall examine the work of Sebastián Miguel Guerrero Herreros and Ignacio María Ruiz de Luzuriaga, two key figures in the anatomical and medical sciences, who theorized vital force during the medical revolution in Spain in the eighteenth century. I borrow the term "medical revolution" from Johnathan Israel, who argues rightly that Spanish medicine entered a more advanced phase beginning in the

7 Perdiguero, "Popularizando la ciencia," 155–78. On this topic of modern and folk medicine in Spain during this period, see Perdiguero's "Medicine in the Spanish Enlightenment," 162–8.

early 1770s, when several universities across the country adopted a number of Boerhaave's and Albrecht von Haller's doctrines on anatomy, physiology, pathology, and medicine, thereby altering how scientific practice was conceived and carried out.[8] In the examination of figures like Guerrero Herreros and Luzuriaga, it becomes apparent that Spanish medical science was more innovative and complex during the Bourbon Enlightenment than has often been contended. To begin with, it was deeply engaged in investigating the nature of vital force and its mechanisms of growth and homeostatic regulation. Secondly, researchers like Guerrero Herreros and Luzuriaga were highly conversant with a broad range of modern scientific literature, including Boerhaave's and Haller's texts, as well as the scholarship of some of Europe's foremost vitalists, such as John Hunter, John Brown, and William Cullen. Without a doubt, Guerrero Herreros's and Luzuriaga's pioneering work on vital force was at the forefront of Spanish science, and provided researchers with unprecedented experimental evidence on the body's microstructures and functions that could be deployed to strategically problematize the definition of life and the boundary between life and death. This research raised for discussion once again the thorny issue of the soul's supremacy over the body. Of particular interest is how the arguments in favour of the soul responded to vitalist theory and its preoccupation with bodily interiority by, in essence, anatomizing the soul.

GUERRERO HERREROS'S *UNIVERSAL MEDICINE*: STOICHIOLOGY AND THE BODY AS LABYRINTH

To gain a better understanding of how Guerrero Herreros's and Luzuriaga's research figures into the medical revolution in Spain, we must take a moment and recognize the role of Boerhaave, and his disciple Haller, in influencing the course of ideas regarding vital force. It was Boerhaave's prodigious erudition that allowed him to develop a plethora of theories on anatomy and physiology, in which the best and most-practical concepts of his predecessors – including those of Hippocrates and Descartes – were effectively synthesized. He furnished medical practitioners with criteria with which to determine the proper treatment of patients that took into account both anatomical and environmental factors, and he also developed his research in myriad fields, including botany and physics. His influence even extended into the field of chemistry in important works like *Elementa Chemiae* of 1732. It was this integrative

8 Israel, "Counter-Reformation," 40.

approach to medical science that placed him at the vanguard of the eighteenth-century drive to understand the body and its relationship with the world. While news of Boerhaave's discoveries had reached Spain by the 1720s, it was not until the 1760s and 1770s that his work became influential in mainstream medical practice when it was adopted in a number of Spanish universities.[9] The physician Antonio Segarra had in fact translated portions of Boerhaave's aphorisms on inflammation in 1772, and these translations facilitated the dissemination of Boerhaave's anatomical principles more broadly. However, it was Juan Galisteo y Xiorro's popular translations of Boerhaave's multivolume *Aphorisms of Surgery of Herman Boerhaave* between 1774 and 1779 that firmly established his reputation in Spain.[10]

In his orations "On the Use of Mechanical Reasoning in Medicine" of 1703, and "On Attaining Certainty in Natural Philosophy" of 1715, Boerhaave expounded the core concepts of the iatromechanism that would prevail in his work for most of his career. In the same period that Georg Ernest Stahl had devised his influential concept of animism (the belief that a sensitive soul directed the physical and chemical actions of vital force in the body), Boerhaave was examining the bodily processes associated with sustaining life, which he claimed were dependent on a series of mechanical movements of liquids and fibres. He argued that "only the mechanicians are entitled to claim that they are dealing with their proper subject; and there exists nothing in the whole of the body, in as far as it is solid, which does not belong to this. We should only listen to *them*."[11] For Boerhaave, the body functioned hydraulically through a series of membranous pipes, while fibres served as the body's most rudimentary structural unit, and combined in multiple interconnecting ways to form all types of tissues, membranes, and blood vessels. He believed

9 Feijóo had referenced Boerhaave in his *Universal Critical Theatre* and *Curious and Erudite Letters* on various occasions. In his *Supplement to the Critical Theatre*, he referred to him as "the celebrated Boerhaave" (323). Martín Martínez also made a few passing references to Boerhaave in his *Complete Anatomy of Man* of 1745 (37, 486).

10 Examining the text as a work of translation, Josefa Gómez de Enterría underscores the popularity of Galisteo's edition of Boerhaave's aphorisms during this period: "It is worth mentioning specifically Juan Galisteo's (1774–1779) version of *Aphorisms of Surgery of Herman Boerhaave*, given the great influence that it exerted on the Spanish medical class during the Enlightenment, which is apparent in the numerous editions that were published in the last decade of the century" (41–2). Segarra's translation is titled *Historical Translation on Inflammation and Its Remedies According to the Mechanism of the Human Body. Translated from the Surgical Aphorisms of Herman Boerhaave, which Baron Van-Swieten Commented Upon.*

11 Boerhaave, "On the Use of Mechanical Reasoning in Medicine," 102.

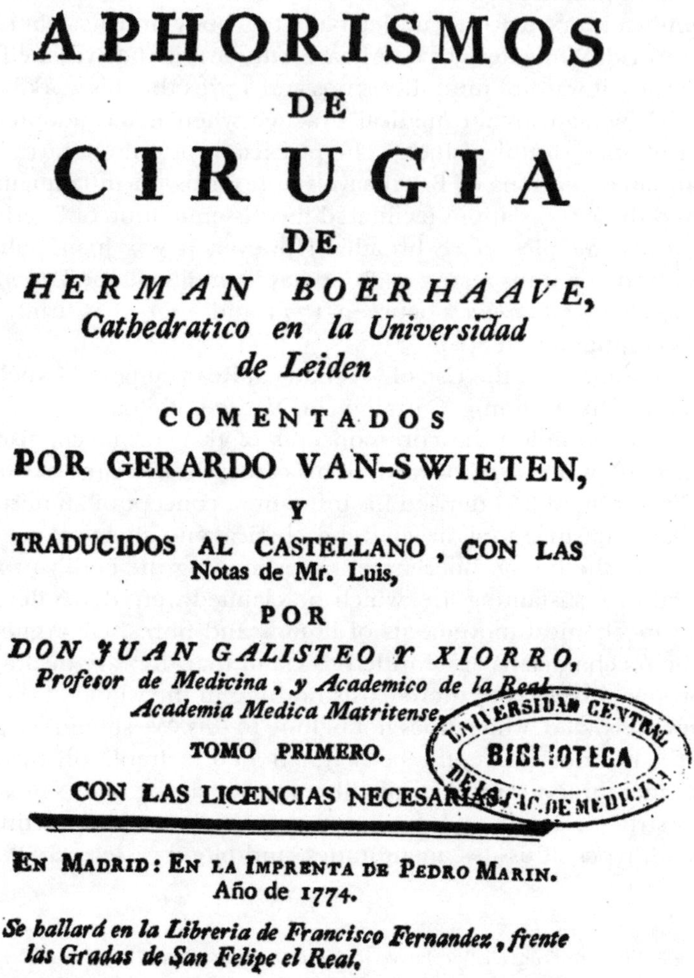

APHORISMOS
DE
CIRUGIA
DE
HERMAN BOERHAAVE,
Cathedratico en la Universidad
de Leiden
COMENTADOS
POR GERARDO VAN-SWIETEN,
Y
TRADUCIDOS AL CASTELLANO, CON LAS
Notas de Mr. Luis,
POR
DON JUAN GALISTEO Y XIORRO,
Profesor de Medicina, y Academico de la Real
Academia Medica Matritense.
TOMO PRIMERO.
CON LAS LICENCIAS NECESARIAS.
EN MADRID: EN LA IMPRENTA DE PEDRO MARIN.
Año de 1774.
Se hallará en la Libreria de Francisco Fernandez, frente las Gradas de San Felipe el Real.

3.1 Title page of the 1774 Spanish translation of Herman Boerhaave's *Aphorismi de cognoscendis et curandis morbis in usum doctrinae domesticae digesti*, 1708.

the minutest blood vessel was analogous to a nerve, and permitted microscopic particles to circulate through it only for the production of sensation and muscular movement. In his conception of anatomy, the body's interior was constructed with intricate meshes of microscopic fibres, and he sustained that "the simplest diseases" could be traced back to these simplest fibres.[12]

For historian Klaas van Berkel, Boerhaave always conceived of the body as an elaborate mechanical system, and thus, "[n]ewer, more vitalistic concepts hardly received mention in his lessons."[13] Yet, as Hubert Steinke has shown, Boerhaave's mechanism underwent a notable turn toward a vitalistic outlook in the 1730s, when he began investigating cardiac motion.[14] In the 1734 edition of *Institutiones Medicae*, Boerhaave added several observations on the workings of the heart, noting, as did Descartes before him, that "[t]here is an amazing and occult tendency in the heart to repeat the systoles and diastoles, alternatively, also after death and even in the excised heart, and actually in single parts of the dissected heart."[15] In a 1736 lecture, he elaborated further on the heart's bewildering post-mortem movement, and he supposed that a vital property unique to the cardiac tissues themselves must therefore necessarily exist. "I will call it its irritability," he declared, adopting terminology that anticipated Haller, "and by this name I understand its innate aptitude due to its fabric, thanks to which it easily and promptly contracts upon the application of … stimulating causes."[16]

Haller's physiological theories were likewise significant in shifting critical views in Europe on vital force. He reasoned at length that science would benefit most from devising a precise animal mechanics, as he called it, capable of describing vital phenomena accurately and efficiently. In his widely read *De Partibus Corporis Humani Sensibilibus et Irritabilibus*, presented at the Royal Society of Sciences in Göttingen in 1752, he outlined his general principles of irritability and sensibility. Drawing on the work of Giorgio Baglivi and his mentor Boerhaave, Haller posited that irritability and sensibility were in fact distinct and independent forces in the body: the force of irritability originated from the capacity of muscles and fibres to contract when stimulated, while the force of sensibility was a distinct property of the nervous system and brain. His perspective on the irritability/sensibility distinction challenged traditional mechanistic theories on physiology and life on several fronts by proposing that, firstly, the force of irritability that made muscles and fibres expand, swell, harden, and contract were inherent to the muscles and fibres

12 Quoted in Knoef, "Practicing Chemistry," 73.
13 Van Berkel, "Science in the Service of the Enlightenment, 1700–1795," 70.
14 Steinke, *Irritating Experiments*, 32–4.
15 Ibid., 33.
16 Ibid., 34.

themselves, as Boerhaave had anticipated; and secondly, this force had nothing to do with the activities of the nerves, much less the soul.

While Haller eliminated purposive agents from his physiology, he nonetheless shifted the general focus of physiological theory from hydraulic forces to immanent forces, and from "the vessel to the fibre – the structural unit whose anatomical and chemical organization was, in his view, more properly suited to house those forces."[17] For Marquis de Condorcet, Haller's trail-blazing research on immanent forces and fibrillar theory had sparked nothing less than "a revolution in Anatomy."[18] Haller's notion that a confluence of obscure forces lurking in fibres animated the human body was especially appealing to Enlightenment scientists and thinkers, who began to speculate how these forces were impacted, supplemented, differentiated, or unified with those apparent in nature. For the physician Joseph-Clément Tissot, for instance, the magnitude of Haller's discovery was clear enough: the theory of irritability and immanent force had furnished science at long last with the basic principles that governed nature's vital system. Furthermore, it was thanks to Haller that "NATURE, this very famous word in medicine, the word about which we talk that often and which we understand so little, will finally be determined; it is the sum total of the powers of the vital principle, a principle which has not been known until now."[19]

In Spain, Boerhaave's and Haller's work on anatomy, physiology, and medicine had a special relevance to the scientific community. The anatomist and physician Guerrero Herreros, a leading figure in Seville's progressive Royal Society of Medicine and Other Sciences, had closely followed Boerhaave's and Haller's work. In fact, Boerhaave's aphorisms were openly debated in the Royal Society as early as the 1730s, well before they gained any meaningful attention in university classrooms.[20] Guerrero Herreros had earned acclaim in Spanish medical circles for his human dissections in the society's anatomical theatre, and the bulk of his scientific investigations on anatomy and physiology, particularly in his later works, relied heavily on fibrillar theory. For López Piñero, Guerrero Herreros's research provided the most rigorous contribution

17 Vila, *Enlightenment and Pathology*, 20.

18 Quoted in Roe, "*Anatomia Animata*," 293.

19 Quoted in Steinke, *Irritating Experiments*, 158.

20 See *Various Medical, Theoretico-Practical, Anatomo-Surgical, and Chemico-Pharmaceutical Dissertations Formulated and Defended in the Royal Society of Seville* (1736). Boerhaave's "De Morbis," "De Sanitate hienda," "De methodo medendi," and seven volumes of his *Aphorisms* were adopted in the Royal Society of Seville's anatomical and medical curriculum in 1769. See Hermosilla, *Cien años*, 106.

to stoichiology – the study of bodily tissues and their cellular components – in Spain during the second half of the eighteenth century.[21] The historian of science María Luz Terrada Ferrandis echoes this assessment in her brief entry on Guerrero Herreros's life and work.[22] Terrada Ferrandis demonstrates that Guerrero Herreros formed part of a more concerted push toward developing fibrillar theory and microscopy in Spain in the eighteenth century. This included the likes of Andrés Piquer, who remained skeptical, nevertheless, of microscopic analysis in medicine.[23] As an anatomist, Guerrero Herreros dedicated years to elucidating the various means of putrefaction and decomposition in various types of body tissues. He collected a great many of his observations in *On the Putrefaction of Humours and the Means to Correct Them* of 1772, in which he argued that, firstly, putrefaction remained an intrinsic part of all biological processes, and secondly, life was best ideated as mired in a continual and ceaseless battle against the forces of decay. While he considered himself an adherent of Boerhaave and exalted the Dutch anatomist and physician, he conceded in his two-volume *Universal Medicine, or Medical, Surgical, Chemical, and Pharmaceutical Academies* (1774–77) that "Boerhaave's medicine is perfect overall, particularly with Haller's exposition and [van] Swieten's commentaries."[24] In terms of Haller, he added: "In the year 1747, Albert Haller [sic] published his little book on the basic ideas of Physiology, where you can read a summary of what I have stated at some length. Later, in 1754, he entreated the public with *Elements of Physiology* where he discusses these topics more extensively than I do, and we owe this author the extensive knowledge we have of cellular tissue."[25]

It is worth examining *Universal Medicine* more closely, since it opens a fascinating window into the ways Boerhaave's – and, to a lesser extent, Haller's – work broadened the definition of vital force in Spain. What motivated Guerrero Herreros's research, as he admitted in the treatise's prefatory remarks, was "a resolute keenness to know this living and most perfect body among all the created bodies."[26] As with several medical treatises that circulated throughout Europe during this period, *Universal*

21 López Piéro, *Santiago Ramón y Cajal*, 30.

22 Terrada tells us: "One of the more mature expressions of Spanish stoichiology can be found in the work of the Sevillian Sebastián Miguel Guerrero Herreros Morales y Reina. He is an author whose important contributions merit a detailed study" ("La teoría," 197).

23 Ferrandis, *La anatomía*, 43–8.

24 Guerrero Herreros, *Medicina Universal*, vol. 1, n.p.

25 Ibid., 170.

26 Ibid., n.p.

Medicine is structured rhetorically around a series of discourses (or academies) between a medical authority – the President – and a number of subordinates, who represent diverse communities of medical and philosophical thought. These discourses dealt primarily with the state of medicine in Spain, and the subordinates offer contrary opinions, elicit clarifications, and question the veracity of the President's assumptions on a range of medical practices and their effectiveness. *Universal Medicine* also probed various pressing topics that were being raised for discussion at the time in medicine, such as the rampant and seemingly worsening (at least in Guerrero Herreros's eyes) levels of disease observed in major Spanish cities, as well as the physician's changing role in society. Yet the topic of most concern was the public's deplorably low esteem of the medical profession. According to Guerrero Herreros, one of the major and warranted reproaches cast upon the medical profession had to do with its crippling disagreements concerning curative treatments. Unfounded conjecture and wild speculation burdened the profession in this respect, and he conceded that "medicine finds itself in a most imperfect state."[27] As the title *Universal Medicine* suggests, Guerrero Herreros argued that, if the medical profession could embrace a universally accepted and empirical framework that set a benchmark for therapeutic practice and united physicians far and wide in terms of instruction and assessment, then health care in Spain would radically improve.

To devise and implement a modern framework of this type was by no means a straightforward undertaking, as Guerrero Herreros well knew. It was, however, realizable, if anatomists, physicians, surgeons, chemists, and healers could agree on what exactly constituted the body's most finite and elemental vital structure upon which all others depended, a topic that had been increasingly addressed throughout Europe with developments in microscopy and how to properly visualize and articulate the complexities of the body's interior.[28] If the profession could identify and establish this essential epistemological ground, then the empirical study of the body and disease would advance at an unprecedented rate through a common purpose. In the President's words: "we must at present clarify and make comprehensible those parts of the human body that in anatomical works remain only partially explained and whose

27 Ibid., 16.

28 See Jutta Schickore's *The Microscope and the Eye: A History of Reflections, 1740–1870*. As Schickore demonstrates, the microscope played a crucial role in the changing field of anatomy in the eighteenth century. A good portion of Schickore's study aims to demonstrate that the development of microscopy required that the eye, as well as its unique perception, had to "function" appropriately.

functions are not fully known."[29] Following the path opened up by Boerhaave, Guerrero Herreros was interested in making "comprehensible," to use his word, the various species of microscopic minimal fibres that he was convinced constituted the body's most elemental components of life, and where diseases were thought to take root. If these fibres could be visualized and identified, Guerrero Herreros reasoned, the medical profession would at long last have discovered the universal ground upon which to securely develop new and effective therapeutic treatments. When he observed various tissues of infirm patients under the microscope, he noted with great wonderment how they appeared to be unique, self-sustaining microcosms of life, and from these observations he surmised that "all the material bodies that we can touch, and that can touch us, are full of seminal seeds ... of small animals and insects that brood and fertilize in our liquids."[30] Even with these observations at hand, supplemented by intense readings and various additional experiments, he admitted that he did not have sufficient evidence to prove that this microscopic life contributed directly to disease development, although he was convinced that it played a meaningful role in the process somehow. He had collected, however, enough evidence to argue that cellular tissue is composed of what he insisted were an infinite number of independent and invisible fibres, which functioned holistically in a complex *systema* to supply the body with its living structure and form. The task of anatomizing the body for Guerrero Herreros thus began with conceiving of invisible, submicroscopic, and elementary fibres, and then progressed to the gross structures visible to the naked eye:

> When we register the most primary elements of animals under a microscope, it is known that they are fibres, or inorganic, crude, formless concretions; and the primary and simplest fibres that compose the sensible living body derive from these concretions ... [T]here is no part of the living body that is not formed or composed of fibres, even those parts where our sight does not register them ... But it is constant that only fibres of the most diverse figures and consistencies compose the living body and all of its organization ... In sum, all the parts that constitute, form, and integrate the living body are created and formed by the fibre ... Thus, to treat the human body one must begin by considering the fibre.[31]

29 Guerrero Herreros, *Medicina Universal*, vol. 1, 12.

30 Ibid., vol. 2, 22.

31 Ibid., vol. 1, 15–16.

Through various life-generating processes, Guerrero Herreros believed these submicroscopic and immutable elements bonded into simple and invisible fibres, which amalgamated further to produce the visible fibres of the body.[32]

A substantial portion of *Universal Medicine* is devoted to clarifying the methods by which the scourge of pox and other lethal maladies corrupted the body's fibrillar structure and affected its vital force. The second volume of *Universal Medicine,* for instance, is dedicated entirely to smallpox, and Guerrero Herreros would significantly develop this vein of research in the complementary treatise, *Physical and Medical Report on Smallpox* of 1786, which documented, and left a valuable record of, the devastating impact of smallpox outbreaks in Seville in 1784 and 1785.[33] When it came to the vital force that supplied minimal fibres with the energy to resist disease progression, Guerrero Herreros could not say exactly, except that God clearly had a hand in it (a response also common in Haller's anatomical investigations when he was faced with clarifying how a fibre's particular microstructure managed to produce an animating force in an entire muscle). In the second volume of *Universal Medicine,* Guerrero Herreros pondered how a vital force was capable of animating both the human body and living organisms in nature. As he explained it, every person's body was unique at the fibrillar level (he had observed under the microscope the prodigious diversity and complexity of identical tissues taken from different patients), which meant that an individual's vital force had to be likewise distinctive and incomparable with another individual's. He considered this distinctiveness to be crucial in properly appreciating the role of anatomical knowledge and body functioning in medicine, given that "the intrinsic construction of man is almost as different as his extrinsic construction, and consequently, the

32 "[A]nd these parts that form the fibre, which are not divisible into smaller parts, are the elements of the fibre. Each one of these parts on its own does not create the fibre, but must bond with others ... But this minimal fibre makes invisible bonds with other minimal fibres to form the sensible, tangible, visible fibre that constitutes the first known part of the body" (ibid., 20).

33 Based on Boerhaave's and John Huxham's chemistry, Guerrero Herreros recommended a blend of antimony and mercury as a cure-all for various maladies: "I must acknowledge that in being guided by Boerhaave's and Huxham's chemistry, I have found that the mix of mercury and antimony produces a medicament, which is singularly effective in curing syphilis [Gálico], not only the simple and solitary [kind], but also the more compound and complicated [kinds] with any other disease ... [T]he most extraordinary cures that this medication has demonstrated have promised the desired happiness that great men have aspired to obtain" (vol. 1, n.p.).

functions within different men should also be different."[34] This simple, yet far-reaching, insight would take on great importance in Guerrero Herreros's thinking. Indeed, his epistemic method in *Universal Medicine* aimed to shed light on this unique submicroscopic realm of concealed forces of attraction and repulsion, of generation and decay, which acted upon the individual fibre, the body's most elemental unit of life. He declared that anatomy had not progressed in any great measure in discovering the origins of vital force, since it had not yet examined microscopically enough the body's interior:

> How can Mathematics perfect knowledge of man if all we know of the body's construction is what manifests itself to sight; the rudimentary arrangement of organs, the large intestine, the big vessels; and within these large parts there are hidden many minute functions that are conducive and necessary to life and have a great influence on diseases. These functions often delay or prevent how treatments work ... It is true that the potencies of living bodies cannot be calculated.[35]

Guerrero Herreros was convinced that detecting the origin of vital force in fibrillar tissue was of paramount significance in determining what exactly sustained the body economy and protected it from the ravages of disease. The more his mind wrestled with the microstructures of human anatomy visible under the microscope, the more he conjectured about the concealed dominion beyond the detections of microscopy, a dominion that defied mechanistic reductionism and which he imagined was comprised of an aqueous and life-giving gluten coursing throughout the body. Following Haller's observations on fibrillar arrangement, he speculated that the presence of this life-giving gluten in the fibres might very well yield the true biological referents of irritability: "Haller also demonstrates that this same gluten gives the fibre its elasticity and probably its irritable quality."[36] Yet he also acknowledged that "physiologists agree that muscle fibres are divided into smaller filaments that no microscope can ever discover."[37] An internal cause, what can be understood as an *intrinsic* vital force, operated in the gluten and continually organized, rearranged, and supported the elementary and invisible particles that went into sustaining the individual fibres: "Once this is assumed and established, I say that the solid parts of the fibre were contained in liquids or fluids, and they differentiated and juxtaposed themselves

34 Guerrero Herreros, *Medicina Universal*, vol. 1, 58

35 Ibid., vol. 2, 56–7.

36 Ibid., vol. 1, 37.

37 Ibid., 43.

mutually by the force, efficacy, operation, and exercise of life. These fibres also combined with the benefit of a very fine gluten, either aqueous or greasy, for of both nature exist and form the minimal fibres, which are most simple, terrestrial, and almost immutable by causes, and work within us throughout our entire life."[38] In line with Haller's theory of connective tissue (*tela cellulosa*), Guerrero Herreros dedicated ample space in his treatise to explain how various types of minimal fibres combined and integrated to produce the gross tissues of the living body: "The modern physiologists, especially from the Boerhaavian school, call *Tela cellulosa* – and we call *cellular tissue* – that most ample part of the human body that is composed of two genres of fibres that were already described, and that are the stamens and laminates, both of which are well intermixed in different proportions ... One can find much of everything in the living body."[39]

Guerrero Herreros's research consistently theorized the nature and life energy of various tissues. In so doing, he was one of the first Spanish scientists to intuit the revolutionary role that the vitalist undercurrents of fibrillar theory played in explicating vital force, and he exploited the rich aporias of microscopy in an attempt to fix its precise bodily origins. What is perhaps most compelling about his work is that his explanatory method hinged on the uneasy complementarity between what we could call a constructive visibility and a dissolving invisibility. That is to say, even when the microscope rendered visible the astonishing fibrillar construction of life beyond the detection of the naked eye, it also pointed beyond its threshold of resolution to a submicroscopic and concealed realm – the invisible building blocks of the fibre, the imperceptible minimal fibres themselves, and the diaphanous and life-giving gluten – where diseases loomed and threatened the fibre's structural integrity through a host of unknown processes. It was in this *terra incognita* where the true causes of life and death originated, and *Universal Medicine* focused as much on mapping the body's microscopic anatomy through the scientific eye as imagining its liminal landscape beyond the frontiers of all possible observation. "Despite much study and work," Guerrero Herreros humbly admitted, "the human body will always remain a labyrinth in which the further one travels the more one remains at a loss."[40]

In the resulting tension that underpinned this transaction between constructive visibility and dissolving invisibility, Guerrero Herreros immersed himself fully in the scientific episteme of the Enlightenment that

38 Ibid., 19.
39 Ibid., 56.
40 Ibid., 50.

Foucault theorized through the developing (and increasingly institutionalized) anatomical and medical disciplines.[41] Ironically, the research Guerrero Herreros argued would revolutionize pathological knowledge and provide a firm foundation for a universal comprehension of the body and disease is tethered ultimately not to the realm of the immediately visible, but rather the labyrinthine realm of the invisible, which was also the dreaded realm of wild speculation that he attempted to overcome. This difficulty notwithstanding, anatomical research for Guerrero Herreros required a rigorous stoichiological approach to vital force that continually sought out connective lines between the visible and invisible, the micro- and macroscopic, and the knowable and unknowable capable of illuminating the body's most rudimentary level of life, where deadly diseases originated. From this angle, he was an innovator who opened new forms of microscopic inquiry that altered how research into vital force was conducted in the more progressive spheres of Spanish science at the time.

It goes without saying that Boerhaave's and Haller's influence on medical practice and micro-anatomical research in Spain was palpable and significant. Firstly, their work was often interpreted to finesse the popular argument, already apparent at the end of the seventeenth century in physicians like Juan de Cabriada covered in Chapter 1, that the anatomical principles of the ancients needed to be modernized, particularly those of Hippocrates. The field of medical science, they believed, was simply overburdened with speculative theories that muddled the relationship between the body's vital force and the environment. This revisionist argument resonated widely in the Spanish medical community, and we need only recall to what degree early treatises like Boix y Moliner's *Hippocrates Defended* of 1711 and *Hippocrates Clarified* of 1716, or Martín Martínez's *Skeptical Medicine* of 1722, represented calls to arms for a modernization of Hippocratic empiricism (calls to arms, it should be noted, that unleashed a storm of polemics and put Scholastic metaphysics on the defensive throughout the eighteenth century).[42] Secondly, neither Boerhaave nor Haller was a full-blown mechanist, and each exploited areas of ambiguity in their definitions of vital force to

41 Foucualt, *The Order of Things*, 259.

42 The publications extolling Hippocrates' modernity continued throughout the eighteenth century in Andrés Piquer's *The Most Select Works of Hippocrates* (1757–1770), Guerrero Herreros's own *On the Utilities and Practical Doctrines That Should Be Learned from the Book on Glands by Hippocrates* (1774), and Francisco Rubio's *Hippocratic Medicine; or, the Art of Curing Diseases Using the Rules of Observation and Experience* (1774), to name a few. See López Piñero, "Andrés Piquer y el hipocratismo en la España de la ilustración," 9–37.

accommodate the actions of obscure energies within the body at the (sub)microscopic level. Put another way, Boerhaave's and Haller's discoveries were flexible enough within a diverse set of medical applications to allow for interpretive latitude and critical disaffection when it came to explaining vital force. In this respect, Àlvar Martínez-Vidal notes that:

> Herman Boerhaave's work was going to exert a tremendous influence on Spanish medicine during the eighteenth century, but not by way of orthodox followers of his system; rather, this influence was felt through the vigorous current of antisystematization that began to manifest itself in the first years of the eighteenth century. In other words, the assimilation of the great physician of Leiden's work was not an acritical undertaking; even though a system might be rejected, its "observations and reasoning" could be used, just like its ideas on the organization of science and medical instruction and assistance.[43]

Lastly, Boerhaave and Haller retained the workings of God in their theories of body functioning, which is something that could not be easily said about the atheistic science emanating from France from figures like Baron d'Holbach, whose *The System of Nature* flatly denied the existence of a deity. For Boerhaave and Haller, God had designed the physical universe, and only He could gift the germ of life in the human body. In a theological sense, Boerhaave and Haller provided the Spanish scientific community, be it the more conservative establishment or the progressive spheres of Seville's Royal Society and Madrid's Royal Academy of Medicine, with a familiar source of references with which to more narrowly advance or refute the concept of vital force.

BLOOD, RESPIRATION, AND LIFE: LUZURIAGA'S *ON RESPIRATION AND BLOOD*

What developed across Europe from the debates on vital force was the idea that, while God may determine the ultimate cause of life, the concrete, bodily self was directly bound to the vital forces of nature in observable ways. By the time Guerrero Herreros had written *Universal Medicine*, life was beginning to be rationalized in epigenetic terms within certain niches of the scientific community as a continual state of development toward higher degrees of perfectibility. In 1781, J.F. Blumenbach further clarified his concept of a *Bildungstrieb*, or formative force, in the

43 Martínez-Vidal, *Neurociencias y revolución científica*, 68.

second edition of *De Generis Humani Varietate Nativa* to address how a teleological dynamism acted upon an embryo so that it could develop and mature in an organized manner. He had noticed that while plants and animals within the same species varied in shape and size, they nevertheless shared a similar structural organization. He also emphasized the ways in which the *Bildungstrieb* allowed the organism to adapt to diverse environments over time, and in this sense it served as a powerful explanatory concept of natural history.[44] The larger dilemma of matter and life in the eighteenth century – a dilemma Guerrero Herreros had intuited would stimulate the development of modern epidemiology – increasingly brought under scrutiny nature's extraordinary vital force at the micro- and macroscopic levels of analysis.

On the cusp of the eighteenth century in Spain, Ignacio María Ruiz de Luzuriaga, a prominent anatomist, physician, chemist, and member of the Royal Academy of Medicine in Madrid, was examining the mystery of vital force and extending his theories on the subject beyond Guerrero Herreros's anatomical framework and Boerhaave's and Haller's views on fibrillar structure. From his early childhood, Luzuriaga had been enthralled by the complexities of human physiology and disease. He was barely seventeen when he translated a treatise on naval hygiene by John Pringle, the so-called father of military medicine.[45] In 1777, Luzuriaga enrolled in the Royal Patriotic Seminary in Vergara, an academy for children of noblemen and elites, where he first learned chemistry from Joseph Louis Proust and Pierre-François Chabaneau. Between 1781 and 1785, he studied anatomy, botany, medicine, and surgery in Paris with leading figures, including Antoine Fourcroy, Pierre-Joseph Macquer, Antoine Portal, François Chopart, Pierre Desault, and Louis Daubenton. While in Paris, he not only published his first scholarly treatise on the chemical effects of atmospheric air on lead (a treatise of considerable value at the time, given that it tackled the obscure causes of lead poisoning), but also established an enduring friendship with Phillipe Pinel, who was known for his innovative methods in caring for psychiatric patients and for establishing one of France's first inoculation clinics in the Pitié-Salpêtrière Hospital. Pinel's research would greatly influence Luzuriaga's interests in vaccination at the turn of the nineteenth century, particularly in his *Impartial Report on the Protection against Smallpox* of 1801, in which Luzuriaga advocated for the establishment of a State-sponsored vaccination committee in Spain to oversee mass inoculations. Through his

44 Lenoir, *The Strategy of Life*, 21.

45 See Mikel Astrain Gallart's "The Unpublished Manuscripts by Ignacio María Ruiz de Luzuriaga (1736–1822) on Naval Hygiene," 437–63.

research and publications on inoculation, he would become the leading figure in hygiene literature in Spain during this period.[46]

After his years in Paris, Luzuriaga relocated to Scotland, where he earned his medical degree from the Edinburgh Medical School in 1786 with a dissertation titled *Medical Essay on the Reciprocal and Mutual Action of the Blood and Nervous Systems*. In this dissertation he first defended the argument that the circulatory system is the origin of vitality in animals. In terms of his extensive education in Paris and Edinburgh, it should be noted that he was the first Spanish physician in the eighteenth century to complete his entire academic training abroad.[47] Edinburgh Medical School at the time was one of Europe's foremost research centres and had maintained a long tradition of vitalist physiology with figures like Robert Whytt, Joseph Black, and John Brown, among others. Yet it was William Cullen – another eminent physician at Edinburgh Medical School, often remembered for his vitalist theory involving what was known as "nervous fluid" – who made a lasting impression on him. Luzuriaga often referred to the Scottish physician as "my venerated master Doctor Cullen."[48] As documented by his friend and colleague the physician Francisco Fabra Soldevilla: "With great pleasure Luzuriaga remained in Edinburgh for two years perfecting the teachings of the wise physicians Monroe, Gregory, Black, Hope, Home, and Duncan, and studying practical medicine with the eminent doctor Cullen, whom he always venerated and deeply loved as a master and friend, and from whom he received repeated demonstrations of regard."[49] Once Luzuriaga completed his degree in Edinburgh, and after he was named a member of the city's Society of Medicine and Society of Natural History, he sojourned in London to train in anatomy with John Hunter, who was recognized as a rigorous anatomist and a pioneer in syphilology and venereal diseases. While in London, Luzuriaga likewise trained with the chemists Bryan Higgins, William Saunders, and Adair Crawford at Guy's and Saint Thomas's hospitals.[50] At the time, Hunter had published his well-received treatise *Observations on Certain Parts of the Animal*

46 de Ros and Gallart, "Una carta inédita," 308–11. On Luzuriaga's role in vaccination programs in Spain, see also Antonio Rumeu de Armas's *On Art and History*, 218–32. Luzuriaga's *Dissertation on the Colic of Madrid* (1796) was an influential treatise that advocated for improved hygiene conditions in the workplace and better health-care standards. For more information on this topic, it is worth consulting José Tuells's "The Unpublished Essay on Vaccines by María Ruiz de Luzuriaga (1763–1822)," 459–80.

47 Granjel, "Perfil histórico de la ciencia vasca," 29.

48 Luzuriaga, *Disertación médica*, 16.

49 Soldevilla, *Elogio histórico*, 11.

50 Gago and Carrillo, "La obra fisiológica de Ignacio María Ruiz de Luzuriaga," 94.

Oeconomy, in which he defended his research into the remarkable powers of what he called the "living principle." For Hunter, the living principle was a ubiquitous force that subsisted in the blood and preserved "the body from dissolution with or without action, and is the cause of all its actions."[51] With Paul-Joseph Barthez and Blumenbach, Hunter was one of the most vocal proponents of late-eighteenth- and early-nineteenth-century vitalism. "[His] type of vitalism," François Duchesneau clarifies, "seems to have induced a trend towards radical antireductionism in the early nineteenth century, with the advent of various kinds of spiritualist and idealist biophilosophies, and more especially with the rise of *Naturphilosophie* in Germany."[52]

Before returning to Spain in early 1788, after his extensive medical training in Edinburgh and London, Luzuriaga returned to France to acquaint himself with Montpellier's School of Medicine, which endorsed a comprehensively vitalist framework in the understanding of the body and disease. As Elizabeth Williams points out, what is known as Montpellier vitalism exerted a tremendous influence on scientific development in the late Enlightenment. In effect, it served not only to challenge prevailing epistemological notions of perfectibility undergirding Enlightenment thought (thereby opening the door to new discourses on ethnic and gender differences), but it also carried on – and immeasurably enriched – the tradition of skepticism concerning the spiritual origins of the body's vital force.[53] There is no doubt that Montpellier vitalism informed Luzuriaga's own developing views on anatomy and pathology. In his *Historic Praise* of 1822, Soldevilla recalled its tremendous influence on Luzuriaga: "He remained in that city [of Montpellier] for a long time to examine the teaching method that the wise professors used in that school. He observed their hospitals closely, [and] he observed with pleasure that the medical doctrine that was taught then had several points of

51 Hunter, *Observations*, 167.

52 Duchesneau, "Vitalism in Late Eighteenth-century Physiology," 259–60.

53 Williams, *A Cultural History*, 148. Williams adds: "The Montpellier physicians did not break with the Enclyclopedists or put themselves beyond the pale of 'Enlightenment' ... All the Montpellier physicians continued to embrace commitments – to the primacy of observation, to practical science, to change in institutions and orthodoxies that inhibited medical progress – shared by diverse Enlightenment figures. But the Montpellier physicians rejected many elements of a model of science committed to determinism and discernment of universal laws of nature, a science that was anti-teleological and anti-religious in spirit and hence tied to critiques of the intellectual and social foundations of the Ancien Régime ... [M]edical vitalism represented a different kind of Enlightenment science" (*A Cultural History*, 148).

contact with the doctrine he had acquired."[54] It remains clear, then, that Luzuriaga, through his extensive training and learning, was well versed in contemporary vitalist theory years before he began his association with the Royal Academy of Medicine in Madrid in the early 1790s.

Luzuriaga served as a conduit for vitalist thinking more generally during this period. In his treatise *On Respiration and Blood Considered as the Origins and First Principle of Vitality in Animals* (a treatise that appeared in 1790 and was later republished with honours in the Royal Academy's *Proceedings* of 1796), he tackles a problem that had plagued the debates on the circulatory system as far back as William Harvey's *De Motu Cordis*: the relationship among respiration, blood oxygenation, and vital force. Luzuriaga draws on an impressive array of scientific sources to give form to *On Respiration and Blood,* including Haller's doctrines on respiration, Hunter's theories on the living principle, Antoine Lavoisier's and Pierre-Simon Laplace's measurements of the body's heat production and carbon-dioxide output, and Adair Crawford's models on animal heat and combustion. In the treatise's introductory pages, he presents his readers with accessible yet instructive accounts of animal experiments that demonstrate the life-giving properties of atmospheric air, a few of which he had conducted in Edinburgh as a medical student. Most of these experiments, however, he had conducted during his stays in London with the assistance of the physician Edmund Goodwyn, who was known mostly for his study *The Connection of Life with Respiration; or, an Experimental Inquiry into the Effects of Submersion, Strangulation, and Several Kinds of Noxious Airs on Living Animals* of 1788. Each experiment documents what happens exactly when animals are deprived of atmospheric air, and each builds upon the findings of the previous to reveal new aspects of atmospheric air's life-giving properties. Luzuriaga begins by noting that "if a small animal is enclosed in a glass bowl with a determined amount of atmospheric air and with no supply of exterior air, it gets sleepy at first, it then shakes breathing painfully and quickly, and then dies slowly with convulsions."[55] He notes further: "The animal's pulse slows the more it breathes the same air until its pulse ceases altogether, thus suspending all the other functions [of the body]. It is also noteworthy that the same symptoms occur when respiration is impeded in the animal. What connection might there be among these observations?"[56]

Luzuriaga documents similar experiments with dogs, in which he attempted to clarify, firstly, how atmospheric air is absorbed into

54 Soldevilla, *Elogio histórico,* 13.

55 Luzuriaga, *Sobre la respiración y la sangre,* 6.

56 Ibid., 9–10.

pulmonary blood, and secondly, how the lungs produce carbon dioxide. The experiments consisted in injecting nitric gas into the external jugular veins of dogs, since nitric gas remains unaltered until it combines with oxygen, or atmospheric air, at which point it produces red vapours that easily stain tissues.[57] In his estimation, the nitric gas would flow into the dogs' lungs through the circulatory system and blood within a matter of seconds and corrode them upon contact with the atmospheric air that the animals respired. In carefully dissecting the dogs' lungs after these experiments, he observed that they were "hard and compact, yet also extremely crumbly, and they were stained throughout with the colour that nitric acid or aqua fortis leaves on your hands, which is orangish."[58] Given that the nitric gas most directly affected the dogs' lungs and not their hearts, livers, or other major organs, he concluded that the oxygen already present in the blood did not contribute in any remarkable way to the reaction. With Dr Goodwyn's assistance, he devised more experiments of this nature, in which he asphyxiated dogs and cats, opened their chests, and observed the colour of blood in the pulmonary artery and veins. The animals were then resuscitated by pumping atmospheric air into their lungs using bellows, and the change in colour in venal blood was monitored and recorded.[59] "Being that this [change in colour] is an incontestable principle," Luzuriaga states, "we should examine in what way, or by what mechanical means, air is directly absorbed into the blood, if by way of absorbent veins, or by chemical attraction."[60] He repeated this experiment with slight modifications, including injecting different gases (hydrogen, for instance) into the animals' veins after they were resuscitated.

Luzuriaga tells us that after dozens more experiments he arrived at the conclusion that there existed "a peculiar attraction" between oxygen and blood during respiration that maintained the optimum conditions to yield life in the organism, including cardiac motion, muscle irritability, body temperature, and so on.[61] He explains this rapport, declaring: "I have demonstrated with these … experiments [on animals] that injecting gases that are not conducive to the processes of oxygenation leads to the destruction of muscular irritability, the movement of the heart, and the circulation of blood."[62] How oxygen and blood mingled exactly

57 Ibid., 12.
58 Ibid.
59 Ibid., 13–14.
60 Ibid., 15.
61 Ibid., 28.
62 Ibid., 33.

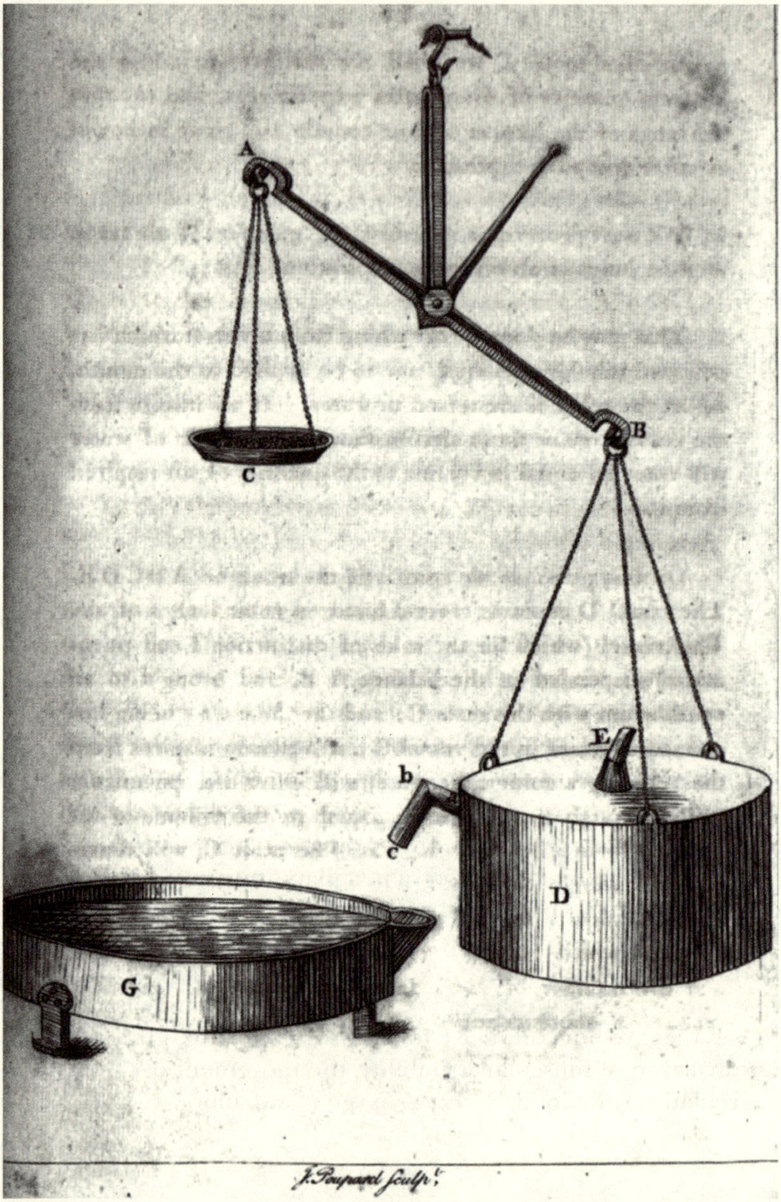

3.2 Illustration of a contraption to measure the quantity of air taken into the lungs during normal breathing from Dr Edmund Goodwyn's *The Connexion of Life with Respiration*, 1788.

to maintain the homeostatic mechanism at the cellular level eluded Luzuriaga, yet there is little doubt in his mind given his observations that the blood was invested with a vital principle much like Hunter had anticipated. Following Haller's general distinction between irritability and sensibility, he postulates that the nervous system could not be solely responsible for vital force in the body, as many physicians had argued, since the nerves to a limb could be severed with no great effect to the continued health of the limb. After describing a slew of experiments by John Floyer, Goodwyn, Stephen Hales, Hunter, and Thomas Kirkland, he asks: "Is it possible that in all these experiments and observations the blood works as an inert matter deprived of all vitality when everything conspires to prove the opposite?"[63]

In the final section of *On Respiration and Blood,* Luzuriaga outlines the practical applications and insights of his experiments on blood and vital force, which include a sharper understanding of such fundamental physiological phenomena as body heat, circulation, digestion, respiration, and cardiac motion. Knowledge of asphyxia and resuscitation is also suggestively illuminated in his numerous experiments. He notes that an animal does not expire immediately upon the cessation of breathing, given that its vital force continues to exert its influence throughout the body for a brief time. He cites French scientist and naturalist René-Antoine Ferchault de Réaumur's astonishing reports about human beings who had been resuscitated after being pronounced dead from drowning. These individuals had clearly died from drowning, and all vitality had fled their bodies, and yet they were brought back to life and were none the worse for the experience. Ferchault de Réaumur's reports on resuscitation were later collected in a brief treatise, which circulated widely throughout Europe and became a sensational success. Of note is the fact that it also offered a how-to guide on resuscitating drowned victims. As Jan Bondeson explains, "it did more than anything else [during the period] to increase uncertainty about the currently used signs of death."[64] Armed with his observations on resuscitation and various supplementary readings, such as Ferchault de Réaumur's treatise, Luzuriaga advances the controversial idea that the boundary between life and death is not as absolute as had often been assumed. In fact, life and death can very well coexist in the same body: "Physiologists have believed for a long time that to live is to breathe, and to not breathe even for a few moments is to die. There was only the two general accepted conditions of life and death

63 Ibid., 55.

64 Bondeson, *Buried Alive,* 80–1.

… But by looking at the observed effects of asphyxia, it seems that they indicate an *intermediate state* between life and death."[65] The fact that a body could be resuscitated after death from asphyxia or drowning within a given time interval only bolstered Luzuriaga's claim that the core elements of vital force must act through the special properties of oxygenated blood and the heart. At this juncture in *On Respiration and Blood*, he defines life, stating: "[w]e can therefore define life in the more perfect animals, saying that it is the coursing of fluids by circulation, as well as by the innate force of the heart and the direct stimulus the blood acquires with its oxygenation in the lungs."[66] He concedes that modern science, particularly under the stewardship of great scientists like his mentors Cullen and Hunter, was beginning to provide concrete evidence of a holistic vital force that preserved the body's functions, beginning with the fundamental actions of the heart and blood. He affirms: "the phenomenon of natural heat that derives from the vital force of the animal economy and the phenomenon of the vitality of the blood are beginning to yield significant evidence."[67] Thus, he arrives at the conclusion that mechanistic theories of circulation cannot satisfactorily explain life phenomena, nor can several of the prevailing anatomical and medical theories that attributed far too much importance to the role of the nervous system in the operations of vital force:

> In examining the annals of our profession, we find among the authors of systematic doctrines the argument that the blood system produces its effects by mechanical means … without noting that the blood itself contains within it a principle of vitality … On the other hand, by denying an active property in the blood system, others argue that the nervous system is responsible for stimulus and the only means of life in the animal … In this way, philosophers ridicule nature and our credulity.[68]

Although Luzuriaga is little remembered today, he was instrumental in extending Spanish science beyond the boundaries of mechanistic reasoning into a broader sphere of vitalist inquiry and experimentation during the Bourbon Enlightenment. As a leading member of the Royal Academy of Medicine who had served in various of the institution's administrative posts, including secretary and vice-president, his work on respiration, resuscitation, and vital force was highly influential. Moreover,

65 Luzuriaga, *Sobre la respiración y la sangre*, 57. My emphasis.
66 Ibid., 59.
67 Ibid., 61.
68 Ibid., 50.

he was one of only a handful of Spanish scientists in the eighteenth century who established transnational dialogues with leading scholars in the fields of anatomy and physiology.[69] Manuel Usandizaga explains that "Luzuriaga's works during this period were of great importance. Of note in this respect is that Morveau, Kirwan, Goodwyn, Hamilton, Crawford, Hope, Adair and Guirtraner commented upon and repeated his experiments ... without acknowledging him."[70] Indeed, Luzuriaga's experiments were impeccably documented, and his language was lucid, sharp, and shot through with the objective empiricism that characterized the most rigorous science of the period. As Usandizaga sees it, Luzuriaga claims the honour of being the first scientist who examined and properly documented the body's chemical processes of respiration.[71] Conversely, for critics like Ramón Gago and Juan Carrillo, Luzuriaga's experiments on respiration were unimaginative and represented a plagiarism of Adair Crawford's scientific work.[72] Gago and Carrillo confirm that in *On Respiration and Blood* Luzuriaga did quote passages of Crawford's treatise on animal heat and a few from Lavoisier's *Elementary Treatise of Chemistry* without acknowledging his sources. They argue, moreover, that Luzuriaga was conceited, boastful, and prone to self-aggrandizement. They propose that he took every opportunity to promote his reputation while abroad.[73] It bears noting in this respect that Luzuriaga was only twenty-two years old when he arrived in Edinburgh. The fact that he was accepted into one of the leading medical schools in Europe and surrounded by some of the eminent physicians of the day certainly made an impression on him, as his correspondence makes clear.[74]

While Usandizaga does overstate Luzuriaga's impact on research into respiration in Europe, there is little doubt that Luzuriaga's findings on blood oxygenation, cardiac functioning, vital force, and the remarkable *intermediate state* between life and death were largely his own. As might be expected, the vitalist theories he assimilated during his medical training with anatomists, chemists, and physicians like Crawford, Cullen, Goodwyn, and Hunter deeply coloured his findings. For López Piñero,

69 In *On Respiration and Blood*, Luzuriaga mentions those portions of his experiments and treatises that had an impact abroad.

70 Usandizaga, *Los Ruiz de Luzuriaga*, 70.

71 Ibid., 71.

72 Gago and Carrillo, "La obra fisiológica de Ignacio María Ruiz de Luzuriaga," 89.

73 Ibid., 92–3.

74 In an undated letter written sometime between 1785 and 1787, he states: "On July 11, I came to the capital of Scotland, the place ... of Medical Science most renowned in Europe, where there is an abundance of students from all nations and pensioners from all courts" (Riera Palmero, "Los estudios," 280).

the importance of Luzuriaga's contribution lies in the fact that "he proposed a theory which conceived the combination of oxygen and carbon in the blood itself. In the history of respiratory physiology, it represented a first step in the research that in the long run would demonstrate … that respiration is an intercellular process."[75] When considering the topic of plagiarism in the late-eighteenth-century context, we must also keep in mind that several of the scientists and physicians across Europe who were examining respiration and blood oxygenation were not only acquainted with this field of research in other countries, thanks to improved communications (the commercial literary market that takes form during the period, for instance), but also reached similar conclusions by improving upon documented experiments. In *On Respiration and Blood*, Luzuriaga openly tackled the question of plagiarism, noting that several researchers in Europe were in fact reproducing each other's experiments and publishing their findings.[76]

Luzuriaga's experiments on animals, which provided the bulk of his observations in *On Respiration and Blood*, sought to shed light on how vital force was generated within the body (oxygenated blood, of course, was of singular importance in this respect). The first lines of his treatise summarize his fundamental thesis that elucidating this special property of vital force – what he calls the origin and principle of vitality – should be regarded as the greatest challenge that the still-emergent sciences of anatomy and physiology faced in Spain at the turn of the nineteenth century:

> *To determine that respiration and blood are the origin and first principle of vitality in animals.* The advances in anatomy have not been sufficient to solve this problem, which is the most important one that faces Physiology today. Since a few years ago, several chemical experiments have been used to solve this problem with admirable success. These experiments have clarified many difficulties and discovered a multitude of phenomena without rejecting the ancients or believing it is useless and chimerical to investigate life in animals. The great Haller could undoubtedly see that the lights of chemistry would take little time to clear up such a challenging matter, which he could not decipher himself with his portentous wealth of knowledge … Let us see, then, what are the purposes of respiration and the action of air.[77]

75 López Piñero, *Diccionario*, 277.

76 Luzuriaga, *Sobre la respiración y la sangre*, 17–20.

77 Ibid., 1.

What Luzuriaga and Guerrero Herreros bring to light is that the question of vital force was not only open for critical debate in Spain, but it blazed bold new paths of research. In the hospitable confines of Seville's Royal Society of Medicine and Other Sciences and Madrid's Royal Academy of Medicine, two of the most progressive institutions for the advancement of science and medicine in Spain throughout the eighteenth century, all kinds of vitalist theories were expounded and critiqued. It should be noted that Guerrero Herreros and Luzuriaga were not alone in exploring vital force and expanding upon and improving scientific innovations from abroad. A few notable physicians who pursued similar work include José Ponce de León, the founder of Granada's botanical and chemical academy and author of *Chemical Physiology of the Human Body* (1804), a treatise that also broadened the definition of vital force in Spain through an analysis of the blood's "electric fluid."[78] In Ponce de León's treatise we read: "There is in the body of all living beings proportionate liquids that have an affinity with the principle of life in which they combine, and it can be deduced from the various combinations, compositions, and decompositions that can be verified in it."[79] He goes on to point out that "blood, charged with electric fluid, serves as the stimulus of the heart's movement and the whole system of blood."[80] This electric fluid exists in the blood and tissue and is continually recharged through oxygenation, circulation, and cardiac motion. For de León, it is responsible for every vital operation in the body. Reminiscent of Cullen's "nervous fluid" and John Brown's theory of excitability, this mysterious and electrically charged fluid could be excited or degraded through multiple means, and it influenced practically everything in the body, from digestion to cognitive ability.

In *Physiological Compendium, or Knowledge of the Physical and Vital Man* (1817), the physician Juan Vicente Carrasco – a noted proponent of Charles-Louis Dumas' vitalism – likewise examined a gamut of biological processes in the body, beginning with respiration. In his assessment, the body was traversed with all manner of mutually reinforcing vital phenomena, and he did not refrain from remarking on them at every turn: "vital resistance," "vital economy," "vital movement," "vital temperature," "vital heat," "vital energy," "vital unity," etc. In his research on medicine

78 Ponce de León, *Phisiología chímica*, 231. Before *Phisiología chímica*, de León also published a treatise titled *On the Animation of Man*. Unfortunately, I have been unable to locate it. De León refers to its contents briefly in *Phisiología chímica* on page 85.

79 Ibid., 172.

80 Ibid., 231.

in late-eighteenth-century Madrid, Costa Carballo has also established that David Macbride's *A Methodical Introduction to the Theory and Practice of Medicine* of 1772, a treatise which was translated into Spanish in 1798 and inspired by Cullen's vitalist research, was adopted in Madrid's San Carlos College of Surgery. Thanks to the adoption of this text, and thanks to professors like José Severo López, who integrated several vitalist theories into the curriculum, it is possible to speak of a vitalist current of thought running through this historic institution leading into the nineteenth century.[81]

THE PERIL AND PROMISE OF THEORIZING VITAL FORCE IN THE ENLIGHTENMENT

While Guerrero Herreros's and Luzuriaga's innovative work remains largely unknown, it testifies to what extent a part of Spanish scientific culture not only dialogued with numerous vitalist philosophies throughout Europe, but also challenged mechanistic reasoning, while nevertheless availing itself of its profitable elements. There is no question that mechanism had come under sustained assault in Spain by the mid-eighteenth century. Renowned physicians like Andrés Piquer, who were once eager mechanists, were beginning to condemn its principles and methodologies and calling for sweeping reform of medical science. In *Discourse on the System of Mechanism* of 1768, Piquer had stated in the introductory paragraph that mechanism in the anatomical and physical sciences should be done away with once and for all. "The system of mechanism," he continued, "which was first introduced into Philosophy, passed to Medicine … In my youth I followed it, yet I have recognized with time and study that this system is false … The mechanical system should be banished from Physics and Medicine."[82]

As representatives of the more rigorous, informed, and progressive Spanish science during this period, Guerrero Herreros and Luzuriaga sought to advance knowledge of a vital force in the Spanish context, even though this enterprise carried sacrilegious implications and was subject to vigorous opposition. A case in point was the great controversy that raged in the Royal Academy at the turn of the nineteenth century concerning the therapeutic ramifications of John Brown's vitalist theories. Brown deemed that diseases originated in a surplus or deficiency of vital force in the body, or what he called the "principle of excitability." The

81 Costa Carballo, "El vitalismo en la enseñanza de la medicina," 86.

82 Piquer, *Discurso*, 1.

key to proper health consisted in effectively balancing the vital force in the body and regulating the external stimuli acting upon it: insufficient excitement produced asthenic ailments (dyspepsia, rheumatism, typhus, etc.), while excessive excitement produced sthenic ailments (palsies, tuberculosis, catarrh, etc.). It was the physician's task to restore the pathological body to the proper state of vital equilibrium, which could be accomplished through exercise, diet, and various medicinal preparations of alcohol, ether, opium, and other drugs. For many traditionalist physicians in Spain, Brown's system was not only unscientific (Brown advised his readers in *The Elements of Medicine* that they should learn only the bare essentials of human anatomy and nothing more), but also immoral and unsafe.[83] The fact that Brown's system, or Brunonianism, was held in high regard in liberal spheres in France in the fateful year of 1789 greatly politicized his work, and several Spanish physicians – Luzuriaga included – ended up condemning it.[84] All the same, Brunonianism gained popularity in Spain in the early-nineteenth century – so much so, in fact, that François-Joseph-Victor Broussais often referred to Spanish physicians as "Brownians" as late as the 1820s.[85]

Other vitalists like Cullen – the physician who exerted the greatest influence on Luzuriaga in Edinburgh – were similarly maligned for

83 Brown, *The Elements of Medicine*, vol. 1, 71–2.

84 "A topic that was particularly debated [at the Royal Academy of Medicine] had to do with the translation of works that explained John's Brown's 'vitalist' doctrine, which was based on the concept of 'excitability' that was recommended in the French Convention (1789). This concept of 'excitability' advanced a generic explanation of the states of health and infirmity. This ideological influence [from France], which carried political repercussions, could have possibly elicited negative criticisms from Francisco Durand and Antonio Franseri in 1802, from Juan Bautista de Soldevilla and Vicente Mitjavila in 1803, and from Ruiz de Luzuriaga in 1805" (Granjel, *Historia*, 136). It should be noted that Luzuriaga might have had a more personal reason to condemn Brown. It was well known in the European medical community that Brown and Cullen had been at odds for years. We must recall that Luzuriaga was Cullen's pupil in Edinburgh and cited him often and with great veneration in *On Respiration and Blood.* Tellingly, there is not a single reference to Brown in Luzuriaga's treatise.

85 Hurtado de Mendoza, *Vindicación y explicación*, 218. In the final years of the eighteenth century, the physician Joaquín Serrano Manzano introduced large portions of Brown's work into Spain when he translated Brown's *Errors and Prejudices of the Spasmodic System of Dr. Cullen* in 1796, and *Medical Elements of the Doctor John Brown* in 1800. Serrano Manzano also translated the German physician Melchior Adam Weikard's *Prospectus of Simple and Human Medicine, of The New Doctrine of Brown* in 1798. In *Vindication and Explanation of Physiological Medicine* of 1826, Manuel Hurtado de Mendoza notes that José Severo López was not only the most ardent disseminator of Brunonianism in Spain, but also a key figure in the reform movement of Spanish medicine in the early-nineteenth century (218).

advancing what one critic at the time called "a very damaging system to the medical advancements [in Spain]."[86] When Cullen's works were approved for instruction in 1788 in the University of Valencia – one of Spain's most progressive universities and a key centre of Enlightenment thought that had counted among its faculty such luminaries as Andrés Piquer and Gregorio Mayans y Sicar – it gave rise to considerable polemics and controversies about the efficacy of modern vitalist medicine.[87] The physician Juan Rajoó's translation of J.B. Lafon's *Introduction to the Medicine of Cullen, with the Physiological Ideas of the Nervous System and the Principle of Life* (1793) helped to popularize and disseminate Cullen's work in Spain and to deepen the disagreements on the merits of vitalism in the spheres of physiology and pathology.

Francisco Llansol, a well-respected Valencian physician associated with Barcelona's medical academy, was an early and strident critic of vitalism and what he reckoned to be its corrupting influence on the tried-and-true methods of Spanish medicine. In *Letter to Don Antonio Hernández on the System of William Cullen* of 1782, he argued that Brown's and Cullen's vitalist theories on the actions of heat and cold in bodily functioning were flawed, for the simple reason that they defied established views of how solids and liquids behaved in the body. He chided Brown especially for his arrogance and the "violence" his theories had introduced into the Spanish medical community.[88] In his extensive treatise on Brown's theory of excitability, *Discourse on the Uncertainty and Prejudice of Doctor John Brown's System* of 1803, Llansol reiterated that Brunonianism was not only potentially lethal for diseased and debilitated patients, but also detrimental to the good practice of medicine in general.[89] His *Discourse* represents one of the most scathing critiques in Spain during the period of modern vitalism, or what he called the "new doctrine" of vital force that progressive physicians like Luzuriaga and Severo López were developing and teaching in Madrid's Royal Academy and San Carlos College of Surgery. In principle, Llansol believed in a homeostatic vital force that animated the body, as outlined in Hippocratic texts, yet he vehemently disagreed with how vitalist science attempted to determine its physical

86 Llansol, *Carta a don Antonio Hernández*, 4.

87 For more information on these polemics see Bartolomé Piñera y Siles's foreword to *Elements of Practical Medicine of the Doctor William Cullen* (1799), titled "Prologue by the translator, in which after addressing the objections made on Cullen's work published in gazettes and newspapers, the rationale for the new notes added to the second volume will be described," i.

88 Llansol, *Carta a don Antonio Hernández*, 11.

89 Llansol, *Discurso*, 3.

font and define its complex workings in the body. More troubling still was the fact that the soul was subordinated to physiological determinants in the new paradigms of vital force, which had to be accounted for, according to Llansol, when considering all types of life-giving energies in the body:

> Our body, composed of solid and fluid parts, and joined with the spiritual, immaterial, and intelligent substance of the soul, should not have only one faculty of life, but lots of them. When these many noble faculties are joined together they contribute to the support of life and the exercise of mental operations … Mobility and sensation are potencies that are affected and receive impressions from stimulations. These potencies serve as the sensations of consciousness in which the soul, by way of a hidden energy, stimulates the nerves in a way that is still unknown to our present-day understanding.[90]

For Llansol, physicians should not waste their time with vitalist medicine – or any theory of vital force for that matter – that failed to address the soul's true workings in the body. Rather, physicians would do best to tend to their patients:

> We do not know with any certainty where the vital principle resides, or whether it is only the proper order of the animal economy, or something more that results from the force of its composition and nature. And, we do not need to know [where the vital principle resides], given that the physician's obligation in the curing of diseases is to re-establish the lost order of those corporeal functions and dispositions that ensure the perfect state of life, or what we could also call health.[91]

While there is no evidence of a vitalist school in Spain per se, there is little doubt that a faction of progressive anatomists and physicians were deeply intrigued by the idea of a vital force capable of elucidating the body's economy in terms of inherent energies and without direct recourse to mechanical causality or the operations of the soul. The common thread that connected vitalist theories was the notion that while each individual body was anatomically homologous at a macroscopic level (human beings have two legs, two arms, a head, a torso, and so on), at the microscopic level it was highly idiosyncratic and like no other body, a point Guerrero Herreros reiterated in his *Universal Medicine*

90 Ibid., 12–14.
91 Ibid., 14.

from a stoichiological perspective. The fundamental assumption behind this reasoning, which dovetailed neatly with the pre-Romantic rhetoric of autonomy and individuality, was that each individual body was distinctive and not only generated its unique vital force, but also perfected its own self-correcting capabilities when it came to health and disease. Indeed, these ideas played a crucial role in how the physician-patient relationship evolved during this period (the shared contract, so to speak, between the physician and patient, within the burgeoning field of medical ethics), and the manner in which disease itself was conceived and the ways cures were administered. There was also increasing biochemical evidence, as Guerrero Herreros and Luzuriaga both argued, that the body's interior was directly bound to nature's awesome workings, since both human beings and organisms in nature progressed through analogous cycles of growth, stability, upheaval, and decay.

The more physicians like Guerrero Herreros and Luzuriaga directed their attention toward the body's (sub)microscopic interior and its vital force, the more their imaginations accommodated the macroscopic exterior that linked human vitality and well-being to the grand system of nature. Treatises like *Universal Medicine* and *On Respiration and Blood* exemplify to what extent progressive spheres of Spanish science participated in that fundamental shift away from both Cartesian mechanism and the metaphysics of the soul by the turn of the nineteenth century. In fact, a number of physicians and scientists began to explore concepts of vital force that gestured toward the more comprehensive organicist reasoning that would characterize Romantic science and philosophy, particularly given the increased separation after 1790 between the disciplines of anatomy (the study of the physical structure of the body and its parts) and physiology (the study of the systemic functions and activities of living organisms). In *Universal Medicine*, for instance, Guerrero Herreros had already acknowledged that modern science had to first bow before nature and yield to its demands if it ever aspired to discover the mysteries of life in the human body.[92]

Throughout the Enlightenment in Spain, theories of vital force infiltrated the university sphere and influenced research practice and curriculum development. Moreover, they offered a framework for scientific

92 Guerrero Herreros puts it as follows: "What the practices of this period of Enlightenment have allowed us to see with clarity is that if we are not friends and in agreement with Nature, we will never be happy in our dealings with her. Disabused of my ignorance, I finally became a pupil of this fine lady, and I promised her to be humble, loyal, and her perpetual servant if she only showed me her ways and methods of working" (*Medicina Universal*, vol. I, n.p.).

opposition to an ideological order – both within and beyond academia – that had redoubled its efforts in the eighteenth century to demonstrate that only the soul animates and vivifies the body. These theories effectively opened the authority of reactionary science and its practices to scrutiny, a manoeuvre that called into question the established distinctions between pathology and environment, body and soul, self and society, individual and nature, and life and death. Not surprisingly, the topic of vital force and the soul aroused renewed condemnation and criticism among religious apologists, not just in Spain but across Europe. In her work on the touchpoints between science and religion in the early Enlightenment, Ann Thomson has demonstrated that the discussion regarding the soul's vital actions in the body was widespread in Europe. What is more, it had significant ramifications for theories tackling the body-soul nexus during this period. It was in the early Enlightenment that "a new view of human nature was emerging, inextricably linked to thinking about the soul."[93] For Thomson, the spread of materialism (and not just mechanism) was crucial in this respect, yet she clarifies that materialism was a "specter haunting any reflection on human nature in the eighteenth century … [A]n analysis of the debates on the soul demonstrate that materialism was not necessarily fuelled by atheism or even deism, but was also an unintended consequence of certain, admittedly unorthodox, Christian beliefs."[94] In theorizing beyond the soul's life-bearing properties, late-seventeenth-century figures like Francis Glisson and Thomas Willis were able to dispense with the soul altogether in discussing the rapport between matter and life.[95]

In the multivolume *The False Philosophy or the Atheism, Deism, Materialism and Other New Sects* (1774–1776), and the encyclopedic *God and Nature. Historical, Natural, and Political Compendium of the Universe in Which the Existence of God Is Demonstrated* (1780–1791), the religious apologist Fernando de Cevallos y Mier, and the priest and legal reformer Juan Francisco de Castro, combatted the spread of sacrilegious science in Spain and deployed the age-old arguments in favour of a Divine Creator. They both argued – particularly de Castro – that matter and spirit obeyed

93 Thomson, *Bodies of Thought*, 1.

94 Ibid., 2.

95 "In his 1672 work Glisson denied that matter was dead and lifeless, claiming that it possessed an energetic nature and not only the capacity to move of itself but also, most importantly, 'natural perception.' The different vegetative, animal, or sensitive functions were accounted for by differences in organization, but all bodies have natural life … His underlying belief was that 'instead of a soul that is superadded to and acts *on* the body, there is only matter that is alive and acts by virtue of the impulse inherent *in* it'" (Ibid., 70).

essentially different laws, and that the union of matter and spirit in man (the spirit being perfect) was proof enough of God's union with His creation. The physician Francisco Javier Garrido took refuge in Hippocratic doctrine in his *Philosophical Discourse on the True Notions of Human Nature* (1799) to argue that "we ignore the first agent of vital movement, and we find ourselves bereft of the most illuminated knowledge about the principles and faculties upon which it depends."[96] Following Garrido, the Jesuit, philologist, and noted scholar Lorenzo Hervás y Panduro interjected himself into the vitalism debate in 1800 with *The Physical Man, or Physical-Philosophical Human Anatomy,* in which he assailed Brown and his troop of lackeys for their inability to offer explicit evidence of the phenomenon of excitability. How is it, Hervás y Panduro asked, that the great discoveries of Enlightenment science and reason, discoveries so often inimical to theological truths and the Good Book, could not demonstrate where vital force was generated in the body? After observing that individuals who suffered from severe birth defects, brain damage, lung deficiencies, and missing limbs not only survived, but also managed to flourish, he advanced the classic argument that the immortal soul must regulate vital force in the body. To declare, therefore, that vital force originated in a single organ or system in the body was simply preposterous:

> No part of the human body contains, or consists of, the principle of vitality. We now know, and we have witnessed, that the human body remains vitalized even though it lacks parts of its brain, cerebellum, lungs, heart, or head. Thus, with evidence and certitude, we can infer that neither vital force nor its font resides in any one part of the body ... The more noble parts of the human body receive their vitality from an entity that exists in the body, but is not part of it.[97]

What is of interest in Hervás y Panduro's response to Brunonianism is clearly not the doctrinal argument in favour of the soul as the true principle of vitality, but rather how it evinces one of theology's most powerful objections to vitalism at the turn of the nineteenth century. In his attempts to anatomize the soul and fully integrate it into the physio-biological processes of the human body, Hervás y Panduro laboured to turn the requirement of objective proof – the cornerstone of the Enlightenment's project of scientific empiricism – against itself through what he believed were sound and methodical principles. Yet, after surveying various anatomical structures and bodily functions, the

96 Javier Garrido, *Discurso filosófico,* 27.

97 Hervás y Panduro, *El hombre físico,* 261–2.

only proof he himself could articulate in support of the soul as the body's animating entity was the idea that it *must* exist, given that life was apparent throughout the entirety of the body and in no one specific organ.[98] He concluded, much like Llansol, that science and medicine would be best served if the troublesome question of vital force was abandoned altogether:

> This philosophically rigorous reasoning drags us and leads us directly to the altar of a sincere confession with which we declare as follows: in the human body, the principle of vitality is the spiritual entity of the soul. In the body, there is no spring or material origin of vitality, because it does not exist ... The anatomical physics as of late has also allowed us to know and see that vitality does not depend on the more noble parts [of the body]. With this new knowledge, we cannot establish vitality in any part of corporeal matter, which obligates us to locate it in the invisible entity that animates the body ... What a useful reform would be undertaken if we could banish from the physical-anatomical books the pointless questions on the material principle of vitality![99]

Treatises of this kind, which attempted to marshal scientific data to argue in favour of the soul, increased during this period and continued well into the nineteenth century. The truth was that anatomists and physicians like Guerrero Herreros and Luzuriaga were conducting empirical and reproducible experiments, in which the precise functions of the heart, blood, circulatory system, and various tissues in animals and humans were demonstrated to support and improve life in the body. In 1816, the traditionalist Agustín Cortiñas published *Physical Demonstration of the Spirituality and Immortality of the Soul* not only to refute deist and atheist philosophers like Julien Offray de La Mettrie and d'Holbach, but also to challenge modern physiological vitalism in Spain and argue once and for all that the soul was empirically demonstrable. The emphasis placed on empiricism and the soul in Cortiñas's treatise, which is also perceivable in Llansol's works and in the scholarship of other traditionalist scientists and philosophers of the period, appears in direct response to the perceived threat that vitalist epistemology posed to established notions of the body-soul nexus. Invoking the latest discoveries in racial differences, Cortiñas takes aim at modern anatomy and the current debates surrounding human and animal bodies. He explains how a growing number of anatomists have maintained that humans and orangutans

98 Ibid., 265.
99 Ibid., 262–3.

share the same internal organs and external parts, which had fuelled the sacrilegious notion that life – and possibly other social and moral faculties – must derive from the body's anatomical structure. Indeed, the bulk of Cortiñas so-called physical demonstration of the soul involves showing that, while humans and orangutans may prove to be identical anatomically speaking, humans are far superior, since it is the soul, working in and through the particularities of human anatomy, that grants them an innate awareness of God. He adds: "regardless of how matter is modified, organized, and combined, it is absolutely impossible to form a being gifted with the attributes of man in terms of his spirituality, or the divine ray that constitutes his soul."[100] He goes on to criticize that class of delusional naturalists (he was referring to those naturalists sympathetic to Denis Diderot, La Mettrie, and d'Holbach) who had simply lost sight of the fact that God intervened directly and continually in nature and its vital current. The scientific inquiry into vital force and the human body had done nothing but obfuscate the fact that the perfect soul is responsible for the individual's intelligence and greatness.[101]

Issues such as the origin of life in the body and the anatomization of the soul were intensified and repeatedly revisited as theories of vital force developed in the late-eighteenth and early-nineteenth centuries and laid the groundwork for Romantic organicism. Within Spain's reactionary scientific establishment, the idea that vital force originated in flesh, tissues, organs, and blood was considered too injurious to the established socio-political and theological order. If vital force originated in the corporeal itself, then the soul would remain in a subordinate position to the flesh with respect to all types of vital and intellective activities, which in turn would call into question doctrinal claims concerning the soul's supremacy over the body. In *Philosophical Enlightenment in Favour of the Truth and the Religion of the Nation that the Doctor Vicente Fernández Valcarce Delivers to the Public* of 1787, the physician Vicente Fernández Valcarce also addressed those offensive scientific discoveries associated with resuscitation that added an entirely new dimension to vital force and effectively opened up for debate what happened to the soul of patients who had died and were brought back to life. Luzuriaga's research

100 Cortiñas, *Demostración física*, 230.

101 Cortiñas declares further: "Man dominates all the creatures in the world, and these creatures are his servants. The elements, obeying only the Supreme Being, recognize Your Sovereignty and obey Your precepts! Nature, that abyss of power and fecundity that, in receiving directly from the Creator its virtue and activity, animates, conserves, and directs the Universe and all of its beings, and alters its laws to obey those that are imposed upon it!" (Ibid., 112).

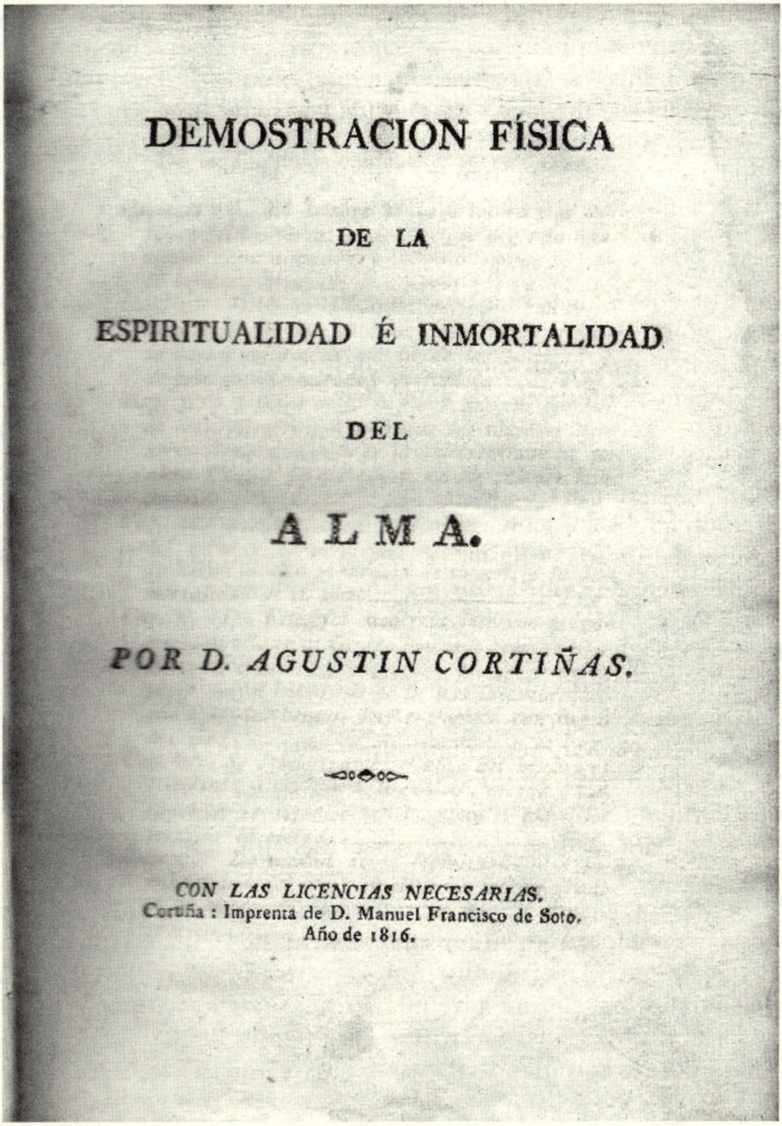

DEMOSTRACION FÍSICA

DE LA

ESPIRITUALIDAD É INMORTALIDAD

DEL

ALMA.

POR D. AGUSTIN CORTIÑAS.

CON LAS LICENCIAS NECESARIAS.
Coruña : Imprenta de D. Manuel Francisco de Soto.
Año de 1816.

3.3 Title page from Agustín Cortiñas's *Demostración física de la espiritualidad é inmortalidad de alma,* 1816.

had demonstrated beyond a shadow of doubt that there existed an *intermediate state* in the human body, which inextricably bound life and death. The questions his research raised included: Did the soul vacate the body as the body passed through this intermediate state? If so, where did it go exactly? And if it vacated the body, did it return in a perfect state when the body was revived? Fernández Valcarce clearly had these considerations in mind when he asked: "Who knows if there are in nature … forces to resuscitate the deceased? asks Rousseau, Freret, and others. These insufferable examples are presented here so that the reader is warned of how malicious is the pretext to doubt, and how with these doubts we do not advance our knowledge."[102] The political and economic deficiencies that had beleaguered Spanish science throughout the eighteenth century clearly did little to nurture theories of vital force. We must also keep in mind that the Inquisition, while not as powerful as it used to be by this stage, still exerted an influence on Spain's medico-scientific community (it added 2,600 books to its Index in 1777). The Inquisition also played a hand in the partial dismantling of the Spanish Enlightenment under Charles IV's reign, a period wracked by the crisis of the French Revolution during which reform-minded intellectuals such as Gaspar Melchor de Jovellanos, Conde de Campomanes, and Pablo de Olavide were exiled or imprisoned.[103]

With the French occupation and War of Independence between 1808 and 1814, and Ferdinand VII's absolutism between 1814 and 1833, Spain's medico-scientific community unravelled. During this period, theories of vital force receded, yet managed to remain relevant, as we shall see in the following chapter. Liberal and progressive scientists, the pioneers of vitalist theory, were persecuted for several years. French forces arrested Luzuriaga in 1809, shortly after the beginning of the War of Independence.[104] He would eventually sympathize with the Napoleonic regime, and, after its fall in 1814, he retreated into obscurity.[105] Indeed, the years running from 1808 to 1833 were devastating for Spain's intellectual culture, given the great number of artists, intellectuals, scientists, physicians, and writers who fled to England, France, and Germany during Ferdinand VII's repressive regime. These years brought

102 Fernández Valcarce, *Desengaños filosóficos*, 33.

103 It should be noted that Olavide was also charged with heresy by the Inquisition during Charles III's reign for owning prohibited books and for his criticisms of religious ceremonies.

104 Luzuriaga was detained for a month and then released. See Granjel, *Historia*, 148–9.

105 Tuells, Duro Torrijos, and Díaz-Delgado Peñas, "Anotaciones," 130.

about what López Piñero has termed a "collapse" of the country's scientific frameworks, particularly those that had advocated for modernization and pushed the boundaries of established paradigms of knowledge.[106] While vitalism never took root as firmly in Enlightenment Spain as it did in other countries, theories of vital force played a pivotal and still largely undocumented role in opening a space of critical inquiry in which to advance the science and meaning of life.

106 López Piñero, González Blanco, and Jiménez Blanco, *Historia*, 74–5.

4

The Subjective Self and the Sublimity of Nature's Vital Force in Gaspar Melchor de Jovellanos

> Sweet nature,
> like a loving mother,
> roused my frozen heart.
>
> Juan Meléndez Valdés, *Poesías*[1]

IN HIS TRAVEL CORRESPONDENCE OF 1782 to the author, painter, and travel writer Antonio Ponz, Gaspar Melchor de Jovellanos reflected upon Spain's vast wealth and natural resources. As he ventured into Asturias's remotest regions during this period, Jovellanos marvelled at the nation's potential for economic growth, social development, infrastructural investment, and educational improvement. He likewise recognized the ignorance and inefficiencies that militated against realizing any such things. The Enlightenment aspiration of sweeping modernization and nation-building in Spain, as he soon realized, was fraught with shortcomings at every step. "I am well aware," he shared with Ponz in his letters, "that the Enlightenment on its own cannot do it all."[2] It was in Asturias's lush and beckoning landscape that he made one of the most momentous discoveries that would influence the course of his thinking: reform could not come about from on high by merely improving institutions or introducing new economic policies; rather, it had to take root with the individual and his direct relationship with nature. To be sure, the realm of nature educated the individual, it elevated him, and it endowed him with the preciously rare ability to apprehend the complex diversity and unity of life, which was absolutely essential in envisioning the continued progress of society.

1 Meléndez Valdés, "Dedicatoria – A una señora" in *Poesías*, vol. 1, 156.
2 Jovellanos, *Cartas del viaje a Asturias*, vol. 2, 18.

For late-Enlightenment thinkers like Jovellanos, who stood on the cusp of Romantic renewal, nature and its influence on the individual and society opened new possibilities for exploring the mysteries of life, and no account of the relevance and diffusion of theories of vital force in Spain is adequate without taking this point into consideration. The question I want to raise in this chapter is: how did a reappraisal of the direct contact between the embodied self and nature's vital force at the end of the eighteenth century in Spain challenge the authority of reason and lay the groundwork for a new understanding of the world? This is not a new question, nor can it be answered simply, yet it is a question that has not been sufficiently addressed in the Spanish context. With this question in mind, I will examine Jovellanos's treatment of nature, principally in his travelogues, diaries, and his eloquent *Oration Pronounced in the Asturian Institute on the Study of the Natural Sciences* of 1799, inspired in part by Comte de Buffon's vitalist ontology. My primary interest is to consider in what sense Jovellanos, as one of the pre-eminent builders of the heterogeneous movement known as *la ilustración*, or the Spanish Enlightenment, engaged the formidable dilemma of the individual's identification with an animated and inscrutable nature.

As discussed in previous chapters, the complex shift in thinking that transformed how nature was valourized and regarded in Spain with respect to vital force begins to take form in the late-seventeenth and early-eighteenth centuries with Cabriada, Martín Martínez, Gutiérrez de los Ríos, and Feijóo, among others. Throughout the eighteenth century, traditionalists and religious apologists of all stripes did everything in their power to resist the steady march of vitalist theories into Spanish science and intellectual culture. Indeed, pioneers like Guerrero Herreros and Luzuriaga, covered in Chapter 3, developed innovative approaches to elucidating the body's dynamism that redefined nature's vital order and the individual's place within it, which often struck at the very heart of Catholic metaphysics and the primacy of status-quo conservatism. It becomes evident when we turn to Jovellanos that he foreshadowed key tendencies of vitalist connection with nature's universal spirit associated with what Robert J. Richards labels the "romantic conception of life," a topic that still requires much more attention as it relates not only to Jovellanos's oeuvre, but also to the tangled concepts of *ilustración* and Spanish Romanticism more generally.[3] Until recently it has been par for the course to interpret Jovellanos, whether it be through his efforts as magistrate, diplomat, essayist, poet, or reformer, as representing the

3 Richards, *The Romantic Conception of Life*, xvii. I am referring to Robert J. Richards's *The Romantic Conception of Life: Science and Philosophy in the Age of Goethe*, which explores, among other topics, the scientific and philosophical practices associated with examining

exemplary *ilustrado*, or the enlightened thinker, committed to neoclassical ideals, educational reform, the empiricist tradition, and the doctrine of liberty. The critical literature on his life and work has sought to define what *ilustración* means exactly within the broader scope of European Enlightenment to thereby establish more compellingly just how "Jovellanos [was] the incarnation of the Enlightenment philosopher."[4] While this scholarship has proved critically important, it becomes evident on closer inspection that Jovellanos's thinking was instinctively dialectical and powerfully shaped by a diverse range of viewpoints, some of which did not square so neatly with what is generally understood as Enlightenment philosophy. In many respects, the richness of his thinking rests, as I argue, in how it assimilated and consolidated the incongruities and tensions that undergirded the cultural shifts marking late-eighteenth- and early-nineteenth-century Europe. Pedro de Silva said it well: "Jovellanos was an intellectual of the Spanish Enlightenment who spiritually and ideologically remained on the frontier ... between two centuries ... He was a man of transition."[5] Appraised through the lens of transition, Jovellanos's thinking takes on a rather different guise and evinces more subtlety and reflexivity than appears at first blush.

On the topic of nature's vital force in Jovellanos's oeuvre, we find that various lines of inquiry – from the scientific and political to the aesthetic and subjective – problematize the image of Jovellanos as the fervent exponent of Enlightenment values. Through figures like Jovellanos, we can determine how the question of vital force in Spain not only was applied to discerning the intimate – and, at times, irrational – bonds that connected the embodied self to nature, but also cleared a path toward conceiving of the natural realm as an arcane system of subjective fulfillment and renewal. This reappraisal of vital force provided the basis for a new approach to organic unity in Spain that participated in the so-called revolt against the authority of reason, which comes about in the mid-to-late eighteenth century and signalled the shift "from the expectation and desire of fixity [characteristic of the Enlightenment] into desire and expectation of change [characteristic of Romanticism]," to use Jacques Barzun's succinct definition of the dominant currents of thought during

nature in German Romanticism. Richards's central claim is that "concepts of self, along with aesthetic and moral considerations ... gave complementary shape to biological representations of nature" (xviii).

4 Souto Rodríguez, *El siglo XVIII español*, 137.

5 Quoted in Cabezas, *Jovellanos*, 11.

this period.[6] This reappraisal only complemented the development of Romantic science and its epistemology of experience, intuition, and becoming, and it provided a malleable framework for the rediscovery of a natural realm that was *alive* and brimming with awesome power.

THE REALM OF NATURE/THE REALM OF PROGRESS

With the expansion of mechanism in the eighteenth century, proponents of vitalist theories advanced world views that challenged the notion that the essence of living matter was extension. Scientists working within what the historian Peter Reill has labelled "Enlightenment vitalism," who appear on the scene shortly after the turn of the eighteenth century, sought to "reformulate the concept of matter, along with those of force, power, and connection in their construction of a natural philosophy that respected natural variety, dynamic change, and the epistemological consequences of skepticism."[7] Catherine Packham, for her part, has paid particular attention to the touchpoints between vitalism and Romantic organicism during the Enlightenment. For Packham, the mid-to-late eighteenth century represented a critical transitional period of scientific creativity that effectively established the epistemological basis for the Romantic encounter with nature. The vitalist themes in the work of Adam Smith, Mary Wollstonecraft, Robert Whytt, and Erasmus Darwin, among others, directly informed the larger discourses that tussled with life's obscurities and the role of nature in the ascendancy of the self-reflexive subject.[8] Packham is right to argue that the Romantics did not disavow Enlightenment epistemology when it came to addressing the means by which reason and rationality impinged on the question of vital force. On the contrary, Romanticism both reacted to, and blossomed from, the great discoveries and misconceptions of Enlightenment rationalism. Robert J. Richards takes up this point specifically in his assessment of Romantic conceptions of life, suggesting something more provocative: "[m]any of the Romantics might, rather, be classified as hyperbolically rational in that they believed the scientific mind could

6 Barzun, "Romanticism: Definition of a Period," 243. I use the term organic unity and organicism throughout within a Romantic frame of reference to refer to the interdependence and unity of all life, or the idea that each living organism participates in, and constitutes, a single, integrated whole (Nature), which remains in a continual process of growth, movement, and becoming. This whole, furthermore, represents more than the sum of its parts.

7 Reill, *Vitalizing Nature*, 6.

8 Packham, *Eighteenth-Century Vitalism*, 210–16.

penetrate into the deep structures of reality, a path overlooked by most Enlightenment thinkers."[9] By 1800, and thanks in great measure to vitalist models of organic change that were being investigated in the life sciences, the concept "nature" was deployed not only to overcome the aporias that plagued science concerning the fundamental mystery of vital force, but also to reimagine the natural realm as a dynamic framework of change that had a direct and visible impact on the body and day-to-day life. Within this framework, nature was progressively sentimentalized and interpreted beyond the constraints of mechanist philosophy and utilitarian rationality, and its generative splendour, colours, diversity, and textures were aestheticized and celebrated through the critical eye of the self-conscious subject in an effort to disclose the "productive activity," to use Friedrich Schelling's phrase, that connected its ceaseless activity to the intimate sphere of lived experience.[10]

As nature was increasingly valourized, Spanish poets like José Cadalso, Juan Meléndez Valdés, Manuel José Quintana, and Nicasio Álvarez de Cienfuegos began meditating upon its mysterious works and subverting neoclassical assumptions about the natural environment as a way to interrogate the Enlightenment's project of Reason and its faith in mind over body. The works of Edmund Burke, Comte de Buffon, David Hume, Jean-Jacques Rousseau, Carl Linnaeus, Antoine Lavoisier, and Joseph Priestly were circulating throughout the Spanish academies, salons, and learned societies and influencing the order and character of the discussion on the obscure processes of change in the body and nature. For the *ilustrados*, there was no question that nature mirrored God's perfectibility, and thus commanded utmost reverence. Its laws and flora had to be dutifully observed, enumerated, classified, and understood to realize its potential benefits and utilities, and once these benefits and utilities were charted, it could be more aptly cognized as a productive force in the service of progress. There was a real sense that reason alone could provide the basis for an efficient and optimistic understanding of nature's order. Clearly, any and all sciences that shed light on the intricate workings of nature's vital force promised to revolutionize society. In his famed *Report on the Agrarian Law* of 1795, Jovellanos declared: "[The sciences] will open … the door to the examination of nature; the sciences, whose object is this great mother, will discover her forces and her immense

9 Richards, *The Romantic Conception of Life*, xvii.

10 Schelling, *System of Transcendental Idealism*, 12. Of note is that with the dissemination of Schelling's *System der Naturphilosophie* of 1798–99, the great chain of being was also irrevocably turned on its head, so that nature could also be ideated as accommodating evolutionary models of development and progress.

treasures; and the Spaniard, enlightened by both, will come to learn how many riches he squanders by not studying the prodigious fecundity of the land and clime in which Providence has placed him."[11]

The natural sciences in particular – their language, philosophy, empirically based methodologies, and the institutional spaces that sprang up to house their new and alluring discoveries – exerted a great attraction for the intellectual culture in Spain. Like never before, the natural sciences and institutions of scientific learning dedicated to the investigation of nature were being poetized and exalted, and particularly evocative in this respect was the ecclesiast and botanist José de Viera y Clavijo's verses extolling the wonders of germination, plant respiration, aerostatic balloons, and the incredible powers of chemistry.[12] In his "Epistle to Eymar," Jovellanos bestows praise on the Royal Cabinet of Natural History, founded in 1776 on the second floor of the Royal Academy of the Three Noble Arts of San Fernando in Madrid. With patriotic emotion, he lauds Charles III for accomplishing the seemingly impossible: gathering the totality of known nature from the globe's farthest reaches and placing it on display in this exemplary institution. In the Royal Cabinet, nature's fascinating creations could be scrutinized and catalogued with the attention they deserved, and they could be made comprehensible to specialists and the general public alike. Jovellanos cannot contain his wonderment at witnessing nature's miracles, monstrosities, and many exotic marvels in the confines of the Royal Cabinet. These creations of nature, displayed within this singular space in the heart of urban Madrid, did nothing if not emblematize Charles III's political reach and Spain's grandeur:

Come with me to the vast house
where the miracles of art and nature
are found. Dear friend!
See here objects worthy of your attention.
What is created in the vast sphere
of one hemisphere and another in the air, land,

11 Jovellanos, *Obras de Jovellanos*, vol. 7, 151.

12 Viera y Clavijo published various poems throughout his life on a wide range of topics. He collected several of his bucolic poems in *Green Fruit of Parnassus*. His better-known poems include "Plant Weddings," "The Aerostatic Balloon," and "Fixed Gases." He is remembered primarily for *News of the General History of the Canary Islands* (4 vols., 1772–1783) and *Dictionary of Natural History of the Canary Islands: Alphabetic and Descriptive Index of Its Three Kingdoms: Animal, Vegetable, and Mineral* (2 vols., 1866 and 1869). See Victoria Galván González's *José de Viera y Clavijo's Literary Works*.

fire, and sea, you will witness here.
Sate your thirst, and over the many classes
of beings, be they perfect, or monstrous,
precious, rare, beautiful, or terrible,
cast your expert and penetrating gaze.
Charles has reduced all of nature
to this most modest of spaces.[13]

What also breathes through Jovellanos's verses is Spain's colonial economy and the notion that the domination of nature in territories throughout the globe ("one hemisphere and another") represented true socio-economic progress. Indeed, the expansion of global trade in the early-modern period, coupled with various technical advancements (metallurgy, cartography, etc.), stimulated new methods to grasp nature and perfect the discourses with which to communicate its value in the building of empire.[14] The linkages between travel and nature writing from 1768 to 1840 demonstrate further the complex ideological biases at work in reducing living environments to calculable constructs that could be readily exploited (the Royal Cabinet Jovellanos poetizes above speaks to the institutional forces behind this type of calculability).[15] It must be noted that Spain, with its extensive overseas possessions, was directly invested in developing the natural sciences and the epistemological suppositions underlying them during this period, which contributed greatly to the new methodologies with which to study nature. For Juan

13 Jovellanos, "Epístola a Eymar" in *Colección*, 5–6. See Cañizares-Esguerra's discussion of marvels and their influence on the advancement of Iberian natural philosophy, particularly in relation to the figure of José de Acosta, in *Nature, Empire, and Nation*, 25–6.

14 The project of building empire informs Daniela Bleichmar, Paula De Vos, Kristine Huffine, and Kevin Sheehan's *Science in the Spanish and Portuguese Empires, 1500–1800*, particularly as it concerns the methods of scientific knowledge production and its circulation within the colonial matrix of power. See, in particular, Nuria Valverde and Antonio Lafuente's contribution to the volume, titled "Space Production and Spanish Imperial Geopolitics," which traces the touchpoints between cartography and geopolitics in the Spanish Enlightenment (198–215). Paula De Vos's article "Natural History and the Pursuit of Empire in Eighteenth-century Spain" is likewise relevant, and explores questions related to political administration and the ability to chart and read nature in the eighteenth century (209–39). For an informative summary of late-Enlightenment epistemology in Spain in the developing field of natural history, see Jaume Josa Llorca's "Natural History in Nineteenth-Century Spain: Botany and Zoology," 109–52. I have also consulted Pamela Smith and Paula Findlen's excellent volume *Merchants and Marvels: Commerce, Science, and Art in Early Modern Europe*, and, in particular, their essay "Commerce and the Representation of Nature in Art and Science," 1–28.

15 Smethurst, *Travel Writing*, 1–5.

Pimentel Igea, the eighteenth century witnessed the last great effort to modernize the imperial structure of the baroque monarchy. "On the scientific plane," he argues, "the imperial projects [of the Bourbons] focused to a large extent on a renewed program of travel and scientific expeditions. It was through these expeditions that Newtonian physics, Linnaean botany, and other products of European science reached overseas territories."[16] The resources the Spanish Crown committed to long-haul expeditions of investigation between 1775 and 1800 were substantial, and conjured up the geographic horizons – real and imagined – alluded to in Jovellanos's verses. Cataloguing nature only complemented the Crown's political ambitions throughout the globe, which held the key to advancing Spanish society well beyond the Enlightenment.[17] The voyage of the botanists Hipólito Ruiz López and José Antonio Pavón to Peru and Chile between 1778 and 1788 was a case in point, which resulted in the identification and classification of hundreds of wondrous specimens, collected in the works *Florae peruvianae, et chilensis prodromus* (1794), *Systema vegetabilium florae peruvianae et chilensis* (1798), and *Flora peruviana, et chilensis, sive descriptiones, et icones* (1798–1802). Also significant was Alejandro Malaspina's expedition around the globe between 1789 and 1794; his "mobile science" attempted to restore Spanish prestige on the global stage through scientific endeavours.[18] Martín Sessé and José Mariano Mociño's more extensive fourteen-year voyage, beginning in 1787, took them from southern California to Guatemala and onwards to the Caribbean, and resulted in the classification of fifteen hundred botanical species.[19] Miguel Barnades's and Antonio Josef Cavanilles's publications on botany also went a long way toward elevating the emerging plant sciences in Spain.[20] Cavanilles was instrumental in describing nature's prodigious diversity not only in

16 Pimentel, "The Iberian Vision," 27.

17 De Vos, "Natural History," 230.

18 Withers, *Placing the Enlightenment*, 96.

19 López Piñero and Tomás, *La influencia de Francisco Hernández (1515–1587)*, 220–1.

20 Miguel Barnades is most remembered for *Principles of Botany Derived from the Best Works and Translated into the Castilian Language* (1767). Antonio Cavanilles's oeuvre is more extensive, and includes *Dissertatio Botanica de Sida* (1785), *Quarta Dissertatio Botanica de Geranio: 128 Species Complectens, 49 Tabulis Incisas* (1787), *Monadelphiae Classis Dissertationes Decem* (1785–1790), *Collection of Papers on Botanical Controversies* (1796), and *Plant Descriptions that Don Antonio José Canavilles Showed in the Public Lessons of 1801* (1802). The journal *Annals of Natural History*, founded in Spain in 1799, also contributed to disseminating the scientific methodologies that were altering the perception and worth of nature. For more on early modern botany, see also Cañizares-Esguerra's *Nature, Empire, and Nation*, 27–9.

4.1 Sketch of Huerta de Alicante from Aigües in Antonio Josef Cavanilles's *Observaciones sobre la historia natural, geografía, agricultura, población y frutos del Reyno de Valencia, Tomo II,* 1797.

Spanish colonies and other distant territories in the Pacific, but within the peninsula itself. Greatly influenced by Linnaean principles, his *Observations on Natural History, Geography, Agriculture, Population and Fruits of the Kingdom of Valencia* (1795–1797) demonstrated that the peninsula – and the region of Valencia specifically – was a cauldron of natural diversity every bit as worthy of scientific study as remote territories.

LETTERS FROM THE JOURNEY TO ASTURIAS: ANIMATED NATURE AND THE ENLIGHTENMENT TRAVELLER TURNED CONTEMPLATOR

Jovellanos was not immune to the rationalist ardour for nature, and he himself became a dilettante naturalist during his many years travelling throughout Spain. While he upheld neoclassical values of stability, harmony, moderation, and probity in much of his work, several of his treatises and literary texts evince his eager curiosity about nature's dynamic unity, which has prompted critics to rightfully identify in his oeuvre a pre-Romantic sensibility.[21] His *Letters from the Journey to Asturias* of 1782, a travelogue of the Asturian region commissioned by Antonio Ponz, reveal his rationalist and objectivist approach to nature (or what he himself called his "analytical observation" of the natural realm), which yielded a wealth of data about the land.[22] Even in this early travelogue, as we shall see, his analytical observation finds itself grappling with its own shortcomings when faced with the task of articulating the expansive wonders of nature's vital force.

Read in conjunction with the later *Diaries* and *Oration*, the *Letters* serve as a basis for tracing how Jovellanos's narrower rationalist and objectivist approach to nature begins to fray and give way to a subjectivist aesthetic. In considering the later *Diaries*, there is little doubt that they are devoted to translating Spain's northern periphery into useful data that could be mined to justify undertaking concrete public works and socio-economic projects. The *Diaries* also bring forth something else that is of great importance: an intimate subjectivity that is produced and reaffirmed in the speaker's direct contact with nature's vital force, a subjectivity that is already apparent, although more tentatively, in the earlier *Letters*. In effect, the *Diaries* document the progressive shift in Jovellanos's attunement to nature during the 1790s, a period that witnessed, as Packham has demonstrated through Erasmus Darwin's botanical works, "a recurring fascination with modes and forms of vital animation which exceed a narrowly

21 While the discussion concerning Jovellanos's Romantic ties has continued to this day through an assortment of theoretical frameworks, critics like Ivy McClelland, Russell P. Sebold, and David T. Gies have traced the contours of a pre-Romantic vein of production in Spain in which Jovellanos certainly contributed and participated. See Sebold's "The Romantic Disillusionment of Jovellanos," 277–80, as well as his invaluable *Trajectory of Spanish Romanticism: From the Enlightenment to Bécquer*, also McClelland's *The Origins of the Romantic Movement in Spain (A Survey of Aesthetic Uncertainties in the Age of Reason)*; and David T. Gies's "The Theater in Romantic Spain" in *The Cambridge History of Spanish Literature*, 350–5.

22 Jovellanos, *Cartas del viaje a Asturias*, vol. 1, 65. The *Letters* are imbued with the spirit of Enlightenment travel writing, one of the most prevalent and popular literary genres at the time. Antonio Ponz had popularized travel writing in Spain in the 1770s, when he was commissioned to tour Andalucia and document its artistic riches and cultural heritage. What began with a simple tour of Andalucía, blossomed into an odyssey throughout the country, and the entirety of Ponz's observations were published in the multivolume *Journey of Spain; or, Letters That Report on the Most Significant and Worthy Things that Lie Within It* (1772–1794). Ponz's travel writing directly inspired Jovellanos's travelogue, which was published posthumously in Havana in 1848.

religious or scientific context."[23] At critical junctures in the *Diaries*, the natural world slips from being a passive and immediate space, subservient to the authority of reason, to an encompassing, animated, and, on occasion, sublime space that integrates the embodied self into the vitality of its splendours. The *Diaries* illuminate instances of dissonance in Jovellanos's reformist agenda, in which his rationalist outlook (the "inescapable monotony," as del Río refers to it, of the text's copious observations stemming from analytical observation) appears in tension with the intimacy and subjectivity that comes to the fore with directly experiencing nature's vital force.[24] In these moments, Jovellanos's direct commerce with nature demands an ulterior language and perspective. More concretely, it requires a revised method of observing and describing the world that transgresses the constraints of analytical observation. This reorientation establishes both the conceptual and emotive basis for the profound revelations documented in his *Oration* of 1799, where, in a clear foregrounding of Romantic organicism, Jovellanos identifies with a natural world conceived of as a sphere of immeasurable transformation, flux, and vital force.

To trace this significant shift in Jovellanos's thought, let us begin with his early *Letters* and analyze the dialectical rapport between objectivity and subjectivity that informs his evolving concept of nature. It is well established that Jovellanos advanced the Enlightenment tradition of travel writing, of documenting from the objective standpoint the country's customs, traditions, hardships, and landscapes. From the first pages of his *Letters*, Jovellanos is conscious of his official mission to textualize the Asturian landscape as accurately as possible for the policy-makers of the court in Madrid, and the truth-value effect of his descriptions is carefully crafted. He has observed the region first-hand, and his letters can dispel any false notion his readers may have of its socio-economic potential: "The country I saw and observed is certainly not the one it is believed to be, and the idea that many have of it is incorrect and imperfect … [T]his error needs to be corrected."[25] His primary motive in writing the letters is to present his courtly readers with first-hand data that can be exploited to fashion a precise and true image of Asturias.[26] He explains further:

23 Packham, *Eighteenth-Century Vitalism*, 3.

24 del Río, "El sentimiento de la naturaleza," 632.

25 Jovellanos, *Cartas del viaje a Asturias*, vol. 1, 56–7.

26 Jovellanos recalls the following: "It was Mr. Ponz's intention to take advantage of the news presented in my letters and diary and publish a volume or two that would come after his general journey. Death … deprived him of the perfection which his simple and amusing style … would have added to my humble works. Lost with such a good friend is

"To know objects, one needs to observe them carefully, and ask, inquire, and indicate their most notable details. If the observer does not proceed in this fashion, he exposes himself to great errors and inaccuracies."[27] Of note is that the sheer spectacle of nature presented in the Asturian landscape, with its verdant life and seemingly infinite horizon, does not at the outset provoke in Jovellanos any emotional reaction, fascination, or state of contemplation. In fact, this bounteous unfolding of land and sky thwarts his observational task, for it throws off his sense of scale: a vista of nature with no structural peculiarities or evidence of human intervention lacks "even an object that indicates and divides the spaces and fixes the limits of observation."[28] Jovellanos, nevertheless, is committed to documenting what he witnesses of the land, and his fifth, sixth, and seventh letters, titled "Topographical Description of the Principality," "Agriculture and Properties of Asturias," and "Industry of Asturias," demonstrate his adherence to the analytical observation he outlines in the introduction.

The *Letters*, however, begin to exhibit a sympathy for nature that resists the instrumentalizing logic of analytical observation. As he proceeds with his journey through Asturias's more remote and verdant regions, his impressions manifest a greater subjective regard for nature, as aesthetic judgments and intimate feelings progressively colour his observations. These impressions have the effect of displacing the dominant objective voice with that of the trail-blazing excursionist and nature enthusiast, or what he himself describes as "a curious contemplator of nature."[29] One such case arises during his leg from León to Oviedo, as he enters into a luxuriant valley and is staggered by its life and beauty. Revealingly, the overwhelming experience transcends all classification: reason is powerless to convey the true feeling roused in him with this vision of nature. Jovellanos states: "It is *inexplicable* what an agreeable sensation its pleasantness causes in the spirit of those who come from Castile's arid fields. As it runs from north to south, the Bernesga River traverses and fertilizes a narrow and fresh valley … The setting participates in all of these objects, and wounds the traveller's senses to such a degree that it excites in his soul pleasant sensations and fills it with peace

---

this precious hope [of publication], and after being persuaded that the public might be interested in restituting such hope, I began thinking if I was capable of undertaking this enterprise. I felt that I had the strength to complete it, and thus I made up my mind and planned to edit and publish my letters" (*Cartas I*, 55–6).

27 Jovellanos, *Cartas del viaje a Asturias*, vol. 1, 67.

28 Ibid., 65.

29 Ibid., 105.

and happiness for *no rhyme or reason*."[30] Unsurprisingly, this part of the journey solicits the poet in Jovellanos. His self-described "little poem," titled "Epistle to Bátilo" – Bátilo being the moniker for his good friend the poet Meléndez Valdés – provides an image of the lush Bernesga plains.[31] Gerardo Diego noted correctly that in this epistle Jovellanos's poetic-descriptive talents transcend the scope of the Enlightenment picturesque, for they aspire to evoke the full grandeur of nature: "Let us affirm that in the poetry in our language there is nothing that surpasses this epistle in its evocative power and its descriptive accomplishments."[32] Neoclassical poetic conventions of the idyll, grounded in the Arcadian *locus amoenus* tradition that privileged values such as harmony, love, and beauty, structure the first verses of Jovellanos's epistle. These opening verses paint an image of the concrete environs of the Bernesga plains, and the poetic voice emanates from their midst and appeals directly to the senses:

Verdant fields, flowered and broad plain
through which the Bernesga benevolently spreads
its crystalline waves; joyful meadows,
ancient and tall poplars. Oh, what pleasure!
How my soul feels contemplating you!
How my merry eyes spill
upon such beauty![33]

The speaker goes on to exalt the Bernesga River's delicate symphony of murmurs and splashes as it flows through islets populated with shrubs, flowers, thickets, and elms. The vigour and tranquility of the scene inundate the speaker's soul with an ineffable delight, allowing nature and self to harmonize. In this idyllic space, the speaker finds meaning in nature's wonders and is at peace with the world.

In her study on the idyll, Gitta Hammarberg notes that spatialization in the *locus amoenus* trope within neoclassicist poetics is largely restricted to the immediate and present environment surrounding the speaker.

30 Ibid., 102. My emphasis.

31 The poem was later included with his observations of the San Marcos convent. As Caso González noted, the poem, which was penned during his travels, was in all likelihood added sometime around 1789. See Jovellanos, *Escritos literarios*, 276. For more on Jovellanos's relationship with Meléndez Valdés, see Gaspar Gómez de la Serna's *Jovellanos, the Lost Spaniard*, 86–95.

32 Quoted in Jovellanos, *Cartas del viaje a Asturias*, vol. 1, 83.

33 Jovellanos, "Epístola a Bátilo," 89.

"What occurs outside the *locus amoenus*," she points out, "is simply not relevant … Spatial parameters in idylls are reduced to understandable dimensions and do not, in general, include abstract structures … but are limited to what is accessible to the poet's senses."[34] In "Epistle to Bátilo," however, the space of the idyll portrayed at the beginning turns unstable as the speaker's imagination exceeds its spatial boundaries in order to perceive a much loftier and abstract dimension: the animated universe. The hospitable Bernesga River and its immediate milieu appear now as a pretext to contemplate nature's design and the forces of life surging throughout it. The speaker urges Bátilo to join him in discovering nature's unifying vital force, in which concepts such as self, creation, universe, and God are inextricably bound:

Its sphere is most noble: the universe
is a code; study it and be wise.
Enter first into yourself; contemplate and inquire
into the essence of your being and its lofty destiny.
Know thyself, and the origin of other beings
will be revealed to you. Search and examine
the common order; admire the whole,
and revere the Almighty through His works.
These skies that spread like a vault
across this humble globe; this perennial
font of light that illuminates and gives life to
all creation …[35]

Jovellanos's view of nature in "Epistle to Bátilo" immeasurably surpasses the boundaries of the spatio-temporal setting as it poetizes the dynamic system of the Absolute, a system that shapes and nourishes the self and brings it into an awareness of nature's remarkable life and inexhaustibility. The firmament itself – the origin of divine light – breathes life into the world and vitalizes all creation. The initial quiescence and objectivity that envelope the speaker and nature presented in the introductory verses are swiftly collapsed by the reciprocal movement between a subjective interiority ("Enter first into yourself; contemplate and inquire / into the essence of your being," "Know thyself") and a soaring exteriority ("universe," "the whole," "the Almighty," "these skies," "globe"), which now governs the self-nature relationship. Nature is

34 Hammarberg, *From the Idyll to the Novel*, 47.
35 Jovellanos, "Epístola a Bátilo," 90–1.

radically transformed at this stage: it is no longer a passive space anchored to the sensorial present, nor is it simply a bountiful vista that kindles emotions in a localized here and now, but rather it is conceived as a vital force of infinite radius that shapes and empowers the subjective self. The verbs "enter," "inquire," "know," "examine," "illuminate," and "gives life" elicit this active sense of formational movement.[36]

There is a continuity and identification among speaker, nature, and God in these verses, and while the poem does not offer any outspoken pantheistic imagery, it does emphasize the universe's divine unity. What is more, the universe is considered a "code" – what the *Dictionary of the Castilian Language* of 1783 defined as "a collection of laws, or constitution of a sovereign" – and understood more intimately as the animated order that weds the speaker and God.[37] This transcendent aspect of nature's vital force, as Jovellanos poetizes it in "Epistle to Bátilo," makes it superior to anything man is capable of creating, even something as noble and pure as fine art. The subordination of Art to nature in the following verses of the poem demonstrates Jovellanos's divergence from neoclassicist beliefs that artistic genius – the prophetic man of genius whom Diderot often extolled – could perfect the beauty and, likewise, the ugliness apparent in nature:

Are there such fools
who prefer the beauties of art,
– those not accurately copied from you, oh, nature! –
to you, their source and saintly model?
Oh, what blindness! Oh, what foolish delirium!
Oh, you wretched mortals! Sighing,
you pursue bliss endlessly, and while
you blindly pursue a hollow shadow,
you distance yourself from the very centre where it hides.[38]

36 As a counterpoint to this vision, Jovellanos's evocation of nature in "Epistle from Fabio to Anfriso, Written from El Paular," written during the same period as "Epistle to Bátilo," is measured and securely moored to a specific locus. The speaker inhabits the natural realm adjacent to the monastery of El Paular to rediscover the peace and equanimity that once rested in his soul. While the natural realm is subjectivized and comes to mirror, subdue, and even augment his inner turmoil in true Romantic fashion as Sebold argues ("Disenchantment," 277–80), it never quite manages to steer the mind in the ascendant to the infinite firmament, or offer the intellect a more encompassing concept of nature's vital force or its cosmic unity and mutability.

37 *Diccionario de la lengua castellana*, 252.

38 Jovellanos, "Epístola a Bátilo," 90–1. From this angle, we can properly situate what Sánchez Corredera terms Jovellanos's "transcendental pragmatism," or the manner in which he conceives concepts of utility involving more than the rational subject and its

While the self-nature relationship is a mainstay in neoclassical poetics, the natural realm is often framed by the "understandable dimensions" – to quote Hammarberg once again – of the spatio-temporal order surrounding the speaker. Certainly, the neoclassicist mind favoured restraint and laboured to envisage a world subordinated to symmetry and limits. This poetic image, however, diverges from the encompassing vision presented in "Epistle to Bátilo," which plumbs nature's vital force and unity and calls to mind the great chain of being that Arthur Lovejoy traced from antiquity to the Romantic period. For Lovejoy, the ambition to identify a vitalist plenitude in nature that is capable of unifying man and God left its mark on several of the foundational metaphysical narratives that informed Western thought. As Lovejoy explains: "The conception of the universe as ranging in hierarchical order from the meagerest kinds of existents through every possible grade up to perfection has, in one form or other, been the dominant official philosophy of the large part of civilized mankind through most of its history."[39] Critics have demonstrated to what degree this philosophical outlook infiltrated eighteenth-century Spanish poetry through the ideas on sublimity that figures like Jovellanos and Meléndez Valdés articulated in response to Alexander Pope's philosophical poem *Essay on Man* and the popular works of early English nature poets like Edward Young and James Thomson who were all the rage.[40] Also influential in this respect was Jean-François de Saint-Lambert's popular *Les Saisons, poëme*, brimming with an invigorating and profound adoration of nature, a work that Jovellanos had read in 1777 and found very much to his liking. Charles Bonnet's two-volume *Contemplation of Nature*, a treatise that figured in Jovellanos's library as early as 1778, was also important, given that it judged every living organism in nature as existing along a harmonious and continuous *scala* from lowest to highest.[41] Much like Jovellanos,

---

immediate socio-economic and political milieu. There is little doubt that the ideal of utility for Jovellanos required restraint, knowledge, moral reflection, and the socio-political triumphs of progress, yet it also brought into the discussion "certain elements that are essential to the relations among men (here lies the transcendental) capable of connecting … with Nature (here lies the nexus between the transcendental and the transcendent) and God (here lies the transcendent)" (Corredera, 675). With reminiscences of a Rousseauian sensibility, Jovellanos suggests that the individual's progression to truth and happiness rests in his relationship with nature in some measure, a point he will make more forcefully in his *Diaries.*

39 Lovejoy, *The Great Chain of Being*, 26.

40 I am referring to the following studies: Delgado and Domenge i Mesquida, "Preliminar," 83–4; García Calderón, "La poesía inglesa de la naturaleza en el XVIII," 519–41; Lorenzo Álvarez, *Nuevos mundos poéticos*, 247–80.

41 See Francisco Aguilar Piñal's *Jovellanos Library (1778)* for a complete listing of Jovellanos's books.

Meléndez Valdés also poetized a transcendental and vitalized nature in his famed "Order of the Universe and Admirable Chain of Its Beings: Dedicated to Jovellanos" and "Immensity of Nature and the Ineffable Goodness of its Author." In these poems, the speaker regards nature as a divine and living totality in which the subjective self is both an observer and participant of its wonders. In fact, every organism along the chain of being, from plants, insects, animals, and humans, and all the cyclical and geological forces of transformation that breathe life into them, are entwined in a mysterious teleological unity.

Ultimately, Jovellanos's reason and logic in the *Letters* dialogues with the sense of inexplicable wonder about nature's vital force that inspired his poetic flight in "Epistle to Bátilo." We must keep in mind that Jovellanos is, as he himself confessed in his letters, "seized [arrebatado] with enthusiasm at the sight of the beautiful valley of Bernesga."[42] The verb "arrebatar," from the Latin *arreptus*, meaning seized, snatched, delirious, or possessed, conjures up the intensity of the domineering emotions that subordinate reason to sensation and sentiment. The emotion and grandeur of the lush Bernesga plains clearly gets the better of him, and he finds himself compelled to survey nature's vital force beyond the purview of his analytical observation. The particular experience of wonder, as Stephen Greenblatt argues in *Marvelous Possessions*, resists by its powerful and elusive nature the "recuperation, containment, [and] ideological incorporation" that frames the colonizing rhetoric of rationality. Not surprisingly, Jovellanos's analytical observation gives way in the *Letters* when he is faced with the task of actually textualizing his potent, subjective response to nature's pulse.[43] Indeed, this subjective rapport with the world establishes the foundation upon which Jovellanos will advance his ideal of nature well beyond neoclassical conventions and principles of utility and progress.

NATURE'S VITAL FORCE: SUBLIMITY AND THE UNFATHOMABLE IN THE DIARIES

Jovellanos's *Diaries* covering the period from August 1790 to January 1801, document his life in Asturias, where he was quietly (and unofficially) exiled for attempting to prevent the dismissal of his friend and

42 Jovellanos, *Cartas del viaje a Asturias*, vol. 1, 89.

43 Greenblatt, *Marvelous Possessions*, 17.

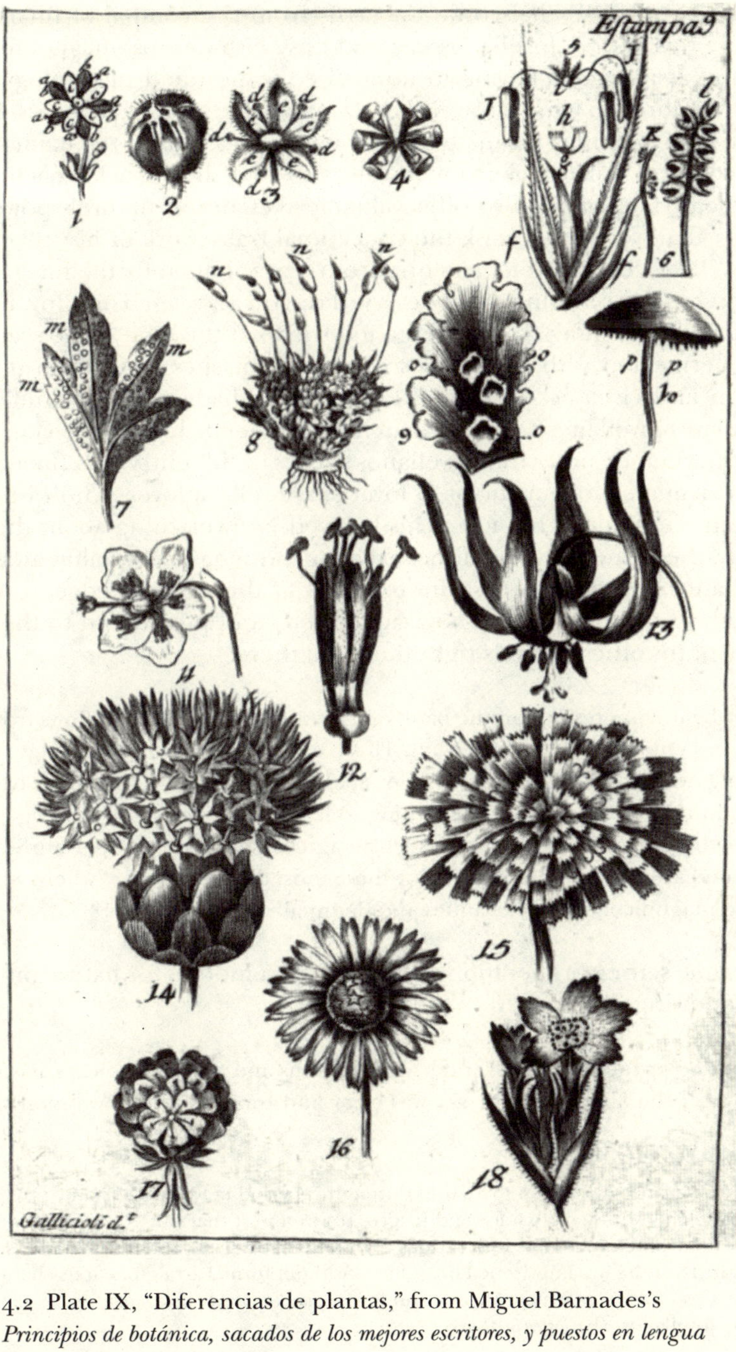

4.2 Plate IX, "Diferencias de plantas," from Miguel Barnades's *Principios de botánica, sacados de los mejores escritores, y puestos en lengua castellana*, 1767.

liberal reformer Francisco de Cabarrús from the council of finance.[44] During this period, Jovellanos was kept busy with various obligations and routine assignments having to do with education and mineralogy that often required extensive travel. The *Diaries* tackle a range of topics, from Spain's socio-political climate to personal impressions of the hamlets he encountered during his many journeys by foot, horseback, coach, and riverboat. The *Diaries* also offer valuable sketches of nature's powerful vitality that work to unmask the conceptual framework of his subjective voice. Take, for example, an entry from 1792 that crafts the image of a weary traveller relishing a well-deserved rest on a stream bank (Jovellanos was in fact travelling from Teverga to Oviedo at the time). The scene itself, permeated with the echoes of gentle splashes from the running stream and circumscribed by the protective shade of a hazelnut tree, stimulates Jovellanos to link it to an intimate poetic logic. Caso González is right when he notes that Jovellanos speaks in this entry with the nostalgic yearning characteristic of "a lover's farewell," a lover "who wishes to remain eternally at the side of his beloved."[45] Everything about the felt reality, the immediacy and direct exchange with nature's vitality, awakens Jovellanos, and it all urges him to linger at the stream's edge, to commune with Nature's glory (now capitalized) and put an end to the nuisance of his official travels right then and there:

> Heavy heat. I am resting on the bank of a most fertile stream that flows from on high and enters the river on the left. This is a delicious place on the edge of the rushing waters, and covered by the shade of a beautiful hazelnut tree … Everything here is poetic … I am going to leave this place soon, although I am sorry I must tear myself away from such an agreeable situation. Oh, Nature! How wretched are those who cannot enjoy these most delicious scenes where you unfurl so magnificently your beauties and flaunt all of your majesty![46]

The same sense of veneration and rapture of emotion for nature informs the following excerpt of 1795:

> All around us there were tall and leafy field elms and plenty of foliage; it was the twilight of the afternoon; the sky was clear and tranquil; the new moon shone

44 Jovellanos did return to Madrid during this period between 1797 and 1798 when he was named Minister of Grace and Justice. It was a post that caused him considerable turmoil and put him at odds with various high-ranking officials in Manuel Godoy's inner circle. In 1801, he was imprisoned in Mallorca without formal arraignment or charges.

45 Caso González, Canga Meana, and Piñán, *Jovellanos y la naturaleza*, 33.

46 Jovellanos, *Diarios*, vol. 1, 283.

sweetly high above; the nightingale's song, the sound of the water, the shade of the tall trees. Oh, Nature! Oh, delicious rustic life! And to think that there are madmen who prefer other scenes to these; scenes whose wise magnificence is crafted by the intelligent and generous hand of Nature![47]

Nature's vital force remained constantly on Jovellanos's mind throughout the 1790s. Like many late-eighteenth-century naturalists, geologists, painters, and poets, he was captivated by those powers in nature – particularly volcanoes and earthquakes – that wrought the earth's surface. The landscape surrounding his birthplace of Gijón, where he remained for the most part during his years of exile in Asturias, was one of sharp contrasts: lush open fields, forest blooms, wave-battered sea cliffs, gentle hillocks, and, hovering in the distance, rose the mountain slopes of Pico San Martín and Peña de los Cuatro Jueces. The Cantabrian Sea – infinite and beckoning – remains an invigorating backdrop in the *Diaries*. Jovellanos remarks: "What a delicious scene presents itself when one leaves Gijón and its countryside; the town in the foreground, and the extensive sea on either side!"[48] This diverse geography around Gijón captivates him and he begins to ponder on the generative processes of climate and vegetation and their impact on the development of civilization. It also piques his curiosity about the origins of volcanoes, earthquakes, and other geologic phenomena. From his earliest years as one of the principal magistrates of the Royal Household and Court beginning in 1778, he had been dispatched to evaluate road works, agricultural developments, pastoral practices, and coal and iron prospects in northern Spain, with an eye toward expanding production and improving lines of communication and distribution.[49] Undoubtedly, he had become adept at assessing the land and surveying its geology and resources, and had acquainted himself with the latest theories in natural history, particularly those of Buffon, which influenced him greatly, as we shall see in the following section.[50] In speaking of Jovellanos's preoccupation with the origins of geologic forces, Sánchez Corredera points out that "one can see that his mental coordinates are Buffonian and not

47 Ibid., vol. 2, 73–4.

48 Ibid., vol. 1, 418.

49 In his *Address to the Royal Economic Society of Asturias* of 1781, he favoured the expansion of iron mining. In his *Report on the Benefits of Carbon Rock and Utility of Its Trade* of 1789, he outlined the feasibility of increased coal production in Asturias. In 1789, he also penned his *Proposal for a School of Mineralogy in Gijón*.

50 See also Sánchez Alonso's "Jovellanos and Geology," and "Jovellanos Seen by a Geologist."

biblical."[51] On an outing in 1792, for instance, Jovellanos comes upon a coal seam encrusted with fossilized ferns, and his imagination is inflamed by visions of primordial volcanoes.[52] A similar curiosity about comprehending the forces that lift mountains and shape hard rock led him to surmise that volcanic activity must have played a pivotal role in the Earth's formation.[53] During an excursion in the vicinity of Gijón, he also admires the peculiar placement of a range of hills, cliffs, and plains adjacent to a windswept beach, which makes evident that other powerful forces such as erosion also contributed in forming the Earth's surface.[54] Foreshadowed in these passages is the concern for the universalized vision of history that would surface more explicitly with the Romantics, in whose work nature's active powers were seen to be directly shaping not only the landscape, but also society and culture.

The concept of sublimity presented in the *Diaries* allows us to establish further linkages between subjective self and world that add depth to the speaker's communion with nature's vital force. As early as the *Letters*, Jovellanos had documented the intense experience of confronting the tremendous scope that nature so prodigally displays at times. At one point during his 1782 journey to Asturias, he comes upon the Puente Tuero pass and documents his encounter with the sublime. He applies the term *sublime* to refer to the splendour of the scene, but he also employs it to reference the Burkean "natural sublime," in which the enormity of nature that the individual is confronted with can be "whatever is in any sort terrible ... or operates in a manner analogous to terror."[55] The sheer length and breadth of the vista, and the pass's forbidding drops, reveal one of nature's most awe-inspiring and terror-provoking phenomena:

51 Sánchez Corredera, *Jovellanos y el jovellanismo*, 695. We must recall that, during the period of the *Diaries*, geology was an emerging science. Buffon had published his enormously popular *Epochs of Nature* in 1778, which Jovellanos knew well. Moreover, Feijóo's *Addendums* had appeared in print and included a disquisition on earthquakes directly inspired by the Lisbon tragedy of 1755, a tragedy that instigated a flurry of debates on everything from devil worship to planetary motion and would radically alter how geologic forces came to be interpreted. J.G. Herder's *Conjectures on the Beginning of Human History* (1786) and *Ideas on the Philosophy of the History of Mankind* (1784–91) had also appeared, and delivered a geologically dynamic vision of earth, characterized by violent volcanoes and earthquakes. For his part, Sir William Hamilton had recorded Mount Vesuvius's volcanic activity beginning in 1766 and wrote *Observations on Mount Vesuvius, Mount Etna, and Other Volcanos* (1772), a popular text that circulated widely throughout Spain in Italian and French translations.

52 Jovellanos, *Diarios*, vol. 1, 274.

53 Ibid., 457–8.

54 Ibid., 456.

55 Burke, "A Philosophical Enquiry," 131.

The sloped path of Villamanín that comes after leads to a greater altitude. Before ascending it, one has to enter on its flank by way of an extremely narrow pass leading through the rock, which forms the celebrated Puente Tuero crossing. If you could only see the sublimity of form and height of the two enormous quartz rocks there; if you could only see the perpendicular drops. It is a crossing that produces anxiety in fearful and inexperienced people, given that the lofty summit that can be seen from one part, and the deep precipice that drops to the river that runs in the deepest area of the other part, fills people unaccustomed to these types of situations with horror and fright. However, to the curious contemplator of nature, the feeling is quite the opposite! Those extremely high rocks, those venerable monuments of time that bring to mind the first ages of the world ... fill the spirit with profound and sublime ideas.[56]

In "Lessons on Rhetoric and Poetry," included in *The Curriculum on Castilian Humanities* of 1794, Jovellanos had expressed his affinity for the sublime, which he understood as an intense personal experience in and of itself, and as a stylistic device.[57] The "Lessons" likewise demonstrate that he had acquainted himself with the primary texts on the sublime published throughout the period, principally Edmund Burke's popular *Philosophical Enquiry into the Origin of Our Ideas of the Sublime and Beautiful* (1757).[58] For Jovellanos, the sublime is most apparent when the mind attempts to ponder the wondrous and ungraspable, which included nature's extraordinary display of vital force and its superior and divine status. Indeed, the imperfect movement of the mind toward the unfathomable is what exposes man's frailty.[59] In her study on Jovellanos's concept of the sublime, Ana Rueda establishes in what measure his appreciation of sublimity in the *Diaries* was tethered to "an important shift

56 Jovellanos, *Cartas del viaje a Asturias*, vol. 1, 104–5. When Jovellanos travels through the Puente Tuero pass years later in 1790, in the opposite direction, he would report once again on the sublimity of the scene. See Jovellanos, *Diarios I*, 121.

57 As Paul don Abott points out, Jovellanos's *Course on Castilian Humanities* was greatly informed by Hugh Blair's *Lectures on Rhetoric and Belles Letres*, particularly in terms of the definition, function, and style of poetry (279). See also John H.R. Polt's *Jovellanos and His English Sources: Economic, Philosophical, and Political Writings* for a more comprehensive view of the English influences on Jovellanos. Yvonne Fuentes's "British Aesthetics and the Picturesque in Spain: Jovellanos's Affinity with England" is also a valuable reference, 210–19.

58 "One author believes," Jovellanos points out in a critique levelled against Burke's *Philosophical Enquiry*, "that terror is the origin of the sublime ... We cannot agree with this opinion, since even though terrible objects of great sublimity exist, there are others that can cause considerable terror and not be sublime in the least" (*Obras de Jovellanos*, vol. 4, 282). Edmund Burke sustained that "terror is in all cases whatsoever ... the ruling principle of the sublime" (131).

59 Jovellanos, *Obras de Jovellanos*, vol. 4, 282.

toward a subjectivity (epiphanic) that is channeled by emotion as a formative principle."[60] For Rueda, Jovellanos inquired into those phenomena in nature that could potentially call into question the rational project and inform a deeper yearning for self-knowledge. She concludes that Jovellanos never teases out the full consequences of the sublime experience, since it is repeatedly truncated and veers in the end towards a scientific-utilitarian aesthetic based on the ideal of infinite (material) progress.[61] While there is little doubt that Jovellanos's notion of sublimity is informed by his reformism, we must consider that its very presence in his *Letters* and personal *Diaries* raises poignant questions concerning the self-nature divide and the knowability of nature's vital force itself. The sublime experience, insofar as it confronts the individual with a natural phenomenon that exceeds the limits of the imagination, necessarily involves imponderable extremes of scale. That is to say, it inserts into questions of the individual-nature divide the element of the incalculable, which is critical in coming to terms with Jovellanos's idea of a vitalized nature in which the subjective self is confronted with making sense of an experience that radically problematizes rationality and scientific culture. The essential sublimity of nature – its awesome vital force and the grand spectacle that Jovellanos comments upon in the *Letters* and *Diaries* – resists objectification and knowing: measurement, quantification, classification, and resolution are all frustrated. What we are left with is an aporia (or the abstract totality, in Kantian terms) that demands us to modify the way we cognize the world.

For Jean-François Lyotard, the sublime confronts us with an ungraspable abyss. He focuses specifically on Kant's notion of *Ernst*, or "seriousness," in which he identifies the notion of lack as an originary aspect of the sublime.[62] What he called the *differend* – the incommensurability that arises between the imagination and reason – is to be found "at the heart of sublime feeling: at the encounter of the two 'absolutes' equally 'present' to thought, the absolute whole when it conceives, the absolutely measured when it presents."[63] The *differend* transforms the sublime

60 Rueda, "Jovellanos en sus escritos íntimos," 491.

61 Ibid., 492–3.

62 Lyotard, *Lessons on the Analytic and the Sublime*, 75–6. Lyotard explains: "This is what must be understood in the *Ernst*, the 'seriousness,' with which Kant qualifies the activity of the imagination in the sublime. It is the seriousness of melancholy, the suffering of an irreparable lack, an absolute nostalgia for form's only always being form, that is, limitation ... Even as it deploys an unlimited field of proliferating forms before thought, the imagination remains a slave to its finitude, because each of the forms it invents and adds to the others remains limited by definition" (75–6).

63 Ibid., 123.

into "the transport that leads all thought (critical thought included) to its limits."[64] The point for Lyotard is that the *differend* makes apparent an "irreparable lack" in the sublime that need not be a negative aesthetic, but rather, in its resistance to knowing, can urge us forward, emblazon the yawning gap, reveal a horizon of possibility, and beckon us to reflect on language and new paradigms with which to engage the self-nature divide.[65] While Lyotard is theorizing the concept of the sublime from the perspective of postmodern criticism and its basic tenets of multiplicity and instability of meaning, his point concerning the manner in which the sublime signals and undercuts the very notion of limit is valid in the discussion of Jovellanos's concept of sublimity. Certainly, some of Jovellanos's most evocative, commanding, and so-called pre-Romantic discernments of nature's vital force are generated precisely in sublime moments when the instrumentalized logic of analytical observation runs aground.

We can proceed now to one of Jovellanos's oft-quoted passages in the *Diaries* dealing with nature's vital force, which for many readers unmistakably foreshadows a Romantic sensibility. All too often, however, the epistemological implications of Jovellanos's insights go unheeded, and what is most celebrated in this passage is his portrayal of an impending tempest:

> Clouds, calm … There was a doubtful and sad light in the sky; the extension of the sea was revealed from time to time by formidable lightning bolts that broke the distant horizon; the muted sound of the waters breaking against the rocks at the foot of the mountain could be heard; the solitude, calm, and silence of all living things made this moment sublime and magnificent beyond all comprehension … Man! If you want to be prosperous, contemplate nature and discover it. The source of the scant pleasure and happiness that were given to your being can be found in [nature].[66]

Jovellanos faces the impending tempest that is soaring on the horizon and is struck by nature's awesome force. Of note is that the sublime experience – the phenomenon which exceeds "all comprehension" – ironically mediates his powerful connection with the natural realm. Revealingly, Jovellanos the observer, the advocate of logic and reason committed to the useful sciences and its methods, acknowledges that observation alone is insufficient to determine nature's workings. Nature

64 Ibid., x.
65 Ibid., 75.
66 Jovellanos, *Diarios*, vol. 1, 467–8.

must be experienced: "contemplate nature and discover it."[67] This statement in itself is illuminating of his progressive shift in conceptualizing the self-nature relationship. That is, the individual must not remain satisfied with the ocularcentrist project of reason, but should strive to also attain a more immediate knowledge of nature (even if it exceeds all rational comprehension) and explore the subjective sphere of sensibility.

What Jovellanos seems to suggest here and in other parts of the *Diaries* is that when nature, in all its arresting and vitalized power, urges the individual forward to the threshold of his conceptual capacities in moments of sublimity, it discloses a new synthesis of the self-nature relationship. This new synthesis is mapped out from within the unity of nature when the subjective self is experientially brought into awareness of the animated totality it cannot possibly come to know, and in which, nevertheless, it directly participates. As Meléndez Valdés poetized it in "Immensity of Nature and the Ineffable Goodness of its Author": "So much sovereign union/that the human mind cannot fathom."[68] This paradoxical tension, so Romantic in its outlook, makes apparent the possibility of a deeper self-understanding in communing with nature, and it also opens the subjective self to a renewed vision of what Emily Brady calls the "complex side of environmental experience," in which "we grasp nature as something that cannot be appropriated."[69] Thus, the experience of sublimity collapses objective and subjective spheres and makes evident that an embodied engagement with a dynamic, vitalized nature can indeed forge a new understanding of the world.

ORGANIC UNITY IN *ORATION PRONOUNCED IN THE ASTURIAN INSTITUTE ON THE STUDY OF THE NATURAL SCIENCES*

What is foregrounded in the *Letters* and *Diaries* is not only the concept of mystery in nature that the Romantics found so compelling, but also the idea that there can be no certain answers to questions concerning the immanent forces of life that bind the subjective self to the natural realm. As Russell Sebold has demonstrated in his work on Spanish Romanticism, various Romantic precepts were beginning to take form in Spain during this period, such as man's emergent sense of individuality and preoccupation with self, the disenchantment and melancholia with one's lot in

67 Ibid., 468.

68 Meléndez Valdés, "Inmensidad de la Naturaleza," 164–5.

69 Brady, "The Environmental," 182.

the world, and the obsessive treatment of life and death.[70] The individual's estrangement from nature is in fact problematized in several areas of Jovellanos's thought. For critic Ramos Gorostiza, there are two distinct personas, as it were, that condition Jovellanos's thinking on nature: there is Jovellanos the economist, and Jovellanos the pre-Romantic. While Ramos Gorostiza acknowledges that both personas obviously coexist within Jovellanos's thinking, he believes they are relatively independent. In all likelihood, he argues, "[Jovellanos's] pre-Romantic attitude did not develop beyond an abstract stance, which was restricted almost always to the expression of feelings in the private sphere."[71] My argument has been that Jovellanos's view of the self-nature relationship is more dialogic and integral than it first appears. In other words, nature is elusive, enigmatic, present, and *alive* precisely in those conceptual spaces that seemingly convey its legible, quantifiable, and passive thingness. The analytic appraisal of nature in Jovellanos's *Letters* and *Diaries* stands in sharp contrast to an embodied, subjective awareness rooted in the indeterminate realm of feeling on the one hand, and the abstract realm of the vitalized sublime on the other. It could be objected, as writer and critic Gaspar Gómez de la Serna does, that given the wealth of quantitative data and empirical observations in these texts, these dialogic moments are minor reflections incapable of divulging much about Jovellanos's thinking.[72] Yet, we cannot forget that what frames the quantitative data and empirical observations is always the living landscape itself.[73] These reflections, therefore, are crucially important, for they disclose – particularly embedded as they are at the heart of Jovellanos's world view – something about the epistemological limits of Enlightenment rationality when it comes to vital force.

We can say that, as an object of study, Jovellanos no doubt considers nature as a realm that can be adapted to satisfy human needs and be suitably transformed for the good of mankind. His *Report on the Agrarian Law* develops this type of analytical insight when he argues that nature's "encumbrances" to progress can be duly examined and overcome.[74] Nevertheless, nature also offers itself for a different type of study. Through the embodied experience of nature's vital force and inscrutability, the subjective self can glimpse the universe's "beautiful

70 Sebold, *Trayectoria del romanticismo español*, 13–42.
71 Ramos Gorostiza, "Jovellanos y la naturaleza," n.p.
72 Gómez de la Serna (Gaspar), *Jovellanos, el español perdido*, vol. 1., 282–90.
73 Gracia Noriega, "Jovellanos," 119.
74 Jovellanos, *Obras de Jovellanos*, 7: 160.

construction," to use poet Meléndez Valdés's words.[75] While the Enlightenment creed of self-improvement is operative in this type of study, the subjective experience associated with it not only undercuts the objective stance of the observer, but, just as importantly, it encroaches upon the unknowable as constructive ground for inquiry. This synthetic study informs Jovellanos's thinking from his early years of the *Letters* of 1782 (in "Epistle to Bátilo": "Its sphere is most noble: the universe/is a code; study it and be wise"), to his *Inaugural Oration for the Opening of the Royal Institute of Asturias* of 1794 ("If any study can guide us to truth, it is the study of Nature, of that remarkable order that reigns in it"),[76] to his *Oration Pronounced in the Asturian Institute on the Study of the Natural Sciences* of 1799 ("[C]alled to the study of nature, you will house in this land the precious truths in which the prosperity of nations and the perfection of the human race is determined"),[77] to his *Discourse on Historical Geography* of 1800 ("The knowledge of nature is the objective of all the sciences; but, man cannot ascend to such knowledge if he does not study the planet in which he lives, and if he does not examine the relations that connect him to the universe's grand system").[78]

I have distinguished between two types of study in Jovellanos's thinking – the analytical and subjective – for the sake of clarity. The truth is that the study of nature unfolded for Jovellanos along a gradient from the finite to the infinite, the knowable to the unknowable, the particular to the universal, and the analytical to the subjective. Nature could be grasped through the firm measurements of the useful sciences, as he called them, yet these same measurements, as they encroached further upon their objects of inquiry and attempted to determine greater vital unities and coherences, pointed toward the unfathomable Absolute. He acknowledges in his lecture *Oration Pronounced in the Asturian Institute on the Study of the Natural Sciences* that this larger synthetic study, envisaged in its most encompassing breadth and totality, can be regarded as a new science of nature's vital force; a new science, moreover, capable of guiding humanity to a more perfect knowledge of itself. Delivered in the Royal Asturian Institute on 7 April 1799, the *Oration* admonishes the younger generation of natural scientists that this new science will require of the individual an altogether different disposition and approach to nature:

75 This verse appears in Meléndez Valdés's ode "Vanity of Man's Complaint against His Maker."

76 Jovellanos, *Oraciones y discursos*, 114.

77 Ibid., 177.

78 Ibid., 138.

[Nature's] novelty, grandeur, and very *uncertainty* demand from you a constant effort, a profound pondering, and a heroic patience. The skies, the earth, however far the vast reach of the universe, will be the object of your contemplation; but this splendid, this immense object ... is mute and silent for you. Indeed, it says nothing yet to your reason, and it will say nothing as long as you do not put your minds into commerce with nature itself. *Discover nature to perfect your being* ... [S]ee here the purpose of the new science you will study. It is the science of man.[79]

With the *Letters* and *Diaries* serving as a backdrop, it becomes evident in the *Oration* how Jovellanos's thinking on nature has progressed to accommodate an organicist aesthetic. In many ways, the *Oration* represents one of the high points of Jovellanos's theorizing on the self-nature relationship. He opens the *Oration* by invoking the ancients who first contemplated nature as an extension of the universe. Over the generations, he argues, philosophy transformed into a practice of system-building shot through with conjecture about the forces that governed nature. Moreover, the very idea of observing and experiencing the world firsthand was left in obscurity, and thus, "while the partisan spirit propagated and defended these illusions, nature, abandoned to the disputes and whims of these sects, seemed to have returned to the tenebrous chaos from where it first originated in the beginning."[80] Aristotle was the most egregious offender in this respect for Jovellanos. His notions of quantity and quality and his theory of universals collected in *The Categories*, *Physics*, and *Metaphysics* established a hollow foundation – particularly as Scholastic theology construed it – upon which to build an epistemology of nature and its vital force: "Aristotle led philosophy away from the path of truth."[81] With Francis Bacon's appeal to observation and empiricism at the turn of the seventeenth century, philosophy was finally restored to its rightful place.

Jovellanos admires several figures beside Bacon, including Joseph Priestly, often considered a vitalist for discovering the powers of dephlogisticated air (oxygen) and his subsequent research into the inherent forces of matter. Jovellanos reserves his highest praise for "the immortal Buffon," and it remains clear that he was well acquainted with Buffon's monumental *Natural History*, as many *ilustrados* were during this period. Jovellanos had extolled the text in an earlier writing, where he stated:

79 Ibid., 177. My emphasis. This *Oration* of 1799 should not be confused with the important speech Jovellanos delivered in 1782 at the Society of Friends of the Nation, titled "On the Need to Cultivate the Natural Sciences in the Principality."

80 Ibid., 179.

81 Ibid., 180.

"the celebrated history of the wise Count Buffon … written with elegance, judgment, and a profound knowledge of the natural sciences, has been translated into our language with great fidelity and purity."[82] The translation of *Natural History* that Jovellanos was referring to was José Clavijo y Fajardo's popular translations, which began appearing in print in 1786. Clavijo y Fajardo's "Prologue" to Buffon's *Natural History* was one of the most cited documents on the natural sciences in late-eighteenth-century Spain.[83] In the *Oration*, Jovellanos applauds Buffon for essentially reintroducing nature into philosophy: "The immortal Buffon, returning to the first days of the world, resolving its ancient epochs, illuminating the skies and intermediary regions, and running with the stride of a giant across the earth, crowned that glorious monument that Pliny had erected for nature."[84]

Buffon's *Natural History* was an encyclopedic work in the true sense of the word, and greatly stimulated the advancement of vitalist theory in the life sciences. He sustained that "matter alone, though perfectly organized, can produce neither language nor thought, unless it be animated by a superior principle."[85] He theorized innate means by which life came into existence, and he postulated that myriad living organic parts, which were primitive, incorruptible, and common to all animals and vegetables, combined into an infinite number of assemblages to produce organized, living beings. The implication of Buffon's theory of living organic parts was that nature was not simply synonymous with God, but that inherent within it there existed a number of processes that generated and directed a vital force. His theory of *moule intérieur* (internal mould) argued precisely this point. The *moule intérieur* was the inherent agency of living matter that allowed it to "mould" itself into specific unities to produce complex living organisms. As Buffon explained it: "In the same manner as we can make moulds by which we give to the exterior of bodies whatever figure we please, suppose that Nature can make moulds by which it gives [to living bodies] not only exterior figure but also internal form; would this not be a means by which reproduction could be brought

82 Jovellanos, *Obras publicadas e inéditas*, 185.

83 In Clavijo y Fajardo's prologue, he not only historically situated Buffon within the emerging field of the natural sciences, but also analyzed his major arguments and revealed their underlying complexity in relation to theology. For a more detailed account of Clavijo y Fajardo's influence on Spanish science in this respect, see Negrín Fajardo Olegario's "José Clavijo y Fajardo, Enlightened Naturalist," 139–56.

84 Jovellanos, *Oraciones y discursos*, 183.

85 Quoted in Olson, *Science and Religion, 1450–1900*, 184.

about?"[86] In her work on the influence of vitalist theory on Romantic literature, Denise Gigante has traced how Buffon's complex concept of *moule intérieur* was reinterpreted in different scientific circles throughout Europe in the late-eighteenth century to mean vital force, a change that signalled a "paradigm shift in the study of organic form: life now denoted power rather than structure ... [T]his shift entailed the move from empiricist natural history to a more speculative natural philosophy."[87] Buffon's ideas of vital force were not very well received in certain spheres of the Spanish medico-scientific community, as might be expected. In the *Medical and Surgical Dictionary; or, the Medico-Surgical Manual* of 1807, the physician Antonio Ballano condemned Buffon's observations on anatomy and physiology in particular, and argued that the French naturalist's system of a life-bearing *moule intérieur*, even in its simplest form, was unintelligible. Furthermore, Buffon's oeuvre was filled with "offensive errors," which included such far-fetched ideas as a female seminal fluid.[88]

While Buffon's vitalism was largely ignored by Spanish medicine, it was his sacrilegious theories about the origins of the earth that aroused the greatest criticism. In *Natural History*, and then again in *Epochs of Nature*, Buffon had considered the origins of the solar system and speculated that the planets had come into being as a result of a comet impacting the sun. He believed it was feasible to study the world's surface and determine empirically the ancient and cataclysmic forces that had formed it. In calculating the cooling rate of iron in the supplement "Introduction to the History of Minerals," which was added to *Natural History* in 1774, he postulated that the earth had advanced through seven distinct epochs of transformation spanning roughly seventy-five thousand years. In these works, Buffon, whether wittingly or not, advanced a "countertheology" that not only frontally challenged the Biblical narrative of the earth's creation and its age, but also obviated the Flood.[89] The Faculty of Theology of the Sorbonne had sharply condemned Buffon's *Epochs of Nature* in 1779 for its blasphemy and insisted that he formally retract his findings, which he did.[90]

86 Quoted in Roe, *Matter, Life, and Generation*, 16.

87 Gigante, *Life*, 16.

88 Ballano, *Diccionario*, 347.

89 Brooke, *Science and Religion*, 321.

90 In José María Alea's *The Life of the Count Buffon* (1797), a popular Spanish translation of an anonymous biography of Buffon, we gain a clearer picture of the religious criticisms levelled against Buffon in Spain during this period. In the lengthy "Prologue by the Translator" and "Appendix," Alea lauds Buffon and clarifies various of his more contentious ideas to demonstrate that he was in fact "a true Christian philosopher," who

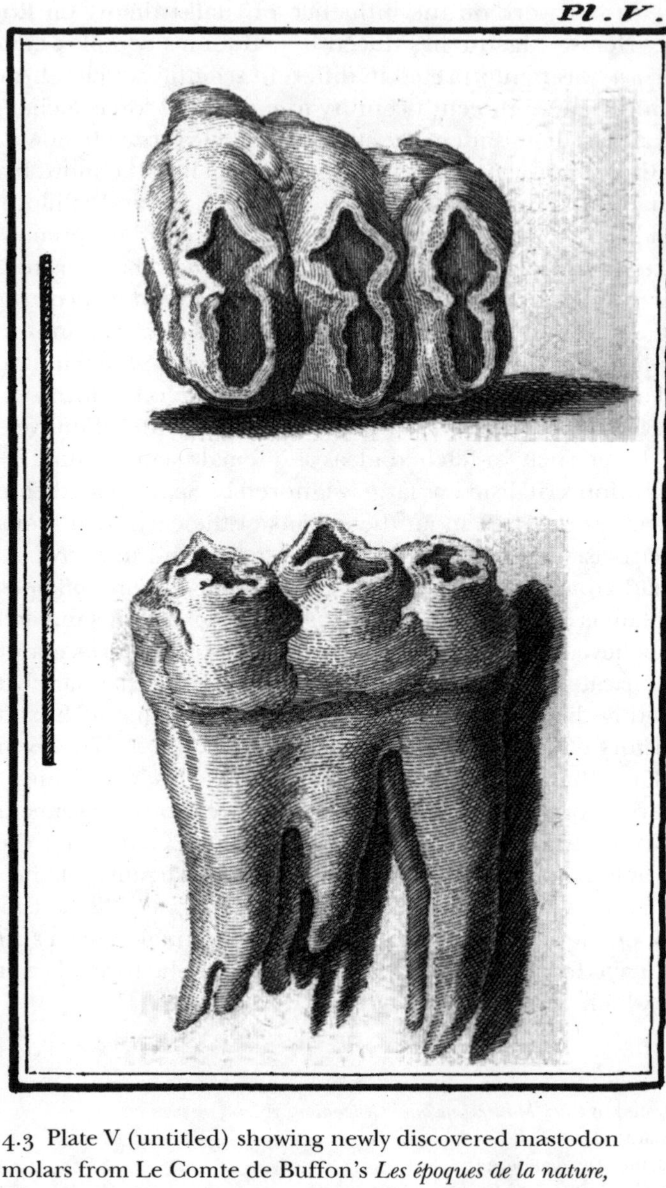

4.3 Plate V (untitled) showing newly discovered mastodon molars from Le Comte de Buffon's *Les époques de la nature, Tome Premier*, 1778.

Jovellanos's applause for Buffon in the *Oration* is more than casual, particularly in light of his references to other renowned naturalists, such as Jacob Theodor Klein, Bernard-Germain de Lacépède, Ferchault de Réaumur, and Carl Linnaeus. As Reill reminds us, Buffon's definition of a natural system served as a powerful stimulus in the development of the life sciences throughout the late Enlightenment, and it radically influenced how nature was interpreted as inherently imbued with vital force.[91] The organic world view Jovellanos examines throughout the *Oration* is permeated with Buffon's vitalist concepts, and it aspires to map out a new science of nature's vital force. Jovellanos begins in much the same manner as Buffon in his *Epochs of History* considering the movements of the solar system and the infinite galaxies that fill the skies. A ubiquitous "active nature," he proposes, impels the universe: it is a vital force generated in the ceaseless activity of reproduction and conservation that traverses every living organism. He entreats his audience at the Royal Asturian Institute to ponder this life-bearing energy: "Do you see that far-reaching region that extends between the sky and earth? It is empty to your eyes, but imagine your surprise when you learn that it is filled and penetrated with an active nature … which is called elemental because it seems to be perennially at work in the successive reproduction of being and the conservation of everything!"[92] The term "active nature" within this context of natural and life sciences conjures up the vitalist active principle that not only Buffon, but also John Needham and Jean-Baptiste Lamarck, theorized directed nature's vital force (Buffon was particularly fond of the word *active* and often employed it in several parts of

---

recognized "the omnipotent and invisible hand of God in all of the workings of the universe, from the largest star to the most imperceptible grain of sand" (92). As Alea goes about defending Buffon as a true man of faith, he addresses the outrage of religious apologists and traditionalists in Spain when confronted with Buffon's notion that natural death is not necessarily painful and should not be feared (this proposition countered the traditional belief that death was painful, given that it was the precise moment when the soul tore away from the body). For Buffon, death was part of life as soon as the body stopped growing, and the moment of death itself marked the cessation of vital functions in the body: "the body therefore dies little by little and in parts, its movement diminishes by degrees, life fades away by successive imperceptible changes" (quoted in Gigante, 170). Alea urges his readers to consider how the French naturalist has been unfairly maligned, since "the sublimity of his philosophical aims and his religious sentiments" were readily apparent if one carefully read his works (121). I would have liked to have consulted Jaume Josa i Llorca's unpublished doctoral dissertation *Buffon in Spain: The Influence That the Scientific Ideas of Georges-Louis Leclerc, Comte de Buffon Had in Spain* (1988) to devise a fuller picture of Buffon's influence during this period, but it was impossible to secure.

91 Reill, *Vitalizing Nature*, 137.

92 Jovellanos, *Oraciones y discursos*, 185.

his oeuvre to emphasize what he called nature's powers of growth, movement, and change, which acted upon the *moule intérieur* and stimulated the constitution of its living form). Within this active nature, the sun for Jovellanos "vivifies all that lives," and its rays penetrate every organism and provide it with a life-giving heat: "And the stirring of this heat and elemental fire, this soul of nature, which is disseminated in all bodies, penetrates them, fills them, and prolongs them. In this way, it resides in everything from the softest clay to the hardest stone ... This most powerful agent moves them and penetrates them, its influence foments and vivifies them."[93] The air is an elemental ether whose "movement forms the salutiferous and purifying winds that conserves existence and life."[94] Water is likewise teeming with "richness and ... life."[95]

Nature in the *Oration* is conceived of as a unifying vital force that directs the growth and complex movements of living organisms. Jovellanos's language is littered with allusions to the vitalist terminology that had infiltrated the life sciences by the turn of the nineteenth century, thanks in large measure to Buffon. Terms like active, agitation, existence, prolong, powerful, vigour, vivify, and life stand out repeatedly. At one point in his lecture, Jovellanos refers to the plant kingdom, noting its unifying "vigour" and "life."[96] When he then muses about "the active and obliging animal kind," he poses the question of human life specifically. With microscopy and embryology on his mind, he maintains that life begets life, given that the human body itself is an extraordinarily complex and wondrous system sustained by its inherent vital force. Every bodily part, and every minutest cell, contains within it its own vital cosmos of life-giving relations: "Life itself is nourishment for life, and living beings are nourishment for other living beings. We ourselves, our flesh, blood, and bones contain within them many families of living beings, which perhaps contain and give shelter and nourishment to many other living beings."[97] The body's construction, then, not only reflects, but intimately participates in, nature's vital force, and he exclaims: "[H]ow portentous is [nature's] force!"[98]

Once again, Jovellanos tackles the notion of epistemological limit as an affirmative and constructive factor in the study of nature. The mysteries of nature's vital force do not undercut objectivity and measurement

93 Ibid., 186.
94 Ibid.
95 Ibid., 187.
96 Ibid., 189.
97 Ibid., 188.
98 Ibid., 191.

per se, but rather perfect them insofar as they urge the individual to develop a deeper and more integral understanding of the world. Thus, he has no qualms at this stage in acknowledging "*man's feeble reason*."[99] In his study on Jovellanos and the life sciences in eighteenth-century Spain, Horacio Capel writes that what Jovellanos articulates with clarity in his *Oration* is the "bankruptcy of mathematical methods and generalizations in the study of nature … as Buffon had defended," and the idea that observation and description merely represent "where the study of nature begins."[100] Indeed, the *Oration* intersects late-eighteenth-century vitalism and advocates that nature should be discovered through observation *and* intuition, and not solely through the methods of empirical reasoning. While Jovellanos employs terms like "nature's ladder" and "immense chain of beings," which conjure up the hierarchized and static composition of nature associated with the great chain of being, he similarly extends the meaning of terms like grand system, relations, animation, and movement to convey nature's vital becoming and how it can be observed, intuited, and reflected upon, but never fully known. Though he may believe in a hierarchical ordering of beings in nature, he nevertheless places these beings in complex interrelations and dynamisms, which speak to the pervasive vital force that is apparent even in the most microscopic of organisms and links them to the immensity of the animated universe. He raises the rhetorical question: "Is there an organism [in the plant kingdom] that does not have the means to conserve life and propagate its species?"[101]

What Jovellanos draws from Buffon is clearly not the Enlightenment dream of crafting a complete and unified history of the natural world. Rather, he homes in on those aspects of Buffon's thinking and disposition toward the world that emphasize not only the grandeur of nature, but also its dynamic vital force, which the French naturalist described as "the wonderful harmony and connection that subsists between all the different branches [of nature]."[102] As Ashton Nichols has demonstrated, these vitalist aspects within Buffon's concept of nature will directly influence Romantics likes Coleridge, Wordsworth, Keats, and Shelley.[103] Throughout his *Oration*, Jovellanos repeatedly challenges his audience of young natural scientists at the Royal Asturian Institute to commune with nature and observe its life-giving movements, investigate its vital

99 Ibid., 184. My emphasis.
100 Capel, "Filosofía y ciencia," 78.
101 Jovellanos, *Oraciones y discursos*, 196.
102 Buffon, *Natural History*, abridged, 530.
103 Nichols, "The Loves of Plants and Animals," n.p.

properties, contemplate its dynamic ebbs and flows, and examine its wealth of living forms with intention and enthusiasm (it bears noting that Jovellanos followed his own advice here and penned a work on botany in 1801 titled *Treaty of Mallorcan Botany, or Medicinal Flora of Valldemossa*).[104] The study of nature, he declares, demands more than the Enlightenment's classification systems of organisms, a point Buffon himself underscored at various points in his *Natural History*. For Jovellanos, this type of "museum order of nature," as Paul Smethurst calls it, is clearly limited.[105] To begin with, it affords copious data about nature without really asking the most searching question of all: what exactly animates it? Jovellanos asks:

Who can explain the nature of a magnet ... or the attractive and repulsive quality of amber[?] ... Who can say why the fire that melts platinum leaves asbestos unscathed, or why platinum stubbornly resists the hammer, which can extend an atom of gold to incalculable distances? ... Who can explain the virtues of this world we tread upon, which is the cradle and the grave of all that exists upon it? ... Here is how the simple observation of nature will guide you to deeper investigations of natural philosophy, because you must know that your spirit will never be content with the counting and classification of beings, but will aspire to understand their properties.[106]

Jovellanos contends that the zeal for classification that characterizes Enlightenment thinking is really man's misguided compulsion to organize the world, to make it completely comprehensible, even though such comprehensibility remains beyond reach. He does not directly address the bitter quarrels over taxonomy that marked the Enlightenment period, yet he makes it clear that classification divides nature in artificial and detrimental ways and provides no real insight into the vital unity of its processes. Indeed, this vital unity, as Jovellanos argues, must become the fundamental focus of the natural sciences, given that it sheds much needed light on the linkages between matter and vital force in the extraordinary fact of existence:

These classifications are our doing, not [nature's]. Nature only produces individuals, whose numbers, properties, and the relations that join them, we only understand in a very limited sense. Without a doubt, everything is connected in

104 According to Ángel Dotor, Jovellanos's *Treaty of Mallorcan Botany or Medicinal Flora of Valldemosa* "constitutes one of the classic texts in the bibliography on Mallorca" (138).

105 Smethurst, *Travel Writing*, 5.

106 Jovellanos, *Oraciones y discursos*, 190.

the great work of creation … Is there, by chance, anyone who can fathom the intermediary essences that the Almighty placed between feeling and animation, animation and life, and among life, movement, and existence?[107]

In considering nature as a unified "empire of existence," as Jovellanos refers to it at one point, the individual would be well equipped to contemplate a dynamic world formed and sustained by a unifying vital force.[108] He also uses the term "ecstasy" in the *Oration* in all its transcendent power to indicate the passionate sentiment roused in the individual who is capable of entering nature and apprehending, if only fleetingly, the sheer scope of this force. There is also a very real moral and socio-epistemological significance in grasping nature's connectedness. As Jovellanos suggests, a re-evaluation of nature's unifying vital force would open a window into the complex processes of the individual's concrete environs, interpersonal relations, bonds to social communities, and, ultimately, the ideal of subjective self as inflected through the Absolute. Through nature, then, the individual could work toward ulterior and improved models of society and acquire an ever-expanding knowledge of the ties that bonded the particular and the universal. This subjective rapport with nature will powerfully inform the Romantic aesthetic that was beginning to emerge in Schelling's *System der Naturphilosophie*, Friedrich Schlegel's *Athenaeum Fragmente*, Novalis's *The Novices of Sais*, and Wordsworth's *The Prelude* at the turn of the century, precisely when Jovellanos wrote his *Oration*. Furthermore, Jovellanos's desire to instruct future natural scientists in the marvels of nature's vital force can be said to dovetail with the Romantic pedagogical project of disseminating an active world view erected upon personal discovery, self-development, social improvement, and infinite becoming:

You are fortunate if, in the middle of the depravity of this century in which superstition and impiety quarrel over the empire of knowledge, you can follow the only path that [knowledge] lays out for you to reach its temple! … You are fortunate if your spirit is enlightened with the understanding of the truths that nature provides, and in perfecting your heart with the virtues to which it leads, you can reach the true wisdom that will ensure your happiness, improve your being, and accelerate the perfection of the human race![109]

107 Ibid., 193.
108 Ibid., 183.
109 Ibid., 205.

Read together, Jovellanos's *Letters*, *Diaries*, and *Oration* offer one of the most compelling pictures of nature's vital force in late-eighteenth-century Spain, a picture that is profoundly dynamic and presages concepts of organicism and becoming that would find mature expression with the Romantics and their fascination with life. Indeed, these texts not only add a richness and depth to our historical understanding of the multiformity of pre-Romantic thought in Spain, but also establish an important claim within the Spanish context for a more evocative concept of animated nature than has been suggested up to this point. Simply put: nature's vital force entwined self and world in a way unlike any other, a way that was intuitive, synthetic, poetic, and revelatory. This view of nature's vital force, whose significance in establishing a bridge between Enlightenment and Romantic thought has remained largely unaddressed in the Spanish context, would connect with Spanish Romanticism in the 1830s.[110] For various socio-political reasons, which include the turmoil of the last years of Charles IV's reign, the War of Independence, and Ferdinand VII's repressive reign, the organic expression of nature in Spanish literature and science in the early decades of the nineteenth century paled in comparison to that in Germany and England. That said, there is no question that it was certainly felt beyond its original time and place and left its imprint on the Spanish cultural imaginary in the work of José de Espronceda, Gustavo Adolfo Bécquer, Rosalía de Castro, Julián Sanz del Río, Francisco Giner de los Ríos, Antonio Machado, and Juan Ramón Jiménez, to name only a few. For Morales Moya, who has devoted some attention to the liberal impulses of the Spanish Enlightenment, one of the aspects that makes Jovellanos's thinking on nature so prescient and modern in this respect is its palpable "ecological sentiment *avant la lettre*."[111]

110 To provide one notable example in the sciences, the liberal physician and surgeon Juan Mosácula Cabrera would write his *Elements of Special or Human Physiology* in 1830 predicated on an organicist teleology that rooted the fundamentals of human physiology in nature's vital force. Inspired by French vitalists like Anthelme Richerand, Mosácula Cabrera invokes the hierarchy of organisms to imagine the harmony that unites all life forms: "In effect, the simplest and seemingly formless mineral and the most perfect individual on the scale of living beings are intimately connected. A consistency and harmony dominates everything. Moreover, each object, and each individual, examined in and of itself, offers the naturalist and physiologist the opportunity to observe that everything is exactly balanced. Each object, and each invididual, is also of interest when examining the formation of simple beings of almost imperceptible life, as well as [complex] beings constituted by various elements and whose vital phenomena are as palpable as they are portentous" (1). See also Josep Barona Vilars's "The Physiological Work of Juan Mosácula Cabrera," 5–28.

111 Morales Moya, "Jovellanos," 49.

What becomes apparent in tracing Jovellanos's progression from the *Letters* to the *Oration* is his awakening to what A.N. Whitehead called the grand "protest on behalf of the organic view of nature," an awakening that promised the individual a new appreciation of the natural order that was empowering and fundamentally challenged the authority of reason.[112] The productive irony that reverberates throughout Jovellanos's works and extends to later treatises like *On English Architecture and So-called Gothic* of 1805 is likewise inescapable, and, in many ways, it is what imbues them with such Romantic expressiveness and significance. Indeed, while his thinking is seemingly anchored in the authority of reason and its analytical observation, it nevertheless gestures repeatedly toward the enigmatic "formed incomprehensibility," as Novalis referred to it, that Romantics admired everywhere in living nature.[113] Nature's vital force, we could say, opened Jovellanos to the subjective potentialities of plumbing the world beyond the limits of reason, and as he himself admitted, he was the better for it.

112 Whitehead, *Science and the Modern World*, 118.

113 Quoted in Behler, *German Romantic Literary Theory*, 200. In *On English Architecture and So-called Gothic*, we find a similar privileging of the subjective experience of nature. In this letter, Jovellanos speaks more confidently about "what is sentimental," which refers to the vitality and mystery of nature capable of stirring powerful emotions in the observer that defy objectivist assumptions. On this point, Yvonne Fuentes notes how this subjective experience established a unique counterpoint with reason and objectivity in this letter: "Despite the classical bias attributed to Jovellanos, this essay of 1805 clearly indicates a preference toward melancholy, ambiguity and mystery, toward what the writer calls the 'sentimental.' 'Sentimental,' then, depends not on rational perception and/or objective criteria, but on emotions provoked by the senses and the imagination, and thus utterly internal and subjective" (215).

PART THREE

From Neo-Hippocratism to the Avant-Garde

5

Pursuing the Modern at the End of an Age: Positivist Materialism and the Krausist Ideal in Pedro Mata y Fontanet and Julián Sanz del Río

The vital power is merely the *vis medicatrix naturae.*
Anthelme Richerand, *Nouveaux éléments de physiologie*[1]

NINETEENTH-CENTURY SPAIN offers a unique picture of the modern processes of change that positioned the body at the centre of aesthetic and philosophical discourses. During this period, the question of vital force acquired a new significance, not only in Spain, but throughout Europe, particularly given the topographies of force that permeated nineteenth-century culture with the spread of Romantic science, industrial development, technological progress, and the emergence of positivism and evolutionism. It should be noted, however, that Spanish science entered a period of crisis early on with the War of Independence and Ferdinand VII's absolutist reign. Between 1808 and 1833, many of Spain's most illustrious minds either fled the country or were imprisoned. The turmoil with France, coupled with the loss of Spanish colonies in the Americas, had precipitated an economic crisis, which played a decisive role in the impoverishment of the country's intellectual and scientific life. This included the near-collapse of its hospitals, medical academies, and surgical schools.[2] The ill-fated Constitution of 1812 and the liberal agenda it promised also played a hand in instigating the profound and drawn-out social crisis that isolated Spain from the rest of Europe and restricted its potential to stimulate political reform and sustainable

1 Richerand, *Elements of Physiology*, 44.
2 López Piñero, "Enfermedad y medicina," 25.

development. "The return of Ferdinand VII [in 1814]," as Barona Vilar explains, "meant more than the return of a dynasty: it represented a step backwards [for the country], the re-engagement of a set of values and a social model that were already mortally wounded."[3] Several of the substantive cultural and scientific gains made in the Enlightenment were reversed during this period: the country's wide-ranging inoculation programs, for instance, which were the result of progressive legislation inspired by the British and French sanitary movements of the late-eighteenth century, fell into neglect. Needless to say, the consequences of this neglect were far-reaching and painfully apparent in urban areas. The scarcity of scientific funding during the period also hampered the elaboration of well-articulated and innovative research. The censorship and repression of journals, media, and foreign print materials and ephemera also made it difficult for Spanish scholars to dialogue with their counterparts abroad and foster the atmosphere of openness and rigour necessary to inspire original scholarship.

With the consolidation of María Cristina's regency in 1833, the country began to make meaningful strides in modernizing its scientific infrastructure and its institutions of higher learning.[4] By the 1840s, Spain's intellectual culture had improved notably with the return of exiles from abroad, as well as with the easing of censorship laws and the expansion of the literary and scientific print industry. Yet, there was significant resistance to what was perceived as the expansion of liberal and Romantic ideals in Spain after the death of Ferdinand VII and the subsequent fall of the *antiguo régimen.* In his study on Spanish Romanticism, Philip Silver is right to remind us that Spanish Romantic thought in the nineteenth century was predominantly conservative and Biedermeierian. However, from the moment Juan Nicolás Böhl de Faber famously expounded on A.W. Schlegel's admiration for Calderonian theatre in 1814, there emerges in the following three decades a Romantic awakening grounded in radicalism, community action, and labour participation.[5]

The Spanish nobility was especially concerned with losing more political ground during this period, and it actively worked to ally itself with the

3 Barona Vilar, *La doctrina y el laboratorio,* 27.

4 The Liberal Triennium represented a bright spot during the pre-1833 period that saw the founding of three medical journals and the publication of over one hundred articles and books on modern science and medicine. There were also several proposals to overhaul Spain's scientific and medical institutions, but they were met with resistance, and finally failed with the restoration of Ferdinand VII's government in 1823. See José Javier Viñes, "La sanidad," 31–2.

5 Zavala, *Historia de la literatura española,* 302–3.

up-and-coming middle class. In many respects, the symbolic *nobleza-burguesía* alliance resonated with the spirit of Prime Minister Ramón María Narváez's conservatism during the 1840s and 1850s. During this period, Narváez devised a *moderantista* solution to Spain's socio-political development that was capable of quelling liberal radicalism, restricting the expansion of new scientific movements deemed heretical or extreme, restoring the full powers of the noble class and its Church, and promoting the type of stable modernization that fell in line with the State's conservative policies. The *moderado* years represented a balancing act of institutional reforms conceived around the shared socio-political objectives of the *nobleza* and *burguesía* and their anti-liberal agenda. As historian Charles Esdaile points out, the Spanish constitution of 1845 was "[p]repared by a committee consisting of Narváez and a variety of *moderado* worthies, [it] deemed sovereignty to rest not with the people, but with the monarch and the *cortes*; increased the power of the throne; proclaimed Spain to be Catholic; declared civil liberties to be subject to 'regulation.'"[6] Yet, liberalism and scientific positivism gained momentum during the *moderado* years, despite the opposition. Between 1835 and 1868, Spanish liberal ideals acquired more concrete political form and introduced into the country a wealth of scientific views from abroad, including the latest vitalist theories that were revolutionizing physiology, hygiene, and homeopathy. In Spain, like elsewhere in Europe, the significant socio-political shifts, instigated in part by new currents of scientific discovery during the *moderado* period, increasingly legitimized the narratives of reform and weakened the Church's ideological appeal. We need only consider the proliferation of progressive publications in Spain at the time, such as *El Dominé, La Antorcha, Revolución*, or *La Abeja*, to appreciate how scientific discourses challenged Church-sponsored *moderantismo* and played a hand in clearing a path to the 1868 revolution and its ideological program of freedom of religion, free association, the expansion of the university curriculum, and universal suffrage, among other things.

During this period of great friction and upheaval, neo-Hippocratic theory gained ascendancy and provided familiar conceptual frameworks with which to assimilate and challenge the scientific advancements sweeping across Europe. Throughout Ferdinand VII's reign, scientific communities in Spain had in fact remained largely committed to the neo-Hippocratic vitalism that had characterized the best of French science. After 1840, however, as these various currents of liberal and

6 Esdaile, *Spain in the Liberal Age*, 86.

scientific thought began to infiltrate Spanish society more freely, a much-more-complex picture emerged. By the late 1850s, as we shall see, leading materialists like Pedro Mata y Fontanet had advocated for an aggressive agenda of reform. In analyzing what came to be known as the Great Debate on Hippocrates, it is possible to ascertain how positivism and its liberal surrogates attempted to deal a final blow to neo-Hippocratic vitalism, while at the same time issuing a call for a radical shift in Spain's cultural policy with respect to science and innovation. Around this time, Spanish Krausism also began proposing new approaches to scientific and cultural reform through the lens of harmonic rationalism, a liberal, ethically oriented mode of existence in which the question of vital force was not only revisited, but deemed instrumental in building the ideal society of the future, a society unhampered by the conservatism of State-sponsored development.

Against this backdrop, I have two aims in this chapter. One is to draw out some of the complexities concerning how the question of vital force was framed and discussed during the bleak period between 1808 and 1840. It is often overlooked that the neo-Hippocratic vitalism that informed French physiology permeated Spanish scientific culture during these years of pronounced socio-economic and scientific decline. The emerging science of physiology, as Anthelme Richerand defined it in his popular *Elements of Physiology* of 1801, was first and foremost "the science of life, [where] the term life is applied to an aggregate of phenomena, which manifest themselves in succession, for a limited time in organized bodies."[7] My second aim is to examine how the powerful ideal to modernize Spain through positivist and Krausist perspectives between 1840 and the early-twentieth century was inextricably intertwined with the question of vital force. It must be said, however, that this period witnessed the emergence of numerous forms of vitalism – far too many to discuss in detail here – that left their mark on a range of fields in the arts and sciences in Spain. I have limited my focus to neo-Hippocratism, physiology, positivism, and Krausism specifically, since not only were these philosophies and fields of study decisive in shaping Spain's cultural progress at the highest levels of government in the nineteenth century, but they provided intriguing windows onto the complex socio-political realities of the country's modernization.

7 Richerand, *Elements of Physiology*, 1.

THE NEW PHYSIOLOGICAL MEDICINE AND THE SCIENCE OF LIFE

While the early-nineteenth century offers a desolate picture of Spain's scientific culture, there were a number of Spanish scholars who attempted to assimilate and develop the latest science conducted in the rest of Europe, particularly in France. Spain's relationship with France during this period was problematic to the say the least, but given the close ties between both countries, it is not surprising that French science had a notable impact on the country's cultural landscape during this period. During the French occupation between 1808 and 1814, for instance, Spanish physicians and scientists who were apologetic toward France – those known as the *afrancesados* – were granted special dispensation to travel to Paris to learn the latest advancements in various fields of research.[8] Undeniably, Spain had always remained both receptive to, and critical of, the vitalist theory emanating from Paris and Montpellier, which came to be known generally as "the new physiological medicine." By this time, several of the major French texts on physiology had been translated into Spanish. A few of the most notable included Jean-Baptiste Lafon's *Medical Philosophy*, a treatise greatly aligned with William Cullen's, Paul-Joseph Barthez's, and Pierre-Joseph Desault's vitalist theories, which was translated and published in Spain in 1802 and generated considerable debate. Charles-Louis Dumas's *Principles of Physiology* was also an important work that appeared in Spanish in 1803, thanks to Juan Vicente Carrasco, a physician well-acquainted with French medicine. Vicente Carrasco would later become a formidable exponent of Montpellier vitalism in Spain with the publication of his two-volume *Compendium of Physiology; or, Knowledge of the Physical and Vital Man* between 1817 and 1822.[9] Anthelme Richerand's widely popular *Elements of Physiology* appeared in 1803, and in 1806 the physician Tomás García Suelto translated Xavier Bichat's *Physiological Investigations on Life and Death*, which famously upheld that life represented "the totality of those set of functions which resist death," and that the processes of vital force in every part of the body remained mired in a relentless struggle against degeneration and decay.[10] Between 1807 and 1814, Ramón Trujillo translated Bichat's landmark *General Anatomy Applied to Physiology and Medicine* in four volumes. Important works that appeared in Spanish some years

8 López Piñero, "Las ciencias," 206.

9 For more on J.V. Carrasco, see Josep Lluis Barona Vilar's *La doctrina y el laboratorio*, 73–80.

10 Bichat, *Physiological Investigations*, 1–2.

later, during the Liberal Triennium and after, included François-Joseph-Victor Broussais's *Fundamental Principles of Physiological Medicine*, translated by Cayetano Lanuza (1822), Louis-Jacques Bégin's *General Principles of Pathological Physiology*, translated by Lorenzo Sánchez Núñez (1822), and François Magendie's *An Elemental Compendium of Human Physiology*, translated by Ramón Fran and Juan Trias (1828).

What did developments in the new field of physiology promise exactly during this challenging period in Spain? And why did they generate such considerable appeal? Barona Vilar's seminal study on physiology in nineteenth-century Spain sheds much-needed light on the socio-historical factors that influenced physiological thinking during Ferdinand VII's reign. Barona Vilar argues rightly that, with the general acceptance of the experimental method and the progressive institutionalization of laboratory sciences across Europe leading up to the mid-nineteenth century, physiology quickly emerged as a distinct discipline.[11] The first concrete signs of its emergence as a proto-discipline, however, appear predominantly in Enlightenment France with the so-called sciences of life. As it was advanced during this period, physiology attempted to elucidate life's organic functions and their underlying causes by integrating new procedures of empirical observation and experimentation with established models of anatomo-pathological interpretation. While Spanish scientists participated in the hybrid empirical/doctrinal framework that propelled physiology during the early-nineteenth century, they sorely lacked the infrastructure and resources to undertake experimental research with any degree of efficiency. Thus, they relied heavily upon established models of anatomo-pathological interpretation, which had a tendency toward eclecticism and emphasized, naturally, well-worn epistemological traditions. The truth was that the physiological science associated with Montpellier vitalism, which had grown exceedingly popular in Spain within a few short years, encouraged the hybrid empirical/doctrinal framework. In fact, it censured experimental, laboratory-based research – vivisection in particular, which physiologists like François Magendie and his devotees vigorously defended – given that the techniques and instrumentation of testing fundamentally changed the body's complex vital functions.[12] On this point, the English physician Gabriel de Lys observed the following:

11 Barona Vilar, *La doctrina y el laboratorio*, 65–72.

12 Wolfe, "Empiricist Heresies," 339. In terms of French science, and Montpellier vitalism specifically, Wolfe tells us that "Montpellier vitalism … consistently praises observation and disparages experiment whether the latter consists of anatomical and pathological

The continental physiologists are fond of theory: an adherence even to the old theories characterizes, very remarkably, the works of the most modern foreign writers on Medicine and Surgery, influencing even the practice of the profession in a very unfavourable manner. But this spirit of theorizing, this anxiety to extend individual facts into general principles, is as essential to the progress of the Science, as the zeal in the acquisition of knowledge which prepares its materials.[13]

Early-nineteenth-century physiology in Spain, even given the context of socio-economic and political burdens, did produce a handful of notable studies, including Tomás Ventosa's *Elements of Physiology Arranged in Order* (1818), Juan Ribot y Mas's *Succinct Elements of Physiology* (1822), and Juan Mosácula's *Elements of Special or Human Physiology* (1830). Another study worth mentioning is Baltasar de Viguera's four-volume *The Physiology and Pathology of Women* (1827). Baltasar de Viguera's treatise showcases the great range of topics covered in early physiology in Spain. To begin with, Baltasar de Viguera was a key figure in advancing obstetrics and gynecology on the peninsula, and used physiological concepts to explore not only the differences between men's and women's physical constitutions (even describing female genitalia in detail, which was uncommon for the period), but also their moral characters. Of note is how he praised the female body with respect to its "heightened" corporeal sensibilities, and he proved sensitive to women's plight and demonstrated a keen sense of awareness of the social constraints imposed upon them. In the third volume of *The Physiology and Pathology of Women*, he touched upon what he called monstrous births and fetal monstrosity and attempted to lend insight into the following question: how can the union of a rational male and a rational female produce an animal-like fetus that transgressed the "rational hierarchy" of body proportionality?[14] Especially baffling for Baltasar de Viguera in this respect were two classes of monstrosity: cyclops (as the name suggests, cyclops were fetuses or newborns with a single eye in their foreheads) and acephalics (fetuses or newborns with severe head malformations). Although he admitted he had never witnessed a cyclops first-hand, he referred to case histories archived in the Berlin Academy that purportedly documented the existence of one. The ancients, he claimed further, clearly knew of their existence, since how else could they have possibly placed them in early creation myths. He offered various factors that could contribute to the

studies of corpses, or worse (in their opinion), of the vivisection of live animals. It also tends to include favourable references to empiricism" (339).

13 de Lys, "Translator's Preface," in *Elements of Physiology*, by Anthelme Richerand, viii.

14 Baltasar de Viguera, *La fisiología de la mujer*, 149.

development and progress of physical deformities of all kinds in human development – spinal anomalies, facial dysmorphism, tumoral calcinosis, polymelia, conjoined twins, etc. – a few of which stemmed from the overstimulation or deficiency of vital force in the man or woman during intercourse or conception. He reasoned that physical deformities were likely passed down from the father and were produced from the "the excessive, or incomplete, or imperfect vital impulsion they receive from man's prolific energy [áura]."[15] Yet, he also argued elsewhere in his treatise that life's innate "organizational potency" within the fetus itself could be overstimulated for some reason and exceed its natural bounds, thereby generating compensatory and irregular growth in parts of the developing body.[16]

More valuable than the research itself was the fact that physiology in Spain incited new enthusiasm for the question of vital force, an enthusiasm through which a much-needed renewal of scientific frameworks could be at least envisioned. The reality, of course, was that the obstructions to any such renewal on a national scale were simply insurmountable during Ferdinand VII's reign. Unsurprisingly, the young and up-and-coming cohort of anatomists, researches, scientists, and medical practitioners hailed physiology as a revolutionary science. The much-admired (and, likewise, maligned) founder of what was known as physiological medicine, François-Joseph-Victor Broussais, served as a beacon of hope to those pursuing new approaches to human anatomy and the body's organic functions. Keeping in step with the vitalists of the day, Broussais declared that without a shadow of a doubt mechanism had proven to be grossly insufficient within the medical sphere, particularly in its attempts to reduce life's complexities to physical and chemical laws. With the publication of his controversial *Examination of Medical Doctrines* in 1816, his vitalist ideas were disseminated throughout Europe, and he swiftly became a medical authority, enjoying spectacular success in Paris by the 1820s.

The foundation of Broussais's physiological medicine was rather straightforward, and his admirers often championed the simplicity of his methods with respect to the body and disease. He insisted that inflammation of the gastrointestinal tract produced the overwhelming majority of illnesses in the human body, and it was this basic phenomenon of inflammation in the gastrointestinal region that migrated to other organs via the nervous system and generated a host of new complications

15 Ibid., 164.
16 Ibid., 150.

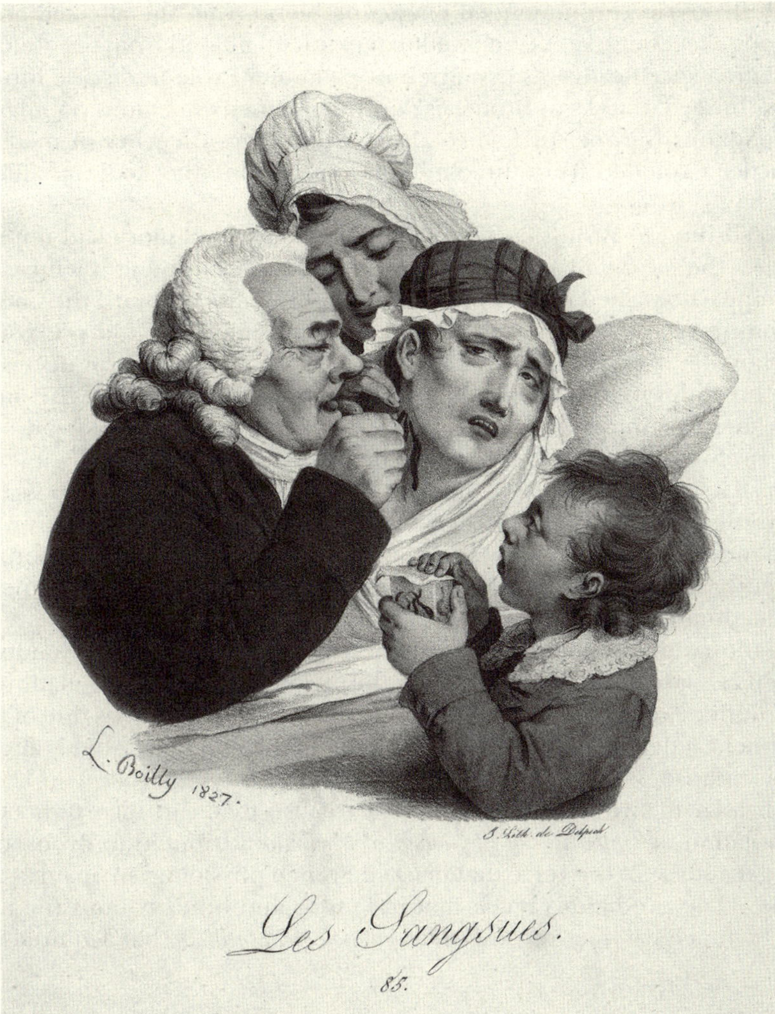

5.1 Lithograph, "Les sangsues," by Louis-Léopold Boilly, 1827.

with their own distinctive symptomatologies. Following established medical theory, inflammation for Broussais stemmed from chronic irritation, and chronic irritation in turn was nothing more than an organ's vital response to stimuli (the presence of impurities, for instance). Thus, eliminating the stimuli at the root of the chronic irritation and inflammation was necessary to eradicate the pathological condition. To this end, Broussais recommended extracting blood from the affected areas through leeching, yet he believed that extracting blood from the abdominal area specifically was key, given its prominent role in disease formation. Indeed, thanks to Broussais, leeching gained enormous popularity throughout Europe. In France alone, the usage of leeches in medical practice exploded from three million annually in 1824 to 41.5 million in 1833.[17]

According to Broussais, the maladies of vanity and glory had not impeded the steady march of the new generation of young scientists in Europe who wished only to put forth their best efforts toward the understanding of the body's vital properties. Drawing upon old criticisms, opponents of physiological science in Spain considered it injurious to the infirm in its anti-mechanism, and argued that the lure of the modern surrounding it was sufficiently seductive to fool "gullible youth" – precisely the same youth who later became its most fervent disciples.[18] For all its apparent novelty and iconoclasm, the truth is that Broussais's physiological medicine did in fact echo not only Brunonianism in its dependence on the general categories of irritation (overstimulation, or sthenic) and debility (understimulation, or asthenic) when it came to conceptualizing disease and its causes, but also Galenism in its preoccupation with bloodletting. The physician Manuel Hurtado de Mendoza, often referred to by his naysayers as the "Broussais of Madrid," had studied under Broussais in Paris between 1815 and 1818 and was one of the staunchest defenders of physiological medicine in Spain.[19] In his apologetic treatise, *Vindication and Explanation of Physiological Medicine* of 1826, dedicated to Broussais's teachings (a treatise that also incorporated a translation of *Catechism of Physiological Medicine* attributed to Broussais), we get a sense of the verve that marked French physiology in Spain at the time: "The prodigious reach that in France and other nations the new French medical doctrine known as *physiological medicine* has acquired is a

17 Thorndike, "A History of Bleeding and Leeching," 477.

18 González Ayensa and Quintanilla, *Refutación*, xvii.

19 As a medical student and *afrancesado*, Hurtado de Mendoza first met Broussais in Spain while Broussais was serving as an army physician during the French occupation. After 1814, Hurtado de Mendoza was exiled to France, where he completed his medical education in Paris, during which time Broussais served as one of his closest mentors. Upon his return to Spain in 1818, he would consistently defend Broussais's physiological medicine, even when it fell sharply out of favour in the 1830s. Consuelo Miqueo points out that, while Broussais was well-known in Spanish scientific and intellectual circles and did generate considerable debate on the merits of physiological medicine in the 1820s, his medical ideas were practised predominantly in rural settings and not in Spain's major institutions of medicine (162).

cause for great admiration among the multitude. It excites in a most notable way the curiosity of the majority of learned men. The following question is being asked in every corner [of the nation]: what is this doctrine that is causing such a stir?"[20]

For Hurtado de Mendoza, Broussais was revolutionizing science with straightforward scholarship based on impeccable reasoning and observation. Just as importantly, he was instigating a reform of medical terminology that would achieve a new level of precision with respect to the body and its vital functions. He railed against Broussais's Spanish critics in *Vindication and Explanation of Physiological Medicine*, highlighting their medical language, which in his opinion was nothing but crude and archaic: "*Putrefaction, pituitary, saburra*; a rank language that leaves one with the aftertaste of humoralism. *Bilious elements, catarrhal mark, rheumatic spirit*; futile and chimerical ontologism."[21] A close analysis of Broussais's work reveals that he was adopting the terminology of dominant vitalist theoreticians during the period to suit his observations, and relied heavily on terms such as contractility, excitability, functions, inflammation, sensibility, and stimulus to articulate the maladies associated with gastroenteritis, which always remained at the centre of his thinking. Broussais naturally relied upon young physicians to advance physiological medicine, Hurtado de Mendoza pointed out, for they were inclined to be tolerant, inquisitive, and far less devoted to the scholarship of the ancients. Even the practice of leeching, which incontrovertibly conjured up Galenic medical doctrine, squared neatly with Broussais's innovative views regarding the therapeutic value of antiphlogistics at the site of inflammation. It was well established, Broussais argued, that leeches reduced swelling and increased blood flow, and should therefore be applied directly to diseased areas.

Physiological science achieved something else of great significance in Spain besides fostering a spirit of enthusiasm for the discoveries of vital force: it introduced new models of body functioning that seemingly confirmed a number of age-old teachings of Hippocrates, one of the most consistently venerated figures in Spanish scientific culture since the late-seventeenth century. Montpellier physicians held Hippocrates in the highest esteem for advocating what they understood as the true methods of observation that had become characteristic of the best and most

20 Hurtado de Mendoza, *Vindicación y explicación*, iii. There is some speculation on whether Hurado de Mendoza or Nicolás José Guitérrez translated *Catechism of Physiological Medicine*, attributed to Broussais. For more on the criticisms levelled against Broussais during this period, see José Antonio Piquer's *On the New Medico-Physiological Doctrine* (1827).

21 Ibid., 7.

practical empiricism. In Montpellier teaching, "Hippocratism represented genuine 'empirical' medicine as opposed to the false 'empiricism' of the tradition-bound medicine still taught in most medical schools."[22] There were various ideological reasons why Montpellier came to be known as a hub of Hippocratic learning in the eighteenth and early-nineteenth centuries. Among other things, Montpellier physicians of the stature of Théophile de Bordeu and Barthez repeatedly invoked Hippocrates to assault iatromechanism and its overreliance on system-building and complex and obscure theories in which the practical observation of the patient was all but neglected. This was not a new tactic. As we saw in Chapter 2, physicians like Boix y Moliner and Martínez in Spain had strategically interpreted Hippocratic teachings in the early eighteenth century to counter the official medical doctrines of the university system, particularly on this question of patient interaction. In his famous *Discourse on the Genius of Hippocrates*, delivered at the Montpellier medical school in 1801, Barthez lauded Hippocrates for his sagacity and inventiveness and for articulating the clear therapeutic principles that effectively divided medical science from philosophy. For Barthez, it was evident that, in the dawning of a new century of great scientific innovation anchored in physiological research, Hippocrates remained "the founder of the true science of medicine."[23]

Neo-Hippocratic doctrine in Spain was indeed sympathetic to the Barthezian vital principle to explain health and the abnormalities of disease. Cristóbal Tomás's 1808 translation of Barthez's *Treaty and New Curative Method of Gout and Rheumatism* was instrumental in popularizing Barthezian medicine among a wide audience. For Barthez, the vital principle had nothing to do with the rational soul or occult powers of any kind, nor was it an entirely material substance within the body. Rather, it was an observable "faculty attached to the combinations of movement and matter of which the living body is formed."[24] The vital principle for Barthez was not only sensitive to the exterior environment (the so-called local context), but it was observable and operated everywhere in the body to establish a complete, living unity. Following Hippocrates' method, Barthez also emphasized close observation of the pathological body and the precise description of disease formation and progression. While the theory of humours was done away with for the most part, body

22 Williams, *The Physical*, 65.

23 Barthez, *Discours*, 5–6. See Elizabeth Williams's "Hippocrates and the Montpellier Vitalists in the French Medical Enlightenment" for the political underpinnings of Barthez's *Discours* and its image of Hippocrates.

24 Quoted in Williams, *The Physical*, 47.

functioning in Barthez's thinking was still understood holistically in terms of sympathies and discords between various active forces, including motor forces, sensitive forces (such as irritation), and those related to pulsation, heat, circulation, and blood chemistry. Overall, Barthez's general approach to the body economy and disease resonated with Hippocratic doctrine when it came to the primacy of observation and the crucial body-environment transaction.

More than a passing phase in nineteenth-century Spanish medicine, neo-Hippocratic vitalism served as a bedrock of scientific thinking that sustained eclecticism and the dialogue between ancient and modern in terms of body and disease. Traditionalist and conservative factions of Spanish science embraced it for decades throughout the nineteenth century and found a safe harbour in its teachings, from which they could effectively adopt or reject new ideas. As late as 1872, for instance, the *Medical Press Circular* of London published a short piece titled "Notes on Current Topics," in which it highlighted to what extent Spanish medical science "remains true to a moderate Hippocratism; and is always disposed to make the tendencies of the traditional school symmetrical with those newly won."[25] Unlike the case in other European countries, neo-Hippocratic vitalism in Spain evolved and endured, and it provided a formidable counterbalance to the so-called liberal excesses of emerging scientific trends, such as positivist determinism, well into the 1880s. Moreover, it offered Spain's knowledge establishment with time-honoured beliefs with which to undercut radical currents that it deemed critical of traditional scientific practices. If anything, neo-Hippocratism's long-standing orthodoxies in Spain provoked the following question anew: What constitutes modern science?

THE GREAT DEBATE ON HIPPOCRATES: SCIENCE, REFORM, AND THE MODERN

Spheres of Spanish medicine and science eschewed neo-Hippocratic vitalism and advocated for the materialist world view that was making significant headway in England, France, and Germany by the mid-1850s. Adopting John Dalton's scientific proof of atoms, nineteenth-century materialism held that matter represented the fundamental substance in nature, and its unique and infinite organization was responsible for all phenomena, including the complexities of life. Much like neo-Hippocratism, its genealogy could be traced back to antiquity in

25 *Medical Press Circular*, 501.

philosophers like Democritus and Leucippus and their theories of atoms and void. By the 1850s in Spain, it was possible to discern the contours of what the medical historian Francesc Bujosa Homar labels "a scientific battle" between neo-Hippocratic vitalism and materialism.[26] For Pedro Mata y Fontanet, one of Spain's leading materialists, whose influence on Spanish science was profound in the 1860s and 1870s, vitalism was, at best, shoddy science, at worst, outright obscurantism.[27] In his estimation, the history of vitalism, beginning with Hippocrates, demonstrated civilization's misguided propensity to entertain supernatural explanations for life phenomena. In his treatise *Critical Examination of Homeopathy* of 1852, which collected various of his early scientific lectures in Madrid's Athenaeum, he had railed against vitalism and, more concretely, Samuel Hahnemann's core belief in vital dynamisms as regulators of the body. The doctrine of homeopathy and the principle ideas of its founder Hahnemann were "absurd" and merely a rehash of "the secular doctrine of all the vitalists schools ... There have existed schools that have explained health and infirmity by means of a vital force in a very similar way [as homeopathy]."[28] What doomed vitalism to failure, according to Mata y Fontanet, particularly in light of the burgeoning field of atomistic medicine in Europe that demanded the uncompromising proofs of observation and measurement, was its underlying unscientific logic:

> In each century vitalism has flown from hypothesis to hypothesis – each more arbitrary than the last – searching for a name to give the mysterious spirit that it has elevated to the status of idol of the sect; an idol which, once created, has taken on the attributes of a real being endowed with everything that the most poetic fantasy can imagine. Even so, vitalism has never transcended the useless category of the peripatetic *occult quality*. It can never aspire to be anything but a *flatus vocis*, as Roselino would say.[29]

26 Bujosa Homar, *Filosofía*, 117.

27 In Ángel Carracedo and Luis Concheiro's entry dedicated to Spain in *The Global Practice of Forensic Science*, we read: "Pedro Mata y Fontanet (1811–1877) ... was the most important figure of Spanish legal medicine in the nineteenth century. His book *Theoretical-Practical Treatise of Legal Medicine and Toxicology* was a key reference text in Spain well into the twentieth century. However, of most importance was his influence on the structure of forensic science because he was the architect of the figure of *forensic physicians*, public servants of the Ministry of Justice, assigned to the courts, including those in rural areas, with the main function of assisting judges in any type of medicolegal issues" (262).

28 Mata y Fontanet, *Examen crítico*, 11.

29 Mata y Fontanet, *Compendio*, 108.

Mata y Fontanet was a methodical and self-assured man with a flair for the dramatic. As a professor in Toxicology and Legal Medicine at the Royal Academy of Medicine in Madrid, he took the opportunity at the inaugural lectures of the 1859 academic year to very publicly lambaste neo-Hippocratic vitalism in favour of a materialist world view. In his lecture *Hippocrates and the Hippocratic Schools*, he stunned his colleagues at the Royal Academy when he argued from the lecture platform that life could be substantiated in materialist terms.[30] It is worth pausing on Mata y Fontanet's lecture, since it sparked a fiery, years-long debate that grew far beyond the Royal Academy and would not only frame contemporary discussions in Spain on the practice and meaning of science in society, but also draw a stark distinction between ancient and modern in terms of scientific learning and epistemology. As one critic put it: "Mata y Fontanet's inaugural lecture was barely read and in print before it produced a general uproar among Hippocratists on the peninsula; it was if a bomb had gone off at close range."[31] Indeed, the ensuing lectures, rebuttals, and assemblies on the subject of Hippocrates and vital force at the Royal Academy, which extended from January to July 1859, attracted the attention of the popular press and the general public, as well as high-ranking figures in Spanish healthcare, including Francisco Méndez Álvaro, the Secretary of Health Services, and Juan Drumen, physician to the royal family.[32] In fact, the debates at the Royal Academy drew such large crowds that they were held in the medical school's auditorium, rather than in the assigned lecture hall. The lectures themselves served as the basis for the collected volume written by the Royal Academy's medical faculty and titled *Defence of Hippocrates, the Schools, and Vitalism* (1859), as well as the treatise *Vindication of Hippocrates and His System* (1859), authored by Tomás Santero y Moreno, also a faculty member. They would also provide Mata y Fontanet with the inspiration to compose his almost thousand-page tome *The Spanish Medico-Philosophical Doctrine Upheld during the Great Debate on Hippocrates and the Hippocratic Schools* (1860), which represented a complete and rigorous exposition of Spain's misguided commitment to neo-Hippocratic vitalism in medicine throughout the ages. Yet, this tome was more than a lengthy condemnation of neo-Hippocratic vitalism. It was also a declamatory text imbued in parts with the rhetorical force of a political manifesto, and it was aimed

30 Mata y Fontanet, *Hipócrates*, 9.

31 Ramos, "La polémica hipocrática," 158.

32 For a detailed summary of who participated and the topics covered at the various lectures, rebuttals, and assemblies, consult Tomás Ramos's "The Hippocratic Polemic in Spanish Medicine during the Nineteenth Century," 115–61.

squarely at enlightening Spanish youth on the truths of modern science. In addition, it issued a call to arms for positivist science in Spain to tackle what Mata y Fontanet called the "vast realm of life" and upend the socio-political status quo: "Here is the object of this book. Its intention is to establish a *positive medicine*, and it directs Spanish youth in medicine toward progress and work. It is *positive* medicine because the banner we raise on January 16 reads on its ribbon: Down with the idols! Freedom of thought! War to ontological fictions! Let the physical and chemical sciences proceed into the vast realm of life!"[33]

The debate Mata y Fontanet had begun with the faculty of the Royal Academy on modern science in Spain extended well into the late 1860s in various spheres. It inspired an array of publications that sought to firm up vitalist science in Spain more generally, such as the physician Ezequiel Martín de Pedro's *What Are the Practical Advantages of the Vitalist School Compared to the Organicist and Anatomic?* of 1865, which railed against the falsehoods of the growing organicist movement of Jean-Baptiste Bouillaud and the belief that vital force originated in the body's structural systems and chemical composition.[34] One of Mata y Fontanet's primary objectives in his inaugural lecture was to expose the irrelevancy of neo-Hippocratic vitalism in comparison to the modern method of positivist science. Hippocratism within the medical community, he averred, was based upon blind faith, and not upon facts. Rather than advancing rigorous scientific claims about the body, it dressed up ancient and speculative theories on vital force in a new guise. In his opinion, Hippocratism was not a science properly understood, but a species of religion, with its attendant ceremonies and dogmatic agenda: "If we were to agree with the impassioned aspirations of certain apologists, we would have to venerate Hippocrates' works just like the Hindus venerate the *Vedas*; the Jews the *Babylonian Talmud*; the Christians the *Sacred Works*; the Muslims, the *Koran*."[35] In terms of neo-Hippocratic vitalism, Mata y Fontanet contended that it served no purpose in modern medical theory and practice to rely on a vital force to clarify physiology and disease. On this point, he added: "What good is it to consider life a positive

33 Mata y Fontanet, *Doctrina médico filosófica española*, 7.

34 Martín de Pedro asserted the following: "To conclude: The great efforts of organicism – the illegitimate child of cold materialism – to avoid accepting the idea of vital force and its attributes not only puts it in contradiction with its own principles, but also makes evident that matter is not enough in the creation of the organic realm. It is necessary to accept independent, and sometimes even contrary forces, to those that are material" (54–5).

35 Mata y Fontanet, *Hipócrates*, 7.

thing, and the living being a substance, if when we look for the relations of action and reaction within the diverse objects in nature, we begin with an ontological concept; an ontological concept that we imbue with a vital and belligerent force so that it can battle with another similarly conceived concept called disease, and whose defeat comes about through a culinary analogy … [in] the *coction* of humours."[36] For Mata y Fontanet, the era of blind conjecture had passed, and what was required in Spanish science to truly comprehend the body' vital complexities and functioning was the observation and fact-based analysis of the emerging laboratory sciences. Consequently, he contended, only that which is directly evident to the senses and which can be subjected to the methods of hypothesis and data analysis is valid in the scientific sphere. This stance evidently echoed Auguste Comte's belief that real science, as he referred to it, must not take root in arbitrary and chimerical "fantasies" that cannot be objectively validated.[37] Mata y Fontanet concluded that "[t]he hypotheses of Hippocrates are not born from experience, because they are false. His theories are flawed, and his system is ridiculous in our day and age."[38]

What was so irreverent and radical about Mata y Fontanet's denouncements of Hippocrates – and what provoked such a visceral reaction from the scientific establishment in Madrid – was that they levelled a sharp critique against Spain's conservative establishment during a period of hard-fought scientific modernization (we must recall that Mata y Fontanet was also persecuted for his liberal politics during the 1830s and was jailed and forced into exile in France between 1838 and 1840, which certainly conditioned his views on authority).[39] Hippocratism did not mean progress for many progressive researchers and scientists open to transnational co-operation and experimental research. In reality, it was synonymous with intellectual lassitude, superstition, conformity, conservatism, institutional dysfunctionality, and, especially, the *unmodern*. The unmodern for Mata y Fontanet meant not simply scientific practice that had become outmoded or obsolete; rather, it brought to the fore the inertia that cut deep into Spain's epistemic fabric and was steering the nation into ruin. Behind the "mask" of neo-Hippocratic theory and its vitalism, he saw only the socio-political lethargy characteristic of the type of *moderantista* conservatism that had infected institutions like the Royal Academy and impeded true scientific progress and reform in the country.

36 Ibid., 18.
37 Comte, *The Positive Philosophy*, 187
38 Mata y Fontanet, *Hipócrates*, 15–16.
39 Manso, et al., "Bicentenario," 87.

In his own words: "Hippocratism is the mask used by all those [scientists] who feel in their conscience the weakness of their hypotheses; it is the medal that a system awards itself when it has no confidence in the reputation of its personality; it is the seal that some use to secure obedience, particularly for those who need of a higher authority to gain respect; it is the *exequatur* that opens a path to those who are worried that doors of approval will be closed to them."[40] For Mata y Fontanet, to take up the cause of neo-Hippocratic vitalism was analogous to repudiating modernity. He invoked the masquerade metaphor once again to propose that Hippocratism is merely the disguise that veiled a much larger national degeneration, a type of intellectual and moral infirmity that the realist Benito Pérez Galdós would bring to life with great mastery in novels like *Mrs Perfect* (1876), *Marianela* (1878), and *The Family of León Roch* (1878), in which he would lay bare the unyielding "national inertia ... this paralysis that is later translated into ignorance, envy, and poverty."[41] In his lecture's concluding remarks, Mata y Fontanet went a step further and directly correlated Hippocratism with State-sponsored religious dogmatism, which had not only thwarted the march of intellectual change in Spain, but had also become irreconcilable with all things modern: "Spanish physicians who aspire to be something in the vast and difficult field of practical medicine!: do not allow yourselves to be dragged by the reactionary torrent that descends from politics to philosophy, and from philosophy to medicine; do not fall in the perfidious trap that the Hippocratic disguise has set for you."[42]

The truth is that Mata y Fontanet's assault on neo-Hippocratic vitalism in his lecture was not without irony. To begin with, he argued that positivist materialism was the true foundation of modern science. Yet, rather than lauding his Spanish or European contemporaries who constituted the scientific and medical vanguard, he lauded the ancients like Thales, Anaximander, Anaximenes, Heraclitus, Democritus, and Leucippus, who studied the universe through the obscure actions of atoms. With this nod to materialistic atomism, Mata y Fontanet appealed to an ulterior vein of ancient authority to legitimize his arguments, for the knowledge claims of this vein of ancient authority, he believed, were being duly validated in contemporary positivist research. This move carried profound meaning and symbolic relevance in Spain for conservatives and theologians alike. Nineteenth-century materialistic atomism, invigorated by Enlightenment rationalism, had offered a persuasive explanation of

40 Mata y Fontanet, *Hipócrates*, 24.

41 Galdós, *Episodios Nacionales. Mendizábal*, 286.

42 Mata y Fontanet, *Hipócrates*, 26.

the cosmological order – including creation and life phenomena – that effectively eliminated the need for an omnipotent God or Prime Mover.

Since the time of Leucippus, atomism had sought to explain – either theologically (through divine Reason) or materialistically (through the environment and the laws of probability) – how the collision and interaction of minute, indivisible, and indestructible atoms could elucidate the infrastructure of the universe. At its core, "[a]tomism constitutes an original attempt to resolve ... the nature of coming into being and of change."[43] It was the English chemist, physicist, and meteorologist John Dalton who moved the debate into new realms of scientific understanding in 1808 and 1810. In these years, he published the two parts of his landmark *A New System of Chemical Philosophy*, which transformed atomism into a major theme of classical physics. In devising a coherent theory of atomic weights, Dalton had at long last provided the scientific community with empirical evidence of atoms.[44] Needless to say, the implications of this new-found evidence were far-reaching. Thanks to Dalton's research, scientists now had at their disposal a *measurable* means of grasping the world's atomic organization and the carbon-based life thriving within it. As the understanding of atomism advanced in the nineteenth century, with Michael Faraday, John Tyndall, and other positivist scientists, the door was left open to prove scientifically how natural and empirical laws ordered atoms, and how these laws did not require the intervention of any divine creator whatsoever. For conservatives and religious apologists, as might be expected, this science was one of the great heresies of modernization.

The type of materialistic atomism that informed Mata y Fontanet's positivism during the Great Debate on Hippocrates, and that would only become more pronounced after the 1868 Revolution, was so reviled and evoked such deep-seated fear among Spanish conservatives that it made its way into all types of partisan literature, even the literature of domesticity. The staunch conservative author Ángela Grassi wrote her popular novel *The Snowflake* in 1876 not only to lambaste Mata y Fontanet's materialism, but also to caution her female readership about the perils of atomism and the question of vital force more generally. The literature of domesticity served as a crucial vehicle to properly educate the so-called domestic angels – the guarantors of conservative values in Spanish society – regarding the most pressing social and religious issues associated with Spain's modernization. What is of particular interest is that in

43 Pullman and Reisinger, *The Atom*, 31.

44 Purrington, *Physics in the Nineteenth Century*, 113.

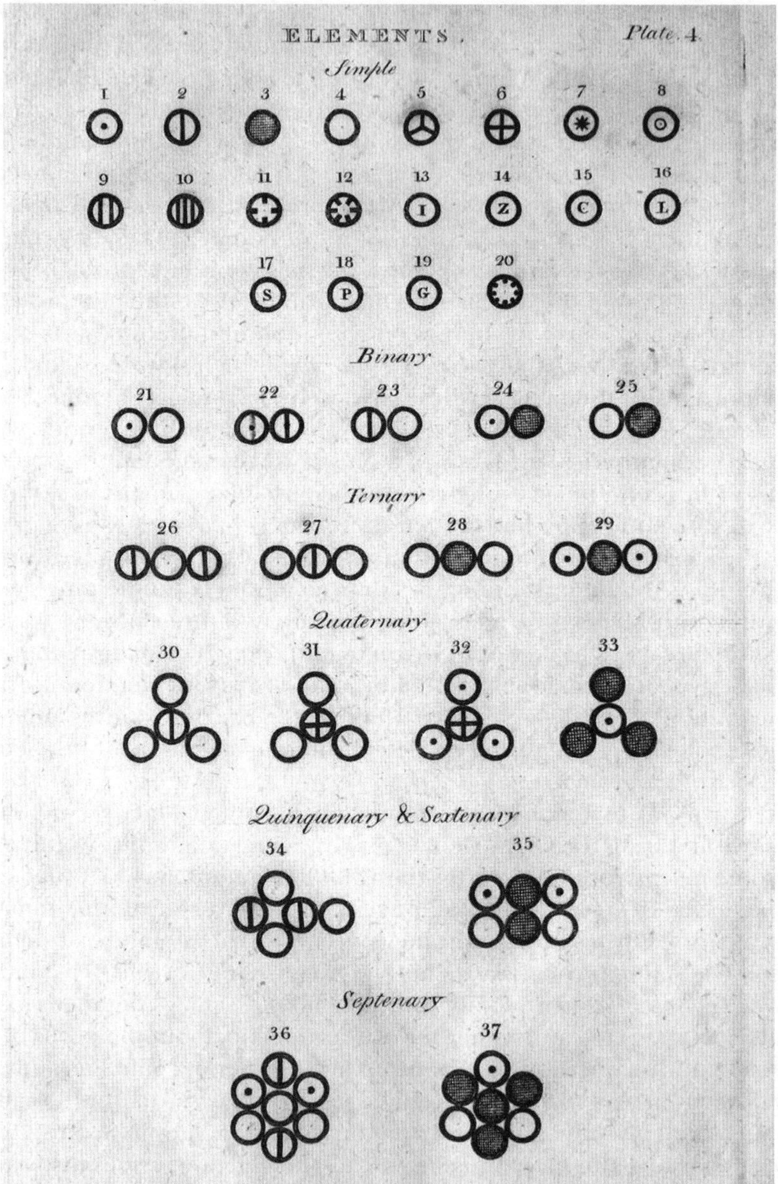

5.2 Plate IV, showing symbols of chemical elements in John Dalton's *A New System of Chemical Philosophy, Part I,* 1808.

strongly religious literary works like *The Snowflake*, featuring a righteous heroine falling under the perfidious spell of modern science, it is possible to gauge to what extent conservatives in Spain were desperately attempting to stem the tide of change and preserve a way of life and its system of beliefs. Ironically, the more Grassi condemns materialistic atomism in *The Snowflake*, the more she is obliged to explain it, to command its idiom and claims, and thus educate her female readership concerning the broader philosophical framework of materialism. When Grassi has a morally corrupt and atheist character cite a poem of one of Spain's vilest philosophers on the material origins of life, she is in fact attacking Mata y Fontanet. While Grassi does not name him in the novel, the reference would have been clear at the time, given that his poetry was quite controversial and had been published in various popular outlets. Mata y Fontanet was in fact a recognized poet in his day, and had published a volume titled *Intimate Photographs* in 1874. In the prologue to this collection, he notes that a number of his poems had appeared in newspapers throughout the years (where in all probability Grassi had come upon his poetry), and that they were generally criticized for their inflammatory scientific and philosophical content. In his poem titled "Posthumous Life" of 1870, which Grassi condemns in *The Snowflake*, death for the speaker is celebrated as a joyous material decomposition.[45] Once lifeless, the body's atoms gradually come undone to fertilize the earth once again:

Once my cadaver is undone, its vapours
will circulate throughout the lofty spheres
of the open firmament.
The white earth will collect
from my solid parts its salt,
and the tranquil irrigation of rain waters
will nourish a hundred seeds.
My residues thus transformed into vital sap

45 Xavier Vall references the same poem used by Grassi in *The Snowflake* and attributes it to Mata y Fontanet (19–20). On the inflammatory content of his poetry, Mata y Fontanet remarked: "I have not felt any unease whatsoever when they have considered me a poet, since I have laughed at those fools who have considered me a *meddler in literature* and even *ignorant in poetry*" (*Fotografías*, xii). As Vall points out, Mata y Fontanet confronted his conservative critics, who accused him of being impious, a materialist, and an atheist, in public literary forums (20n11). Like Vall, Sánchez Llama points out the poem's allusions to Epicurean atomism in Lucretius's *De rerum natura* (*Galería* 170n65).

will flow through parched rootlets
to conquer, with mallow and fennel,
the shores of my final dwelling place.[46]

The image of a bodily breakdown after death into finite elements and residues is captured in the generative rain and seed imagery in verses six and seven. In *Treaty on Human Reason in Its Intermediate States*, Mata y Fontanet had stated that "life … [is] a mode of being of matter … What separates organic and inorganic matter … is only the circumstances and conditions in which their atoms exist and combine."[47] The body's breakdown reappears more strikingly in the poem's closing verses. Grassi, however, did not include these verses in her novel, perhaps because they allude more directly, as the title "Posthumous Life" suggests, to an atomic re-embodiment – or reincarnation – in a cosmic life/death cycle. In a sense, the body – and, it seems, some part of its consciousness – returns organically to the *systema naturae* after death. The remainder of Mata y Fontanet's poem reads as follows:

Thus returned to the life cycle,
I will be scattered in a thousand different beings,
I will return to think in fiery minds,
I will return to feel in the unsettled
and passionate sea of ardent hearts
that will beat with my substance.[48]

Appearing in the same year in which Galdós harshly condemned orthodox religion in *Mrs Perfect* and in which the ultra-conservative Carlist movement effectively passed into history, *The Snowflake* brings a sense of moral urgency and nostalgia to the spiritual aims of a *moderantista*-styled conservatism. It was precisely during the 1860s and 1870s that the State sought to advance, through an appeal to historico-nationalist Romantic ideals, various moral and spiritual objectives under the guise of educational reform and political justice. Conservatives like Grassi censured Mata y Fontanet's materialistic atomism primarily because it conjured up what the conservative scholar and historian Marcelino Menéndez y Pelayo called "the perverse monstrosities" of modernity, which questioned God's role within the social and cosmological scheme.[49] Yet it also

46 Grassi, *El copo de nieve*, 170.
47 Mata y Fontanet, *Tratado de la razón humana*, 73.
48 Quoted in Vall, "La ciència," 19–20.
49 Menéndez y Pelayo, *Historia*, vol. 2, 24.

aroused in individuals a moral free will that powerfully subjectivized such things as virtue and good and evil. If there is no divine creator, as Grassi points out in her novel through the mouthpiece of the despicable atheist, or if the divine creator is absent from worldly life in a form of deistic scheme, each atom's – that is, individual's – raison d'être must therefore obey the causal laws of the environment. Thus, the atheist arrives at the following realization: "Life is a dream, life is an exhalation … I am an atom, and atoms move at the will of the wind. The responsibility remains with the environment."[50] It must be said that Grassi believed in modernization insofar as it was subservient to the established order. As she understood it, God remained the source of all progress, and it was His works that nourished the individual and opened a path to improvement in all areas of life. Thus, when nineteenth-century materialists like Mata y Fontanet advocated for a positive science intrinsically inimical to religious dogma, it was no wonder that she put pen to paper to condemn the atheistic implications of his work.[51]

The larger conflict between religion and modernity that undergirds novels like Grassi's *The Snowflake* was very much on the minds of Mata y Fontanet and his adversaries during the years spanning the Great Debate on Hippocrates and beyond. In his 1866 lecture at the Royal Academy of the Sciences, the famed dramatist and mathematician José Echegaray bemoaned Spain's marginalization when it came to modern science, and he condemned the country's conservatism and religious establishment for impeding scientific progress at every turn. "And in our Spain," he declared, "reason, the most noble faculty of the thinking being, languishes and declines, and with it, everything languishes and dies in the end."[52] It bears noting that Pope Pius IX's *Syllabus of Errors*, condemning eighty errors of the modern world – a number of which had appeared in earlier papal writings – began circulating in 1864, just as the Great Debate on Hippocrates was intensifying. The *Syllabus* marked a turning point in the religion-science controversy in Spain – or what can be translated more generally as the growing conservative-liberal divide – insofar as it scuttled any real possibility of a reconciliation between the Church

50 Grassi, *El copo de nieve*, 169.

51 In her novel *Palmas y laureles*, Grassi stated it as follows: "While wise men remain absorbed in their great accomplishments and scrutinize the physical world, they lose sight of the moral world. While they count and analyze the atoms on earth, they remain blinded to the stars shining in the sky … When man elevated mechanism [la mecánica] to such prodigious heights, he believed he had accomplished it all; he believed he had thrown God from his pedestal to pay tribute to a foolish and selfish cult" (366).

52 Echegaray, *Discursos*, 29.

and the cultural mechanisms of progress and change. Just over a decade earlier, the Concordat of 1851, signed by Isabella II's government and the Vatican, had solidified Catholicism's case regarding Spain's official religion, a manoeuvre that was nothing if not the Church's expression of its deep anxieties concerning the country's steady advancement toward more liberal socio-economic policies (of note, too, is that in this same period in which the Concordat was approved, Jaime Balmes's prescriptive *Letters to a Skeptic on Religious Matters* put in believers' hands an arsenal of defences against the evils of skepticism). Indeed, the progressive deamortization program of the 1830s – revisited during the Liberal Biennium of 1854–56 – which led to the confiscation and public auction of Church property, was still fresh in the minds of conservatives at this point. In truth, the battles waged between the Church and the proponents of progress in Spain had a long precedent, yet with the expansion of liberalism and scientism after 1833, the gulf that had separated science from religion only widened.

In his fateful lecture, Mata y Fontanet not only sparked one of the first modern debates in Spain concerning the powerful role medical science played in progress narratives, but also instigated the demise of neo-Hippocratic vitalism as a viable foundation upon which to build a so-called national medicine (José de Letamendi y Manjarrés, one of Mata y Fontanet's harshest critics, whose last major work, *Course on General Clinical Medicine*, appeared in 1894, was for all intents and purposes Spain's last great Hippocratic physician). Rather than conceiving of medical science as a practice of conjecture wedded to vitalist theory, Mata y Fontanet understood it within the progressive trends of professionalization that were transforming nineteenth-century science, thanks to figures like Comte and Claude Bernard. In his mind, and as he explained it to the hundreds of students who passed through his lecture room over the years at the Royal Academy of Medicine in Madrid, neo-Hippocratic vitalism delivered no practical solution to the modern scientific challenges that were appearing everywhere in society. On the contrary, to filter medical science through the vagaries of an intrinsic vital force was not simply archaic and misguided, but fundamentally flawed.

The reality, of course, was a bit more complex. Theories of vital force were in fact infiltrating science and philosophy by leaps and bounds. What Mata y Fontanet could not see with clarity was the extent to which vitalist theories were being assimilated and reinterpreted through the emerging discourses of evolutionism, hygiene, calisthenics, homeopathy, and psychology, discourses that would fundamentally modernize culture and science across Spain and Europe in a few short years. Nietzsche's

EL DOCTOR SANGREDO

GALERÍA HUMORÍSTICA DE «EL Dr. SANGREDO»

EL Dr. LETAMENDI

Soy poeta, y orador,
y músico, y catedrático,
y pintor, y matemático,
y médico, y escritor.
Soy un ente original,
sobre todo, en mis axiomas,
poseo muchos idiomas
y doy tertulias *Duval*.
Dicen, y me importa poco,
que yo mismo me confundo;
si soy loco para el mundo,
el mundo para mí es loco.

5.3 Caricature of the vitalist physician José de Letamendi y Manjarrés by Ramón Cilla that appeared in *El Doctor Sangredo*, 1883.

Birth of Tragedy, for example, which articulated the core principles of the Dionysian vitalism that would not only inform much of his philosophical thinking thereafter on the body and *décadence*, but also serve as a powerful beacon of renewal for modernist intellectuals, would appear in 1872.

It could very well be that Mata y Fontanet's vitriol against vitalism betrays more about his own anxieties over an increasingly dynamic modernity that embraced the indeterminate, irrational, and unknown than anything else. And in fact, it was not the inherent shortcomings of neo-Hippocratic vitalism that troubled him the most (he had said as much in his inaugural lecture), but rather, how this species of vitalism, appropriated and adapted in the service of the conservative State by fanatical Hippocratists, had become sharply politicized and wielded as an instrument of power.

One of Mata y Fontanet's singular accomplishments with the Great Debate on Hippocrates was to "unmask" – a term he very much liked to use – how deeply the question of vital force had become integrated into a set of socio-political and economic interests in Spain that sought to safeguard the status quo. In the fourth edition of his popular *Treatise on Legal Medicine and Surgery, Theory and Practice, Followed by a Compendium on Toxicology* of 1866, he summed up his position, stating: "As a philosopher, you will always see me defending the experimental method guided by reason. As a physiologist, I will be an irreconcilable enemy of fictitious entities, of abstractions considered as entities, of unwarranted hypotheses, of vital forces that do not exist and that are different in essence from those that preside over the phenomena of the world."[53]

BODY CULTURE: THE KRAUSIST HARMONY OF THE WHOLE

In the same year, 1860, which saw the publication of Mata y Fontanet's *The Spanish Medico-Philosophical Doctrine*, the philosopher and jurist Julián Sanz del Río translated and published a book that would become one of the seminal works in nineteenth-century Spanish philosophy. The title of this book was *Ideal of Humanity for Life*, and it introduced Spain to Karl Christian Friedrich Krause's idealism. Beginning in the early 1860s, the movement that would eventually be known as *krausismo* had a far-reaching and profound impact on Spanish culture well into the twentieth century. Much like positivism, Krausism sought to reform Spain's scientific frameworks, and it likewise tackled the question of vital force as a point of departure to address larger socio-political and epistemological issues. In step with the major tenets of German Romantic idealism and *Naturphilosophie*, Krause's early-nineteenth-century harmonic rationalism laid out a framework for building a new ideal of humanity, beginning

53 Mata y Fontanet, *Tratado de Medicina y Cirugía Legal*, 8.

with the individual. As Krause argued, before the individual could consider the social and ethical dimensions required to grasp the ideal of humanity – these included the development of communal relations, sweeping pedagogical reform, upholding the dignity of otherness, and the personal quest for transcendence, among other things – he had to first undergo a process of self-discovery capable of perfecting the operations and activities of the mind and the body. Krause maintained that, to perfect society, it was necessary to perfect the individual, a notion that became the philosophical cornerstone of Spanish *regeneracionismo* – the progressive Regenerationism movement – and its program of socio-political reform during the late-nineteenth and early-twentieth centuries.

The healthy and invigorated body capable of harmonizing with nature's order remained at the centre of Krausist philosophy. As Sanz del Río outlined it in the prologue to *Ideal of Humanity for Life*, "man ... is the harmonic composite of Nature and Spirit."[54] The object of all philosophy, he added, "is to get close to life and penetrate it."[55] An intimate and thorough understanding of bodily life and nature revealed a path to the ideal society. It stands to reason why he believed that "[t]o attain this goal and rehabilitation of life ... we must first return to the deepest knowledge of our nature in its permanent reality, in its equality among men, and in its harmonic relation with all beings."[56] The body, as a composite of nature and spirit, had to be nurtured spiritually, through a rational inquiry into God's perfectibility, and nurtured physically, through an emphasis on healthy behaviours, hygiene, calisthenics, and moderation of the appetites. The idea was that the body's vital force, if it was perfected in states of physical activity and well-being, could harmonize more completely with nature's rational order, which would allow the individual to better recognize – and thus contribute to – the resolve of reason in every sphere of action, ranging from personal to institutional relationships. The active and healthy body, therefore, was deemed superior and more beautiful, since it was most attuned to nature's rational order, while the inactive and unhealthy body was considered ugly and exposed the incongruity, so to speak, that existed between self and world:

> It is, therefore, the law of humanity that man educate his body and maintain it in a state of health, force, and beauty, and that he listen and follow his natural instinct in as much as this instinct agrees with the harmony of the whole. He must establish among all of his forces and corporeal senses ... a reciprocal and living

54 Sanz del Río, "Prólogo," xii.

55 Ibid., xvi.

56 Ibid., xxi–xxii.

relation in accordance with the health and beauty of the whole body and all of its organs. The body also requires exercise to keep it healthy, vigorous, worthy, and beautiful in the exterior. It requires exercise of all of its systems ... and of all of its senses in the form of a gymnastics appropriate for the individual and the relation among the many ... To neglect the culture of the body, or to destabilize its forces or abuse them, is a sign of an ignorant and vulgar soul, and it reveals an ingratitude to nature.[57]

The concept of vital force, understood holistically as the alignment of the body and soul with nature, underscored Krausism's practical interest in experiencing nature first-hand, and it was crucial in laying the ideological groundwork for the expansion of the naturist movement in Spain, beginning in the 1890s.[58] From Krause's perspective, "[s]pirit and body, intimately joined in man, express the dignity of reason and the vitality of nature: both form a sustained chord, a healthy real-ideal organism, where all forces function in a balanced way."[59] Krausism's notion of the "harmony of the whole" undergirded not only the belief in exercise and health, but also the desire to synchronize the body's vital force with the world through direct commerce with it. From this notion derived the importance in Krausist pedagogical doctrine of experiencing nature's wonders through long and invigorating hikes and nature walks. Krausism's preoccupation with body culture more generally anticipated and informed the modernist aesthetics that would become evident in the following decades through the expansion of sport and improvements in hygiene, particularly among the emerging *burguesía.*

Francisco Giner de los Ríos, one of the most venerated Krausist educators and the founder of the progressive school known as The Free Institution of Learning, was a firm advocate of *excursionismo* (excursionism), and, thanks to his efforts, various theories that exalted the superior status of nature were introduced into Spain. Through the institutional framework of The Free Institution of Learning, he offered a new lens with which to observe and appreciate nature's invigorating powers – one that incorporated the distinctive and reformist characteristics of the

57 Krause, *Ideal de la humanidad,* 89.

58 The many practices and ideas that made up the Naturist Movement in Spain owed a great deal to the spread of anarchism in the late-nineteenth and early-twentieth centuries. The anarchist Juan Montseny Carret (also known by the pseudonym Federico Urales) proposed a naturist way of life based on the harmonic integration of body and nature: "We want to unify the individual's life with the life of Nature. What's more, we want man to be Nature itself, just like the other animals who are bound by natural laws" (quoted in Lázaro Lorente, 318).

59 Krause, *Ideal de la humanidad,* 91.

landscape perspective developed in nineteenth-century geography.[60] Yet, there was more to Giner's approach to body and nature than just perspective. In conceiving of the body's inherent attunement to nature, Giner offered a way of guarding oneself from the hazards of modernization, a way of discovering natural and productive energies to reinvigorate one's physical-spiritual life. The environmental historian Santos Casado de Otaola explains that "[i]n the purity and spontaneity of nature, Giner and his disciples sought an antidote against hopeless materialism, against the hollow sophistication and crude mercantilism of a society heading towards the primacy of industrial capitalism."[61] At the centre of Giner's philosophy of nature stands the idea that body and environment were indissolubly entwined at the most elemental, enriching, and edifying level of vital force. In his words: "[B]ecause the body carries like a spirit the seal of its divine origin, we must cultivate it, know it, love it, desire its well-being, and direct and discover its forces ... The body's well-being, development, and health is impossible without Nature's well-being and health."[62] This same impulse to harmonize body and nature would profoundly influence the landscape aesthetics of Krausist-educated modernists like Antonio Machado and Juan Ramón Jiménez at the turn of the twentieth century. In his 1917 prologue to his landmark *Lands of Castile* (also translated as *Fields of Castile*), Machado orients his readers to the true wellspring of his poetic compositions: "Many poems respond to a patriotic concern; others respond to the simple love of Nature, which for me is infinitely greater than the love of Art."[63]

Key figures within the Krausist movement would venture into the biological and evolutionary sciences. Enrique Serrano y Fatigati and Salvador Calderón y Arana's *Studies on Natural Philosophy: Total Organization of Matter* (1870), represented one of Krausism's earliest forays into the history and philosophy of biology (in fact, through this biological lens, Krausism morphed into Krauso-positivism, as it inevitably engaged the experimentation and objectivity of positivist science).[64] Fatigati and Calderón y Arana set out to investigate organized bodies, not in terms of their form per se, but rather, their function. In a clear rebuttal of

60 See Ortega Cantero, "Paisaje, historia e identidad nacional," 187–8.

61 Casado de Otaola, *Naturaleza patria*, 34.

62 Giner, *Estudios de Literatura y Arte*, 17–18.

63 Machado, *Campos de Castilla*, 79. See Elena de Jongh-Rossel's *Krausism and the Generation of 1898*, 149–51.

64 Antonio Jiménez's García's "The introduction of Krausopositivism in Spain" provides a useful summary on the subject, 649–59. See also José Luis Abellán's "Philosophy of the Free Institution of Learning: Krausopositivism," 405–18.

materialist philosophy, they stressed the wondrous and complex organization of matter and theorized that nature, by means of a fundamental life principle, aspired to continually perfect itself and teleologically advance toward higher states of functional unity. In a review of Fatigati and Calderón y Arana's work, the Krausist Alfredo Calderón summed up their thesis, stating: "organization contains within it a type of providential and divine ambition, and this mysterious force allows bodies day after day, and one by one, to advance from the unformed chaos of the inorganic, to the varied and generative functions of life."[65] Fatigati and Calderón y Arana's *Studies on Natural Philosophy* did not strive to identify evolutionary causalities, yet they advanced the idea that nature was imbued with a vital force that did in fact evolve toward higher degrees of rational organization (the human being, of course, represented nature's most highly organized organic system). This teleological organicity echoed Thomas Huxley's belief that man was the product of "nature's great progression, from the formless to the formed – from the inorganic to the organic – from the blind force to conscious intellect and will."[66]

Other Krausist scientists, such as the distinguished Augusto González de Linares, would tackle the divide between the organic and inorganic, postulating that all living matter constantly evolved toward larger and more perfect vital unities. To state, as materialists did, that life was simply a by-product of organized matter "erases the hierarchy of life … It conceives vital force as pure ethereal dynamism, or mere atomic collisions. It does away with the bond of unity from which the various parts of the organism blossom and live."[67] In many respects, Fatigati, Calderón y Arana, and Linares were arguing for a view of the organic – its generation and development – that accommodated the mysterious workings of a vital force, a proposition that ran contrary to what the anatomist, physician, and great defender of Haeckelian evolutionary materialism Peregrín Casanova proposed in his *General Biology* of 1877: "No one, absolutely no one, has demonstrated the existence of a *vital force* … [A]ll the properties presented in living bodies are not products of singular beings … but rather are caused by the special properties of the chemical

65 Calderón, "Una idea," 187–8. "More than a formal unity," Sala Catalá notes of Fatigati and Calderón y Arana's conclusions, "organized matter was characterized by a *functional unity* … This allows them to abandon a basic premise of German *Naturphilosophie* and incorporate into their research the Comparative Anatomy of the French school, as well as the paleontology of the period" (57).

66 Quoted in Ruse, *Monad to Man*, 209.

67 Linares, *Obra completa*, 402.

elements that enter their composition, and, above all, by the great variety of combinations of that Proteus of the organic realm, carbon."[68]

Krausism faced harsh criticism from the Church and conservative groups in Spain for emphasizing the individual's vital potentialities in matters of reason and faith. Krause himself prophesied that the most rational and perfect stage of human development depended on forging a new alliance between the healthy, embodied self and God, and not surprisingly, the *Ideal of Humanity for Life* was placed on the Index of Forbidden Books shortly after its publication. One of the most momentous pieces of legislation that the Krausist-inspired government enacted after the 1868 liberal revolution in Spain was precisely the separation of Church and State and the freedom of religion. The Free Institution of Learning was erected upon the principles of personal liberty, tolerance, and self-improvement (Article 15 of its Statutes, for instance, stressed the requirement of freedom of thought, without regard to state or religious authority). Yet, we must be clear on this point: Krausism was by no means the profane philosophy it was made out to be. Quite the opposite. The immanence of God, according to Krause, was apparent in every facet of existence. Krausism's intriguing amalgam of panentheism and harmonic rationalism encouraged a very personal search for God's transcendence and, just as importantly, an edifying and *embodied* engagement with the world. The question was this: how could the individual ever aspire to harmonize with greater spheres of rational perfection in his day-to-day life if his constitutive vital force was not realized to its full potential? In *Ideal of Humanity for Life*, Krause condensed his philosophy into twenty-three precepts, of which precepts four and five spell out this crucial point: "4. You should live and work as a human whole [exercising your] full understanding, faculties, and forces in all your relations. 5. You should know, respect, and love your spirit, body, and both as one, always maintaining each one, and both, pure, healthy, and beautiful, and living in them as a harmonic being."[69] As interpreted through the lens of Spanish Krausism, a body attuned to reason and its teleology was a healthy body, whose vital force had to be duly nurtured and perfected. The essence of Spanish Krausism, then, was rooted not in a scientific approach to man and nature per se, but rather in the embodiment of a *Weltanschauung* in which life energy – the individual's, the community's,

68 Peregrín Casanova, *La biología general*, vol. 1, 27.

69 Krause, *Ideal de la humanidad*, 100.

and the nation's – was directed toward building the ideal society of the future, or what came to be known as the New Spain.[70]

It cannot be overlooked that, with the rise of positivist science and Krausism, vitalism greatly expanded in scope in this post-1868 period. The meaning of vital force was explored in Spain and across Europe through everything from intuitionism to irrationalism, and naturism to avant-gardism. As Richard Lofthouse explains in his study on vitalism and modern art, "the end of the nineteenth century and the years leading up to 1914 witnessed vitalism in its most intense form."[71] Indeed, vital force was theorized by luminaries like Henri Bergson (élan vital), John Burroughs (new vitalism), Samuel Butler (vital unity of life), Hans Driesch (vital teleology of life), John Haldane (vitalistic physiology), Nietzsche (Dionysian vitalism), Johannes Reinke (neovitalism), Bernard Shaw (metabiological vitalism), and José Ortega y Gasset (ratiovitalism), to name only a few. In fact, Ortega y Gasset went on to erect an entire philosophical system in Spain around the same fundamental rapport between rationality and vital force that preoccupied the Krausists. In an attempt to overcome the limitations of a positivist-materialist ontology and to place the body at the centre of the problem of modern subjectivity, he claimed that the individual's particular experience within the larger social context constituted his world, his authentic reality. For Ortega y Gasset, the individual could be thought of as a vital aspiration ("pretension vital"), a body-self in a continual state of movement and vital becoming. "I am not a thing," he declared, "but a drama, a struggle to become what I need to become."[72]

As theories of vital force gained currency, they found expression in artistic and literary practices and fuelled modernism's fascination with corporeality and bodily aesthetics, as we shall see in the following chapter. They played a pivotal role in conceiving of the body – and not just the realm of the intellect – as the font of true creative energy. What is

70 I am referring to what the author Antonio Zozaya tells us in 1922 of Giner de los Ríos's impact on Spanish culture: "The *new Spain* is the daughter of Giner" (quoted in Rama, *La crisis*, 69). Likewise, the politician Fernando de los Ríos declared in 1926 that Giner de los Ríos was "the spiritual father of the new Spain" (177).

71 Lofthouse, *Vitalism in Modern Art*, 14. Hvidberg-Hansen and Oelsner's edited volume *The Spirit of Vitalism: Health, Beauty and Stength in Danish Art, 1890–1940* is framed around a similar argument: "Vitalism as a period is associated with certain specific developments betweent 1890 and 1940 ... Vitalism is viewed in this context as a modern project with the aim of recreating a healthy and vital culture which in the longer term might perhaps dare to measure itself against the cultures of the past" (14).

72 Ortega y Gasset, *Obras completas*, vol. 5, 339.

more, they informed a wealth of discourses on health and sexuality and were deployed to frame discussions of degeneration, social pathology, and the far-reaching rhetoric of sickness well into the twentieth century.[73] Artists, dancers, filmmakers, poets, and novelists heeded the modernist call for body intelligence, and mounted a counter-critique to the maladies of tradition and the legacies of mind-body epistemology that they fervently believed had no place in the new age of self-determination.

73 Here I am referring to Barbara Spackman's excellent study *Decadent Genealogies*. Spackman analyzes the discourses of disease and sickness in decadent writers and demonstrates how it extols the "counternatural" as a way of opening new critical spaces in which to explore gender, corporeality, otherness, and virility (viii). I explore this topic in more depth in Chapter 6.

6

Degeneration, Regeneration, Corporealization: What the Lived Body Can Do According to Miguel de Unamuno, Pío Baroja, and Ramón Gómez de la Serna

As long as science fails to discover
the sources of life
…
there will be poetry!

Gustavo A. Bécquer, *Rimas*[1]

I stripped your petals like a rose,
to see your soul,
and I did not see it.
But everything on every side
– horizons of land and sea –,
everything, even the infinite,
became suffused with an immense
and living essence.

Juan Ramón Jiménez, *Diario de un poeta reciencasado*[2]

IN HIS 1876 LECTURE "POSITIVISM AND CIVILIZATION," the philosopher and jurist Gumersindo de Azcárate stood before a packed house at Madrid's Athenaeum and confirmed what everyone already knew: "Positivism is entering Spain through two open doors."[3] Azcárate was not

1 Bécquer, *Rimas y leyendas*, 9.
2 Jiménez, *Diary of a Newlywed Poet*, 180.
3 Azcárate, "El positivismo y la civilización," 234.

mistaken when he insisted on the reach of positivist science in Spain in the 1870s. The number of university students pursuing a scientific degree had more than doubled between 1857 and 1878, while the number of students pursuing a medical degree specifically had more than quintupled in the same period.[4] Increased foreign investment and industrial development during this period only stimulated positivist science, which presented itself as the Religion of Humanity that Comte had prophesized would change the world. With the translation of Ludwig Büchner, Pierre Jean Georges Cabanis, Comte, Darwin, Haeckel, and Kant into Spanish during these years, and with the introduction of the latest laboratory research and the experimental method in various disciplines, vital force was increasingly reduced in scientific literature to the functions of physical and chemical relations. Within certain spheres of the Spanish scientific community, there was a real sense that the fundamental question of life was being systematically emptied of any trace of vitalist metaphysics. In his *Reform Plan of General Pathology and Its Clinical Application*, published a few years after Azcárate's lecture, the physician and vitalist José de Letamendi sharply condemned positivism within the medical profession for attempting to downplay and even ignore the complex vital phenomena that regulated the living body. From his perspective, positivism was attempting to relegate to "total obscurity ... the real and practical notion of *living individuality*."[5] The most ancient and essential medical practice of general pathology, he maintained, had undergone such profound transformations in a few short years in Spain, and had adopted positivist methodologies so tyrannically, that it had lost sight of its true purpose: assessing the individual body and its life functions in relation to the origin, nature, and progress of disease:

> Modern general pathology seeks its foundation in experimental observation. What is good about this tendency is the wealth of concrete ideas it provides; what is bad about this tendency is its anarchic spirit that buries the immutable principles of science in a troubled storm of empirical truths. Ancient general pathology was based on observation and synthetic experiences of the whole individual, which is the aim and purpose of [good] medicine.[6]

In his study on physical culture, Harold Segel has examined the ways in which corporeality and action gained currency in the late-nineteenth

4 Peset and Peset, "Las universidades españolas," 37.
5 Letamendi, *Plan de reforma*, 29.
6 Ibid., 32.

and early-twentieth centuries with the rise of the modernist movement. The disenchantment with science and intellectual culture in general fostered a profound skepticism concerning the rapport between language, epistemology, and cultural reform. "Modernist anti-intellectualism," Segel asserts, "favoured action over contemplation and the passive culture of the word … Experience is what mattered most; that was how the world was to be learned, not through intellectualization and language."[7] The emerging world of pantomime, modern dance, sport, and the cult of the athlete also generated a new awareness of physicality and action, particularly during this period that saw the launch of the first modern Olympic Games in 1896 and its celebration of the Greek ideal of body culture. Segel accepts, for the most part, Theodor Adorno's premise that modernist aesthetics – including avant-garde fragmentation and skepticism – represented a trenchant critique of the mass-culture industry and commodity capitalism that positivist rationality helped build. Yet, the issue is more nuanced on closer inspection, as Segel recognizes. What his study brings to light clearly is that the life of *action* at the heart of modernist culture, which inspired adventurers and writers such as Ernest Hemingway, Theodore Roosevelt, and Henry de Montherlant, participated in, and depended on, the very socio-cultural forces it often repudiated. The larger revolution of how corporeality was perceived in the late-nineteenth century – a revolution inconceivable without the vitalist assault on positivism and rationality that allowed the body to be reconceptualized as a dynamic, living system of powerful energies and impulses – buttressed the crucial notion that the body, *my* body, was one of the most effective means of accessing the truth about the world.[8]

The scientific penchant for reducing life to facts and quantities fuelled modernism's complex and, at times, chaotic revolt against positivism, and brought into relief the need to reaffirm the body and its creative powers.[9] Modernism's bold praise of the body and its potentialities was presaged in Spain not only in Krausist practical philosophy, as we saw in the previous chapter, but also in the anarcho-syndicalist movements of personal liberty and self-sufficiency that began taking

7 Segel, *Body Ascendant*, 5–6.

8 Armstrong, *Modernism*, 2. See especially Chapter 1, titled "Electrifying the Body," in which Armstrong demonstrates how advancements in electrical science, neurology, and physiology were employed to regulate the body and its energies, 13–41.

9 See Rene Wellek's chapter, "The Revolt against Positivism in Recent Literary Scholarship," in *Concepts of Criticism*, 256–81. Also relevant is H. Stuart Hughes's chapter, "The Decade of the 1890s: The Revolt against Positivism," 33–66.

form in the 1870s with the rise of anarchism and socialism, movements that greatly informed the debates in Spain concerning everything from eugenicist science to women's liberation.[10] Also significant were the free love, homeopathic, naturist, and spiritualist movements that were coming into their own by the 1890s in response to the perceived erosion of agency in modern society and the growing physical maladies of urban life, which were vividly documented by realist authors like Benito Pérez Galdós and Juan Valera. Catherine Bellver has demonstrated further how the rise of the jazz scene in Spain, as well as the expansion of the dance-hall craze and the advent of sports as a democratizing cultural spectacle, likewise played a decisive role in elevating the corporeal between 1900 and 1930. As she points out, these developments depended largely on a new awareness of the body's inherent dynamism, as well as a general reverence for youthfulness and its association with boundless change.[11]

My aim in this chapter is to consider the influence that theories of vital force exerted on Spanish philosophy and letters and the role they played in widening the dialogue on regenerationism and human subjectivity in the late-nineteenth and early-twentieth centuries. What I argue is that the epistemological basis upon which it was possible to know the body shifted radically throughout this period. There was a push in various fields toward a more holistic conception of the body, in which it was not simply reduced to anatomical or physiological characteristics, or abstracted from theological doctrine, medico-biological practices, or positivist reasoning. Rather, it was valued as a *lived* body. The term "lived body" has its origins in Edmund Husserl's *The Basic Problems of Phenomenology* and brings into focus to what extent the I-experience depends upon the body's vital capacities and processes. "Everyone relates his I-experience," Husserl explains, "and, in general, his specific I-possessions to the lived body. Thus, he *localizes* them in the body."[12] The lived body encompasses more than organs and flesh. Indeed, it becomes the vital ground, so to speak, for all experience, for all consciousness, and thus serves as the organic, existential medium (the "central member" for Husserl) through which the individual relates to the world. For philosopher Max Scheler, what differentiated the lived body from the objective and material

10 See Martha A. Ackelsberg's *Free Women of Spain*, 37–52; also Richard Clemison and Francisco Vázquez García's *Hermaphroditism: Medical Science and Sexual Identity in Spain, 1850–1960*, 35–108.

11 Bellver, *Bodies in Motion*, 111.

12 Husserl, *The Basic Problems of Phenomenology*, 4.

thing-body is that it provided the unique and underlying form that conjoined organic sensations (the body's vital states and perceptions) and consciousness (the mind) into a "whole ego in its total manifold."[13] That is to say, the lived body, conceptualized as the complete integration of life energy and mind, constituted the total ego. Maurice Merleau-Ponty greatly expanded the meaning of the lived body in the post–Second World War period into the realms of psychology, ontology, physiology, and, of course, phenomenology. Echoing Scheler's core argument, what made the lived body so remarkable for Merleau-Ponty was that it acted as the intermediary between consciousness and everything else, and it was thus the all-important organic nexus that fundamentally negotiated subjectivity (inside) and world (outside).[14] To sum up, then, the lived body is a body "bound up with, and directed toward, an experienced world … a being in relationship to that which is other: other people, other things, an environment … [a body] that helps to constitute this world-as-experienced … [a body that] is not just one thing *in* the world, but a way in which the world comes to be."[15] The emerging concept of the lived body became a pivotal resource in Spain with which to combat tradition, science, and religion, while opening new vistas into the study of complex behavioural and psychic processes and experiences. With Unamuno, Baroja, and Gómez de la Serna, it is possible to appreciate just how the lived body brimming with health and vitality – or conversely, degenerate, infirm, and drained of its vital force – laid the groundwork for new critical paradigms of subjectivity that propelled modernist aesthetics in Spain.

KNOW THYSELF: INWARDNESS AND PROTOPLASMIC THEORY IN MIGUEL DE UNAMUNO

Let us begin exploring pre- and early-modernist expressions of the lived body and vital force in Unamuno's writings. While his oeuvre has elicited generous commentary and inspired diverse theoretical inquiries spanning a broad set of philosophical and literary domains, there are various questions concerning its treatment of the lived body and vital force that remain to be addressed, particularly with respect to his early essays on gymnastics, as well as his socialist publications and landmark collections *On Casticism* (1895) and *The Tragic Sense of Life* (1912). Clearly, a compelling vitalist undercurrent traverses Unamuno's thinking from his earliest period and informs practically every area of his work. It is so pervasive, so

13 Scheler, "Lived Body," 181.
14 See Merleau-Ponty's *Phenomenology of Perception.*
15 Leder, "A Tale of Two Bodies," 25.

integrally embedded in his thinking, that it reveals unambiguously that the potentialities of the lived body were always on his mind. This vitalist undercurrent, as we shall see, is variegated rather than homogenous, nuanced rather than formulaic, and its progression in Unamuno's thought remains relatively uncharted.

The complexity surrounding the lived body in Unamuno's oeuvre has prompted readers to attribute myriad meanings to it. For Octavio Ruiz-Manjón, for instance, Unamuno found in the heterogeneous currents of nineteenth-century *vitalismo* a strategic implement for both critiquing and transcending the positivism that had so powerfully influenced his formative years during the 1880s and early 1890s.[16] In a similar vein, Pedro González Cuevas holds that Unamuno's early writings amount to a "vitalist reading" of Hippolyte Taine's positivist arguments, a vitalist reading that progressively elevated the bodily self in the face of positivist reductionism.[17] Unamuno had indeed sung the praises of Taine, just as he had G.W.F. Hegel and Herbert Spencer, and it is often claimed that his first serious approximation to any vitalist ontology came about as he distanced himself from positivist historicism after the 1897 spiritual crisis that sharpened his philosophical insights into death, nothingness, and Being.[18] Yet, in his essay "The Influence of Gymnastics on Building Character" of 1886, and later in the essays collected in *On Casticism* of 1895, it becomes clear that his affinity for the question of vital force not only antedates his break with positivism and his crisis considerably, but also establishes a thread of continuity from the 1880s well into the twentieth century.

Readers like Stephen Roberts have appreciated the vitalist perspective in Unamuno's oeuvre and considered it an integral facet of his philosophical project, which was conveyed – and poignantly so after 1897 – in a very personal struggle between the irrational optimism in life and the rational order of experience.[19] Unamuno's *Intimate Diary* documents his 1897 crisis in painful detail. It was a crisis that came about when he attempted to reconcile himself to the idea of nothingness and annihilation, yet could not forsake the prospect of God and the afterlife. The erratic emotional states reflected in the diary range from euphoria to anxiety to phobic dread, and reveal the very real physical toll they

16 Ruiz-Manjón, "Notas sobre Miguel de Unamuno," 277.

17 González Cuevas, *El pensamiento político*, 54.

18 In the short essay "Taine, Caricaturist" of 1907, Unamuno criticized positivists like Taine for having never believed in "individuality or the soul" and for having reduced individuals to "instances of exemplification of abstract theories" (*Ensayos*, vol. 2, 137).

19 Roberts, *Miguel de Unamuno*, 126.

exacted on his body. The finality of death distressed Unamuno greatly, and it was with this finality in mind that he stated: "One should attempt from time to time to conceive oneself as non-existent, feel oneself not being. Out of such horror comes the fear of God – and hope."[20] For her part, the critic María de la Concepción de Unamuno Pérez focuses on Unamuno's more elaborated ideal of vital force in *The Tragic Sense of Life* with Henri Bergson's philosophy in mind, noting that Unamuno's philosophy offers a rather different vitalist sensibility than Bergson's. "Unlike Bergson," she argues, "[Unamuno] is interested not in the harmonic development of human existence, but rather its struggles, its anguish."[21] The convergences and divergences between Unamuno and Bergson have long been recognized, for both philosophers reacted against positivism through a vitalist disavowal of the cult of quantification and empiricism and a recognition, nonetheless, of the ultimate necessity of reason and its principles.[22] More comprehensively, the philosopher and scholar Luis Jiménez Moreno points to a loose-textured "vitalist order" within Unamuno's philosophy that engages and, likewise, resists reason and logic to provide a safe harbour for the individual in his despairing aspiration for immortality.[23] While he makes a convincing case for Unamuno's affirmation of life and his vitalist discernments, he confines the bulk of his critical remarks to *The Tragic Sense of Life* and does not explore how this "vitalist order" extends to other areas of Unamuno's oeuvre.

Clearly, there is little consensus on the depth and character of the vitalist bent in Unamuno's oeuvre, and few efforts have been made to document its impact on his early publications before 1897. W.D. Johnson's early study of Unamuno's ontology tackles an issue of great relevance that all too often has been overlooked and serves as a guiding framework in this respect. What Johnson proposes is that Unamuno's fundamental methodology for approaching the lived body rests upon a straightforward and yet profound hypothesis: the reality around us is not what determines our lifeworld, but rather, it is our lifeworld, in all its vital possibility, that determines the reality around us.[24] Each individual being constitutes a reality unto itself, and its concrete and ever-unfolding existence – the actual *living* that defines it – generates this reality. Thus, it is the continuity, action, and surge of life mediated through a body

20 Unamuno, *The Private World*, 40.

21 Concepción de Unamuno Pérez, *Miguel de Unamuno*, 116.

22 See Benjamin Fraser's "Unamuno and Bergson: Notes on a Shared Methodology."

23 Jiménez Moreno, *Prácticas del saber*, 74.

24 Johnson, "Vida y ser," 9–11.

(*this* body, *my* body) that matters, and not our abstract beliefs or thinking about what existence could be. In her psychoanalytic reading of Unamuno's concept of self, Alison Sinclair touches upon this corporeality, pointing out that "the presence of the body, with man's being always contingent upon it, predicated by it, is a shadowy and consistent area of emphasis in Unamuno's writing."[25] Sinclair's understanding of Unamuno's preoccupation with race, origins, lineage, and individuality more generally (a preoccupation that other modernists like Baroja shared, as we shall see in the following section) shifts our attention to the lived body and its signifying surfaces and vitalist meanings. There is no question, as Sinclair contends, that Unamuno advocated for a "return to the world of the body," yet it was precisely this fragile and ephemeral world of corporeality that radically problematized his yearning for immortality.[26] For Paul Olson, Unamuno's thinking is indeed founded upon the "primacy of the body," and he echoes Sinclair in the basic premise that the lived body subsumes a vexing realm of incongruities for Unamuno, in which "the joy of existence and of anguish deriving from its limitations" are brought into dialogue and conflict.[27]

Francisco La Rubia Prado's study on Unamuno's organicism merits our attention here. La Rubia Prado's *Allegories of the Will* has made the most convincing case thus far for the organic view that guides Unamuno's inquiries. As he demonstrates, an organicist thinking informs Unamuno's oeuvre through and through, and takes its coordinates primarily from Samuel Taylor Coleridge's poetry and philosophy, particularly his theory of the imagination, and from *Völkerpsychologie*, the ethnic psychology founded in the 1860s and grounded in Romantic approaches to the *Volk* and cultural nationalism. With the publication of *On Casticism* in 1895, Unamuno transitioned, according to La Rubia Prado, from a positivist-mechanist world view to an "organic vision of the universe" in which key concepts, such as biological teleology, pantheism, and vital principle, were increasingly marshalled in support of his literary ambitions.[28] Unamuno developed what he himself called *viviparismo* (a zoological term meaning to give birth to living young rather than eggs) to conceive the literary craft as a spontaneous and natural process in which the seed of a work gestated in the author's mind and was birthed, as it were, in a generative flash of inspiration. Obviously, this approach to literary production presented new tensions between literary form and content,

25 Sinclair, *Uncovering the Mind*, 228.
26 Ibid., 71.
27 Olson, *The Great Chiasmus*, 11–13.
28 LaRubia Prado, *Alegorías de la Voluntad*, 66.

tensions that Unamuno exploited masterfully in complex ways in his own particular genre of novel, which he termed *nivola*. The strength of La Rubia's study is that it plants Unamuno's literature firmly in organicist theory and its vitalism. What is downplayed in his study, however, is how Unamuno channelled a host of vitalist assumptions into those fundamental concepts of individuality and corporeality that framed his thinking on bodily life, including ancient Greek philosophy, the nineteenth-century physical-education movement, Spanish regenerationism, and *fin-de-siècle* protoplasmic theory.

Unamuno's preoccupation with the lived body and vital force took root in his earliest writings. It is well established that he suffered from poor health throughout his youth, and grew concerned at a very young age with the rapport between soma and psyche. What is not widely recognized is how much he fretted about the degree to which his physical health declined with the cultivation of his intellect. As he remembered it, "I became depleted in a childhood ardour of thirsting to know, which was like a premature and unnatural gloom that brought about physical debility."[29] Elsewhere, he added: "In my ascendant march through school, my body grew weak with the ardour of my intelligence."[30] In the words of one biographer, Unamuno lived in isolation from the world throughout most of his childhood, and was, for all intents and purposes, "a bay-window child," a reclusive youth who interacted little with his home city of Bilbao and devoted himself instead to family, school, religious obligations, and the books collected in his father's library.[31] Unamuno did in fact seek refuge in reading. He read voraciously in biology, history, logic, philosophy, and natural science. It was through binge readings of the philosopher and priest Jaime Balmes during spells of feverish insomnia that he first discovered those paragons of reason – Descartes, Kant, and Hegel – who would accompany him for the rest of his life. From the beginning, then, the fruits of intellectual exertion for Unamuno were intimately wedded to a range of bodily states of fatigue and illness.

In one of his earliest and more-curious writings, dating to 1886 and titled "The Influence of Gymnastics on Building Character" – a series of three short essays published in *Gymnastics Review* that resonate with the same *fin-de-siècle* cult of physical education characteristic of the Krausist movement and the debates on societal health and hygiene across Europe – the twenty-two-year-old Unamuno meditated upon the ties between

29 Unamuno, *Escritos bilbainos*, 184.

30 Unamuno, *Recuerdos*, 63.

31 Juaristi, *Miguel de Unamuno*, 61–2.

body and mind. By this time, he had completed his studies in literature and philosophy in Madrid, which had been a wearying endeavour, given that it was during his university years between 1880 and 1884 when he began grappling with his religious identity and duty to God. "It was the period of my greatest internal struggles," he recalled, "because while I wished to think of God and the afterlife, all I thought about was … this life."[32] Since childhood, he had sporadically followed exercise regimens in hopes of strengthening his poor constitution, but by 1886 he had intensified his physical activity and began frequenting Bilbao's New Hygienic and Therapeutic Gymnasium. Opened in 1875, the New Hygienic and Therapeutic Gymnasium was a state-of-the-art facility that boasted modern exercise machines and comfortable and stylish dressing rooms, including spacious studios for music, fencing, and other sports. Unlike the smaller gymnasiums and recreational centres in the city, it offered the latest hydrotherapy treatments, which were all the rage throughout Europe and responded to the emerging middle class's concern for hygiene and physical well-being. The gymnasium had come under the management of Felipe Serrate, the founder of *Gymnastics Review* and a pioneer in the Spanish physical-education movement, who had travelled extensively around the country preaching the transformative benefits of the nascent sport of modern gymnastics. In fact, the Serrate family had made a name for itself since the early-nineteenth century in the circus world – one of the main performative arenas from which modern gymnastics emerged during these years – and the family was celebrated for its gymnastic acts, which included death-defying somersaults over lions and tables laden with sharp objects.[33] As an avowed admirer of the hygienist José Gil y Fresno – a proponent of calisthenics and medical hydrology and author of *The Physical and Moral Hygiene of the Bilbaino* of 1871 and *Hydrological Medical Guide to Vizcaya* of 1879 – Felipe Serrate upheld the therapeutic value of exercise and maintained that the kinetic body was an indubitable source of pleasure and overall health. In Serrate's words: "[M]ovement is life and everything, absolutely everything, moves in the universe, and without movement existence would be impossible. Movement brings us life, and paralysis brings us death."[34]

Serrate had clearly made an impression on the young Unamuno. In the first essay of "The Influence of Gymnastics on Building Character," titled "Valour" and dedicated to "my *maestro* Felipe Serrate," Unamuno opens with a laudatory preamble praising Serrate for his "intelligent

32 Quoted in Rabaté, *Miguel de Unamuno*, 38.

33 Torrebadella-Flix, "Del espectáculo acrobático," 71.

34 Arroyo Parra and Hernández Vázquez, "Ilustración Gimnástica," n.p.

6.1 Drawing of the Nuevo Gimnasio Normal, Higiénico y Terapéutico of Bilbao that appeared in *La ilustración española y americana*, 1875.

mentorship."[35] There is no denying that valour was an odd topic of analysis for a journal devoted to gymnastics and the practical application of physical education, yet upon closer inspection it becomes apparent that Unamuno is chronicling his own very personal journey from the morass of physical debility and trepidation of his youth to the invigorating courage and general salubriousness of his early adulthood:

> I know a lad – and so do you [Felipe Serrate] – who used to be apprehensive, even though he never let on that he was this way. After a spirited race, he would fall to the ground drowning in intense palpitations ... He often breathed with difficulty ... [H]e tossed and turned in bed, unable to sleep, preoccupied with a certain stinging sensation close to his left nipple. He used to grope his chest-box, and he

35 Unamuno, *Escritos bilbainos*, 100.

lived in constant worry. He began doing gymnastics ... Today, after completing a series of pectoral flexions or any other type of violent exercise, he sits easy with his heart at rest or not very agitated. He also laughs at his old fears and gives thanks to gymnastics, to you, and to himself, for having accomplished so much.[36]

Unamuno invokes the instruction of the ancient Delphic Oracle to extol the "active, energetic, and serene valour" that blossoms naturally in the individual who comes into awareness of his bodily self, which of course included one's plethora of physical energies.[37] What he seeks to convey in this essay is that, through the conscientious cultivation and management of the body's innermost vital force, the individual can transform himself – just as the lad Unamuno had done – and conquer the debilitating frailties of temerity and apprehensiveness to thereby act more effectively, even more ethically, in the face of adversity:

Gymnastics not only provides us with strength, but it distributes and regulates it and teaches us how to understand and manage it. The man who understands the limits of his physical vigour, who considers his forces and becomes master over them, has an appreciable advantage over other men. There are lots of people who are unaware of the force they can muster and who are ignorant of the real treasures of physical vigour that such a force can bring ... One of the greatest enemies of the body is apprehension. To do away with it, there is nothing better than to know thyself.[38]

As might be expected, philosophy is never far from Unamuno's mind. In the second essay, "Reason and Imagination," he draws upon the ancient Greek philosophical tradition once again – principally Aristotle's belief in the shared nature of body and soul in *De Anima* – to contend that the body's intrinsic forces and those of the soul are wholly complementary. Thus, when the body is debilitated from excessive work, for instance, so too is the soul, which has the unfortunate result of unleashing those unhappy vagaries of the imagination that deplete the body even further. It follows that when the imagination – itself an organic function for Unamuno – and not the sober faculty of reason commandeers the body, the individual is disposed to lapse into an infirm and hallucinatory state characterized by amnesia, hyperesthesia, deliriums, visions, and chills. He clarifies further: "When the body is weak, the soul is ill ... To debilitate and castigate the body is to unbridle the imagination and work

36 Ibid., 101.
37 Ibid., 100–1.
38 Ibid., 101.

toward losing dominion over oneself."[39] Unamuno frames this essay more generally in relation to the ancient ideal of *mens sana in corpore sano,* which called for the harmonious development of body and soul.[40] In his estimation, the body that remains sovereign over its forces through reason, the body that is vigorous, resilient, and even triumphant without falling prey to monomaniacal regimens, is the body whose vital force is not only cultivated through physical activity, but also appropriately harnessed toward productive and moral ends. In his dissertation *On the Origin and Prehistory of the Basque Race* of 1884, he had already hinted at this aesthetic when he correlated outward physical beauty with inner constitutional fortitude within the context of the Basques' racial character, a topic of great interest to him throughout the 1880s and 1890s: "If there is such a thing as beauty, gentlemen, then beauty is the man who displays his forces, who instructs his ingenuity, who jumps and runs; the energy of the soul, as well as that of the body, are beautiful."[41] We can better appreciate why Unamuno concludes the essay by suggesting that maladies such as moral perversion and even something as nebulous as the soul's corruption oftentimes originated from the body's systemic enfeeblement.

In the third and final essay "Good Humour" – an essay in which *humour* has little to do with the comical or amusing, but rather with one's positive disposition and sound physical constitution – he offers his closing thoughts on vital force. Fittingly, he alludes to the Aristotelian concept of *eudaimonia,* what is often translated as "happiness" or "human flourishing," and projects the most desirable form of life – that is, of living and acting – for the individual. For Aristotle, *eudaimonia* remains out of our grasp so long as we disregard reason and its guiding hand in life, for it is reason and its virtue and excellence that motivates all of those worthwhile actions in the world that make for a full life. In *Nicomachean Ethics,* he declares that "if there is an end for all that we do, this will be the good achievable by action … Happiness, then, is something final and self-sufficient, and is the end of action."[42] Although in "Good Humour" Unamuno merely sketches his ideals of *vivir* (living; the continuous day-by-day existential becoming) and *obrar* (acting; the actualization of one's life through action and will), which appear so prominently in his later

39 Ibid., 102.

40 In Book 3 of Plato's *Republic,* Socrates ponders on the proper education in the Just State and illuminates Glaucon on the two necessary arts – music and gymnastics – for the harmonious conjunction of body and soul/mind.

41 Unamuno, *Obras,* vol. 6, 222.

42 Aristole, *Nicomachean Ethics,* 369.

work, his sympathy for these key concepts is clearly visible in this early essay and tethered to the body's intrinsic vital force:

> Among the many pleasures there is no greater pleasure than living [vivir] and acting [obrar]. This pleasure is none other than activity manifested freely, namely, the inner force that acts upon the exterior world without any hindrances or obstacles ... The man who has within him a force that is balanced, well-distributed, and eager to obey the will, has cause to enjoy to ever-greater extents all the simple and human pleasures, especially the pleasure of living.[43]

What is so compelling about Unamuno's essays in "The Influence of Gymnastics on Building Character" is threefold. Firstly, they provide a more intimate portrait of the young Unamuno's engagement with the so-called working body and the discourse of fatigue that remained looming shadows in the nineteenth-century imaginary. By the 1890s, the problem of fatigue was considered "the paramount manifestation of the body's limit to produce work. Fatigue ... was a greater threat to the future of the modern civilized nation than either rapacious capital or the atavistic worker lacking in discipline and time sense."[44] Through the framework of gymnastics and bodily health, Unamuno gives voice to the conviction that the demands made on the body in modern society were not only exhausting, but also increasingly onerous – to the point of depleting it of its vital force and rendering it pathological. Interestingly, the working body he envisions in these essays is not that of the urban labourers Marx and Engels portray in *The Communist Manifesto*, who must peddle themselves as commodities and become toiling appendages of modern industrial machinery. Rather, he envisions a working body that resembled his own in childhood: a body consumed in intellectual pursuits – he offers as an example what he considers to be the sedentary occupation of an attorney – that requires some form of corrective corporeal exertion (i.e., gymnastics) in order to return the integral body-mind system to a state of vital equilibrium.[45] Secondly, it becomes apparent in these essays to what extent ancient Greek philosophy and its emphasis on the rapprochement between body and soul undergirded his early philosophical approach to vital force. In short, he sets up, however schematically, the framework for the dynamic kinship – and likewise,

43 Unamuno, *Escritos bilbainos*, 104–5.

44 Rabinbach, *The Human Motor*, 121.

45 In his *Intimate Diary*, written more than a decade later, he remained steadfast that "intellectualism is a terrible illness" (*The Private*, 36). This idea resurfaces throughout his entire oeuvre.

antagonism – between body and soul that will frame his later theorizations on the seemingly insoluble contradictions of embodied existence. Thirdly, in these essays Unamuno gestures toward what will become his expansive ontological project of life, which aimed at consolidating *vivir* and *obrar*. In the 1900 essay "Inward!" he reiterated that no preconceived plan or formula made for a good life. In other words, one had to master life by *living* it, and it was only through the lived body and its actions that the individual discovered meaning and purpose.[46] In *The Tragic Sense of Life* of 1912, this idea remained very much intact: "that to be is to act, and that only whatever acts, what is active, exists, and only insofar as it acts."[47]

It has long been acknowledged that Unamuno's early sympathy for science, evolutionism, economics, and sociology shaped his concept of life and played a hand in his definitive turn toward socialism shortly after he obtained the professorship of Greek at the University of Salamanca in 1891. We know from recently published writings that he was well acquainted with the science of anthropometrics – the gathering of measurements of the human body that was common in the nineteenth century in the fields of phrenology, hygiene, eugenics, and criminology – and had even offered his own body for measurement at the Natural History Museum in Madrid in 1888.[48] It was in Salamanca, though, where he tackled the problem of individual human existence more fully. For Unamuno, the essential conditions of history – their constitution, exegesis, and functioning – were always present in his thinking when it came to *el individuo*. The great irony of his historicism was that capitalized History, understood in the broad sense as the endeavour to record and account for events in time, was of little interest to him. In 1910, a certain Schopenhauerian pathos inspired his critique of History, as he took up a point he had articulated more persuasively in his *On Casticism* of 1895, as we shall see shortly. This point was that History functioned as a looking glass, reflecting the turbulent upheavals of mankind and its institutions, but said precious little about the individual's lifeworld in the here and now. "I have always been more interested in individual human

46 Unamuno, "¡Adentro!" 315.

47 Unamuno, *The Tragic*, 161.

48 Along with recording copious body measurements, Unamuno gives us some indication of the scientific texts he was reading at the time, particularly in physiology and psychology. These texts include Henry Maudsley's *The Physiology of Mind* (1876) and *The Pathology of Mind* (1879), Léon A. Dumont's *Theórie Scientifique de la Sensibilité: Le Plaisir et la Peine* (1875), Julian Ochorowicz's *Mental Suggestion* (1887), Paul Gibier's *Spiritualism or Fakirism: Historical, Critical, and Experimental Study* (1886), and William Thierry Preyer's *The Mind of the Child* (1882). See Rivero Gómez's "Cuaderno 26," 220–1.

souls than social institutions," he admitted.[49] It was this fundamental question of *el individuo* and his vital engagement with the world that served as a wellspring, not only for his ruminations about what he called intra-history (the silent, day-to-day existence of individuals whose way of life remained immune to the vagaries of History), but also for his philosophy and literature and their richly complex interweaving.

The critic John Butt has contended that "Unamuno simply argued the individual out of existence, defined him as a dimension of nature, i.e. the unconscious ... [H]e deprived man of his freedom and creativity and argued himself into a totally enclosed view of the world."[50] On the contrary, Unamuno conceived of the individual brimming with life, and it was precisely this profusion of life at the core of his being that kindled his irrational yearning to extend it into the infinite. Similarly, it is also what transformed death – the cessation of all life in *my* body, and thus, of all hope whatsoever in *me* – into such a profoundly personal offence for the individual. To be sure, Unamuno considered the insult of death the bedrock of any vitalist outlook. For Unamuno, to live, nourish, cultivate, and feel one's vital force in every cell of the lived body at the inevitable precipice of nothingness revealed faith and God as absolute necessities of life, yet this revelation was likewise laden with agony, struggle, contradiction, and *tragedia* (a term that has little do with ancient Greek aesthetics or philosophy and instead conjured up the irreconcilable inner conflict that accompanied any attempt to rationalize life at the precipice of nothingness). Unamuno's concept of the individual, therefore, much like his allied concept of life, was not a metaphysical abstraction moulded out of categories of understanding and models of subjectivity and self-awareness à la Kant. The individual was conceived of as a concrete and temporal being, a thoroughly embodied and vitalized organism, a "man of flesh and bone, the man who is born, suffers and dies – above all dies; the man who drinks and loves; the man who is seen and heard; one's brother, the real brother," as he put it in the oft-quoted opening paragraph of *The Tragic Sense of Life*.[51] In this same work he clarified that "the end of History and Humanity is man, each man, each individual ... The individual is the end-purpose of the Universe."[52]

During his early socialist period in the 1890s, Unamuno ruminated on the ways capitalist production and the worship of technique diminished the individual and depleted his vital force. Lily Litvak is correct in

49 Unamuno, "Educación por la historia," 1059.

50 Butt, "Unamuno's Idea of Intrahistoria," 53.

51 Unamuno, *The Tragic*, 3.

52 Ibid., 339.

claiming that there is an essential contradiction between the forces of nature and those of industrial civilization in Unamuno's thinking. She tells us that "[h]e finds in nature a harmony and peace lacking in the modern world – a sensibility and sincerity struggling with the latest modern achievements … All these scientific and technological developments are concealing the panorama of natural life from modern man."[53] Unamuno maintained that, in the face of the ever-growing cult of quantification and empiricism, socialism stood as humanity's one true religion, capable of uniting and vivifying the loftier teleological project of social perfectibility. From this standpoint, one need not wonder why he endorsed socialism as a dynamic science whose vitalist impetus did nothing if not steer the individual toward the living spirit of the collectivity. As he proposed in one of his earliest socialist articles, "[t]o study politics … one has to swim in the currents of life."[54] Modern modes of production, similarly, had not sufficiently addressed the topic of human will, which was crucial to any consideration of the individual's life and character within the socio-economic order. As the origin of the body's physical and psychic energies, the enigmatic sphere of human will remained for Unamuno relatively immune to the technical apparatus of modern production, and it thus injected an indeterminate variable into the labour equation that resisted measurement and mechanism: "A factor of great importance intervenes in labour within the economy of production which is human will; be what it may with regard to liberty, it introduces [into the economy of production] a variability of the indeterminate and uncertain."[55] What it all came down to was that the fundamental severance of science from humanity's vital core had come to a tipping point. "Man," he argued, with his mind pinned on the cold positivist reason that regulated capitalist production, "is more than reason supplied with organs."[56] Put another way, the individual was a rational, living being, whose fundamental vital force had to be accounted for to illuminate any socio-economic change, present or future.

For Unamuno, then, there was capitalized *Life*, which had become a hopeless abstraction, an idol of science and logic, used to rationalize and order existence; there was also *life*, the tangible and organic existence irrevocably marked by the passage of time and, finally, death. Yet life was not confined to the dimension of human existence for Unamuno (although it certainly permeated his thinking), but it

53 Litvak, *A Dream of Arcadia*, 159.
54 Unamuno, *Escritos socialistas*, 68.
55 Unamuno, "Socialismo," 92.
56 Ibid., 97.

extended to encompass a vital current – an eternal essence of Being, as it were – that traversed, as La Rubia Prado has demonstrated from an organicist perspective, every living organism in nature within a continuity of generation and finitude. Repeated with variations throughout Unamuno's oeuvre is the age-old assumption that life is continued creation and consummation.

In *On Casticism*, a work comprising five essays that vary in approach and critical orientations, published between February and June of 1895, Unamuno mused on this vital current as an entry point into the living dialectics of tradition and progress that had landed Spain in what he understood as an infirm state. He employed a rich pathological vocabulary to diagnose and describe the ailing national body, including anemia, atony, atrophy, abulia, contagion, hyperesthesia, and paralysis. Clearly, his thinking in *On Casticism* intersected with, and drew upon, the progressive movement of *regeneracionismo* that had picked up steam with the Bourbon Restoration in 1874 and sought to identify the origins of Spain's national degeneration. He was convinced, moreover, that to properly comprehend the nation's infirmity it was imperative to engage the concept of intra-history, which he defined as follows:

> [Intra-history represents] the life of millions of people without history who at all hours of the day and in every nation around the globe rise at dawn and head to the fields to resume their gloomy, silent, daily, and eternal labours; much like suboceanic madrepores, these labours form the base upon which the islets of history are erected ... Upon the immense and silent humanity stand those few who cause the rowdy uproars in history.[57]

What is often overlooked in readings of *On Casticism*, and what bears examining here, is the degree to which it drew its coordinates from vitalist theory and various concepts of the lived body. The intra-historical framework at the heart of Unamuno's ideal, for instance, depended upon a vitalist outlook, in which the primary and constitutive essence of a people was transmitted in an "eternal tradition," or a type of present-past incarnated in individuals that both preserved and invigorated the nation's vital substratum. Each individual, Unamuno contended, preserved in his body a living soul, within which inhabited the souls of his ancestors, souls that, although dormant like seeds and buried in the chasms of the self, were likewise alive. For Unamuno, the eternal tradition established an encompassing metaphysics of life moored to a

57 Unamuno, *En torno*, 40–1.

familiar body-soul dualism: a materiality (individual living bodies in the present here and now), and an immateriality (the ancestors' past wisdom, pains, and striving that were passed on in these individual living bodies from generation to generation). The ideal Unamuno aspired to here reminds us, at least temporally speaking, of the organic history at the heart of *Völkerpsychologie* that La Rubia Prado analyzes throughout *On Casticism,* in which the dynamic impetus of the past poured through the present in a continuous flow of vital creation.[58] In Unamuno's words:

> When we understand the present as a single moment of the total series that constitutes the past, we begin to appreciate the living within the eternal from which the total series originates. There is one more step to complete this understanding, which is to seek the raison d'être [razón de ser] of the "present historical moment," not in the past, but in the *total* intra-historical present, and to observe the causes of living historical facts for clues [revelaciones] about their substance, their eternal cause.[59]

At this point in *On Casticism,* Unamuno turns to Spinoza's *conatus* – the body and mind's striving or vigour to persevere in existence above all else – and advocated for something akin to an intrinsic vital force within all living and embodied beings, the sole purpose of which is to generate, perpetuate, and improve life through action. "Spinoza," he explained, "expressed the essence of being in an eternal way, which is the perseverance of being in itself. Afterwards, others have referred to it in a thousand different ways: 'persistence of force,' 'will to live,' etc."[60] In the *Ethics,* Spinoza had conceived *conatus* as the relentless action and drive of each embodied being to engage harmoniously with its environment to preserve its body, mind, and vital essence. He argued that "[e]ach thing insofar as it is in itself, endeavors to persist in its own being ... The *conatus* with which each thing endeavors to persist in its own being is nothing but the actual essence of the thing itself."[61] Although Unamuno was at times critical of Spinoza's philosophical reflections (he pilloried Spinoza years later in *The Tragic Sense of Life* for being a hopeless intellectualizer, as he put it), the fundamental concept of *conatus* will nevertheless remain a recurring refrain in his thinking. In *On Casticism,* it expanded his ideal of the individual's affirmative will, the same will he had broached in his earlier socialist writings and imbued with Schopenhauerian

58 La Rubia Prado, *Alegorías de la voluntad,* 48–9.
59 Unamuno, *En torno,* 58.
60 Ibid., 43.
61 Spinoza, *Ethics,* 283.

overtones. More than anything else, it powerfully embodied the indeterminate and dynamic of the eternal tradition and drew into its orbit the irrepressible resolve of embodied life, of the vital force of every individual, to thrive, extend life, and make the world its own.

Unamuno's vitalist ideal, as he himself recognized in *On Casticism*, was fraught with difficulties. For one, legions of coercive traditionalists in Spain and across Europe had marginalized the eternal tradition for fear of its socially regenerative potential, and in so doing had suppressed the vital pulse of the living historical present. Others, like professional historians (or the plodding "exhumers of bones"), cast their gaze to a bygone era without giving a second thought to the living historicity of the here and now.[62] They descended into archives with the zeal of archaeologists and unearthed all manner of fossilized facts, which they duly catalogued in books that were neglected in libraries (the knowledge storehouses far removed from the *pueblo*). Reclaiming the past was no trifling task, as Unamuno claimed with manifesto-like conviction in *On Casticism*, yet any practice of historical reclamation that obviated the intrinsic vital force of the present would offer at best a very fragmentary view of the nation's malaise, and at worst become a sterile exercise of mere historical fact-finding. "[T]he best history books," he reasoned after alluding to Augustin Thierry's hugely popular historical works, "are those in which the present comes to life … In the end, it is a most dismal blindness of the soul; it is a sickly hyperesthesia that prevents [the traditionalists] from acknowledging one *fact*, one single fact, but a living fact that forms the throbbing flesh of nature."[63] The conceptual patterns and topoi of vitality (*intra-*, continuity, movement, subordinate, the collective) and sterility (*extra-*, petrification, static, dominant, the traditionalists) that Unamuno espouses in *On Casticism* allow him not only to rebuff late-nineteenth-century positivist historicism and its narrow episteme in favour of a vitalist metaphysics, but also to lay bare the binary asymmetry underwriting Spain's degeneration. The simple point was that Spain had lost sight of the vitalist imperative to engage the living historical present.

While History came and went like the waves of a tumultuous sea, as Unamuno imagined it in *On Casticism*, the vital continuum of life accumulated and endured in the *pueblo*'s daily living and doing. It stands to reason why, in Unamuno's view, the individual had to be roused to the transcendental import of the eternal tradition stirring within his very *body*, a point which constituted one of the essays' overriding

62 Unamuno, *En torno*, 46.

63 Ibid., 48–50.

regenerationist aims. *On Casticism* leverages a host of Romantic influences with its paean to the *pueblo* – the authentic *Volk* – and its faith in a collective soul that made apparent "how the *pueblo* goes about constituting itself from its past in a process guided by an intrinsic internal force."[64] Its socialist humanism is likewise manifest, and so too is its debt to Krausist idealism and *fin-de-siècle* degeneration discourses and pathology narratives. Yet, in the nation-as-body metaphor that lends a certain cohesiveness to the essays, Unamuno's fundamental claim rings clear: the national body's regenerative potentiality has its genesis in the very innermost recesses of its anatomy – the vital *intra* – with the millions of individuals of flesh and blood who effectively constitute its living cells. We note throughout *On Casticism* the cellular mapping that conditioned Unamuno's historical imaginary. For instance, he conceived of the authentic Castilian language coalescing around a geo-cultural "Castilian nucleus";[65] old Castile, moreover, served as the indubitable "nucleus of Spanish nationality";[66] and Spanish individualism – its Quixotic spirit and profundity – had blossomed from "the authentic nucleus of our culture."[67] And, of course, lest we forget: the essays themselves endeavoured to define "[Spain's] authentic nucleus."[68] Unamuno intended to delve microscopically further into the national body's interstices and conceptualize intra-history beyond the cellular threshold as universal "protoplasmic material."[69] His allusion to protoplasm in this cellular-corporeal context is by no means fortuitous and allows us to illuminate aspects of his vitalist thinking that have remained largely unexamined.

Drawing on previous research in the field of plant physiology, the chemist Thomas Graham and microscopic anatomist Max Schultze theorized in the 1850s and 1860s that protoplasm – the colourless, colloidal, and viscous substance contained within all living cells – could very well provide the physical cause of life.[70] Although Ernst Haeckel expanded the concept of protoplasm in *Radiolaria* (1862) and *General Morphology of Organisms* (1866), it was Thomas Huxley's *Protoplasm: The Physical Basis of Life* (1869) that broadcast the protoplasm's extraordinary properties in various scientific contexts and catapulted the term into the mainstream.

64 La Rubia Prado, *Alegorías de la Voluntad*, 53.
65 Unamuno, *En torno*, 64.
66 Ibid., 71.
67 Ibid., 182.
68 Ibid., 189.
69 Ibid., 214.
70 For a brief history of plant physiology in relation to protoplasm, see Randy O. Wayne's *Plant Cell Biology: From Astronomy to Zoology*, 133–6.

Huxley's treatise derived from a lecture he had delivered in Edinburgh in 1868, titled "On the Physical Basis of Life," which was disseminated to much controversy in the widely circulated journal *Fortnightly Review*. In his lecture, Huxley had proposed a materialist account of vital force, in which the complex admixture of carbon, hydrogen, oxygen, and nitrogen, under a given set of conditions, produced that most fundamental building block of life: protoplasm. Protoplasm, he suggested further, interacted with and absorbed environmental energies through various means to structure living physical forms. "Protoplasm, simple or nucleated," he claimed in *Protoplasm*, "is the formal basis of life … [and] thus, it becomes clear that all living powers are cognate, and that all living forms are fundamentally one character."[71] As the building block of life, protoplasm promised to make visible at long last the hidden bond – the singular, physical substance – that linked bio-formational processes in nature capable of generating such diverse organic forms as "the flower which a girl wears in her hair [to the] blood which courses through her youthful veins."[72]

Several subsequent studies developed and critiqued Huxley's findings and introduced the protoplasm into even greater spheres of scientific influence and vitalist discourse.[73] In Spain, Santiago Ramón y Cajal's pioneering research and detailed illustrations of cell types and neural plasticity in the early-twentieth century was paramount in both advancing and problematizing protoplasmic theory. This was particularly true given his early studies on the subject, such as *Contribution to the Study of Involuted and Monstrous Forms of comma-bacilli of Koch* of 1885, dealing with protoplasm's degenerative processes, and *Structure of the Nervous Protoplasm* of 1896, in which he documented his innovative procedures for staining nervous tissue. Aside from stimulating the expansion of the sciences in the *fin-de-siècle* period and opening to scrutiny the wondrous subcellular realm of organic forms, protoplasmic theory also powerfully shaped modernist aesthetics, given how it held up for critical debate

71 Huxley, *Protoplasm*, 7.

72 Ibid., 4.

73 A few of the more prominent studies during this period include Lionel Beale's *Protoplasm; or, Life, Matter, and Mind* (1870); James Hutchison Stirling's *As Regards Protoplasm in Relation to Professor Huxley's Essay on the Physical Basis of Life* (1871); John Drysdale's *The Protoplasmic Theory of Life* (1874); George James Allman's *Protoplasm and Life* (1879), and Johannes Hanstein's *Protoplasm Considered as the Base of Animal and Vegetable Life* (1885). Beale's theory of bioplasm, for example, which focused on what he believed was the cell's living, vitalized matter and excluded the formed matter (or tissue) that was increasingly being included under the term protoplasm, is especially significant in this respect, for it countered Huxley's materialist argument and physical reductionism more generally.

such notions as plasticity, differentiation, and form, notions that were already being re-evaluated in the arts.[74] The discoveries surrounding cellular activity and structure sparked a veritable explosion of interest in the field of physiology, which Unamuno knew well. It is important to note, as we saw in the previous chapter, that, beginning in the 1840s, the very concept of vital force had come under sustained attack in the field as physiologists across Europe began adopting new principles of physical reductionism to challenge vitalist theories. Yet the discoveries surrounding cellular activity and the mystery of protoplasm's vital properties were simply too compelling to be ignored, and opened new avenues of investigation offering what Carolyn Steedman calls "a Romantic quest for unity in diversity, for the common source of life."[75] Between 1885 and 1892, Unamuno had read assiduously on physiological psychology, including the scholarship of Wilhelm Wundt, William James, Alexander Bain, and Théodule-Armand Ribot, and he was conversant with protoplasmic theory and would have certainly been well-acquainted with Huxley's research.[76] He also kept abreast of developments in embryology throughout the 1890s, a field which likewise seeped into his thinking (take his article "The Regeneration of Spanish Theatre" of 1896, in which he declared: "Our national sentiment has to be regenerated and made fertile with new fruits, just like organic cells are made fertile by the polarization of the nucleus, which in embryology is called karyokinesis").[77]

The universal protoplasm Unamuno referenced in *On Casticism* did indeed resonate with Huxley's focal argument in *Protoplasm* concerning the originary site of life, yet it was not the scientific intricacies, much less the materialist approach to vital force, that attracted Unamuno to protoplasmic theory. What most captivated him was its levelling effect on formal differentiations among living organisms (read living individuals) in the name of a fundamental and shared vitalist character, to use Huxley's

74 Brain, *The Pulse of Modernism*, 37–47.

75 Steedman, *Strange Dislocations*, 58.

76 Unamuno's interest in psychology and physiology will continue over the years. He will connect with figures like the biologist, psychologist, and philosopher Ramón Turró in the 1910s who will inspire him to reflect further upon innate drives and the chemical foundations of life (Arias Santos, "Unamuno," 32–4). Unamuno even wrote the prologue to Turró's *Origin of Knowledge (Hunger)* in 1916. The general topics of knowledge and hunger provided Unamuno ample room in the prologue to return to the topic of the body: "Perhaps the special and intimate sensation of self, or the sensation of oneself, which is the basis of knowledge of who we are, is linked to the chemistry of our interior physiological environment through our blood" (11). He adds: "To live is not simply to nourish oneself and reproduce; to live is to act, to exercise, to become a subject" (14).

77 Unamuno, "La regeneración," 249.

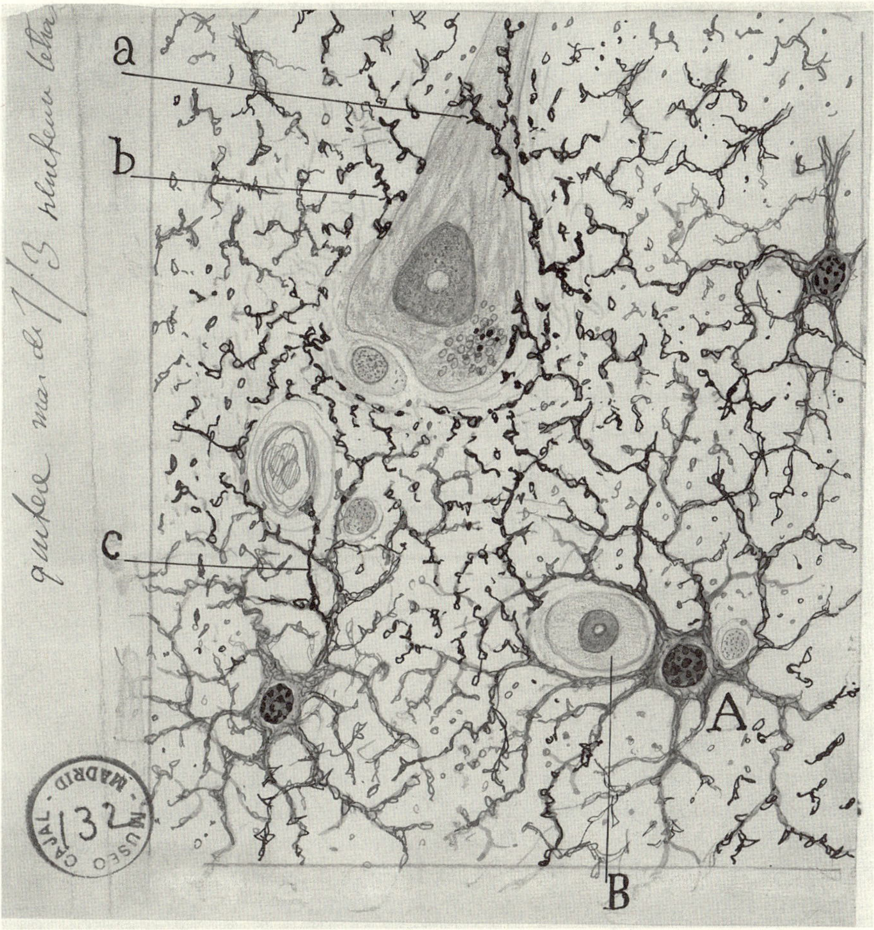

6.2 Santiago Ramón y Cajal's undated drawing of protoplasmic astrocytes from a human cerebral cortex (A: astrocyte; B: neuron [a and b: pericellular pedicles; c: fine perivascular pedicle]).

word. That is to say, every individual for Unamuno, regardless of origin, race, lineage, or class, originated from the same core protoplasmic substance. In the fields of cellular biology and physiology, the encompassing word "substance" (also "life-substance") referred to protoplasm and its little-understood vital processes. In tackling Huxley's definition of protoplasm, James Hutchison Stirling clarified the word's scope and limits, noting that "[p]rotoplasm cannot be denied to be a chemical substance;

protoplasm cannot be denied to be a physical substance ... [Huxley] has simply forgotten the addition to protoplasm of a third structure that can only be named organic."[78] Throughout *On Casticism*, Unamuno employed a similar semantics, in which substance ("sustancia") repeatedly conjured up the *pueblo*'s homogeneous protoplasmic core. A few examples include: "[T]radition is the substance of history. This is the way to conceive it as alive, as the substance of history, as sediment, as the revelation of the intra-historic";[79] "Tradition lives in the depths of the present; it is its substance";[80] "Humanity is the eternal race, the substance of the historical races that are done and undone like the waves of the sea."[81] Likewise, he also used the polysemic term *masa*, which denotes substance, but also mass, crowd, multitude, and totality. With *masa*, he brought to the fore both the one (the individual substance or cell) and the many (the communal body):

> What is original is not the countenance, nor the gesture, nor the *difference*, nor even the original itself. What is truly original is originary, or the humanity in us. What great madness to want to discard our collective core [fondo común], our identical substance [masa], upon which differential forms are moulded and from which proceeds everything that unites us and makes us similar, from all which makes us *fellow men*![82]

In the second essay, Unamuno developed the concept *masa* and expounded on how nations historically attained the sufficient vital energies to constitute themselves as distinct "national individuations," which required plumbing the "*continuous* core of the simple *pueblo*, of the substance [masa] of what all *pueblos* have in common."[83] In the concluding essay, he reiterated that "the *pueblo*, the deep *pueblo*, the one that lives beneath history, is the common substance [masa] to all races, its protoplasmic material."[84] In the closing pages of *On Casticism*, he levelled his most damning critique of the traditionalists and exhorted Spanish youth to open Spain to Europe's modernizing currents. The infirm nation

78 Stirling, *As Regards Protoplasm*, 39.
79 Unamuno, *En torno*, 40.
80 Ibid., 43.
81 Ibid., 53.
82 Ibid., 44. The word "*masa*" throughout this period oftentimes carried negative connotations in Spain in the political rhetoric of both left- and right-wing movements, who used it to conjure up the stark divisions between elites and the masses, yet this is generally not the case in *On Casticism*.
83 Ibid., 68.
84 Ibid., 214.

required fresh air to stimulate recovery. To be sure, Spain would not fall prostrate before Europe, but would stand on equal footing with it by appealing to the unifying, regenerative, and transnational humanism dwelling in every nation's protoplasm:

> [C]ultivating what is merely different in an individual or *pueblo* without subordinating it properly to what is common to everyone ... elevates the mere bud [capullo] of individuality at the expense of the integral personality [of the *pueblo*] ... [I]n the intra-history, with the diffuse and forsaken multitude [masa], there lives the deep principle of international and cosmopolitan continuity, or the universal human protoplasm. Only by opening [Spain's] windows to European winds, only by steeping ourselves in the continental atmosphere ... will we regenerate this moral steppe.[85]

What becomes apparent in *On Casticism* is how Unamuno's approach to Spain's degeneration hinges upon a vitalist metaphysics. This metaphysics threads together a number of concepts – intra-history and eternal tradition; *conatus* and will; cell theory and protoplasm – that intersect, coincide, and pass into each other in a fluid rendering of corporeality. The interplay between these concepts directs our attention far below institutions and political structures to the national body's microscopic innards, from which any true regenerative vital force must spring: day-to-day *life*. In Unamuno's view, the vital force upon which all life depends, be it individual, social, political, or national, is at root bifocal, involving the concrete, organic referent of individuals in the here and now, and the abstract, historical referent of the vital continuity of the collective over time that stands immune to History. These two emphases concretize the diffuse and forsaken multitude described above, yet they also gesture toward a more idealized national becoming, originating from deep within the lived body and capable of bridging borders and cultural barriers. In this broader and ideal sense, this bifocality is evocative of Krausism's supranational *humanidad*, in which, as Julián Sanz del Río theorized, individuals would harmonize from generation to generation with the "universal and permanent relations" of the grand human family.[86] Unamuno's vitalist metaphysics, then, depends first and foremost upon the unflinching discovery of interiority, or that turn inwards to apprehend the (national) body's vital force at its most concrete, innermost, and cellular level. In this light, *On Casticism* serves as a continuation of the vitalist

85 Ibid., 218.

86 San del Río, "Prólogo," xvii.

trajectory that Unamuno had charted in "The Influence of Gymnastics on Building Character," in which coming into awareness of one's bodily self and vital force – the Delphic injunction "Know thyself" – is the requisite first step to any transformative regeneration.

After his crisis of 1897, when his socialist convictions began to wane, Unamuno continued to explore the complex of ideas he had developed in *On Casticism.* In "Life Is a Dream: Thoughts on Spain's Regeneration," published shortly after the end of the Spanish-American War of 1898, he bemoaned with sombre cynicism the fact that the individual had still not dared to gaze inward. What was most discouraging was that Spain, even with the cry of military defeat ringing in its ears, had not come to terms with its intra-history, much less realized that "[t]he destiny of the individual man … is the most human thing that exists."[87] Progress, culture, history, and regeneration were mere fancies if the individual obviated the lived body that imbued these concepts with purpose: "We must live, live to the fullest extension and intensity! We must live because we must all die! We must live because life is an end in itself!"[88] We find a similar argument in "Ideocracy" of 1900, where Unamuno inveighed against the "lethal tyranny of ideas" and admonished his readers that his fellow man was more than an appearance, more than a mere construct of reason, but rather, "a brother, a man of flesh and blood like you and me."[89] In "Inward!" a short piece published in the same year of 1900 and headed with the epigraph "*In interiore hominis habitat veritas,*" taken from Augustine's *De vera religione* (what amounts to Augustine's adaption of the Delphic injunction "Know thyself," which reads: "In the interior of man lives the truth"), Unamuno revisited the basic premise of the eternal tradition and reiterated that the individual does not originate from one ancestor, but from legions of them.[90] In *The Life of Don Quixote and Sancho* of 1905, one of Unamuno's most profound works, dedicated to a chapter-by-chapter analysis of Cervantes's masterpiece, he delved into the intricate rapport between will and truth and took fresh aim at the bounds of reason: "It is not intelligence but will which makes the world … Life is the criterion of truth; logical concordance is not. If my faith leads me to create or increase life, what is the use of submitting it to further proof? When mathematics kills, mathematics is false."[91]

87 Unamuno, "La vida es sueño," 304.
88 Ibid., 305.
89 Unamuno, "Ideocracia," 331.
90 Unamuno, "¡Adentro!" 243.
91 Unamuno, *Our Lord Don Quijote,* 128–9.

Unamuno published a wealth of articles and texts throughout the period, including his second novel, *Love and Pedagogy*, in 1902, and his first collection of poems, titled *Poetry*, in 1907. Yet it is in his landmark *The Tragic Sense of Life*, the conceptual origins of which date to 1899, where he condensed his thoughts on the lived body and vital force.[92] In truth, *The Tragic Sense of Life* can be read as one long disquisition on the lived body and vital force, and a number of its claims are foreshadowed in *On Casticism*. It is composed from a collection of notes Unamuno had gathered over the years to wrestle with "the only real and vital problem, the problem which strikes closest at the root of our being, the problem of our personal and individual destiny, of the immortality of our soul."[93] The framework argument that binds the twelve chapters of *The Tragic Sense of Life* is rather straightforward: the individual who ponders seriously over existence becomes entangled in a tragic struggle – a wounding stalemate, as it were – between rationalizing life and vitalizing reason. Our reason, being what it is, tells us that life is finite, while life – expansive, unrelenting, and ubiquitous – insists on its infinite continuity. What often gets obscured in readings of Unamuno's treatise is its corporeal dimension, which is more than ironic given that it opens with a bluntly titled chapter, "The Man of Flesh and Blood," in which the concept of life is denuded of its lofty conceptions and framed within a vitalist outlook:

> Our man is the other one, the man of flesh and blood: you and I, that man yonder, all of us who walk firmly on the earth. And this specific man, this flesh-and-blood man is both the subject and object of all philosophy ... And to be a man is to be something concrete, unitary and substantive: it is to be a thing, *res* ... And that which determines a man ... is a principle of unity and a principle of continuity. A principle of unity, first, in space, by virtue of his body, and next in action and intention ... We are animated by some purpose at every moment in our life, and it is to this purpose that the synergy of our actions is directed, even though in the next instant we may alter our purpose.[94]

The immortality that both invigorated and tormented Unamuno so profoundly encompassed more than the soul; it involved consciousness, feeling, and every aspect of the lived body's inexorable, vital yearning. As R.L. Predmore demonstrated years ago, Unamuno insisted on physicalizing the soul in his oeuvre, thereby imbuing it with a curious

92 See Paolo Tanganelli's "From Erostratism to the Love of God" for more on the origins of *The Tragic Sense of Life*, 175–94.

93 Unamuno, *The Tragic*, 6.

94 Ibid., 3–11.

"palpability."[95] The philosopher William Barrett likewise observed that "[the] hunger for the concrete and physical ... explains Unamuno's longing for immortality. What he craves is not just the survival after death as pure consciousness or disembodied spirit, but survival in this flesh, these bones, this body."[96] Throughout *The Tragic Sense of Life*, and particularly beginning in Chapter 3, "The Hunger for Immortality," Unamuno elucidated how the yearning for immortality was lived through and experienced corporeally. Reminiscent of Dostoevsky's Underground Man, he argued that consciousness of our mortality was a disease, yet a disease that revealed with excruciating lucidity that what we most desire is the "substance, not the shadow, of eternity!"[97] He even brought the concept of dread into play, stating: "I dread the thought of having to tear myself away from my flesh. I dread still more the idea of having to tear myself away from everything perceptible and material, from everything with substance."[98] Unsurprisingly, affirming the lived body's vital force represented a dominant trend of his thinking, and he employed a tapestry of corporeal terms that not only concretized it in relation to day-to-day life, but also stressed its innumerable vital potencies as it was channelled through sexual desire, longing, sickness, pain, and will. A few of these corporeal terms included sense ("suffering means to sense the flesh of reality; it is to sense the mass and substance of spirit"),[99] feeling ("the irreconcilable conflict between reason and vital feeling"),[100] hunger ("the hunger for personal immortality, the striving [*conato*] to persevere indefinitely in our own being"),[101] thirst ("the thirst for eternity, for survival"),[102] desire ("vital skepticism is brought about by the clash between reason and desire"),[103] and, of course, life ("science and knowledge are forced by the needs of life to place themselves at the service of these needs").[104]

If, as the critic Martin Nozick proposes, *The Tragic Sense of Life* represents "the incandescent confession of a man," then it is a confession that places the lived body's specificity at the very centre of its confessional

95 Predmore, "Flesh and Spirit," 590–1.
96 Barret, "Unamuno," 367.
97 Unamuno, *The Tragic*, 53.
98 Ibid., 53.
99 Ibid., 224.
100 Ibid., 138.
101 Ibid., 42.
102 Ibid., 49.
103 Ibid., 130–1.
104 Ibid., 127.

discourse.[105] The somatic experience for Unamuno, and the sense and awareness of vital force in all its plenitude, served as fixed moorings for approaching Being. The affective-biological basis of his engagement with Being prefigures current theorizing on embodied cognition and its probing of the legacies of Cartesian dualism, in which the body and its vital force are ascribed a far greater role in shaping consciousness than has normally been recognized. In fact, one of Unamuno's most devastating reproaches in *The Tragic Sense of Life* was levelled against the desubstantiation of Being in Descartes' *Discourse on Method*, particularly when Descartes affirmed in section 4: "I concluded that I was a thing or substance whose whole essence or nature was to think, and which, to exist, has no need of space nor of any material thing or body."[106] In Unamuno's eyes, the disembodied cogito was the most whimsical of philosophical constructs, which absurdly erased the lived body from the equation of Being. It was inconceivable for him to even reflect upon the tragic sense of life through the abyss of a bodiless, immaterial self.[107]

In a direct continuation of his previous works, Unamuno did battle against this vein of instrumental reason for its dissolving and pernicious views of the lived body, and he advocated instead for what can be called a bodily consciousness. Echoing his much-admired Schopenhauer, he believed in the double knowledge of the body as representation and will, where will was defined as that distinctive consciousness of the inner life force that opened the individual to nature's innermost vitality.[108] Unamuno held that individuals, if they ever aspired to recognize their own self-deception and embrace the authentic truth about life, had to come to terms with their vital flesh-and-bloodness, and thus with their mortality. Accordingly, they had no choice but to *think* with their "whole body and soul, with their blood with the marrow of their bones, with their heart and lungs and viscera, with their whole life."[109] This picture grows sharper if we consider that this notion of a bodily consciousness dates to early essays like "Ideocracy," in which he maintained that it was through the lived body's vital claim upon the world that the individual could unburden himself of the shackles of dogmatism for a new and

105 Nozick, "Introduction," xviii.

106 Descartes, *Discourse on Method*, 25.

107 Unamuno concluded that "[t]he defect [of Descartes' *Discourse on Method*] lies in his resolving to begin by leaving himself out, omitting Descartes, the real man, the man of flesh and blood, the man who does not want to die, so that he can become a mere thinker, that is, an abstraction" (*The Tragic*, 39).

108 Schopenhauer, *The World*, 104–9.

109 Unamuno, *The Tragic*, 19.

transformative disposition toward life. He implored his fellow countrymen: "Think! Think! And think with all of your body and with all of its senses, innards, blood, medulla, fibre, and with each of its cells, and with your entire soul and all of its forces, and think not only with your mind; think vitally and not logically."[110] Unamuno's notion of a bodily consciousness calls to mind Merleau-Ponty's view of the lived body. As Merleau-Ponty understood it, the individual reflected about, and participated in, the world through the anchor of the lived body, which served as the site of all thought and all meaning. In *Phenomenology of Perception*, he took up the same critique of Cartesianism as did Unamuno to reiterate the simple and yet far-reaching notion that consciousness projects itself into the physical, material world and has a body.[111]

Let us turn now to a passage in *The Tragic Sense of Life* that goes unnoticed in the commentary, in which Unamuno offered insight into the type of consciousness that involved all of one's body and brought into the fold once more protoplasmic theory. The passage in question appears in Chapter 7, "Love, Pain, Compassion and Personality," a chapter in which he reflected upon the fundamental nature of vital force. The question he sought to face in this chapter was this: from where does the longing for life that we feel so powerfully and intimately in our bodies originate? He opens the chapter with assorted observations on different forms of love – sexual, maternal, and spiritual – and upon surveying the ancillary theme of compassion, he enters that most familiar ground of inwardness. Although love and compassion comprised a variety of functions, from procreation and perpetuation of the species to the recognition of collective anguish, they ultimately steered the individual's gaze inward, for it was through love and compassion that the individual discovered "the ardent longing to reach the uttermost, the innermost of all things, [which] is extended to everything in sight."[112] Once again, he hints at Schopenhauer's notion that the individual's recognition of the objectivity of the will (what Unamuno refers to as "longing" in this chapter) is what allows him to appreciate the uniform and innermost nature of all living things. Moreover, through love and compassion the individual could "feel everything within" as he subjectivized the totality of the universe.[113] As is obvious enough from Unamuno's verbiage – longing, innermost, oneself, felt, feel wholehearted, feel everything, extended,

110 Unamuno, "Ideocracia," 329–30.

111 Merleau-Ponty, *Phenomenology of Perception*, 158.

112 Unamuno, *The Tragic*, 151.

113 Ibid., 153.

everything, all – he builds up an intimate physicality and corporeal awareness through which the lived body connects to the world.

After weighing the limitations of Schopenhauerian will and Darwinism in explaining this vital longing, Unamuno reformulated his question in more specific vitalist terms: "For what, after all, is the occult force, the ultimate agent, which impels organisms to perpetuate themselves, to fight to persevere and propagate?"[114] He reasoned that sympathy, understood as the capacity of a living organism to identify with another organism at the most fundamental level of Being, must predispose the individual to discern this occult force in some fashion. And this force, clearly, was channelled in a primary aspiration toward consciousness, an aspiration that swelled within even the simplest of living organisms.[115] As he had done in *On Casticism,* he directed his mind to the lived body's microscopic interiority and conjectured that this occult force was very likely responsible for "mov[ing] and activat[ing] the very cells of our own corporeal organism … [I]t moves the very globules of our blood."[116] Each individual cell, he contended, much like each individual bodily self, must possess its own concrete purpose, and thus a type of originary consciousness that directs its vital activities:

> To fancy that our cells, our globules, should possess a kind of consciousness, or the beginning of a rudimentary, cellular, globular consciousness, is no more far-fetched than many fancies which pass for valid theories; and neither is it any more fanciful to imagine that they might come to have such consciousness. And now that we are being fanciful, let us imagine that these cells communicate with each other and that one of them would express its belief that it formed part of some superior organism endowed with a personal collective consciousness.[117]

Unamuno's notion of a bodily consciousness functioning at the cellular level does call to mind elements of Romantic organicism (the ideal, for instance, that the integrated whole, or the body's "superior organism," represents more than the sum of its parts, or its "cells"), yet what he was bringing into view was a central concept of protoplasmic theory having to do with the tenuous-yet-profound divide between non-living and living. More precisely, he was responding to contemporary scientific polemics (both the far-fetched and valid theories he alludes to above) concerning what exactly activated the cell's inherent vital properties from

114 Ibid., 163.
115 Ibid.
116 Ibid.
117 Ibid.

which life and consciousness ultimately sprang. What fascinated popular vitalists like Lionel Beale, and what ultimately scuttled hardline materialist arguments like Huxley's, was how protoplasm, the cell's simple, transparent, and protein-based substance, could generate myriad life processes and govern the sophisticated and heterogeneous developmental activities of organic living forms.[118] As we saw in the previous chapter, the Krausist Free Institution of Learning remained a platform in Spain for modern science, and in the pages of its bimonthly *Bulletin of the Free Institution of Learning* the enigma of protoplasm was examined and debated. In the article "Plurality of Protoplasms" of 1886 – an article inspired by Charles Morris's remarks on protoplasm and the possibility of extraterrestrial life in *The American Naturalist* a few years prior – the naturalist José Gogorza y González echoed the idea then gaining steam that "protoplasm … is the only *living* matter, and within it, therefore, we should seek all that commonly goes by the names 'consciousness and life.'"[119] For the renowned biologist and naturalist Alfred R. Wallace, however, the very idea that protoplasm was somehow responsible for consciousness was as implausible as it was naïve. In his reasoning, there was simply no arrangement or quantity whatever of non-sentient substance – or what he called "unconscious matter" – that could generate the marvel of consciousness, and thus consciousness, by necessity, had to occupy matter from without.[120]

What remained in the air in Spain as well as in the rest of Europe throughout the late-nineteenth and early-twentieth centuries was the alluring notion that protoplasm, which for many scientists evolved inexplicably out of non-living nebulosity, as Beale described it, must contain some form of seminal consciousness that directed vital force in

118 The anatomist and histologist Aureliano Maestre de San Juan's *Elemental Treatise on Normal and Pathological Histology* of 1879 tackled this very issue. Maestre's treatise, which was by far one of the most comprehensive studies in Spain at the time on protoplasmic theory and proved instrumental in piquing Ramón y Cajal's early interest in cellular biology, proposed that the cell's protoplasm did in fact exhibit "all of the properties of life; it is the agent of all organic syntheses" (161). Still, when it came to the slippery question of by what means the cell and its protoplasm produced life, Maestre had to concede that this mystery was well beyond the scope of his treatise.

119 Gogorza y González, "Pluralidad de protoplasmas," 200.

120 "We may admit with Professor Huxley," Wallace averred with simplicity, "that *protoplasm* is the 'matter of life' and the cause of organization, but we cannot admit or conceive that *protoplasm* is the primary source of sensation and consciousness" (*Contributions*, 373). Needless to say, Wallace's non-material approach to consciousness, coupled with his affinity for spiritualism (he had published his popular *A Defence of Modern Spiritualism* in 1874), set him at odds with a great many of the leading biologists and naturalists at the time.

structuring organic living forms. Unamuno speculated in *The Tragic Sense of Life* about the remarkable powers of this "globular consciousness." He analogized planets to cells, and galaxies to bodies. He also conjectured that the Milky Way, home to our solar system, is perhaps itself "a molecule … a cell in the Universe, the Body of God."[121] He was simply fascinated with how each cell's distinctive consciousness might participate in a holistic, corporeal one. The implications of this larger consciousness were far-reaching for Unamuno. If he could harness the vital consciousnesses coursing throughout his body, and if he could come into an awareness of their total unity, then the resulting transcendent bodily consciousness would allow him to feel something akin to the Absolute in the sheer grandeur of scale that separated the cellular horizon from the bodily horizon. This supreme feeling, in turn, would surely offer him the most precious gift of all when it came to the organizing question of immortality that inspired *The Tragic Sense of Life*, a glimpse of the infinite in the lived body:

> All the cells of our body combine and concur in their activity in maintaining and arousing our consciousness, our soul; and if the consciousness or the souls of these cells penetrated into our consciousness, into the composite whole, if I possessed consciousness of all that happens in my bodily organism, I should feel the universe happening within myself, and then perhaps the painful sense of my limitation would be erased. And if all the consciousnesses of all beings wholly concur in the universal consciousness, then this consciousness, that is, God, is all.[122]

The proposition of a bodily consciousness embedded in protoplasmic theory not only solidified vitalist arguments against positivist epistemology during the period, but for modernist thinkers also underscored with increasing insistence the limits of science concerning the lived body and its potential. It was through the archway of bodily consciousness that Unamuno assigned to the lived body – the antipode to the immaterial Cartesian cogito he found so inconceivable – a central role in *thinking* about life, which implied not only entering into awareness of vital force, but also adopting a particular disposition toward finitude and action. Since his early writings in *On Casticism*, Unamuno declared that he carried within his own germ plasm his forefathers' vital force. Yet, more imperative still, this germ plasm and its seminal consciousness

121 Unamuno, *The Tragic*, 164.

122 Ibid.

permeated his actions in the here and now. "The whole of me," he claimed, "with all this universe of mine, go into each of my actions … [M]y individual essence goes into my action."[123] And it is action, ultimately, that allowed Unamuno to commit to the struggle against destiny in day-to-day life, to persevere in the face of annihilation, and, most importantly, to deserve immortality. In the final chapters of *The Tragic Sense of Life,* he even tackled the practical problem of action as it concerned one's vocation, and he offered Don Quixote as a model of heroic virtue to live by. Interestingly, he came full circle to the fundamental rapport between lived body and action that he had sketched so many years earlier in "The Influence of Gymnastics on Building Character," in which every act, no matter how insignificant or small, offered the individual purpose, meaning, and, above all, hope.

ON DEGENERATION AND SUPREME HEALTH: PÍO BAROJA'S *THE TREE OF KNOWLEDGE*

Spanish modernists like Unamuno greatly expanded the concept of lived body and made good use of it to reimagine the relational bonds between corporeality and world, as well as to diagnose the chronic infirmities of modernity itself. I would like to further explore modernist expressions of the lived body in the works of Baroja, one of the most prolific Spanish novelists, whose career spanned from roughly 1900 to the 1950s. More concretely, I will dwell on Baroja's *The Tree of Knowledge,* arguably his most accomplished novel, which condenses and integrates with great insight and like few others of the period the various strands of thought that made the lived body relevant in early-twentieth-century Spain.

A cursory review of the critical literature on Baroja demonstrates that the vitalist outlook in his oeuvre has always been a subject of inquiry. For many readers, this outlook is most profitably interpreted through the autobiographical elements of his fiction, which document to a certain extent his personal struggle with modernity. Torrente Ballester's early critiques of Baroja's novels are representative of this approach: "Baroja's ideology lacks objective value. He is not an essayist, but a man who searches in books for a solution to his personal problem … His ideology has a symptomatic and documentary value."[124] In Ortega y Gasset's

123 Ibid., 221.
124 Ballester, *Literatura española,* 240.

opinion, the vitalist outlook in Baroja's oeuvre, while clearly informed by the individual's plight in modern society, offers one of the most revelatory portraits of the deadening *abulia* that plagued European culture in the early-twentieth century. The multiplicity and forms of life presented in Baroja's narratives, which must contend with a cruel network of economic interests as well as a morally bankrupt society, highlight the need for a radical rethinking of the categories of identity and existence. Ortega y Gasset sums up this point, stating: "the feeling of insufficiency which plagues the ideas and values of contemporary culture is the mainspring that moves Baroja's whole soul."[125] Ever since José Martínez Ruiz, "Azorín," mused in 1904 about the philosophical bent of Baroja's literature, critics have also conjectured about whether Schopenhauer's pessimism and concept of will, or Nietzsche's ideal of overcoming, most deeply inspired the author's vitalist outlook.[126] While this either-or line of inquiry has not always been very illuminating, it should be noted that Baroja himself admitted that his readings of both Schopenhauer and Nietzsche, as well as many other philosophers for that matter, profoundly affected his literature.[127]

125 Ortega y Gasset, "Thoughts on Pío Baroja," 428.

126 See Azorín's "Baroja's Philosophy," 85–9.

127 For Luis Lozano, "Baroja's interest in Schopenhauer was perhaps not as intense as his interest in Nietzsche … but it persisted undeniably longer" (53). Félix Vázques argues that Baroja's trademark pessimism reveals that he was a "loyal disciple of Schopenhauer" (183), while for Magdalena Cueto Pérez, "the influence of Schopenhauer on Baroja can be considered definitive" (135). For E. Inman Fox, "Schopenhauer's spiritual influence is overwhelming" (401). For the various critical readings of Baroja's work through the Schopenhauerian lens, consult Carlos Roberto Saz Parkinson's *Positively Negative: Pío Baroja the Essayist* (53–70). Parkinson strikes a conciliatory tone on this question of whether Schopenhauer or Nietzsche was most influential on Baroja's work: "While there is no doubt that Schopenhauer was important for Baroja, Friedrich Nietzsche was almost as relevant for the writer. Even though Baroja became seriously interested in Nietzsche after Schopenhauer … the echoes of Nietzsche in many of Baroja's works are often equal to, or greater than, those of Schopenhauer" (55). In his analysis of Baroja's first articles on Nietzsche between 1899 and 1902, Nelson Orringer contends that Nietzsche was a decisive influence on the author's turn toward modernist aesthetics. For Orringer, Baroja held Nietzsche to be a "philosophical-poetic modernist," whose ideal of the modern project was not only defined by the crisis in thinking and belief encoded in evolutionism, but also privileged action and the individual's life-world over the authority of tradition. Thus, "aestheticism, passionate elitism, anti-Christian Hellenism, anti-bourgeois anarchism, Darwinian Machiavellianism, ruthless egotism, amoral banditry, the Apollonian style of a Valera – All these attitudes harmonize with Baroja's Nietzscheism" (148). In his unpublished dissertation "Aesthetic-Vitalist Factors in Pío Baroja's Oeuvre," Ramón Mandado concurs with Orringer and sustains that Nietzsche's work was the major catalyst that brought about

What has been largely overlooked when it comes to Baroja's vitalist outlook is his treatment of one of the fundamental topics that drove modernism: the lived body. We must recall that Baroja earned a medical degree and was well acquainted with the medical literature of his day on human physiology, infectious diseases, hygiene, and sexuality. His doctoral thesis *Pain: A Psychophysical Study*, published in 1896, demonstrated that corporeality and embodiment had concerned him deeply from the very beginning. He claimed in his thesis that pain is treated too narrowly, as sensory experience, within the scientific sphere. By examining various psycho-biological aspects of pain, he determined that it grants us unique insight into our body and its vital force. There are faint, but perceptible, echoes in Baroja's thesis of Schopenhauer's core argument in *Parerga and Paralipomena*: pain, in all its various forms, structures our awareness of self. He affirmed that "if pain provides us a clear and different idea of who we are, [and] if kinesthesia is a knowledge that we are alive, then pain is a conscious knowledge of life."[128] Baroja had also briefly practised medicine as a country doctor in the mid-1890s, which had a lasting impact on how he portrayed infirmity and bodily suffering in his work.[129] *Sombre Lives* of 1900, his first literary work inspired by his experience as a country physician, is rife with characters who are infirm and in agony. In the short story "Marichu," dedicated to a woman's strange affliction, which crippled her with pain whenever she laughed, we read: "Each

Baroja's philosophical development (this is a well-established argument shared by Luis Lozano in his unpublished dissertation, "Vitalism and the Concept of the Hero in Pío Baroja: The Influence of Nietzsche") (288). Above all, the Nietzschean will to power increasingly takes cêntre stage in Baroja's oeuvre after 1910 in how the injunction to overcome morality and tradition through *action* is revisited and expanded. (It should be noted that Mandado Gutiérrez's study is more a philosophical reflection on the ways Baroja intersects a type of *Lebensphilosophie* than a literary analysis of his work. In fact, he does not analyze any of Baroja's works. Ultimately, he concludes that Baroja's dialogue with vitalism is really a philosophical issue about the meaning of existence in an uncaring world.) According to Sobejano, "Pío Baroja is often considered the Spanish novelist who has most amply incorporated into his work aspects of Nietzsche's philosophy" (*Nietzsche*, 347). Mary Lee Bretz also acknowledges Baroja's debt to Nietzsche's philosophy, yet also points out that Baroja maintains an ambivalent attitude with respect to several of the German philosopher's ideas that comes through in a "partial and contradictory application of Nietzscheism" (146). Yet, Roberta Johnson is right to draw attention to the fact that "if Baroja was saturated with Nietzsche, as has been averred, he was likewise saturated with Schopenhauer, Claude Bernard, evolutionism and the scientific method … Elements of all his favourite philosophers entered into his dialogic format" (57).

128 Baroja, *El dolor: Estudio de psico-física*, 8.

129 See Félix Cabezas García's *Medicine and Physicians in Pío Baroja's Oeuvre*. See also José Luis Puerta's "The Physician Pío Baroja (1872–1956)," 198–21.

town [Marichu visited] was an immense hospital full of sickly flesh and it cried out in delirious shrieks ... [and] tragedy, disease, and death reached every corner [of the country]."[130] While Baroja was critical of certain aspects of the medical profession, he believed science was a transformative force in society and argued over the years that one possible solution to Spain's socio-political crisis rested in scientific innovation. That said, his views on science were far from static, and were riddled with inconsistencies.[131]

While the concept of action elaborated in Baroja's work is often treated more abstractly through notions of self-realization, nihilism, and existential inquiry, the vitalist-corporeal dimension is often inscribed within the frame of physical suffering. For Baroja, the concept of action depended on the complementarity between vital force and will that allowed the individual to transform his reality and overcome social barriers of injustice and prejudice.[132] As I will demonstrate through an analysis of *The Tree of Knowledge*, Baroja's stance with respect to the question of vital force and action is far more complex and subtle than it first appears.[133] In his rendering of bodies in various states of health and infirmity, he paints a picture of corporeality against which he will argue that effective action in modern-day society requires the vital impetus of the lived body, a proposition that recalls a number of Nietzsche's arguments about supreme health, as we shall see. Through the lived body, as Baroja makes clear, we gain empowering knowledge of the world, and we become *aware* of ourselves, of our instincts and powers, and thus of our bodily potential to overcome our circumstance for a true sense of self. The sticking point for Baroja is that modern-day society found itself in a process of degeneration, and in fact acted against the vast majority of individuals by physically and socially depriving them of any real prospect for self-realization. To be sure, Baroja is channelling not only *fin-de-siècle* theories of decadence and infirmity in his work, but also powerful notions of genetic deterioration advanced in such popular works as Francis Galton's *Hereditary Genius* (1869) and Charles Darwin's *The Descent of*

130 Baroja, *Vidas sombrías*, 65–6.

131 See E.H. Templin's article "Pío Baroja and Science," as well as Alison Sinclair's section on Baroja and science in "Authority of Authenticity? The Battle of the Cultures at the Millennial Crossroads," 137–40.

132 Baroja, *El tablado de Arlequín*, 60.

133 I will be using Aubrey Bell's translation of Pío Baroja's *El árbol de la ciencia*. However, this translation has its shortcomings, and thus I will be supplementing it with my own translations of particular words and phrases. I indicate when I do so.

Man (1871). In the early 1901 article "Ex nihilo nihilo," Baroja employs the familiar organicist analogy between the body's vital force and that of society to contend that modern Spain was effectively powerless to offer the individual any hope for the future:

What is felt today in Spain is not malaise, but rather, something almost the opposite: the absolute lack of vital force, or the inertia that drives one to live a sham existence … Morally speaking, Spain is inexistent. It is a type of gelatin without irritability; there is nothing in our country that has fibre … In my view, Spain now is like a white and feeble body. It is a face that expresses no pain, no anguish, no nothing, but rather, reveals that something has turned rotten inside … And they speak of the future! And they speak of youth! Here [in Spain] where the fetuses are old! It is the eternal fiction, the eternal simulacrum of life.[134]

In 1904, he tackled the issue once again in *Harlequin's Stage*, but adopted a different perspective, which exudes a Nietzschean flavour:

I believe in a renaissance, not in science or art, but in life … We must forget the names of theologians, poets, philosophers, apostles, and all the mystifiers who have saddened life by subjecting it to an absurd morality. We must immoralize ourselves. Our school days are behind us, and now we must live … We are in a transition period from the simple life to the complex life of progress. From here derives our malaise … We must never doubt ourselves; everything we vigorously desire deserves to be achieved. Only the stingy and wretched can condemn and accuse the individual who, flung in a great passion, breaks all laws of society to impose by his strength the right of his sentiment.[135]

Baroja always considered *The Tree of Knowledge* his most polished and complete novel. Set in the 1890s, it follows the young Andrés Hurtado as he earns his medical degree in Madrid and begins to practise in the rural town of Alcolea del Campo and then in the capital itself. As Hurtado advances through medical school and endures its charlatan professors (one of whom is the renowned Hippocratic physician José de Letamendi), and as he ventures out into a squalid world crowded with the sick and despairing, he is overcome with a "curiosity to get at the source of life."[136] In his growing disillusionment with the rampant selfishness and cruelty he witnesses all around him, he turns to philosophy, grasping for solutions. In Hurtado's realization about the inherent callousness of

134 Quoted in Sotelo Vázquez, "Pío Baroja en 1901," 870–2.

135 Baroja, *El tablado de Arlequín*, 59–61.

136 Baroja, *Tree*, 31.

existence, Baroja addresses one of the fundamental questions that permeated modernist culture: What is the most enriching mode of life that would allow the individual to realize his vital potential as a free, self-creating subject, without losing sight of the larger social question? In Hurtado's discussions with his uncle Iturrioz that constitute the novel's philosophical frame, Baroja argues that the individual cannot rationalize life, since life, at its root, is fundamentally irrational. The individual must *act* in the world to give expression and meaning to the lived body. Iturrioz, a physician and Nietzschean figure who advocates accepting life in all its absurdity and barbarism, proposes that "if one believes in something finer and more useful than that one is a parrot, one must affirm one's belief strongly."[137] In the end, Hurtado does not adopt the life of action, but rather attempts to disengage from the world through a state of *ataraxia.* After the loss of his stillborn baby and the subsequent death of his wife, Lulú, he decides to take his own life.

The body and death are dominant and overlapping themes in *The Tree of Knowledge.* In fact, death mediates Hurtado's concept of life from the outset. For all intents and purposes, he lives among the dead and dying, and he even adorns the walls of his room with "the bones of a skeleton given him by his uncle Dr Iturrioz."[138] During his years in medical school, he learns that his privileged and selfish classmates share a common "disdain for death, a certain enthusiasm for surgical brutality."[139] He is perturbed that they amuse themselves with bloody body parts and cadavers during anatomy lectures, and he looks on with exasperation as medical-school staff toss piles of corpses from carts and drag them legs first down the flight of steps to the dissection hall. "As the [corpses] fell on the stone," Baroja tells us, "they made a strange, disagreeable sound … [Their] heads knocked lugubriously against the steps." After the cadavers have been dissected, they are discarded into great waste cauldrons, where "one could see a hand close to a liver and brains, or a dark and turbid eye embedded in lungs."[140] The scene in the dissection hall is so ghastly that it resembles "the ending of some prehistoric battle or a fight in the Roman circus, the victors dragging the vanquished at their pleasure." Baroja remarks further that it calls to mind the image of a modern-day *spoliarium.*[141] The *spoliarium* here refers to the subterranean

137 Ibid., 189.
138 Ibid., 24.
139 Ibid., 30.
140 Ibid., 30–1.
141 Ibid.

chambers of gladiatorial arenas, where the dead and dying were dragged to be stripped of their armour and then disposed of.[142]

The related themes of the body and death in the *The Tree of Knowledge*, particularly given the image of the *spoliarium*, intersect a larger discourse on social degeneration. It bears noting that Baroja's experience as a physician of the poor and marginalized profoundly affected his views on this topic. He had always been drawn to questions of heredity, thanks in part to his interest in his Basque heritage, as well as his many readings in social theory and criminology. Max Nordau's tremendously popular *Degeneration* and its pseudo-medical argument of cultural crisis exerted a significant influence on him, most notably in works like "Pathology of the Scoundrel."[143] The *spoliarium* itself articulates an acute social malaise when it is applied later in the novel to conjure up not only the bodily suffering and demise of young women ensnared in a life of prostitution, but also the brutal abortion practices of midwives in Madrid's indigent neighbourhoods. Yet, it acquires its full social gravity when Iturrioz clarifies that society, much like nature, is mired in a ruthless struggle for life, and he analogizes individuals' selfish behaviour with that of wasps, noting that wasps, following their natural instinct, will look after their own and deposit any number of victims into feeding *spoliariums* to ensure the continuation of their species.[144] With this evolutionary frame of reference in mind, what Baroja suggests is that, in the gladiatorial arena of life, so to speak, the physically frail, the fatigued, and the weak are summarily annihilated and end up in modern-day *spoliariums*.

We cannot lose sight of the fact that the great prevalence of death and disease in society kindles in Hurtado that "curiosity" to determine the font of bodily life. In the chapter "A Formula for Life," for instance, he delves into Letamendi's vitalist philosophy to acquaint himself with

142 As Donald Kyle explains: "We know that human casualties were taken from the arena to the *spoliarium* … [It] was a temporary morgue for corpses on their way to some form of ultimate disposal elsewhere" (159).

143 Lozano, "El vitalismo," 58–60. See Lara Otis's *Organic Memory*, 78–84. Baroja had even explored, in one of his earliest series titled *Basque Land*, the relationship between the environment and the individual's fortitude, a theme that would run deep throughout most of his oeuvre. In *The Tree of Knowledge*, Baroja states that every nation has "its own practical rules of life, the result of its race and history and of its physical and moral atmosphere" (9). In terms of literature and degeneration, it should be noted that the essayist, dramatist, and politician Pompeyo Gener had published various articles in *El liberal* and *La publicidad* in the late 1880s on the relationship between decadent literature and disease. In 1894, Gener published *Infirmed Literatures: Studies on Contemporary Literary Pathology*, which included several of these essays.

144 Baroja, *Tree*, 126.

the general tenets of vitalism, yet he recognizes that Letamendi's application of mathematics to vital force is nothing but a ruse. As a medical student, Baroja had indeed studied with Letamendi in Madrid. He recalled that "[t]he desire to approach the world of philosophy as a [medical] student prompted me to read *Pathology* by the physician Letamendi."[145] While Letamendi condemned positivism for shoehorning life into all manner of scientific formulas and empty abstractions, he proceeded to reason out life through very similar means, which is precisely the criticism Baroja levels against him in *The Tree of Knowledge*.[146] Finding no recourse in Letamendi's vitalism, Hurtado will turn to philosophy, but as his uncle Iturrioz reminds him, approaching vital force from cold, philosophical intellectualism is impractical and "will lead you nowhere."[147]

Baroja will intertwine Hurtado's quest to discover life's processes and functions with the realities of an abject and degenerating world that acts upon individuals' bodies and progressively limits, impoverishes, and saps their vital force. A fitting example in this respect is Hurtado's much-loved younger brother Luisito, whose sickly body invokes a familiar modernist trope that structures the novel's city-country dichotomy: that is, the almost Rousseauian yearning to return to the simplicity and harmony of nature to escape the physical decline that accompanies urban life. Luisito's illnesses prompt Hurtado to remove him from the city in favour of the temperate clime of the country, where he can benefit from a "hygienic life" of proper dieting, fortifying sunbaths, nature walks, fresh air, and "every favourable condition to strengthen and develop him."[148] In a

145 Baroja, *Juventud, egolatría*, 151.

146 In his *Reform Plan of General Pathology and Its Clinical Application*, Letamendi devised convoluted equations for life, death, and the general "vital perturbations" in the body and nature. He is best remembered for the equation V=*f*(YC), where Life (V) integrated the body's vital force (Y) with cosmic forces (C). A few excerpts from Letamendi's *Reform Plan* will clarify further: "35) We shall call, then, VITAL PERTURBATIONS the anomalous oscillations of the product (*YC*), in one or more instances, given the *absolute* or *relative* disconformity with *C* or *Y*. Normal oscillations will be called *variations*, as it was stated (29), and are the subject of Physiology. 36) In all VITAL PERTURBATIONS it should be understood that the conditioned or definite factor *Y* is what imprints its character on the phenomenon, given that, since it originates from its spontaneity, it is its inherent resistance of vital force that determines it as an *act* and as a *form* ... 42) – One should note above all that the equation for death *(V=o)* is absolute, while the equation for life *V=(YC)* ... is always positive, and therefore relative, since in any moment there exists the possibility that an alteration in the coefficient *C* will induce perturbations in *V*; and thus, if death is always a fact that agrees with the theoretical equation that we have discovered, life does not, since life can differ from its theoretical or normal equation, with or without appreciable prejudice"(99).

147 Baroja, *Tree*, 184.

148 Ibid., 132.

short time, Luisito's constitutional vital force improves markedly, and he is described as feeling well and strong, yet it is only under Hurtado's scientific supervision that he is able to preserve such vitality. When Luisito and Hurtado relocate to Valencia to spend time with family, the boy remains vigorous under Hurtado's supervision. Yet as Hurtado gazes upon the cityscape, he is tormented with the foreboding thought of "the germs of earth and air and water developing in the heart of the night."[149] Shortly after leaving Luisito behind in Valencia's urban setting, Hurtado receives word that the boy has succumbed to tubercular meningitis.

The news of Luisito's death confirms for Hurtado the cruelty of life and the limits of science and rationality in elucidating vital force (all the health regimens and scrupulous hygiene could not prevent Luisito's inevitable demise), yet it also makes clear that the "healthy individual full of life and strength" manages to survive in modern society.[150] Iturrioz will underscore this point when he admonishes Hurtado that only healthy and vigorous individuals should ever consider procreating. Echoing physician and psychiatrist Bénédict Morel's outlook on social degeneration, Iturrioz claims that a father's and a mother's inherent – and, likewise, inherited – vital forces are one of the most accurate predictors of whether their progeny will thrive within a given social environment. In his widely read *Treatise on Degeneration* of 1857, Morel reasoned that both heredity and environmental factors played a fundamental role in humanity's progressive degeneration, which was apparent in the high rates of alcoholism, venereal disease, mental illness, and crime that characterized modern society. More specifically, he believed that all types of harmful environments, particularly those poorer communities in urban spheres lacking proper hygiene and wracked by violence and crime, acted upon the body and directly triggered its inherited pathological predispositions.[151] We can now better understand Iturrioz's stance when he declares: "The bare possibility of having weak children should be enough to deter a man [from fathering a child]. To propagate suffering seems to me a crime."[152] Iturrioz is likewise alluding to the wealth of eugenic theories and genetic-deterioration doctrines that were part and parcel of

149 Ibid., 155. In Aubrey Bell's translation, the word "gérmenes" of the original is translated as "seeds," but given the context of Luisito's illness and Hurtado's obsession with microbes, it should be translated as "germs."

150 Ibid., 174. Of note is that in the city/country dynamic, Hurtado learns that the country is just as cruel, morally debased, and unforgiving as the city, which confirms Iturrioz's point that the individual is egocentric regardless of environment.

151 See Otis, *Organic Memory*, 49–50.

152 Baroja, *Tree*, 310.

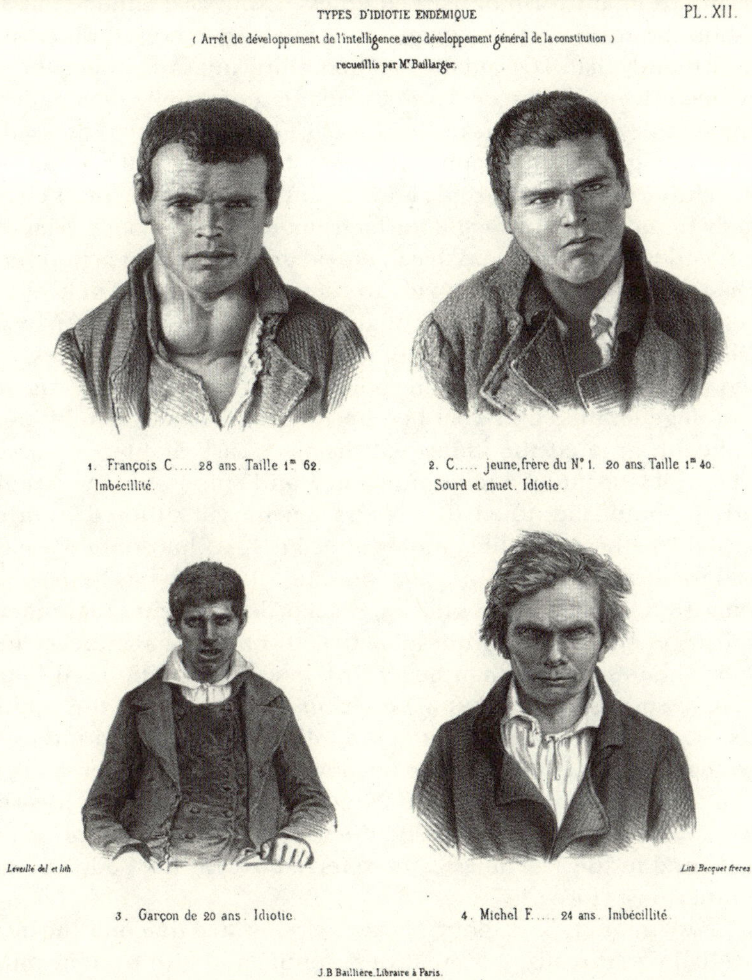

6.3 Plate XII, "Types D'Idiotie Endémique," from Bénédict Morel's *Traité des dégénérescences physiques, intellectuelles, et morales de l'espèce humaine et des causes qui produisent ces variétés maladives*, 1857.

not only Morel's concept of social degeneration, but also those of Francis Galton, Charles Darwin, and Herbert Spencer. In *The Descent of Man*, Darwin held that, as societies progressed and became more civilized, they tended to care for the weak, which allowed this stratum of the populace to procreate and spread. He advised that any man or woman suffering from any form of marked illness or physical and mental disorder should refrain from marriage. It was Spencer, however, who asserted most stridently that "[t]o aid the bad in multiplying, is, in effect, the same as maliciously providing for our descendants a multitude of enemies."[153]

The parade of characters in *The Tree of Knowledge* who are diseased and moribund highlights the rapport between lived body and action that informs Hurtado's quest. Baroja always maintained that the most effective remedy to the painful struggle for life remained in the body itself: bold, wilful, and vigorous action. We can elucidate this ideal of action further in *The Tree of Knowledge* by referring to Nietzsche's appraisal of health and its relation to will to power. Throughout most of his oeuvre, Nietzsche consistently praised the wonders of vital force and healthy bodies, which always served as corrective counterpoints to his ruminations on the maladies of degeneration and what he referred to as *décadence*. In his estimation, health granted the individual the necessary vitality – or what he liked to call "fortitude" – to fashion a new and empowering vision of the world (it should be noted that Nietzsche himself suffered from poor health throughout his life, which affected his philosophical outlook considerably).[154] For too long, he contends, the body has been subordinated within the social and philosophical order to the moral framework of spirit, yet there was no question that the triumphant "belief in the body is always stronger than belief in the spirit."[155] The lived body, as Nietzsche suggested in *Thus Spoke Zarathustra*, provided the optimum vessel, so to speak, through which the will to power – the primitive vital force that urges the individual to become healthier, stronger, and greater – could manifest itself as the unexhausted and procreative life-will.[156] In *The Case of Wagner*, he defended the will to power as "the principle of life,"[157] and in the *Will to Power*, he referred to it as the body's powerful and innermost "force."[158]

In his writings on physiology, Nietzsche reiterated that only the healthy individual could realize his creative potential and give true meaningful expression to the will to power. However, great health, as he called it, necessitated illness (or "sickliness") to flourish: in order for the individual to self-overcome, it was imperative that he *suffer* the sickness of the

153 Quoted in Stewart-Williams, *Darwin, God, and the Meaning of Life*, 237.

154 Karl Jaspers's short and insightful entry on this topic can be found in *Nietzsche: An Introduction to the Understanding of his Philosophical Activity*, 108–15.

155 Nietzsche, *Will to Power*, 348.

156 Nietzsche, *Thus Spoke Zarathustra*, 98.

157 Nietzsche, *Case of Wagner*, 190.

158 Nietzsche, *Will to Power*, 636.

world – the progressive inner decay and disintegration of the body politic and its moral foundations – and experience its symptoms in their most acute form. If the individual could physically and mentally endure such sickness, if he could determine its root and affirm the procreative life-will, he would be well on the path to realizing "the supremest form of health," which involved not only a transformative critical stance toward the falsity that infected day-to-day existence, but also "the co-ordination of the [body's] inner systems and their operation in the service of one end."[159] It comes as no surprise that Nietzsche reflected upon his own real sickness and believed it to be a most positive sign: "Being sick can even become an energetic *stimulus* for life."[160] Sickness could fortify both mind and body, and thus comprised critical and physical dimensions. Sickness and health, then, were by no means antithetical, but rather complementary, and it stands to reason why Nietzsche acknowledged that "we have learned better than to speak of healthy and sick as of an antithesis."[161]

With Nietzsche's proposition at hand, let us examine how Hurtado endures the sickness of the world, and just how it informs the vitalist outlook in *The Tree of Knowledge* with respect to the lived body. In Hurtado's attempts to fathom life's processes and functions through what amounts to his experience of social degeneration, he develops a more profound awareness of his own constituitive vital force. This awareness becomes explicit early on, after he visits Fermín Ibarra, a university acquaintance crippled with chronic arthritis and related diseases: "The absurd thing was that when he left the house of the poor invalid, life seemed pleasant to Andrés. Was this a vile feeling of contrast, that of being healthy as compared to the feeble cripple?"[162] We learn that Hurtado is not so different from Fermín the "feeble cripple" after all, given that he himself is neuro-arthritic since childhood and suffers from articular pain, alopecia, gastroenteritis, hypochondria, and depression.[163] His neuro-arthritis flares up in Alcolea del Campo when he comes to the dawning realization that country life is as callous and morally contemptible as city life. The brutal murder of a woman at the hands of her husband in this small rural town only confirms that "man in his natural state

159 Ibid., 408.

160 Nietzsche, *Ecce Homo*, 224.

161 Nietzsche, *Will to Power*, 430

162 Baroja, *Tree*, 37.

163 Ibid., 162. I have substituted the term "neuro-gouty" in the original translation with "neuro-arthritic." Not only is the term "neuro-gouty" no longer used, but it was also very rare in its time.

is vile, selfish, and idiotic."[164] He withdraws from society and seeks refuge in his readings, yet this disengagement only drains his vital force further. Yet he endeavours to fortify his body as a palliative against a degenerating world turned "madhouse and hospital."[165] Ultimately, he practises an ascetic way of life and disciplines his bodily appetites and sexual desires. As he did in the past, he subjects the world to rational analysis to thereby formulate a workable solution to what exactly is stripping his body of its energies and threatening to bring the world crashing about him. At no point, however, do these correctives compel him to affirm the will to power – the Nietzschean route to the supremest form of health within the lived body – but, quite to the contrary, they set him on the path to inaction and a blissful freedom from worry, or *ataraxia*: "At the end of a month of his new way of life, Andrés felt better. His frugal and vegetable diet, his bath and exercise in the open air were converting him into a man without nerves. His asceticism made him feel free and godlike; he began to have a glimpse at *ataraxia* sung by the Epicureans and Pyrrhonians. He no longer felt anger at either things or persons."[166]

The ataraxic condition is at root a form of mental health in which one suspends judgment, eliminates all worries, and grows unconcerned with the cares of the world. It is "freedom from disturbance, tranquility of the soul (*psychē*) … Among Greek philosophers, *ataraxia* was widely supposed to be true *eudaimonia*."[167] For Hurtado, the therapeutic state of *ataraxia* is indeed short lived. Upon returning to Madrid from Alcolea del Campo, he struggles to readjust to urban living. Everything about his new environs drains his vital force further and "did him harm … he felt like a naked man walking through brambles."[168] The experience of bodily suffering, of enduring his own pain and observing that of others in the urban sphere, brings about a Morelian realization that "[there are] two lines of progress in Madrid, that of the rich becoming finer, stronger … and that of the poor becoming weaker and more degenerate."[169] This knowledge, however, does not prompt in Hurtado a desire for self-overcoming. As he did in the country, he withdraws from society and strives to attain *ataraxia*. He also marries Lulú, a simian-looking woman who lacks "organic strength" (her inherent and inherited atavism presages from the very beginning her inability to produce a

164 Baroja, *Tree*, 261.
165 Ibid., 58.
166 Ibid., 240.
167 Preus, *Historical Dictionary*, 74.
168 Baroja, *Tree*, 282.
169 Ibid., 284.

viable child). What is more, he takes refuge in the domestic sphere and becomes a translator of medical literature:

> Andrés was completely changed. His new way of life, without having to be in the hot sun or go up flights of stairs and see so many wretched sights, gave him a feeling of tranquility and peace. He would have explained the matter like a philosopher, saying that his body as a whole was now passive, quiet, and happy. His bodily comfort gave him a state of mind akin to that perfect intellectual balance that the Greek Epicureans and Stoics named *ataraxia*, the paradise of the unbeliever.[170]

Even though Hurtado attempts by every means to remain in an ataraxic condition, Lulú's death in childbirth and the loss of the baby prove to be insurmountable. With Lulú's lifeless body lying in the next room, he ingests a lethal dose of crystallized aconitine.

What Baroja, with great ingenuity and skill, brings to the fore in *The Tree of Knowledge* is not only that the concept of vital force was firmly embedded in modernist discourses ranging from medicine to degeneration theory, but also that there was a particular manner in which it informed notions of the lived body. Let us not forget that Hurtado's quest to discover life's processes and functions hinges upon the indissoluble problem of his *own* sense of physical and subjective well-being within a society that is sinking ever deeper into a degenerative state: "What direction should he steer his life? he asked himself with anguish. And with this problem in his mind, the people he met, the things he saw, the sun itself seemed to lack reality."[171] Iturrioz, serving as Baroja's mouthpiece, reiterates that the philosophy, empiricism, analytical dissociation, and scientific reasoning that Hurtado trusts will guide him to a stable subjectivity and offer him rational meaning to the so-called sickness of the world are sterile without action. That is, the lived body had to be capable of properly harnessing and channelling its transformative vital force through action to survive. In *Intermedios*, Baroja suggested as much: "One achieves more in life through the will than through reasoning."[172] The novel's title, taken from the Book of Genesis, conjures up the problematic frontier between mind and body that has defined philosophical inquiry well before Cartesian dualism came into view. In the chapter "The Tree of Knowledge and the Tree of Life," Iturrioz urges Hurtado not to lose sight of this duality and to come to terms with the embodiment of subjectivity, no matter how painful it may be: "[W]hen we begin to leave those

170 Ibid., 320.
171 Ibid., 128.
172 Baroja, *Intermedios*, 331.

simple sciences and enter the sphere of life, we find ourselves in a labyrinth … One must live."[173] We are afforded here a powerful glimpse of one of the fundamental premises of the modern subjectivity that will define twentieth-century thought: the constitution of self involves more than the realm of the intellect, but also a lived body full of capabilities that must interact with a world brimming with pain, disease, cruelty, injustice, and death.[174]

Ironically, Hurtado's inability to transform his reality through action hastens his demise. In Hurtado's tragic end, Baroja gives voice to modernism's anxieties concerning "the complex life of progress" he had alluded to in *Harlequin's Stage* and the formidable socio-economic interests that actively worked against the lived body in modern society. Certainly, theories of physical decline, exhaustion, debility, and fatigue permeated *fin-de-siècle* culture and were given wide currency. Morel, one of the earliest to theorize about social degeneration, claimed that environmental factors contributed greatly to physical and mental decline, as we have seen, and had produced a subclass in society he called "the invalids of civilization."[175] Nordau's *Degeneration*, which Baroja knew well, argued at length that the cumulative demands of modern life drained the individual of his vital energies and opened the door to all types of ailments, including hysteria and neurasthenia. What is more, modern life imposed on the larger social body "exigencies greatly surpassing its strength."[176] For his part, Nietzsche admitted that "nothing has occupied me more profoundly than the problem of *décadence*," which he understood as a crippling morality that "impoverished life."[177] Others, like Émile Tardieu, author of the widely read *Ennui: Psychological Study*, and Charles Féré, known for his theories on degeneration and emotion in *Degeneration and Criminality* and *The Pathology of Emotions*, advanced the belief that the origin of all types of social pathologies could be found in profound bodily fatigue. In Spain, the loss of the Spanish-American War, a topic Baroja tackles tangentially in *The Tree of Knowledge*, served as a cruel reminder of the larger national degeneration. In *On the National Disaster and Its Causes* of 1899, the regenerationist Damián Isern gave voice to the popular charge that Spain's degeneration had everything to do with the nation's

173 Baroja, *Tree*, 180–2.

174 As Freud put it, "the Ego is first and foremost a bodily Ego" (16). This claim, which Baroja clearly supports, announces the core phenomenological premise that "we are our body … we are in the world with our body" (Merleau-Ponty, 239).

175 Quoted in Pick, *Faces of Degeneration*, 32.

176 Nordau, *Degeneration*, 537.

177 Nietzsche, *Wagner*, 155.

corrupt socio-economic system, in which the exploited masses suffered "a gradual diminution of physical forces and a constant predisposition to illness."[178] Indeed, during this period the logic of degeneration was especially prevalent among Spanish intellectuals – Ángel Ganivet, Joaquín Costa, Rafael Altamira, Ricardo Macías Picavea, Antonio Machado – who not only lived the failed experiment of the Bourbon Restoration and the devastating end of Spain's colonial empire, but had also imbibed the doctrine of *regeneracionismo* and its promise to inject new life, as it were, into the national body.[179]

Before Hurtado commits suicide, he makes one last crucial admission: he, too, like the rest of society, had become infirm and had degenerated into something "poisoned" and "rotten" (his neuro-arthritis and his brother's frail health – the familial/inherited pattern of disease – effectively foreshadowed this revelation). Iturrioz's final remark leaves us with the image of Hurtado's bodily defeat: "He had not the strength to live."[180] Baroja brings the novel to a close suggesting that, in committing suicide and denying his procreative life-will, Hurtado in fact transformed into what he enigmatically calls a "forerunner." While the end of the novel has been subject to various readings, I contend that Hurtado's act of self-annihilation demonstrates more than an affirmative act of will in the Schopenhauerian sense, a case of anomic suicide, the sterility of Spanish society, or existential angst and heroism, as has been proposed.[181] Rather, it reveals modernity's acute sickness and signals the emergence of the enlightened visionary, who, in recognizing that the most supreme form of health will forever remain beyond his grasp in a cruel socio-economic order, takes a stand and offers his infirm, wasted, and lifeless body as both an indictment of the present and an appeal to the future. In Hurtado's tragic effacement, Baroja articulates one of the most powerful cautionary tales in Spain about the rapport between

178 Isern, *Del desastre*, 57.

179 See Ricardo Campos and Rafael Huertas García-Alejo's "Biological Degeneration and Social Decadence in Spain: Data for a National Imaginary," 47–66. Of note is that the term "regeneration" itself, particularly as denoting social regrowth or rebirth, derived from late-eighteenth-century medical theories. See Quinlan *The Great Nation in Decline*, 112–13.

180 Baroja, *Tree*, 329.

181 See E. Inman Fox's "Baroja and Schopenhauer" for the Schopenhauerian interpretation here. Fuster García relies on Durkheim's theories in his landmark *Suicide* (1897) to propose that Hurtado's death provides an example of "anomic suicide" (65–74). Navajas Navarro tells us that Hurtado's suicide reveals the insularity of Spain and its lack of a viable future (207–8), while for Bretz, Hurtado's death can be read within the frame of existential angst (390). Finally, Patt argues that Hurtado's demise brings into view the "existentialist hero" who will "affirm life in the face of death" (116).

modernity and the lived body in an era of unprecedented change. If Nietzsche had read *The Tree of Knowledge*, he would have certainly been sensitive to it. In all likelihood, he would have heaped praise on the character of Hurtado for his honourable altruism, for his deeply modern sensibility in coming to terms with the hard lesson about degeneration and vital force. Likewise, he would have pointed out that suicide is a *pharmakon* of sorts: while it is a malady, it can, nevertheless, deliver a much-needed vitalist cure, so to speak, to an ailing world yearning to advance into a new era of prosperity. Put another way: "life itself gains more advantage from suicide than any 'life' of renunciation, anemia, and other virtues – one has freed the others from the sight of one, one has freed life from an objection."[182]

RAMÓN GÓMEZ DE LA SERNA'S LIFE-WRITING: RECONSTITUTING THE MODERN SUBJECT

For Spanish avant-gardists like Ramón Gómez de la Serna, it was a given that the lived body opened the subjective self to new horizons of existence and meaning. While this idea pervaded modernist culture in general, Gómez de la Serna was a trendsetter when it came to drawing on vitalist concepts to develop an aesthetics of authenticity in his experimental life-writing. From the moment he put pen to paper as a teenager, readers and commentators alike have been drawn to this vein in his work. One is hard pressed to find a part of his extensive oeuvre that does not include some form of life-writing, be it short stories, letters, personal essays, articles, and novels. Even in the biographies of artists and writers he wrote over the years, he acknowledged that he was quite often adrift in contemplating his own image when he was engaging the biographical subject.[183] The historian and critic José Camón Aznar goes as far as to aver that one of Gómez de la Serna's most popular biographies, on the painter Francisco Goya y Lucientes, "is almost an autobiography."[184] What makes life-writing so alluring in Gómez de la Serna's eclectic avant-gardism is the manner in which it weaves together a complex of sensibilities, styles, and forms that speak to the dynamic unity of lived body and world. And it is no wonder why he felt so attracted to life-writing and made it a central part of his work: it was a mode of writing that provided the individual the ideal space in which to discover the lived body and its

182 Nietzsche, *Twilight*, 71.

183 In *Cartas a mí mismo*, he explained that "[o]f course I included my own history, my own details, touches, and anecdotes in those biographies" (674).

184 Camón Aznar, *Los libros de arte*, 15.

vital possibilities. The practice of life-writing greatly informed Gómez de la Serna's early works between 1908 and 1914, and it is what makes them so significant in interpreting not only his later literary production, but also the trajectory of the avant-garde movement in Spain leading into the 1920s.

From his earliest writings, Gómez de la Serna was concerned, even fixated at times, with how to convey the subjective self authentically. In the article "Supreme Truth," which appeared in the journal *The Extremaduran Region* when he was only seventeen years old, he declared: "Let the distractions and fanaticisms that cast shade over the absolute transcendence of the *I* come to an end."[185] A great influence on his work during this period – and on the work of countless aspiring writers, as we saw with Baroja in the previous section – was Nietzsche's life philosophy. Gómez de la Serna found in Nietzsche a symbolic lens through which he could filter the many facets of his own evolving identity and personality, his own nascent *Ramonism*, as he would later refer to it. In 1909, he acknowledged that "[w]hen I say Nietzsche … I use the name as a symbol. His philosophical, bold, heroic, and insolent influence does not belong to him, but to the period we are going through."[186] As Gonzalo Sobejano noted in his landmark *Nietzsche in Spain*, Gómez de la Serna will purify Nietzsche's vitalism of its moral, regenerationist, and patriotic implications, and thus transform it into an "almost organic phenomenon: sexual, cellular, and fiery strength; orgasmic creation."[187] For Gómez de la Serna, Nietzsche's autobiography, *Ecce Homo*, served as an ideal blueprint to follow in examining how to engage the world authentically, and it remains clear what attracted him to this work, to the point of considering it a supreme book. Nietzsche's autobiographical persona forged an intense, confessional intimacy of the self with the reader that was rich with emotion and passion: "What is most important about Nietzsche is that his influence is not literary, but rather alimentary, testicular, private."[188] Let us recall that in works like *Ecce Homo*, which appeared in Spain via France in 1909, Nietzsche deploys the autobiographical "I" to claim an unimpeachable space in which to ruminate on his particular experience of the world. To be sure, texts like *Ecce Homo* are overwrought and hyperbolic, yet they allow Nietzsche to demonstrate that the origins of his profound intellectual blossoming over the years (the evolution and steady course of his world view from *The Birth of*

185 Gómez de la Serna, *Obras completas*, vol. 1, 1019.

186 Ibid., 152.

187 Sobejano, *Nietzsche*, 508.

188 Gómez de la Serna, *Cartas a mí mismo*, 354.

Tragedy to *The Antichrist*) had little to do with outside influences per se, but rather with his innate fortitude: his feelings, sensitivity, psychology, intuitions, resentment, and so on.

Gómez de la Serna's preoccupation with authenticity did not lead him down the path of social protest or political action, as it did with so many of his peers. Instead, it allowed him to develop a type of writing that sought to reintroduce the artist into the praxis of life, as Peter Bürger put it. Like Baroja, Gómez de la Serna held that society was in decline. Everything, he believed, from traditional values and the growth of consumerism to the excesses of rationalism and the tyranny of positivism were infecting modern existence. In *Morbidities* of 1908, his first major work and his first autobiography, penned in his late teens, he reasoned that the present age in all its infirmity and decay perverted authenticity and the true expression of the lived body. In this text, it is clear at first blush that he is not interested in regaling the reader with a coherent and temporally ordered commentary about a lived life, nor is he concerned in organizing his memory, but rather his ambition is to elaborate a self-portrait of a writer in the here and now whose acute and newfound sensitivity to the world grants him access to something extraordinary: the naked *truth.* This undertaking elucidates why the spatio-temporal ordering of *Morbidities* is configured as a diffuse-yet-dynamic present, and why the autobiography itself is the product of one continuous thread of thought. *Morbidities* does not begin, therefore, with the question of origins, familial lineage, or the past, but with the psychological and corporeal present of a writer and his circumstance in the world.

What makes *Morbidities* such an illuminating text in light of its autobiographical impetus, is the manner in which the young Gómez de la Serna reflects upon his image as a writer specifically. There is a clear intention on his part to articulate his true self as a way – he tells us – to bequeath to posterity the accurate coordinates of his emerging authorial personality. *Morbidities* is a decidedly self-reflexive text in this respect, for it labours to instantiate this authorial personality at a precise personal/historical juncture. There is little doubt that, when *Morbidities* appeared in 1908, Gómez de la Serna was on the very precipice of a major turning point in his literary endeavours after the publication of his first work, *Entering the Fray* (also translated *Entering the Flame*) of 1904, and his various articles, stories, dramas, and reviews, which circulated in regional journals between 1904 and 1908. He is only months away from founding with his father the short-lived but important periodical *Prometheus,* in which he would not only give life to his alter ego, Tristán, but also publish his influential avant-garde manifesto "The Concept of the New Literature." (*Prometheus* will also introduce Marinetti's Futurist Manifesto into Spain in 1909 – translated by Gómez de la Serna himself – and the larger Futurist challenge to instigate a broad-based cultural renewal in "Futurist Proclamation to the Spanish People" in 1910.) It has also been demonstrated that *Morbidities* stands as a decisive text in Gómez de la Serna's evolving socio-political consciousness, for it displays his discontent with Spanish liberalism (and politics in general) during the dawning years of the twentieth century.[189] Similarly, the generative period he will spend in Paris immediately following the publication of *Morbidities* will be absolutely crucial for the development of his writing. In Paris, we cannot forget, he will define the *greguería*'s basic construct, which will inform his entire literary production thereafter in some form or other (it is later, however, in *Tapestries* of 1912, that his own literary creation of the *greguería* will finally surface in its mature form as the genre of cafés and public benches, to use his words). Several essential aspects that will mark Gómez de la Serna's authorial persona and his ideas on the lived body for decades to come are not only presaged in *Morbidities*, but clearly spelled out.

What strikes the reader of *Morbidities* from the outset is the fact that the figure of the writer is drawn with an utterly uncompromising dose of self-referentiality. In the prologue, Gómez de la Serna refers to himself in the third person, thus establishing a doubled self: he presents a seemingly objective self (the editor of the text) as the mindful, privileged observer of the more impulsive subjective self (the author of the text): "In this book that carries my name, I am only the editor. The reason for this is quite a tale. The nameless author is a youth with a rough appearance carved in the crude, hardened, and sculptural manner of Rodin."[190] In the dialogue that transpires between these two selves, Gómez de la Serna the editor describes Gómez de la Serna the writer as a tormented and somewhat anemic poet of sorts: "You remind me of Heinrich from *The Sunken Bell* by Hauptmann. He, like you, begins as a poet."[191] The purpose of this introductory paratext is to convey that Gómez de la Serna, whether it be the writer, the poet, or even the misfit (he also fashions himself as a loner and an outcast) has experienced a vital and psychic transformation in response to an all-consuming *mal du siècle*. And it is this process of body-mind transformation in a precise locus and moment in time that requires understanding, recognition, and, above all, explanation from the autobiographical perspective.

189 Navarro Domínguez, *El intelectual adolescente*, 65–9.

190 Gómez de la Serna, *Morbideces*, 457.

191 Ibid., 459.

Gómez de la Serna is convinced that society has corrupted him and that its inexorable degeneration is exhausting his precious vital force. The title *Morbidities* points to the assortment of "morbidities" – what he labels the text's symptomatic philosophies, absurdities, dreams, nostalgias, and reflections – that respond to the erosion of contemporary culture. The word "morbideces" from the original Spanish title requires some unpacking. On the one hand, it refers to *mórbido* ("morbid") and *morbidez* ("morbidity"), which denote unwholesomeness, decadence, malaise, and infirmity. On the other hand, it also carries resonances of the artistic term *morbidezza,* or the healthful suppleness, illumination, colour, and smoothness of flesh that we find in Correggio's masterpieces. With the term *morbideces,* then, Gómez de la Serna affirms a duality between infirmity and health, darkness and light, and subjective self and representation (interestingly, the term also resonates with his other major autobiography, *Automoribundia,* published four decades later in 1948). Of course, these dualities serve the purpose of allowing him to plumb his own malady, and he urges his readers not to lose sight of the underlying pathological condition that governs his life-writing: "Its author is still sick from all the illnesses he condemns."[192] The degeneration he portrays so prominently in his work, as one might expect, has larger critical ramifications, since it leads him to privilege the lived body and its regenerative vital force above all else:

> My mind, like that of humanity, was something feudal and absorbent. I reacted against its aristocracy and I did away with its arrogance … I was left alone with my *physiology,* and I looked at things without the expected and traditional pass-key of the guillotined overseer. Everything appeared peaceful, wild, aqueous, eclectic … In this circumstance, and protected by my solitude and silence, I have been able to distill life and I have freed myself … My mind is no longer a deplorable and infirmed burden … Having truly acquired my natural amplitude, I am happy existing in an extended and extraordinary fluidity.[193]

In *Morbidities,* Gómez de la Serna documents his conversion to a new life-writing that aspired not only to throw off the shackles of nineteenth-century epistemic traditions, but also to position the lived body – and not just the so-called aristocracy of the intellect – at the centre of his literary practice. "For Ramón," as one critic points out, "writing became the only way through which he could momentarily escape from the limitations of

192 Ibid., 461.

193 Ibid., 467–9. My emphasis.

society, a way of making sense of existence itself."[194] Echoing a common conviction among the younger writers of the time, Gómez de la Serna declares that literature throughout the better part of the nineteenth century up to the present, with its unwholesome fixation on market forces, readership numbers, literary circulation, and the interminable questions of taste, had been divested of its radical ethos. The contemporary writer had lost sight of what it meant to write authentically and critically about the self-world relation and was ignorant of the lived body's formidable desires, instincts, yearnings, and drives that could channel meaningful literary practice. He concludes that literature had been progressively eviscerated of its most stirring potentialities and been degraded into a vacuous and sterile project. He centres his crosshairs on those specific literary giants of the nineteenth century who have hastened this infirmed condition: "I have read Bécquer, Heine, Victor Hugo … All of it required a mental effort that threw my mind out of its orbit, thus crippling me with a disease that we could call 'intellectual hernia.'"[195] His criticism of Symbolist aesthetics – he names Albrecht Rodenbach and Maurice Maeterlinck, among others – is directed toward its "surreptitious art," which consolidates a mélange of amorphous moods and superstitions that say little about the lived body and world and play into the utterly conventional bourgeois sensibilities of the feeble-minded. When he turns his eye toward Spain and its literary production, his criticism is even more vehement. Spanish writers like Azorín, Baroja, Ramón del Valle-Inclán, Felipe Trigo, Gregorio Martínez Sierra, and Salvador Rueda do little more than rehearse outmoded forms of expression and produce a generic and insipid entertainment literature (including erotica) that falls far short of capturing anything of any real consequence about life.

In the prologue to Gómez de la Serna's theatre piece *Theatre of Solitude* of 1912, we find similar manifesto-like calls to reflect upon contemporary literature and its ties to the lived body and world. He makes clear in this prologue that the struggle of the committed writer in contemporary society must centre on conveying the beauty, variety, and carnality of day-to-day life in all its angst and exquisite randomness. In his view, there is no question that the preoccupation with the lived body is a thoroughly modern phenomenon. Only the most youthful and daring writers can ever hope to discern how the legacies of the past have subjugated the body and buried its radical vitalistic potential beneath layers of social and aesthetic conventions. He sharply condemns many of the

194 McCulloch, *The Dilemma of Modernity*, 9.

195 Gómez de la Serna, *Morbideces*, 513.

same authors he cited in *Morbidities* – Azorín, Baroja, Valle-Inclán, and Martínez Sierra – for their passivity and ignorance, yet he also goes after Unamuno, whom he dubs "the yellow man with no mundanity or initiative, the imitator and gloomy vulgarizer."[196] Clearly, the poses of self-aggrandizement, the iconoclasm, the effrontery, the mordant insights into the literary dynamics of the period that pepper the prologue of *Theatre of Solitude*, as well as many of his previous works like *Morbidities*, are all part and parcel of a young Gómez de la Serna attempting to overcome his anxiety of influence and distinguish himself from his predecessors and peers (the title *Theatre of Solitude* is revealing in itself of his commitment to radical self-sufficiency and independence). Yet the point he insists upon when firing his critical salvos is as poignant as it is telling with respect to the future of avant-garde aesthetics: literature must not only recognize that the very concept of body has fundamentally changed, but it *must* lead the way in defining it. What he succeeds in doing is to draw attention to the body's discursive nature and to the bankrupt norms of intelligibility that attempt to determine its value, function, and purpose within society.

It is fair to say that Gómez de la Serna overlooked (or simply ignored) how *modernismo* and modernists like Unamuno and Baroja were in fact engaging in a similar project of redefining vital force. As we learned in the previous sections, Unamuno and Baroja were crucial in widening the debate on corporeality and life in Spain through their philosophical and literary works, many of which subverted conventions and had an enormous impact on Spain's intellectual climate. Juan Ramón Jiménez's forays into *modernismo* in early poetry collections like *Water Lilies* (1900), *Rhymes* (1902), and *Sad Arias* (1903), and through his labours on the *modernista* journal *Helios* between 1903 and 1904, provided him ample opportunity to survey the corporeality of desire and inquire into how the lived body generated a new awareness of the world. By 1912, he admitted in a letter to Unamuno: "life has no other meaning for me than the meaning I give it with my *ecstasy* and my dreams; what I esteem … is my own *soul* and my own flesh."[197] In this brief snippet, it is possible to make out the main lines of Jiménez's concept of pure poetry that would flourish in his pioneering *Diary of a Newlywed Poet* of 1916, a work that would have been unthinkable without his early and intense sympathy for *modernismo*. As Jiménez conceived it, the poet, as a dweller of the Absolute and sensitive to the vital plenitude of the world, must render legible,

196 Gómez de la Serna, *El teatro*, 155.
197 Quoted in Blasco Pascual, 94.

through direct bodily experience, life's ineffable rhythms in all their awe-inspiring complexity. Indeed, he always insisted that "the poet … is a mystic without a necessary god."[198] Of note, too, is that Rubén Darío, whose influence on Spanish modernism and avant-garde (Ultraism) was decisive, also wrought a poetics ripe with vitalist connotations that allowed the individual to look beyond socio-economic interests, industrialization, materialism, and conventions of all types to the generative ambiguities and perceptions of bodily life that had been obscured in the cultural sphere. In his "Colloquium of the Centaurs" of 1901, he rejected the epistemic realms of science and philosophy when he reflected upon life, or what he called the most "insoluble enigma" of all. Rather, he turned to ancient mythology and conjured up a sweeping dialogue among the centaurs about the function and meaning of vital force. Everything alive, he insisted, is traversed by an arcane vital force that finds its singular expression in the world's natural architecture, including the human body:

ABANTES
Hymns to sacred Nature, from the earth's
bowels to the seed among the rocks,
to the flesh of trees and inside the human form,
it is all the same secret and the same law,
potent and exceedingly subtle, a universal compendium
of the supreme force, of Numen's virtue.

CHIRON
Hymns! Things possess a vital essence; things
have strange appearances, mysterious looks;
every form is a gesture, a cipher, an enigma.[199]

The key assumption that literature had somehow neglected the lived body undergirds Gómez de la Serna's manifesto, "The Concept of a New Literature," of 1909. In this foundational manifesto, he calls for a revolutionary new literature, in which the lived body serves as the wellspring for profound literary creativity. "Literature must labour through the CESAREAN OPERATION," he proposes conjuring up the organic social body, "[l]et us tear from those deadened by life that vital something that is not dead and that throbs in their inner depths."[200] The unthinkable

198 Quoted in Saz-Orozco, *Dios en Juan Ramón*, 68.
199 Darío, *Cuentos y poesías*, 109.
200 Gómez de la Serna, "El concepto," 170.

had finally come to pass, and the craft of literature had disregarded corporeality at its own peril. In an emphatic cry, he concludes: "There is no STATE OF BODY. All of literature is composed of an ethical, logical, canonical, and insufferable repose."[201] What he was getting at is that literature, if it was to meet the challenges of the modern age, had little choice but to realize a bodily aesthetic. The complicity between the literary and the corporeal during this period of technological, scientific, and mechanical revolution required a new perception, Gómez de la Serna claims in his manifesto, and there is no doubt that the explosion of erotica and sexual pseudo-scientific treatises in the following years of the twentieth century across Europe spoke to the shifting boundaries that circumscribed the body/world dynamic. F.T. Marinetti, one of Gómez de la Serna's early mentors, was explicit on this point: "One must imitate the movements of the machine … thereby preparing the fusion of man with the machine."[202] While Gómez de la Serna disagreed with Marinetti on several issues (Futurism's unapologetic misogyny, for instance), he nevertheless agreed with him that the critical appreciation of the lived body and its representation were highly problematic in countries like Spain that were burdened with uneven modernization, traditionialism, and the practices of religion. Given such a state of affairs, the new literature he outlines in his manifesto would not only daringly explore – but also exploit and assert – the lived body and its vital possibilities:

> The primary influence on literature is life: the present life, the awakened, naked, and vigorous life unfolding in an unprecedented deluge of light. [The old literature] lacks that movement and carnal imperative that the new literature provides us … The commonplace has tarnished and deformed life … The new literature does away with the commonplace and unearths the true concept of life. It is reviving the muddled curiosities and overcoming all the constraints that make up the commonplace … The goal of the new literature, therefore, is to allow us to reconstitute ourselves … The new literature can be summed up in what [Friedrich] Lange says about Being: *a specific centre of forces* … It responds to the intimate and functional concept of Being. All its imperatives are carnal in nature, and all its objects establish a sensible, urgent, and *organic* correspondence between the world and the individual.[203]

To better grasp the significance of the body and vital force during this crucial period in Gómez de la Serna's intellectual life we need only turn

201 Ibid., 159.
202 Marinetti, "Manifesto of Futurist Dance," 138.
203 Gómez de la Serna, "El concepto," 151–67.

to his one-act play *The Drama of the Uninhabited Palace,* which he wrote in the same year as his manifesto. Although the play is all but forgotten today, it reveals with unusual starkness the fundamental concerns about the lived body and vital force he outlined in his manifesto. The play is set in the Great Hall of an abandoned palace, which nevertheless has remained relatively intact, with tapestries, coats of arms, majestic paintings, exquisite furniture, and various other objects. What is most striking about this play is that all but two of its sixteen characters – the young peasant lovers, Juan and Rosa, who make a brief appearance at the end – are dead. Thus, the grey and listless spirits of the minor nobility that appear on stage represent nothing more than "carnal longings," or mere projections of their physical bodies that lie decomposing in crypts beneath the small church adjacent to the palace.[204] The play opens with the entrance of The Anonymous Man, who is concealed behind a masquerade mask. Addressing the audience directly before the curtain goes up, he delivers a short introduction, in which he clarifies the macabre setting and beseeches the audience to ponder honestly and openly what is about to transpire on life and death. He also conveys Gómez de la Serna's wish that each audience member "kill the death within you by ripping off its mask, prohibit the *misereres,* and give free reign to your merriment, no matter how ungodly or ravenous it may be."[205] The theme of concealment and deceit, introduced at the outset through the symbolic masks, underpins the entire play, given that the bodily projections in the Great Hall must come to terms with the repressive deception that once stifled their embodied existence (of note, too, is that the play's epigraph is taken from Nietzsche's *Beyond Good and Evil,* which reads: "Everything that is profound loves the mask").

The underlying tension between embodiment and identity in *The Drama of the Uninhabited Palace* is projected further in the setting itself: the uninhabited palace (the physical structure and decomposing bodies in its adjacent cemetery) is in fact inhabited (the non-physical residents and their bodily projections). The entire play, which is devoid of protagonists or any significant action, can be conceived of as a sustained reflection on the meaning of the lived body. Without bodies to engage the physical world, and thus without innate vital drives, the bodily projections simply mill around in the Great Hall and lead a glum existence filled with banal colloquies about what could have been. Almost every character takes up the question of embodiment and fantasizes about

204 Gómez de la Serna, *El drama,* 526.
205 Ibid.

re-engaging the haptic senses once again. A number of characters crave a simple kiss, given that kisses in the realm of the uninhabited palace only imprint shade on one's lips. The viscount Don Pedrín, who is portrayed slumped in a large armchair next to the baron Don Dámaso throughout most of the play, remarks: "We no longer know how to dream and we are left without philosophy, now that we long for our livers and hearts and stomachs and our entire anatomy… This is how we have learned of their worth!"[206] It is the irreverent Jester who flows across the stage and prods his fellow spirits into reflecting upon their squandered lives and the obvious shortcomings of their disembodied present. In the uninhabited palace, where issues of rank, lineage, and propriety no longer hold sway, the Jester badgers barons and duchesses indiscriminately and forces them to confront not only their most insidious transgressions in life (such as Don Dámaso's successful plot to murder his wife, Leticia, for her adultery), but also the fact that God is a myth. In a Nietzschean fashion, an old marquis quips: "The living had it all wrong: God was far away."[207]

The question Gómez de la Serna poses so provocatively in this play, which is reminiscent of one of Unamuno's fundamental concerns in *The Tragic Sense of Life*, explored in the previous section, is this: what good is the immortality of the soul *without* the lived body? When the young peasant lovers Rosa and Juan hide out in the palace to merge in an amorous embrace in the Great Hall, the spirits look on in envy from the shadows. Don Dámaso and Leticia are particularly drawn to the young lovers' bodies, yet when they realize that all hope of physical love is lost, they agree once and for all to leave the palace and go into the garden, where they dissolve into nothingness. There is no mistaking the denouement of the play and its fundamental meaning: the lived body triumphs above all else. Indeed, we are left with the "passionate culmination" of the young lovers' desire, which must be concealed behind a folding screen, before the final curtain.

More than an apology for instinctive life, as one critic proposes, Gómez de la Serna's play dramatizes the carnal imperative he charted in his manifesto.[208] In a society dulled by the so-called mask of conformity, the only life worth living necessitates the defiant recognition and acknowledgment of the lived body and its vital possibilities. The fact that the young lovers are peasants and live free from the nobility's cunning deceptions and cult of appearances certainly adds a compelling social

206 Ibid., 532.
207 Ibid., 536.
208 Sobejano, "Prólogo," 28.

component to the play in this respect. In the play's Prologue, Gómez de la Serna vented his frustration that the modern individual had still not pondered the lived body's complexities or given a second thought to the opportunities it provided to engage not only a new literary aesthetic, but also a rapidly transforming world. When he gazed into the world, all he saw were docile and zombie-like conformists:

> I am surprised when I observe people; they are all blind, disabled, and broken-legged people who look, act, and walk about with organs that have no origin in reality, organs that have no sagacity and are bereft of their clear persuasion ... If man does not soon transform into a corrupting and evil rebel, he will evolve not from the monkey, but from the original lie, which will make him a spectral, weak, trembling, lymphatic, and obsessed being.[209]

Gómez de la Serna will uphold the ideals of the lived body he outlined in his early works throughout his entire literary career. In *My Seven Words* (1910), *The Mute Book (Secrets)* (1910), *Tapestries* (1912), *Breasts* (1917), *Pombo* (1918), *The Incongruent One* (1922), and *Ramonism* (1923), he demonstrated to what extent the writer could create, if he sharpened his "carnal" awareness and managed to tap the body's wondrous vital capacities through intuition, instinct, spontaneity, and impulsiveness, something truly authentic and untarnished by the world's moral epidemics. His invention of the *greguería* – an epigram that combined humour and metaphor to sabotage logic and establish new and unexpected associations between objects and things – relied on the organic correspondence between bodily self and world that is referenced in his manifesto. It was only by interacting with the surrounding world in the here and now, by physically surrendering to life's changeability and vital flow, that the writer could even begin to think about the task of writing about the self. In his manifesto, he had bemoaned the fact that "[e]veryone has forgotten about day-to-day life. How is this possible? Day-to-day life is what is supreme and what wholly consumes us."[210] In each passing and fleeting moment, new possibilities presented themselves to the writer, and thus each new moment was fresh, raw, fortuitous, unpredictable, and *alive*, and thus it demanded its own *greguería*. In *Greguerías* of 1917, he explained further that each *greguería* came into existence spontaneously from a web of fleeting impressions and bodily sensations, sensations that needed to be acknowledged and recorded in their rawest form. More

209 Gómez de la Serna, *El drama*, 704–7.
210 Gómez de la Serna, "El concepto," 162.

than anything else, each *greguería* was the product of "a fruitful gaze that once it burrows itself into flesh blossoms its sprig of words and realities."[211] The subtlety and range of expression in Gómez de la Serna's *greguerías* is thus enormous:

The man who slices sausages is a counterfeiter of coins …
We will never know whether the cockscomb is intended as a crown or a Phrygian hat …
When a star falls, there is a run in the night's stocking …
Do angels carry parachutes? …
When an ape peels a banana, we see that he is the same as man …
I have noticed that one gives advice as one gives duplicate calendars: to get rid of them …
Something that has not been said about the moon? That it gives manicures to women sleepwalkers …[212]

For Gaspar Gómez de la Serna, the *greguería* indeed sprang from the totality of the living human organism. The body, the mind, the senses, every emotional and intuitive system, they all had to be fully engaged in the moment. It is no surprise, therefore, that literary practice for Gómez de la Serna had to encompass a commanding autobiographical dimension, in which the writer could synthesize the highly fluid self/world relation. "We must do everything," he proposed, "as if we were letting ourselves fall, as if we were unbraiding all of our tendons and nerves, as if were falling off a cliff."[213] The creative act was boundless and had to remain an open act, an act that out of necessity created no illusion of totality and channelled the lived body in the production of meaning, no matter how seemingly irrational, ironic, perverted, or critical it appeared. In many ways, the elaboration of this open approach to corporeality and writing in the *greguería* was one of Gómez de la Serna's signature achievements. As he stated in "My autobiography," from *The Sacred Crypt of the Pombo* of 1924: "Me? Me? I have to ask this question incessantly as I consider my autobiography; not because I doubt my existence, but rather, in the skepticism that surrounds us today and that we have to live in like a natural ether, I only encounter myself as a burst of

211 Gómez de la Serna, *Obras completas*, vol. 2, 15.

212 These selection of *greguerías* are taken from *Aphorisms – Ramón Gómez de la Serna* by Miguel González-Gerth.

213 Gómez de la Serna, *Obras completas*, vol. 2, 704.

myself, as something akin to a formless and fluid radioactivity that is congealed momentarily into a form."[214]

Throughout his life, Gómez de la Serna wrote hundreds of *greguerías*, and they can be found embedded in practically everything he ever wrote. The recently released *New greguerías* of 2009 contains dozens of unpublished *greguerías*, many of which he wrote in the years leading up to his death in 1963. As has been well established, Gómez de la Serna's *greguerías* deeply influenced the Spanish avant-garde, and writers like Rafael Alberti, Manuel Altolaguirre, Luis Cernuda, Gerardo Diego, Jorge Guillén, and Federico García Lorca relied on his example when it came to the idea of the lived body and cult of the image that figures so prominently in their work. The reigning idea of upholding first and foremost the lived body and discovering its vital possibilities in the act of defining the self would mark not only Gómez de la Serna's oeuvre, but much of twentieth-century modernist and avant-garde literature across Europe. Futurists, Dadaists, and Surrealists amply demonstrated that the lived body and its vital force held the secret to authenticity. Indeed, the lived body became for modernist writers the undisputed site of creation, spirituality, politics, and truth. It was this lived body, *my* lived body, that reflected and problematized social structures, norms, and values, and thus it became the ground, as Gómez de la Serna intuited, from which to imagine the possible.

214 Gómez de la Serna, "Mi autobiografía," 640–1.

Conclusion

> We accept far too easily that there exists a fundamental conflict between knowledge and life, such that their reciprocal aversion can lead only to the destruction of life by knowledge or to the derision of knowledge by life.
>
> Georges Canguilhem, *Knowledge of Life*[1]

EVER SINCE DESCARTES GAVE FORM to the human automaton consisting of cogs and wheels in *Treatise of Man*, men of learning and letters sought to explain the body's workings through increasingly more empirical methods. Empiricism brought forth facts, quantities, formulas, and, of course, a greater degree of mechanical certainty, or so Descartes argued. In the mechanistic models of human functioning that increasingly informed scientific progress in the seventeenth and eighteenth centuries, the organism's mechanical organization began to supplant its total organicity to such a degree that "the logic of the automaton as a simulacrum displace[d] the priority of the lived, experiential body."[2] This gradual displacement of the lived, experiential body represented a crucial development of modern thought, a development that was only hastened forward with the consolidation of Newtonianism and its zeal to imbue the world (including human anatomy) with distinct and measurable qualities of force. With the decline of humoral theory and the rise of the culture of dissection during this period, the concept of *materia* itself was also re-evaluated beyond Aristotelian arguments (that is, quality, unity, difference, and continuity), which were entering a period of decline.[3] As the body was abstracted further into a complex miscellany of interconnected pieces and parts, and as the essential properties of matter were

1 Canguilhem, *Knowledge of Life*, xvii.

2 Judovitz, *The Culture of the Body*, 69.

3 See Thomas M. Lennon's chapter, "The Problem of Individuation among the Cartesians," in *Individuation and Identity in Early Modern Philosophy: Descartes to Kant*, edited by Kenneth F. Barber and Jorge J.E. Garcia, 13–39. Also relevant is "Part 1" of Udo Thiel's *The Early Modern Subject: Self-Consciousness and Personal Identity from Descartes to Hume.*

debated within a mechanical framework, it is no small wonder that the question of vital force resurfaced with a vengeance.[4]

In my examination of Cabriada's *Letter* and the work of several of the *novatores* during this period in Spain, I have suggested that medicine and philosophy began to approach body functioning through an increasingly diverse set of theoretical lenses. These lenses privileged notions of vital change and renewal that were observable and theorizable, yet not easily measurable. Harvey's theories on circulation and blood properties – the all-important circuit of regeneration that animated every part of the body with "living" fluid – were critical in this respect, and through innovative figures like Cabriada we now have a more compelling picture of how Harvey's and Sylvius's concepts of vital force were strategically interpreted in Spain to counter prevailing Galenic theories and practices. Yet, I have also wanted to call attention to the great relevance of neo-Hippocratic doctrine in vitalist concepts between the late-seventeenth and mid-nineteenth centuries, which was decisive in expanding the very meaning of (bodily) life. It remains clear that neo-Hippocratism not only offered a wealth of expedient principles about body functioning and nature that served as springboards into reinterpreting life energy, but also emphasized the lucid empiricism that characterized the best of modern science (for instance, the observation of, and interaction with, the pathological body, advocated by the likes of Boix y Moliner).

Neo-Hippocratic doctrine was indeed "reinvented," as David Cantor has proposed, and it was wielded to challenge and circumvent not just Galenic authority, but also the New Science of mechanism, which was understood in Spanish medical circles as a type of modernized atomism that tended to theorize away the complexities of life. "Humanist scholars," as Cantor explains, "started to study Hippocratic texts in the late fifteenth century, a study that represented greater reliance on the ancient past, but also led to a repudiation of some parts of that past."[5] Hippocrates' accommodating notion of *impetum faciens*, or the essential vital activities within the body that generated life, was reinterpreted and

4 David Hillman and Carla Mazzio's volume *The Body in Parts: Fantasies of Corporeality in Early Modern Europe* does a magnificent job of bringing to light the various ways in which this process of bodily abstraction unfolded in the seventeenth century. While their volume does not tackle the question of corporeal knowledge in relation to vital force specifically, it does explore what they define as "social and psychic conditions of fragmentation [that] were encoded in practices of bodily partitioning" (xi). Essays of particular relevance include David Hillman's "Visceral Knowledge: Shakespeare, Skepticism, and the Interior of the Early Modern Body," and Gail Kern Paster's "Nervous Tension: Networks of Blood and Spirit in the Early Modern Body."

5 Cantor, "Introduction," 5.

given new stimulus in the anatomical and physiological sciences and the burgeoning field of microscopy. Similarly, the Hippocratic *natura medicatrix* principle, in which nature's healing powers were believed to operate through blood, organs, and fluids, was also critical in determining how the body participated in nature's ubiquitous vital force in direct and dynamic ways. Eighteenth- and early-nineteenth-century models of physiology, and Montpellier vitalism in particular, resonated widely in Spain. These models were instrumental in expanding the *natura medicatrix* principle to address (and modernize) a host of medico-anatomical issues. In many cases, as with the Montpellier vitalists, Hippocrates was often deployed as a tool of vitalist resistance against the excesses of mechanistic reasoning and its authority in key social and institutional spheres.[6] Thanks in large measure to neo-Hippocratic theory – which in Spain, unlike in other European countries, remained a part of the scientific imaginary well into the 1880s, as the Great Debate on Hippocrates demonstrated – vital force became a major focus of medical research and socio-political discourses. Clearly, there is still much to be learned about how Hippocrates, a fifth-century BCE physician, came to play such a crucial role in defining *modern* scientific progress in Spain.[7]

The body's dependency on the soul for vital force, particularly conceived through the framework of Galenic medical theory, was increasingly reaffirmed in Spain. As the body was dissected and scrutinized in progressive institutional spheres, such as Seville's Royal Society of Medicine and Other Sciences and Madrid's Royal Academy of Medicine, and as anatomical experiments and the findings of microscopy generated new knowledge about what animated it exactly, there was growing evidence that vital force originated from the material body and not the spiritual body. Cabriada's observations on circulation and blood properties, which offered a more "democratic" way of assessing the body's vital workings through a universal life-giving energy, was crucial in reducing

6 Williams, "Hippocrates," 159.

7 Teresa Santander Rodríguez's *Hippocrates in Spain (XVI Century)* is still the most comprehensive work on the subject, yet it focuses solely on the sixteenth century. Rodriguez's scholarship and extensive bibliographical sources demonstrate that Hippocrates' *Prognostics*, *Aphorisms*, and *De ratione victus in morbis acutis* circulated widely throughout the university system in early-modern Spain. Also relevant is López Piñero, "Andrés Piquer and Hippocratism in Spain during the Enlightenment," 9–37; and Jesús Ángel y Espinós, "Andrés Piquer and the Neo-Hippocratic Teaching of Medicine in Eighteenth-Century Spain," 461–74. Pedro Laín Entralgo also published extensively on Hippocratic doctrine, particularly in his thorough study *Hippocratic Medicine*, yet rarely did he focus on its influence in Spain. On this point see Luis Gil Fernández's "Pedro Laín Entralgo and the History of Greek Medicine."

Galen's hierarchy of body-soul relations to the level of a holistic vital *system.* What is more, each body at the microscopic level, as Guerrero Herreros argued in *Universal Medicine,* was discovered to be wholly unique and brimming with untold universes of life, which were bonded to nature's cycles of generation and decay in ways that were concrete and observable. Moreover, the living body was imagined as a complex "labyrinth" that resisted not only new methods of quantification, but also the objectivity of the instruments of science (microscope), which promised greater precision in the production of knowledge. Of note is that Guerrero Herrero's research reveals yet another crucial facet of the in/visible distinction that preoccupied early Enlightenment figures like Torres and remained embedded in the question of vital force. While Guerrero Herreros could render visible these universes of life under the microscope to some degree, he also intuited that they depended upon even more microscopic universes of life thriving just beyond the frontier of visibility. It is this very same frontier that haunted not only protoplasmic theory's quest to discover the origins of life in the cell in the late-nineteenth century, but also quantum biology today.[8]

While the great battle over the vitalist interpretation of the body and soul was waged in salons, pulpits, medical *juntas,* cafés, and in all sorts of treatises and ephemera, it is important to emphasize that the polemics they stirred up were more than simple mudslinging between rivals. These polemics had a very real impact on everything from what authors and theories were rejected in the university system to how groups of scientists and intellectuals established knowledge networks to subvert traditional customs and transform social institutions. In many instances, these polemics shed light on the structures (and injustices) of authority, and they also circulated new scientific methodologies and vocabularies and issued direct calls for reform. The unifying thread that runs throughout the texts I have analyzed in Chapters 2 through 4 is the inherent threat that new discoveries about the body posed to religious authority in particular. If vital force could be proven to originate in the idiosyncrasies of the body's fabric, then perhaps other complex human sensibilities (morality, for instance) could also be discovered to be wholly dependent on the corporeal realm. If this were the case, the soul's governance over the body would be greatly reduced, or would evaporate altogether, which would have profound ramifications for the Church and what Foucault has labelled its pastoral power. Torres's *Anatomy* provides a paradigmatic

8 For more on quantum biology and the frontier of visibility, see McFadden and Al-Khalili's *Life on the Edge,* 27–8.

example of how religious apologists vehemently censured these sacrilegious notions by what I have called "anatomizing the soul": the attempt to substantiate that most-elusive boundary between flesh and spirit through the medium of a bodily vital force. These efforts often had the unintended consequence of disclosing to what extent the body-soul nexus was in fact becoming more problematic under the weight of scientific discovery, and how the very exploration of vitalistic agency, which included the evolving questions of autonomy, corporeality, individualization, and self, was considered subversive. The same ambition to anatomize the soul, as I have argued, continued well into the Enlightenment and remained an important proving ground for all sorts of pointed criticisms of vitalist scholarship – Luzuriaga's, for instance – during Spain's medical revolution.

While the revelations of vital force defied key notions about the body-soul nexus, they also cast doubt on the fundamental assumptions that underpinned the individual's relationship with nature. The astonishing fact of resuscitation, of bringing a dead body back to life, demonstrated that the border between life and death was not as sharp as was traditionally thought. Three of the more-challenging questions it raised included: if the soul flees the body upon death, as dictated by Scripture, how is resuscitation even possible on the dead? And, if the soul imbues the body with vital force, does the soul return from its otherworldly journey to inhabit the resuscitated body once again? Lastly, can any lifeless body that has not succumbed to the visible processes of decomposition be resuscitated? The fact of resuscitation, as Luzuriaga well knew, proved devastating to religious apologists. As Stefan Timmermans points out in *Sudden Death and the Myth of CPR*, "[r]esuscitating aims to alter by human means what for most of history has been considered unchangeable divine prerogative … To engage in resuscitative efforts implies that human beings put faith in technical and pharmacological interventions to overcome death."[9] We still do not have a clear picture of how these questions associated with resuscitation and the soul resonated in Spain, particularly from the perspective of Romanticism's fascination with mortality, for instance. That said, there is little doubt that resuscitation radically challenged concepts of how the soul interacted, or could interact, with the body.

The increasingly subjectivist view of life and nature that gained traction with these types of inquiries deeply troubled the Church. The formidable question the subjectivist view raised was: what would a society look

9 Timmermans, *Sudden Death*, 32.

like organized around the individual's direct rapport with the world and its mysterious life energies? In works like *Principles on the Essential Order of Nature*, written by the jurist and philosopher Antonio Javier Pérez y López in 1785, we get a sense of the urgency associated with reinserting *naturaleza* more firmly into theological discussions in Spain during the Enlightenment. With a curious blend of rational objectivism, metaphysics, and mystical theology, Pérez y López affirmed that, in observing nature's vital force and its divine order, the individual would be inspired to eschew the "gangrene" of liberal models of social organization for more traditional ones based on the revelations of the Church and Scripture.[10] In a similar fashion, beginning in 1781, the priest and legal reformer Juan Francisco de Castro, covered in Chapter 3, published the encyclopedic ten-volume work *God and Nature: Historical, Natural, and Political Compendium in Which It Is Demonstrated the Existence of God* to discredit beliefs in a vitalized nature during the Enlightenment. What he attempted to do was reconcile the natural realm with what he deemed was man's innate yearning for religiousness and ethical improvement. Few late-eighteenth-century treatises in Spain marshalled the breadth of theological scholarship in favour of a reassessment of nature as did de Castro's *God and Nature*.

During the eighteenth century in Spain, the question of vital force was fundamental in opening new vistas on that most essential relationship between body and world, with an eye toward making intelligible the dynamics of social change and progress. Everything from human nature and communal milieu to universal history and the rise of secularism were up for consideration. In examining Jovellanos's progression of thought toward an organicist view of nature, we can appreciate in what ways the ideal of nature's vital force in Spain was allied to a subjective, corporeal experience that defied the authority of reason when it came time to "make sense" of the world. In embracing the unknown in nature's vital force (or living nature), Jovellanos essentially reimagined the

10 Pérez y López, *Principios del orden esencial de la naturaleza*, vii. López Silvestre does point out, however, that figures like Castro had a hand in ushering in the fundamental reconsideration and aestheticization of nature during the Spanish Enlightenment:

> Leaving aside Feijóo, what remains understudied is the key role that certain members of the clergy played in introducing new ideas [on natural theology] into Spain … Seen from this angle, we would have probably reached the conclusion by now that somewhere between traditionalism and reform there existed a group that served … a crucial role as intermediary. The natural theology of the eighteenth century – a product of priests and believers who sidestepped dogmatic theology and Scripture to rely on the methods of science and experience – can be seen as a conciliatory gesture on the part of this moderate group. (440–1)

individual's place within the social and divine order and prefigured Romantic attitudes toward life. He likewise expanded the meaning of *progreso* to include an ulterior knowledge derived from the unfathomable of life. Indeed, the unfathomable of life could serve as the necessary complement to reason and open a path to an epistemology of feeling, intuition, and imagination that could improve the individual and advance society. What I have offered on Jovellanos's thought in this respect is merely a fragment, and the image of Jovellanos that I have presented as a transitional figure bridging Enlightenment reason and Romantic subjectivity remains to be fully explored. Certainly, establishing a sharper picture of the touchpoints between Enlightenment and Romantic projects in Spain requires more consideration, and the question of vital force might very well serve as one way to address this issue.

With each new physiological discovery in the nineteenth and early-twentieth centuries, and with each new chemical or iatromechanical breakthrough, science attempted to further demystify the body and make it more straightforwardly knowable. In Spain, positivist and Krausist science advanced this epistemological enterprise and set the tone for the discovery of vital force for decades to come – yet from vastly diverging standpoints. While positivists quantified and measured life and divested it of what the Hippocratic physician Letamendi called its "living individuality," Krausists sought to establish the basis for a new, vigorous society through a rehabilitation of life that involved everything from aesthetics to calisthenics to evolutionary theory. What became apparent to artists, poets, philosophers, and intellectuals in early-twentieth-century Spain was that this rehabilitation of life only went so far in providing a solution to the problem of modern existence. What was required was a profound, intuitive understanding of how the lived body (and not just the mind) served as the medium through which the world was known. For the most part, they claimed that each individual's vital force, which was valued as a formidable and creative activity of the body and mind, was simply beyond the scope of reason. Nietzsche, like Bergson, had elaborated on this important point throughout most of his oeuvre, and his influence in Spain was significant, as I have indicated.[11] The intellect, he believed, was ill-equipped to grasp the fundamental essence of life, yet bodily

11 Henri Bergson also famously elaborated on this important point in *Creative Evolution* of 1907, and his influence in Spain was likewise significant. Bergson's vitalist theories took hold in Spain in the early 1910s, before the First World War, and for this reason I decided to pay more attention to Nietzsche's vitalism, which was felt as early as the mid-1890s and had more visibility and influence on the question of vital force in the early years of the twentieth century. See Benjamin Fraser's *Encounters with Bergson(ism) in Spain*:

intuition, channelled through the imagination and instinct, blossomed from the very form of life. Thus, the lived body could not be quantified or defined in a precise rational or scientific sense, for the simple reason that its vital force was transformation, movement, will to power, and supreme health, a proposition that greatly informed Spanish modernists like Baroja and Gómez de la Serna. I have also suggested that the concept of the lived body often framed not only the plethora of discourses during this period that attended developments in hygiene, epidemiology, and degeneration theory, but also the dominant socio-economic forces of modernity that reacted against life.

In analyzing the question of vital force, I have sought ultimately to add clarity to one of the driving motors of modernity: the practical critique of life. On this crucial point, Foucault's notion of critique has been important to my argument, yet I would like to end this book with Deleuze, one of Foucault's greatest admirers and critics. Indeed, Deleuze has something illuminating to offer on the practical critique of life that neatly ties together the book's overarching aim. For Deleuze, vital force is synonymous with Life: it is the fundamental energy that urges the individual forward, opens new fields of self-reflexivity, resists knowledge practices to generate new ones, and establishes and renews relations between self and world in the repressive face of authority, whatever its guise. What Deleuze proposes with the project of modernity in mind, and what I have underscored through an assortment of lenses, is that "[l]ife becomes resistance to power when power takes life as its object."[12] Within and beyond the limits of power, the question of vital force in Spain has always managed to refigure the very meaning of these *limits* in all their multiplicity and contingency. It is this unfaltering, ceaseless, and increasingly pronounced process of critical self-reflection that provides us with another view of the contradictory nature of reason and the inherently unstable categories of knowledge at the heart of modernity.

Reconciling Philosophy, Literature, Film and Urban Space. Of particular interest for this study is Fraser's readings of Unamuno's and Pio Baroja's dialogue with Bergson's philosophy in Chapters 1 and 2.

12 Deleuze, *Foucault*, 77.

Bibliography

Abellán, José Luis. "Filosofía de la Institución Libre de Enseñanza: el krausopositivismo." In *Masonería, Política y Sociedad*, edited by J.A. Ferrer Benemeli, 405–18. Zaragoza: CEHME, 1989.

Abrams, M.H. *The Fourth Dimension of a Poem.* Foreword by Harold Bloom. New York: W.W. Norton, 2012.

Abril, Pedro Simón. *Apuntamientos de cómo se deben reformar las doctrinas y la manera de Enseñallas.* Madrid: Manuel Fernández, 1769.

Ackelsberg, Martha A. *Free Women of Spain: Anarchism and the Struggle for the Emancipation of Women.* Oakland: AK Press, 2005.

Adorno, Theodor. *Aesthetic Theory.* London: Routledge, 1984.

Alberti, Fay Bound. *Matters of the Heart: History, Medicine, and Emotion.* Oxford: Oxford University Press, 2010.

Albiña, Salvador, and Telesforo M. Hernández. "Comentario en torno a la biografía de Tomás Vicente Tosca." In *Universidades españolas y americanas: época colonial*, 16–56. Madrid: CSIC.

Aldrete y Soto, Luis de. *La verdad acrisolada, con letras divinas, y humanas, padres, y doctores de iglesia.* Valencia: Benito Macà, 1682.

Alea, José María. *Vida del conde de Buffon.* Madrid: Pantaleón Aznar, 1797.

Álvarez de Toledo, Gabriel. *Historia de la Iglesia del mundo, que contiene los sucesos de su creación hasta el Diluvio.* Madrid: Librería del Rey, 1713.

Amo Usanos, Rafael. *El principio vital del ser humano en Ireneo, Orígenes, Agustín, Tomás de Aquino y la antropología teológica española reciente.* Rome: Università Geogiana, 2007.

Ángel y Espinós, Jesús. "Andrés Piquer and the Neo-Hippocratic Teaching of Medicine in Eighteenth-Century Spain." In *Hippocrates and Medical Education*, edited by Manfred Horstamanshoff, 461–74. Leiden: Brill, 2010.

Aquinas, Thomas. *Summa Theologica.* Raleigh: Hayes-Barton, 1971.

Arce, Joaquín. "Jovellanos y la sensibilidad prerromántica." *Boletín de la Biblioteca de Menéndez Pelayo* 36 (1960): 139–77.

– *La poesía del siglo ilustrado.* Madrid: Alhambra, 1981.

Arias Santos, Francisco J. "Unamuno y la psicología científica española." In *Tu mano es mi destino. Congreso Internacional Miguel de Unamuno,* edited by Cirilo Flórez Miguel, 31–6. Salamanca: Universidad de Salamanca.

Aristotle. *De Anima.* Translated by R.D. Hicks. New York: Cosimo, 2008.

– *A New Aristotle Reader. Nicomachean Ethics.* Edited by J.L. Ackrill. Princeton: Princeton University Press, 1987.

– *The Philosophy of Aristotle.* Translated by J.L. Creed and A.E. Wardman. Introduction by Renford Bambrough. New York: Penguin, 2003.

Armstrong, Tim. *Modernism, Technology, and the Body: A Cultural Study.* Cambridge: Cambridge University Press, 1998.

Arroyo Parra, Matilde, and Manuel Hernández Vázquez. "Ilustración Gimnástica: Felipe Serrate (1886–1887)." Museo del juego. Accessed 21 March 2017. http://museodeljuego.org/.

Atlantic Monthly. "French and German." 34, no. 205 (Nov. 1874): 631–3.

Ausejo, Elena. *Las matemáticas en el siglo XVII.* Madrid: Akal, 1992.

Azcárate, Gumersindo de. "El positivismo y la civilización." *Revista Contemporánea* 4 (1876): 234.

Azorín, José Martínez Ruiz. *Clásicos y modernos.* Madrid: Losada, 1951.

– "La filosofía de Baroja." In *Ante Baroja: Edición crítica, revisada y ampliada (1900–1960),* edited by Francisco Fuster García, 85–9. Alicante: Universidad de Alicante, 2012.

Bakhtin, Mikhail. "Contemporary Vitalism." In *The Crisis in Modernism. Bergson and the Vitalist Controversy,* edited by Frederick Burwick and Paul Douglass, 76–97. Cambridge: Cambridge UP, 1992.

Ballano, Antonio. *Diccionario de medicina y cirugía, ó, Biblioteca manual médico-quirúrgica.* Madrid: Imprenta Real, 1805–1807.

Barnades, Miguel. *Instrucción sobre lo arriesgado que es, en ciertos casos, enterrar a las personas, sin constar su muerte por otras señales más que las vulgares.* Madrid: Antonio de Sancha, 1775.

Baroja, Pío. *El dolor: Estudio de psico-física.* Salamanca: Real Academia de Medicina de Salamanca, 1980.

– *Intermedios.* Madrid: Espasa-Calpe, 1931.

– *Juventud, egolatría.* Madrid: Caro Raggio, 1920.

– *Páginas escogidas.* Madrid: Calleja, 1918.

– *El tablado de Arlequín.* Valencia: Sempere y Compañía, 1903.

– *The Tree of Knowledge.* Translated by Aubrey F.G. Bell. New York: Knopf, 1974.

– *Vidas sombrías.* Madrid: Aguilar, 1958.

Barona Vilar, Josep Lluís. *La doctrina y el laboratorio: Fisiología en la sociedad española del siglo XIX.* Madrid: CSIC, 1992.

– *La fisiología: Origen histórico de una ciencia experimental.* Madrid: Akal, 1991.

– "La obra fisiológica de Juan Mosácula Cabrera." *Llull* 7 (1984): 5–27.

– "Las tercianas de su Excelencia: el debate entre tradición y modernidad en la medicina española del seiscientos." *Idée* 23 (1993): 49–66.

Barrett, William. *The Illusion of Technique.* Garden City: Anchor Press, 1978.

– "Unamuno and the Contest with Death." In *The Tragic Sense of Life in Men and Nations: Selected Works of Miguel de Unamuno.* Vol. 4. Translated by Anthony Kerrigan. Introduction by Salvador de Madriaga, 361–74. Princeton, NJ: Princeton UP, 1972.

Barthez, Paul-Joseph. *Discours sur le génie de Hippocrate.* Montpellier: Tournel, Père et Fils, 1801.

Barzun, Jacques. "Romanticism: Definition of a Period." *Magazine of Art* 42 (1949): 243–8.

Bauman, Zygmunt. *Modernity and Ambivalence.* Cambridge, UK: Polity, 1993; 2007.

Beale, Lionel S. *Protoplasm; or, Matter and Life.* Philadelphia: Lindsay & Blakiston, 1874.

Bécquer, Gustavo Adolfo. *Rhymes and Legends (Selection). Rimas y leyendas (Selección).* Edited and translated by Stanley Appelbaum. Mineola, NY: Dover, 2006.

Behler, Ernst. *German Romantic Literary Theory.* Cambridge: Cambridge UP, 1993.

Belilla, Agustín Joseph. *Dissertacion Physico-Chímica Mecánico-Medica.* Zaragoza: Joseph Fort, 1750.

Bellver, Catherine G. *Bodies in Motion: Spanish Vanguard Poetry, Mass Culture, and Gender Dynamics.* Lewisburg, PA: Bucknell UP, 2010.

Benjamin, Walter. *Illuminations.* Edited by Harry Arrendt. Translated by Harry Zohn. New York: Schocken, 1968.

Bergson, Henri. *Creative Evolution.* Translated by Arthur Mitchell. New York: Dover, 1988.

– *Creative Mind.* Translated by Mabelle L. Andinson. New York: Dover, 2007.

– *An Introduction to Metaphysics.* Translated by T.E. Hulme. New York: Putnam's Sons, 1912.

Berlin, Isaiah. *The Roots of Romanticism.* Foreword by John Gray. Princeton: Princeton UP, 1999.

Berman, Marshall. *All That Is Solid Melts into Air: The Experience of Modernity.* New York: Simon and Schuster, 1982.

Bianco, Giuseppe. "The Origins of of Georges Canguilhem's 'Vitalism': Against the Anthropology of Irritation." In *Vitalism and the Scientific Image in Post-Enlightenment Life Science, 1800–2010,* edited by Sebastian Normandin and Charles T. Wolfe, 243–66. New York: Springer, 2013.

Bichat, Xavier. *Investigaciones fisiológicas sobre la vida y la muerte.* Vol. 2. Translated by Tomás García Suelto. Madrid: Real Arbitrio, 1807.

– *Physiological Researches upon Life and Death.* Translated by Tobias Watkins. Philadelphia: Smith & Maxwell, 1809.

Blasco Pascual, Francisco Javier. *La poética de Juan Ramón Jiménez. Desarrollo, contexto y sistema.* Salamanca: Universidad de Salamanca, 1981.

Boerhaave, Herman. *Boerhaave's Orations.* Leiden: Brill, 1983.

Boix y Moliner, Miguel Marcelino. *Hipócrates defendido, de las imposturas, y calumnias, que algunos Medicos poco cautos le imputan.* Madrid: Mateo Blanco, 1711.

Bondeson, Jan. *Buried Alive: The Terrifying History of Our Most Primal Fear.* New York: Norton, 2001.

Bourdieu, Pierre. *Outline of a Theory of Practice.* Translated by Richard Nice. Cambridge: Cambridge UP, 1977.

Brady, Emily. "The Environmental Sublime." In *The Sublime: From Antiquity to the Present*, edited by Timothy M. Costelloe, 171–82. Cambridge: Cambridge UP, 2012.

– *The Sublime in Modern Philosophy: Aesthetics, Ethics, and Nature.* Cambridge: Cambridge UP, 2013.

Brain, Robert Michael. *The Pulse of Modernism: Physiological Aesthetics in Fin-de-siècle Europe.* Seattle: U. of Washington Press, 2015.

Bretz, Mary Lee. *La evolución novelística de Pío Baroja.* Madrid: Studia Humanitatis, 1979.

Brown, John. *The Elements of Medicine.* Vol. 1. London: J. Johnson, 1788.

Bueno, Mar Rey. "Alchemy and Medicine." In *Alquimia, ciencias y pensamientos a través de los libros*, edited by Joaquín Pérez Pariente and Miguel López Pérez, 55–8. Madrid: Universidad Complutense, 2005.

– *El hechizado. Medicina, alquimia y superstición en la corte de Carlos.* Vol. 2: *1661–1700.* Madrid: Corona Borealis, 1998.

Bujosa Homar, Francesc. *Filosofía e historiografía médica en España.* Madrid: CSIC, 1989.

Bürger, Peter. *Theory of the Avant-Garde.* Minneapolis: U. of Minnesota Press, 1984.

Burke, Edmund. "A Philosophical Enquiry into the Origin of our Ideas of the Sublime and Beautiful." In *The Sublime: A Reader in British Eighteenth-Century Aesthetic Theory*, edited by Andrew Ashfield and Peter de Bolla, 131–43. Cambridge: Cambridge UP, 1996.

Burroughs, John. *The Breath of Life.* New York: Houghton Mifflin, 1915.

– "The New Vitalism." *North American Review* 196, no. 6 (1912): 759–71.

Burwick, Frederick, and Douglass, Paul. "Introduction." In *The Crisis in Modernism*, edited by Frederick Burwick and Paul Douglass, 1–12. Cambridge: Cambridge UP, 1992.

Butler, Judith. "Foucault and the Paradox of Bodily Inscriptions." *Journal of Philosophy* 86, no. 11 (1989): 601–7.

Butt, J.W. "Unamuno's Idea of Intrahistoria: Its Origins and Significance." In *Studies in Modern Spanish Literature and Art Presented to Helen F. Grant*, edited by Nigel Glendinning, 13–24. London: Tamesis, 1972.

Cabezas, Juan Antonio. *Jovellanos: El fracaso de la ilustración.* Madrid: Silex, 1985.

Cabezas García, Félix. *La medicina y los médicos en la obra de Pío Baroja.* Bilbao: Beta, 2013.

Cabriada, Juan. *Carta filosofica, medico-chymica en el que se demuestra, que de los tiempos, y experiencias se han aprendido los mejores remedios contra las enfermedades. Por la nova antigua medicina.* Madrid, 1687.

– *Verdad triunfante: Respuesta apologetica escrita por Filiatro, en defensa de la Carta filosofica, medico-chymica del doctor don Juan de Cabriada.* Madrid, 1687.

Calderón, Alfredo. "Una idea. Estudios de Filosofía Natural. Total organización de la materia. Folleto de los Sres. D. Enrique Serrano y Salvador Calderón." *Revista de España* 29 (1872): 187–98.

Camón Aznar, José. *Los libros de arte en la obra de Gómez de la Serna.* Madrid: Maestre, 1968.

Campos, Ricardo, and Huertas García-Alejo, Rafael. "Degeneración biológica y decadencia social en España, datos para un imaginario patrio." In *Imágenes e imaginarios nacionales en el ultramar español,* edited by Consuelo Naranjo Orovio and Carlos Serrano, 47–66. Madrid: CSIC, 1999.

Canguilhem, Georges. *Knowledge of Life.* Translated by Stefanos Geroulanos and Daniela Ginsburg. Edited by Paola Marrati and Todd Meyers. New York: Fordham UP, 2008.

Cañizares-Esguerra, Jorge. "Iberian Science in the Renaissance: Ignored How Much Longer?" *Perspectives on Science* 12, no.1 (2004): 86–124.

Cantor, David. "Introduction: The Uses and Meanings of Hippocrates." In *Reinventing Hippocrates,* edited by David Cantor, 1–18. Burlington, VT: Ashgate, 2002.

Capel, Horacio. "Filosofía y ciencia en los estudios sobre el territorio en España durante el siglo XVIII." *Cuadernos de estudio del siglo XVIII,* no. 5 (1995): 59–100.

Cardona, Álvaro. *La salud pública en España durante el Trienio Liberal, 1820–1823.* Madrid: CSIC, 2005.

Cardona, Dionisio de. "Aprobación." *Carta filosofica, medico-chymica en el que se demuestra, que de los tiempos, y experiencias se han aprendido los mejores remedios contra las enfermedades. Por la nova antigua medicina.* Madrid, 1687, n.p.

Carnero, Guillermo. "Por la emoción a la idea: la poesía filosófica del siglo XVIII." In *La luz de la razón: Literatura y Cultura del siglo XVIII,* edited by Aurora Egido and Enrique Laplana, 121–32. Zaragoza: Excma. Diputación de Zaragoza, 2010.

Carracedo, Angel, and Luis Concheiro. "Forensic Science Practice in Spain." In *The Global Practice of Forensic Science,* edited by Douglas H. Ubelaker, 261–6. Hoboken, NJ: Wiley, 2015.

Carrasco, Juan Vicente. *Compendio de fisiología, o conocimiento del hombre físico y vital.* 2 vols. Madrid: José Collado, 1817.

Carter, Codell K. *The Decline of Therapeutic Bloodletting and the Collapse of Traditional Medicine.* New Brunswick, NJ: Transaction Publishers, 2012.

Carter, Richard B. *Descartes's Medical Philosophy: The Organic Solution to the Mind-Body Problem.* Baltimore: Johns Hopkins UP, 1983.

Casado de Otaola, Santos. *Naturaleza patria: Ciencia y sentimiento de la naturaleza en España del regeneracionismo.* Madrid: Marcial Pons, 2010.

Casalete, José. "Aprobación." *Carta filosofica, medico-chymica en el que se demuestra, que de los tiempos, y experiencias se han aprendido los mejores remedios contra las enfermedades: Por la nova antigua medicina.* Madrid, 1687, n.p.

Casanova, Peregrín. *La biología general.* Vol. 1. Valencia: Ferrer de Orga, 1877.

Cascardi, Anthony. *The Subject of Modernity.* Cambridge: Cambridge UP, 1992.

Caso González, José Miguel. "El sentimiento de la naturaleza en Jovellanos." In *Jovellanos y la naturaleza.* Introduction Jesús Menéndez Pelaez. Edited by Bernardo Canga and Carmen Piñán, 21–65. Gijón: Fundación Foro Jovellanos, 2011.

– "Prólogo." In *Cartas del viaje a Asturias (Cartas a Ponz).* Vol. I: *Gaspar Melchor de Jovellanos,* 11–51. Asturias: Ayalga, 1981.

Caso González, José, Bernado Canga Meana, and Carmen Piñán. *Jovellanos y la naturaleza.* Gijón: Fundación Foro Jovellanos, 2006.

Castejón, Agustín de. *Voces del alma dadas dentro, y fuera de España. Tomo Segundo.* Madrid: Juan de Zúñiga, 1739.

Castillo, Antonio Díaz del. *Hipócrates desagraviado, de las ofensas por Hipócrates defendido: en particular en la curación de calenturas agudas, de dolor de costado, y tercianas.* Alcalá de Henares: Julián García Briones, 1713.

Castro, Américo. *Los españoles: como llegaron a serlo.* Madrid, 1965.

Ceñal, Ramón. "El cartesianismo en España." *Revista de la Universidad de Oviedo* (1945): 3–95.

Clarke, Desmond M. *Descartes: A Biography.* Cambridge: Cambridge UP, 2006.

Clement, Jean Pierre. *Las instituciones científicas y la difusión de la ciencia durante la ilustración.* Vol. 23: *Historia de la ciencia.* Madrid: Akal, 1993.

Clemison, Richard, and Francisco Vázquez García. *Hermaphroditism, Medical Science, and Sexual Identity in Spain, 1850–1960.* Cardiff: U. of Wales Press, 2009.

Clericuzio, Antonio. "The Internal Laboratory: The Chemical Reinterpretation of Spirits in England (1650–1680)." In *Alchemy and Chemistry in the 16th and 17th Centuries.* Edited by Piyo Rattansi, 51–83. Dordecht: Kluwer Academic Publishers, 1994.

Comte, Auguste. *The Positive Philosophy of Auguste Comte.* London: Trübner & Co., 1875.

Comte de Buffon, Georges-Louis Leclerc. *Natural History.* Abridged. London: C. & G. Kearsely, 1791.

Concepción de Unamuno Pérez, María. *Miguel de Unamuno y la cultura francesa.* Salamanca: Universidad de Salamanca, 1991.

Cortiñas, Agustín. *Demostración física de la espiritualidad e inmortalidad del alma.* Coruña: Manuel Francisco de Soto, 1816.

Costa Carballo, Carlos Manuel. "El vitalismo en la enseñanza de la medicina del *Setecientos* madrileño." In *Ciencia en expansión: Estudios sobre la difusión de las ideas científicas y médicas en España (siglos XVIII y XIX)*, edited by Elvira Arquiola and José Martínez-Pérez, 81–105. Madrid: Editorial Complutense, 1995.

Cruz del Pozo, María Victoria. *Gassendismo y cartesianismo en España: Martín Martínez, médico filósofo del siglo XVIII.* Sevilla: U. de Sevilla, 1997.

Cueto Pérez, Magdalena. *Aspectos sistemáticos en la narrativa de Pío Baroja: El árbol de la ciencia.* Gijón: Universidad de Oviedo, 1985.

Cullen, William. *Elementos de medicina práctica.* Translated by Bartolomé Piñera y Siles. Madrid: Benito Cano, 1799.

D'Alembert, Jean le Rond. *Preliminary Discourse to the Encyclopedia of Diderot.* Translated, and with an Introduction, by Richard N. Schwab. Chicago: Chicago UP, 1995.

Darío, Ruben. *Stories and Poems. Cuentos y poesías. A Dual-Language Book.* Edited and Translated by Stanley Appelbaum. New York: Mineola, 2002.

Darwin, Charles. *The Descent of Man.* Vols. 1 and 2. New York: Appleton and Co., 1872.

De los Ríos, Fernando. *El sentido humanista del socialismo.* Madrid: Castalia, 1976.

De Lys, Gabriel. "Translator's Preface." In *Elements of Physiology*, by Anthelme Richerand. Translated by Gabriel de Lys, iv–xviii. London: R. Gilbert 1819.

De Ron, Antonio. "Aprobación." In *Carta filosofica, medico-chymica en el que se demuestra, que de los tiempos, y experiencias se han aprendido los mejores remedios contra las enfermedades. Por la nova antigua medicina.* Madrid, 1687.

De Ros, Guillermo Olagüe, and Gallart, Mikel Astrain. "Una carta inédita de Ignacio María Ruiz de Luzuriaga (1763–1822) sobre la difusión de la vacuna en España (1801)." *Dynamis* 14 (1994): 305–37.

De Vos, Paula. "Natural History and the Pursuit of Empire in Eighteenth-Century Spain." *Eighteenth-Century Studies* 40, no. 2 (2007): 209–39.

Debus, Allen G. *Chemistry and Medical Debate: Van Helmont to Booerhave.* Canton, MA: Watson, 2001.

Del Río, Angel. "El sentimiento de la naturaleza en los *Diarios* de Jovellanos." In *Nueva Revista de Filología Hispánica* 7 (1953): 630–7.

Deleuze, Gilles. *Foucault.* New York: Continuum, 1999.

– "Immanence. A Life…" In *Pure Immanence: Essays on A Life.* Introduction by John Rajchman. Translated by Anne Boyman, 25–33. New York: Zone Books, 2001.

– *Negotiations, 1972–1990.* New York: Columbia UP, 1990.

Delgado, Daniel Crespo, and Joan Domenge i Mesquida. "Preliminar." In *Gaspar Melchor de Jovellanos: Memorias histórico-artísticas de aquitectura,* edited by Daniel Crespo Delgado and Joan Domenge i Mesquida, 13–56. Madrid: Akal, 2013.

Derrida, Jacques. *Of Grammatology*. Translated by Gayatri Chakrovorty Spivak. Baltimore: John Hopkins UP, 1997.

Descartes, René. *Description of the Human Body*. In *The Philosophical Writings of Descartes*. Vol. 1. Translated by John Cottingham, Robert Stoothoff, and Dugald Murdoch. Cambridge: Cambridge UP, 1985.

– *Discourse on Method*. In *The Philosophical Writings of Descartes*. Vol. 1. Translated by John Cottingham, Robert Stoothoff, and Dugald Murdoch. Cambridge: Cambridge UP, 1985.

– *Passions of the Soul*. In *The Philosophical Writings of Descartes*. Vol. I. Translated by John Cottingham, Robert Stoothoff, and Dugald Murdoch. Cambridge: Cambridge UP, 1985.

– *Treatise of Man*. Translated by Thomas Steele Hall. Cambridge: Harvard UP, 1972.

Deutsch, Helen, and Mary Terrall. "Introduction." In *Vital Matters: Eighteenth-century Views of Conception, Life, and Death*. Edited by Helen Deutsch and Mary Terrall, 3–12. Toronto: U. of Toronto Press, 2012.

Diccionario de la lengua castellana. Madrid: Joaquín Ibarra, 1783.

Diogenes Medico. n.p., n.d.

Domínguez, Frank A. "Body and Soul: Jorge Manrique's 'Coplas por la muerte de su padre,' 13: 145–156." *Hispania* 84, no. 1 (2001): 1–10.

Domínguez Lázaro, Martín. "La educación en España en la segunda mitad del siglo XVIII." *Revista Española de Pedagogía* 43, no. 167 (1985): 71–89.

Don Abbot, Paul. "The Influence of Blair's *Lectures* in Spain." *Rhetorica* 7, no. 3 (1989): 275–89.

Dotor, Ángel. *Jovellanos*. Madrid: Compañía Bibliográfica Española, 1964.

Driesch, Hans. *The History and Theory of Vitalism*. London: Macmillan, 1914.

Duchesneau, François. "Vitalism in Late Eighteenth-century Physiology: The Cases of Barthez, Blumenbach, and John Hunter." In *William Hunter and the Eighteenth-century Medical World*, edited by W.F. Bynum and Roy Porter, 259–95. Cambridge: Cambridge UP, 1985.

Eagleton, Terry. *The Ideology of the Aesthetic*. London: Wiley, 1991.

Echegaray, José. *Discursos leídos en la Real Academia de Ciencias Exactas, Físicas y Naturales*. Madrid: Aguado, 1866.

Eknoyan, Garabed. "A History of Diuretics." In *Diuretic Agents: Clinical Physiology and Pharmacology*, edited by Donald Seldin and Gerhard Giebisch, 3–28. San Diego: Academic Press, 1997.

"El gimnasio de Bilbao." *La Ilustración Española y Americana* 19, no. 47 (1875): 399.

Elliott, John H. *The Count-Duke of Olivares: The Statesman in an Age of Decline.* New Haven: Yale UP, 1986.

– *Imperial Spain, 1469–1716.* New York: Penguin, 1990.

Enríquez Gómez, Antonio. *El siglo pitagórico y vida de don Gregorio Guadaña.* Madrid: Antonio Espinosa, 1788.

Esdaile, Charles J. *Spain in the Liberal Age: From Constitution to Civil War, 1808–1939.* Malden, MA: Blackwell, 2000.

Ettinghausen, Henry. "Politics and the Press in Spain." In *The Politics of Information in Early Modern Europe,* edited by Brendan Dooley and Sabrina A. Baron, 199–215. London: Routledge, 2001.

Fajardo Olegario, Negrín. "José Clavijo y Fajardo, naturalista ilustrado." In *Veinticinco ensayos de historia de la educación española moderna y contemporánea,* 139–56. Madrid. UNED, 2013.

Feijóo y Montenegro, Benito Jerónimo. "Al Doctor Martínez." *Teatro crítico universal.* Vol. 2, 355–82. Madrid: Real Compañía de Impresores y Libreros, 1778.

– "Causas del atraso que se padece en España en orden a las Ciencias Naturales." In *Teatro crítico universal.* Vol. 2, 215–34. Madrid: Real Compañía de Impresores y Libreros, 1778.

– "Maravillas de la naturaleza." In *Teatro crítico universal.* Vol. 6, 225–56. Madrid: Real Compañía de Impresores y Libreros, 1778.

– "Racionalidad de los brutos." In *Teatro crítico universal.* Vol. 3, 189–223. Madrid: Real Compañía de Impresores y Libreros, 1778.

– *Suplemento del Teatro Critico o adiciones, y correcciones a muchos de los asuntos, que se tratan en los ocho Tomos de el dicho Teatro.* Madrid: Francisco de el Hierro, 1740.

Fernández, Enrique. *Anxieties of Interiority and Dissection in Early Modern Spain.* Toronto: U. of Toronto Press, 2015.

Fernández Valcarce, Vicente. *Desengaños filosóficos, que en obsequio de la verdad, de la religión y de la patria, da al público el doctor don Vicente Fernández Valcarce.* Vol 1. Madrid: Blas Román, 1787.

Ford, Richard. *A Handbook for Travelers in Spain, and Readers at Home.* Vol 2. Cambridge: Cambridge UP, 2012.

Foucault, Michel. *The Birth of the Clinic. An Archaeology of Medical Perception.* Translated by Alan Sheridan. New York: Vintage, 1994.

– *The Foucault Reader.* Edited by Paul Rabinow. New York: Pantheon, 1984.

– *The History of Sexuality.* Vol 1. Translated by Robert Hurley. New York: Penguin, 1978.

– *The Order of Things: An Archeology of the Human Sciences.* Translated by Alan Sheridan. New York: Random, 1970.

– *Power/Knowledge: Selected Interviews and Other Writings, 1972–1977.* Edited by Colin Gordon. Translated by Colin Gordon, Leo Marshall, John Mepham, and Kate Soper. New York: Pantheon, 1980.

– *The Politics of Truth.* Edited by Sylvère Lotringer. Translated by Lysa Hochcroth and Catherine Porter. Los Angeles: Semiotext(e), 2007.

– *Politics, Philosophy, Culture: Interviews and Other Writings, 1977–1984.* Edited by Lawrence D. Kritzman. Translated by Alan Sheridan. New York: Routledge, 1988.

– *Religion and Culture.* Edited by Jeremy R. Carrette. New York: Routledge, 1999.

– *Security, Territory, Population: Lectures at the Collège de France, 1977–1978.* Edited by Michel Snellart. Translated by Graham Burchell. New York: Picador, 2007.

– *Society Must Be Defended.* Edited by Mauro Bertani and Alessandro Fontana. Translated by David Macey. New York: Picador, 2003.

Fox, E. Inman. "Baroja y Schopenhauer: El árbol de la ciencia." In *Pío Baroja,* edited by Javier Martínez Palacio, 397–408. Madrid: Taurus, 1979.

Fraser, Benjamin. *Encounters with Bergson(ism) in Spain. Reconciling Philosophy, Literature, Film, and Urban Space.* Chapel Hill: U. of North Carolina Press, 2010.

Fraser, Mariam, Sarah Kember, and Celia Lury. "Inventive Life: Approaches to the New Vitalism." In *Inventive Life: Approaches to the New Vitalism,* edited by Mariam Fraser, Sarah Kember, and Celia Lury, 1–14. London: Sage, 2006.

Freud, Sigmund. *The Ego and the Id.* Edited by James Strachey. Translated by Joan Rivere. New York: Norton, 1962.

Fuchs, Thomas. *The Mechanization of the Heart: Harvey and Descartes.* Translated by Marjorie Grene. Rochester: Rochester UP, 2001.

Fuentes, Yvonne. "British Aesthetics and the Picturesque in Spain: Jovellanos's Affinity with England." *Hispania* 87, no. 2 (2004): 210–19.

Fuertes Herreros, José Luis. "La influencia de la metodología cartesiana en Sebastián Izquierdo (1601–81): Para la construcción de una filosofía barroca." *Studia Zamorensia* 8 (1987): 383–405.

Fuster García, Francisco. "'Afinidades electivas' entre literatura y sociología: el suicidio de Andrés Hurtado en *El árbol de la ciencia* como ejemplo de suicidio anómico." EPOS 25 (2009): 61–75.

Gago, Ramón, and Juan L. Carrillo. "La obra fisiológica de Ignacio María Ruiz de Luzuriaga (1763–1822) y su plagio del científico británico Adair Crawford (1748–1795)." *Dynamis* 1 (1981): 87–100.

Galdós, Benito P. *Episodios Nacionales: Mendizábal.* Madrid: Hijos de Tello, 1898.

Galino Carrillo, M. *Tres hombres y un problema.* Madrid: CSIC, 1953.

Gallart, Mikel Astrain. "The Unpublished Manuscripts by Ignacio María Ruiz de Luzuriaga (1736–1822) on Naval Hygiene." *Dynamis* 11 (1991): 437–63.

Gallego, José Andrés. *La crisis de la hegemonía española: siglo XVII.* Vol 8. Madrid: Rialp, 1991.

Galván González, Victoria. *La obra literaria de José de Viera y Clavijo.* Las Palmas de Gran Canaria: Ediciones del Cabildo de Gran Canaria, 1999.

Ganguilhem, Georges. *Knowledge of Life.* Edited by Paola Marrati and Todd Meyers. Translated by Stefons Geroulanos and Daniela Ginsburg. New York: Fordham UP, 2008.

Garber, Daniel. *Descartes Embodied: Reading Cartesian Philosophy through Cartesian Science.* Cambridge: Cambridge UP, 2001.

García Boiza, Antonio. *Don Diego de Torres Villarroel: Ensayo biográfico.* Madrid: Editora Nacional, 1949.

García Calderón, Ángeles. "La poesía inglesa de la naturaleza en el XVIII y su influencia en Meléndez Valdés." *Revista de literatura* 69, no. 138 (2007): 519–41.

Gaukroger, Stephen. *Descartes' System of Natural Philosophy.* Cambridge: Cambridge UP, 2002.

Gay, Peter. *The Enlightenment: The Science of Freedom.* New York: W.W. Norton & Co., 1977.

Genette, Gérard. *Paratexts: Thresholds of Interpretation.* Cambridge: Cambridge UP, 1997.

Giddens, Anthony. *The Consequences of Modernity.* Stanford: Stanford UP, 1990.

Gies, David T. "The Theater in Romantic Spain." In *The Cambridge History of Spanish Literature.* Edited by David T. Gies, 350–61. Cambridge: Cambridge UP, 2004.

Gigante, Denise. *Life: Organic Form and Romanticism.* New Haven: Yale UP, 2009.

Gil Fernández, Luis. "Pedro Laín Entralgo y la Historia de la Medicina Griega." *Estudios Griegos e Indoeuropeos* 14 (2004): 9–14.

Giner de los Ríos, Francisco. *Estudios de Literatura y Arte.* Madrid: Victoriano Suárez, 1876.

Gogorza y González, José. "Pluralidad de protoplasmas." *Boletín de la Institución Libre de Enseñanza* 10, no. 226 (1886): 200–3.

Gómez de Enterría, Josefa. "Notas sobre la traducción científica y técnica en el siglo XVIII," *Historia de la traducción.* Vol. 8. Edited by Brigitte Lépinette and Antonio Melero, 35–67. Valencia: Facultad de Filología de la Universidad de Valencia, 2003.

Gómez de la Serna, Gaspar. *Jovellanos, el español perdido.* 2 vols. Madrid: Sala, 1975.

Gómez de la Serna, Ramón. *Aphorisms – Ramón Gómez de la Serna.* Translated by Miguel González-Gerth. Chicago: Latin American Literary Review Press, 1990.

– *Cartas a mí mismo. Obras completas.* Vol. 14. Edited by Ioana Zlotescu, 667–743. Barcelona: Galaxia Gutenberg, 2002.

– "El concepto de la nueva literatura." *Obras Completas.* Vol. 1. Edited by Ioana Zlotescu, 149–76. Barcelona: Galaxia Gutenberg, 1996.

– *El drama del palacio deshabitado. Obras Completas.* Vol. 2. Edited by Ioana Zlotescu, 703–12. Barcelona: Galaxia Gutenberg, 1996, 523–49.

– *El teatro en soledad. Obras Completas.* Vol 2. Edited by Ioana Zlotescu, 151–223. Barcelona: Galaxia Gutenberg, 1996.

– *Morbideces. Obras Completas.* Vol. 1. Edited by Ioana Zlotescu, 455–532. Barcelona: Galaxia Gutenberg, 1996.

– "Mi autobiografía." *La sagrada cripta de Pombo.* Vol. 2, 640–746. Madrid: Visor, 1999.

– *Obras Completas.* Vols. 1 and 2. Edited by Ioana Zlotescu. Barcelona: Galaxia Gutenberg, 1996.

González, Zeferino. *La Biblia y la ciencia.* Sevilla: Izquierdo y Compañía, 1892.

González Ayensa, José, and José Alonso Quintanilla. *Refutación de las nuevas doctrinas del Dr. Broussais.* Madrid: Miguel de Burgos, 1825.

González Cuevas, Pedro. *El pensamiento político de la derecha española del siglo XX: De la crisis de la Restauración al Estado de Partidos (1898–2000).* Madrid: Tecnos, 2005.

González de Fauve, María Estela. "La práctica de la flebotomía en España a través de algunos tratados médicos (siglos XIV–XVI)." In *Mundos medievales: espacios, sociedades y poder.* Edited by Beatriz Arízaga Bolumburu et al., 1403–16. Santander: Universidad de Cantabria, 2014.

Goodman, David C. *Power and Penury: Government, Technology, and Science in Philip II's Spain.* Cambridge: Cambridge UP, 1988.

Goodwyn, Edmund. *The Connection of Life with Respiration; or, an Experimental Inquiry into the Effects of Submersion, Strangulation, and Several Kinds of Noxious Airs on Living Animals.* London: J. Johnson, 1788.

Gracia Noriega, Ignacio. "Jovellanos, viajero de cercanías y prosista romántico." *Boletín Jovellanista* 5.5 (2004): 115–25.

Granjel, Luis S. *Historia de la Real Academia Nacional de Medicina.* Madrid: RANM, 2006.

– "La medicina vasca de los siglos XVIII y XIX." *IX Congreso de Estudios Vascos,* 127–38. Bilbao: Eusko Ikaskuntza, 1983.

– *La medicina y los médicos en las obras de Torres Villarroel.* Salamanca: Universidad de Salamanca, 1952.

– "Panorama de la ciencia de la ilustración." *Ciencia, medicina y sociedad en la España ilustrada.* Edited by Juan Riera, 101–14. Valladolid: ICE, 1990.

– "Perfil histórico de la ciencia vasca." *Osasunaz* 2 (1992): 21–32.

Grassi, Ángela. *El copo de nieve.* Edited by Sánchez Llama. Madrid: Editorial Castalia, 1992.

– *Palmas y laureles.* Barcelona: Bastinos, 1884.

Greenblatt, Stephen. *Marvelous Possessions: The Wonder of the New World.* Chicago: U. of Chicago Press, 1991.

Grosz, Elizabeth. *Volatile Bodies: Toward a Corporeal Feminism.* Bloomington: Indiana UP, 1994.

Guerrero Herreros, Sebastián Miguel. *Medicina universal, o academias medicas, chirurgicas, chymicas, y pharmaceuticas.* 2 vols. Sevilla: Nicolas Vázquez, 1774, 1777.

Gutiérrez de los Ríos, Manuel. *Idioma de la naturaleza: con el que se enseña al médico como ha de curar con acierto los morbos agudos.* Madrid: Viuda de Eliséo Sanchez, 1768.

Haidt, Rebecca. *Embodying Enlightenment: Knowing the Body in Eighteenth-century Spanish Literature and Culture.* New York: St Martin's Press, 1998.

Hales, Katherine. *How We Become Posthuman: Virtual Bodies in Cybernetics, Literature, and Informatics.* Chicago: U. of Chicago Press, 1999.

Hall, Thomas. "Foreword." In René Descartes, *Treatise of Man.* Translated by Thomas Steele Hall. Cambridge, MA: Harvard UP, 1972.

Hammarberg, Gitta. *From the Idyll to the Novel: Karamazin's Sentimentalist Prose.* Cambridge: Cambridge UP, 1991.

Harvey, William. "An Anatomical Study on the Motion of the Heart and Blood in Animals." In *Medicine and Western Civilization,* edited by David J. Rothman, Steven Marcus, and Stephanie A. Kiceluk, 68–75. New Brunswick, NJ: Rutgers UP, 2003.

– *The Works of William Harvey,* MD. London: Sydenham Society, 1847.

Healy, Margaret. "Anxious and Fatal Contacts: Taming the Contagious Touch." In *Sensible Flesh: On Touch in Early Modern Culture,* edited by Elizabeth Harvey, 22–38. Philadelphia: U. of Penn Press, 2003.

Hedley Brooke, John. *Science and Religion: Some Historical Perspectives.* Cambridge: Cambridge UP, 1991.

Hendry, Petra Munro. *Engendering Curriculum History.* New York: Routledge, 2011.

Herazo, Héctor Rojas. *Rojas Herazo. Obra periodística, 1940–1970.* Tomo I. Edited and with an Introduction by Jorge García Usta. Medellín: Fondo Editorial Universidad EAFIT, 2003.

Hermosilla Molina, Antonio. *Cien años de medicina sevillana (La Regia Sociedad de Medicina y demás Ciencias de Sevilla en el siglo XVIII).* Sevilla: Diputación CSIC, 1970.

Herrero, Antonio María. *Physica moderna, experimental, systematica, donde se contiene lo mas curioso, y util de cuanto se ha descubierto en la Naturaleza.* Madrid: 1738.

Hervás y Panduro, Lorenzo. *Historia de la vida del hombre o idea del universo.* Vol. 3. Madrid: Imprenta Real, 1794.

– *El hombre físico o Anatomia humana fisico-filosofica.* Madrid: Administración del Real Arbitrio de Beneficencia, 1800.

Hill, Christopher. "William Harvey and the Idea of Monarchy." In *The Intellectual Revolution of the Seventeenth Century,* edited by Charles Webster, 160–96. New York: Routledge, 1974.

Hill, Ruth. *Sceptres and Sciences in the Spains: Four Humanists and the New Philosophy (ca. 1680–1740).* Liverpool: Liverpool UP, 2000.

Hillman, David. "Visceral Knowledge: Shakespeare, Skepticism, and the Interior of the Early Modern Body." In *The Body in Parts: Fantasies of Corporeality in Early Modern Europe,* edited by David Hillman and Carla Mazzio, 81–106. New York: Routledge, 1997.

Hillman, David, and Carla Mazzio. "Introduction: The Body in Parts." In *The Body in Parts: Fantasies of Corporeality in Early Modern Europe,* edited by David Hillman and Carla Mazzio, ix–xxvii. New York: Routledge, 1997.

Hollick, Frederick. *The Origin of Life and Processes of Reproduction in Plants and Animals.* Philadelphia: David McKay, 1878.

Hughes, H. Stuart. *Consciousness and Society: The Reorientation of European Social Thought, 1890–1930.* New Brunswick, NJ: Transaction, 2008.

Hunter, John. *Observations on Certain Parts of the Animal Oeconomy.* London: Longman, Orme, Brown, Green, & Longmans: 1837.

– *The Surgical Works of John Hunter, F.R.S.* Vol. 3. Edited by James F. Palmer. London: Longman, Rees, Orme, Brown, Green, and Longman, 1835.

Hurtado de Mendoza, Manuel. *El catecismo de la medicina fisiológica, o diálogos entre un sabio y un médico joven, discípulo del catedrático Broussais.* Madrid: Villalpando, 1826.

– *Vindicación y explicación de la medicina fisiológica en respuesta del escrito de los señores González-Ayensa, y Quintanilla.* Madrid: Fermin Villalpando, 1826.

Husserl, Edmund. *The Basic Problems of Phenomenology, from the Lectures, Winter Semester, 1910–1911.* Translated by Ingo Farin and James G. Hart. Dordrecht: Springer, 2006.

Hutchison Stirling, James. *As Regards Protoplasm in Relation to Professor Huxley's Essay on the Physical Basis of Life.* New Haven: Charles C. Chatfield, 1871.

Huxley, Thomas. *Protoplasm: The Physical Basis of Life.* Melbourne: Peter C. Alcock, 1869.

Hvidberg-Hansen, Gertrud, and Gertrud Oelsner. "The Triumph of Life." In *The Spirit of Vitalism: Health, Beauty, and Strength in Danish Art, 1890–1940,* edited by Gertrud Hvidberg-Hansen and Gertrud Oelsner, 10–45. Copenhagen: Museum Tusculanum Press, 2011.

Ilie, Paul. "El conocimiento a través de los sueños y la ilustración española: un juicio sobre Torres Villarroel." In *Revisión de Torres Villarroel,* edited by Manuel María Pérez López and Emilio Martínez Mata, 37–65. Salamanca: U. of Salamanca, 1998.

Isern, Damián. *Del desastre nacional y sus causas.* Madrid: Minuesa de los Ríos, 1900.

Israel, Jonathan I. "Counter-Reformation, Economic Decline, and the Delayed Impact of the Medical Revolution in Catholic Europe, 1550–1750." In *Health Care and Poor Relief in Counter-Reformation Europe,* edited by Ole Peter Greell,

Andrew Cunningham, and Jon Arrizabalaga, 39–54. New York: Routledge, 2005.

– "'The Decline of Spain': A Historical Myth?" *Past and Present* 91 (1981): 170–80.

– *The Dutch Republic and the Hispanic World.* Oxford: Oxford UP, 1986.

– *Radical Enlightenment: Philosophy and the Making of Modernity, 1650–1750.* Oxford: Oxford UP, 2001.

Izquierdo, José Joaquín. *Harvey, iniciador del método experimental.* México D.F.: Ediciones Ciencia, 1936.

– "On the Spanish Neglect of Harvey's 'De Motu Cordis,' for Three Centuries, and How It Was Finally Made Known to Spain and Spanish-speaking Countries." *Journal of the History of Medicine* (Winter 1948): 105–24.

Jackson, Noel. *Science and Sensation in Romantic Poetry.* Cambridge: Cambridge UP, 2008.

Jaspers, Karl. *Nietzsche: An Introduction to the Understanding of his Philosophical Activity.* Translated by Charles F. Wallraff and Frederick J. Schmitz. Baltimore: Johns Hopkins UP, 1997.

Javier Garrido, Francisco. *Discurso filosófico sobre las verdaderas nociones de la naturaleza Humana.* Madrid: Cano, 1799.

Jiménez García, Antonio. "La implantación del Krausopositivismo en España." In *Actas del IV Seminario de Historia de la Filosofía Española,* edited by Antonio Heredia Soriano, 649–59. Salamanca: U. de Salamanca, 1986.

Jiménez, Juan Ramón. *Diary of a Newlywed Poet.* Introduction by Michael P. Predmore. Translated by Hugh A. Harter. Selinsgrove: Susquehanna UP, 2004.

Johnson, Roberta. *Crossfire: Philosophy and the Novel in Spain, 1900–1934.* Lexington: UP of Kentucky, 1993.

Johnson, W.D. "Vida y ser en el pensamiento de Unamuno." *Crisis* 10 (1956): 9–25.

Jones, Donna V. *The Racial Discourses of Life Philosophy: Négritude, Vitalism, Modernity.* New York: Columbia UP, 2010.

Jongh-Rossel, Elena de. *Krausismo y la generación de 1898.* Valencia: Albatros Hispanofila, 1985.

Jovellanos, Gaspar Melchor de. *Cartas del viaje a Asturias.* Vols. 1 and 2. Edited by José Miguel Caso González. Gijón: Ayala, 1981.

– *Diarios.* Vols. 1, 2, and 3. Edited by Julio Somoza. Oviedo: Diputación de Asturias, 1953.

– "Epístola a Bátilo." In *Cartas del viaje a Asturias,* Vol. 1, edited by José Miguel Caso González, 89–93. Gijón: Ayala, 1981.

– "Epístola a Eymar." In *Colección de varias obras en prosa y verso.* Vol. 1, 1–7. Madrid: D. León Amarita, 1830.

– *Escritos literarios.* Edited by José Miguel Caso González. Madrid: Espasa-Calpe, 1987.

– *Oraciones y discursos.* Madrid: Enrique Teodoro, 1880.

– *Obras de Jovellanos.* Vols. 4, 5, and 7. Barcelona: Imprenta de Oliva, 1840.

– *Obras publicadas e inéditas.* Vols. 1 and 2. Edited by Cándido Nocedal. Madrid: Rivadeneyra, 1858.

Juanini, Juan Bautista. *Discurso político y physico, que muestra los movimientos y efectos que produce la fermentación y materias nitrosas.* Madrid: Mateo Llanos y Guzman, 1689.

Juaristi, Jon. *Miguel de Unamuno.* (Colección españoles eminentes). Madrid: Taurus, 2012.

Judovitz, Dalia. *The Culture of the Body: Genealogies of Modernity.* Ann Arbor: U. of Michigan Press, 2001.

Kamen, Henry. *The Spanish Inquisition: A Historical Revision.* New Haven: Yale UP, 2014.

Kant, Immanuel. *Critique of the Power of Judgment.* Translated by Paul Guyer. Cambridge: Cambridge UP, 2007.

Keevil, J.J., and L.M. Payne. *Francisco de la Reyna and the Circulation of the Blood.* London: Lancet, 1951.

Kemp, Martin, and Marina Wallace. *Spectacular Bodies: The Art and Science of the Human Body from Leonardo to Now.* Berkeley: U. of California Press, 2001.

Knight, David. *The Making of Modern Science.* Cambridge: Polity, 2009.

Knoef, Rina. "Practicing Chemistry 'After the Hippocratical Manner.'" In *New Narratives in Eighteenth-century Chemistry,* edited by Lawrence Principe, 63–76. Dodrecht: Springer, 2007.

Korsmeyer, Carolyn. *Savoring Disgust: The Foul and the Fair in Aesthetics.* Oxford: Oxford UP, 2011.

Krause, Karl Christian Friedrich. *Ideal de la humanidad para la vida, con introducción y comentarios.* Translated by Julián Sanz del Río. Madrid: Galiano, 1860.

Kyle, Donald G. *Spectacles of Death in Ancient Rome.* New York: Routledge, 1998.

La Rubia Prado, Francisco. *Alegorías de la Voluntad: Pensamiento orgánico, retórica y deconstrucción en la obra de Miguel de Unamuno.* Madrid: Prodhufi, 1996.

Lafuente, Antonio, and Nuria Valverde. *Los mundos de la ciencia en la ilustración española.* Madrid: Fundación Española para la Ciencia y la Tecnología, 2003.

– "Space Production and Spanish Imperial Geopolitics." In *Science in the Spanish and Portuguese Empires, 1500–1800,* edited by Daniela Bleichmar, Paula De Vos, Kristine Huffine, and Kevin Sheehan. Stanford: Stanford UP, 2009.

Laín Entralgo, Pedro. "La obra de William Harvey y sus consecuencias." In *Historia universal de la medicina,* vol. 4, edited by Laín Entralgo, 235–49. Madrid: Salvat, 1973.

– "Mecanicismo, vitalismo, y empirismo. (Siglos XV–XVIII)." In *Historia de la Medicina,* vol. 4, 245–386. Barcelona: Salvat, 1978.

Lázaro Lorente, Luis M. "Naturismo, Eugenesia y Educación en España." In *Education, Physical Activity and Sport in a Historical Perspective*, edited by Jordi Montes and Pere Solà i Gussinyer, 318–25. Cataluña: Secretaria General de Deporte, 1992.

Leder, Drew. "A Tale of Two Bodies: The Cartesian Corpse and the Lived Body." In *The Body in Medical Thought*, edited by Drew Leder, 17–36. Dordecht: Springer.

Lennon, Thomas M. "The Problem of Individuation among the Cartesians." In *Individuation and Identity in Early Modern Philosophy: Descartes to Kant*, edited by Kenneth F. Barber and Jorge J.E. Garcia. Albany: SUNY UP, 1994.

Lenoir, Timothy. *The Strategy of Life: Teleology and Mechanics in Nineteenth-century German Biology*. Chicago: Chicago UP, 1982.

Lesaca, Juan Martín de. *Formas ilustradas a la luz de la razón*. Madrid: Juan de Ariztia, 1717.

Letamendi y Manjarrés, José de. *Plan de reforma de la patología general y su clínica*. Madrid: Aurelio J. Alaria, 1878.

Linares, Augusto González de. *Obra completa*. With an introduction by Carlos Nieto Blanco. Santander: U. de Cantabria, 2013.

Litvak, Lily. *A Dream of Arcadia: Anti-Industrialism in Spanish Literature, 1895–1905*. Austin: U. of Texas Press, 2011.

Llansol, Francsico de. *Carta a don Antonio Hernández médico titular de la villa de Benigamin, sobre el sistema de Guillermo Cullen en orden a la causa próxima de la calentura, y su impugnación por el Dr. Juan Brown, con una censura del sistema Browniano*. Valencia: Joseph de Orga, 1802.

– *Discurso sobre la incertidumbre y prejuicio del sistema de doctor Juan Brown*. Valencia: Oficina del Diario, 1803.

Llorca, Jaume Josa. "La Historia Natural en la España del siglo XIX: Botánica y Zoología." In *La ciencia en la España del siglo XIX*, edited by José María López Piñero, 109–52. Madrid: Marcial Pons, 1992.

Loeb, Jacques. *The Mechanistic Conception of Life: Biological Essays*. Chicago: U. of Chicago Press, 1912.

Lofthouse, Richard A. *Vitalism in Modern Art, c. 1900–1950: Otto Dix, Stanley Spencer, Max Beckmann, and Jacob Epstein*. Lewiston, NY: Edwin Mellen, 2005.

Lopez, François. "Los novatores en la Europa de los sabios." *Studia historica. Historia Moderna* 14 (1996): 95–111.

Lorenzo Álvarez, Elena. *Nuevos mundos poéticos: La poesía filosófica de la Ilustración*. Oviedo: Universidad de Oviedo, 2002.

López Pérez, Miguel. "Novatores or Alchemists? A Spanish Historiographical Problem." In *Chymia: Science and Nature in Medieval and Early Modern Europe*, edited by Miguel López-Pérez, Didier Kahn, and Mar Rey-Bueno. Newcastle upon Tyne: Cambridge Scholars Publishing, 2010, 331–66.

López Piñero, José. "Andrés Piquer y el hipocratismo en la España de la ilustración." In *Andrés Piquer: Las epidemias de Hipócrates con observaciones prácticas de los antiguos y modernos*, 9–37. Introduction by José María López Piñero. Madrid: Ministerio de Sanidad y Consumo, 1987.

– *Ciencia y técnica en la sociedad española de los siglos XVI y XVII.* Barcelona: Labor, 1979.

– *Diccionario histórico de la ciencia moderna en España.* Vol. 2. Barcelona: Península, 1983.

– "Enfermedad y medicina en la España del siglo XIX." *Aula-Historia Social* 7 (2001): 18–43.

– "The Faculty of Medicine of Valencia: Its Position in Renaissance Europe." In *Universities and Sciences in Renaissance Europe*, edited by Mordechai Feingold and Víctor Navarro-Brotóns, 65–82. Dordrecht: Springer, 2006.

– "Harvey's Doctrine of the Circulation of the Blood in Seventeenth-century Spain." *Journal of the History of Medicine* 28 (1973): 230–42.

– "Juan de Cabriada y el movimiento *novator* de finales del siglo XVII: Reconsideración después de treinta años." *Asclepio* 45, no. 1 (1993): 3–53.

– "Juan de Cabriada y las primeras etapas de la iatroquímica y de la medicina moderna en España." *Cuadernos de la Historia de la Medicina Española* 2 (1962): 129–54.

– "La iatroquímica de la segunda mitad del siglo XVII." In *Historia universal de la medicina*, edited by Pedro Laín Entralgo, 279–95. Barcelona: Salvat, 1973.

– "Las ciencias médicas en la España del siglo XIX." In *La ciencia en España del siglo XIX*, edited by José López Piñero, 193–240. Madrid: Marcial Pons, 1992.

– *Santiago Ramón y Cajal.* Valencia: Universitat de València, 2006.

López Piñero, José, and José Pardo Tomás. *La influencia de Francisco Hernández (1515–1587) en la constitución de la botánica y la materia médica moderna.* Valencia: CSIC, 1996.

López Piñero, José, Pedro González Blanco, and José Jiménez Blanco. *Historia y sociología de la ciencia española.* Madrid: Alianza, 1979.

López Silvestre, Federico A. "Dios y la naturaleza. El desarrollo de la Teología Natural en España y en Galicia en el siglo XVIII." *SEMATA* 14 (2002): 417–53.

López Terrada, María Luz. "The Control of Medical Practice under the Spanish Monarchy during the Sixteenth and Seventeenth Centuries." In *Beyond the Black Legend: Spain and the Scientific Revolution*, edited by Víctor Navarro-Brotóns and William Eamon, 283–94. Valencia: CSIC, 2007.

Lorenzo Álvarez, Elena de. *Nuevos mundos poéticos: la poesía filosófica de la ilustración.* Oviedo: Universidad de Oviedo, 2002.

Lovejoy, Arthur O. *The Great Chain of Being: The Study of the History of an Idea.* Introduction by Peter J. Stanlis. New Brunswick, NJ: Transaction, 2010.

Lozano, Luis. "El vitalismo y el concepto del héroe en Pío Baroja: la influencia de Nietzsche." PhD dissertation, University of Tennessee, 1973.

Luzuriaga, Ignacio María Ruiz de. *Disertación médica sobre el cólico de Madrid inserta en las memorias de la Real Academia de Medicina de Madrid.* Madrid: Imprenta Real, 1796.

– *Sobre la respiración y la sangre consideradas como origen y primer principio de la vitalidad de los animales.* Madrid: Imprenta Real, 1797.

Lyotard, Jean François. *Lessons on the Analytic and the Sublime.* Translated by Elizabeth Rottenberg. Stanford: Stanford UP, 1994.

MacArthur, Elizabeth J. *Extravagant Narratives. Closure and Dynamics in the Epistolary Form.* Princeton: Princeton UP, 1990.

Machado, Antonio. *Poesías completas.* Edited by Manuel Alvar. Madrid: Austral, 2001.

Macherey, Pierre. *A Theory of Literary Production.* New York: Routledge, 1978.

Maestre de San Juan y Muñoz, Aureliano. *Tratado elemental de histología normal y patológica precedido de una técnica de laboratorio.* 2nd ed. Madrid: Nicolás Moya, 1885.

Magallón, Jesús Pérez. *Construyendo la modernidad: la cultura española en el tiempo de los novatores (1675–1725).* Madrid: CSIC, 2002.

Malthus, Thomas Robert. *Population: The First Essay.* Foreword by Kenneth E. Boulding. Ann Arbor: U. of Michigan, 1959.

Mandado Gutiérrez, Ramón E. "Factores estético vitalistas en la obra de Pío Baroja." PhD dissertation, Universidad Complutense de Madrid, 1992.

Manning, Patricia W. *Voicing Dissent in Seventeenth-century Spain: Inquisition, Social Criticism, and Theology in the Case of* El Criticón. Boston: Brill, 2009.

Manrique, Jorge. "Copla por la muerte de su padre." In *An Anthology of Spanish Poetry,* edited by John A Crow, 22–31. Baton Rouge: LSU Press, 1979.

Manso, Josep Arimany, et al. "Bicentenario del nacimiento del profesor Dr. Pere Mata i Fontanet." *Revista española de medicina legal* 37, no. 3 (2011): 87–9.

Maravall, José Antonio. "El pensamiento político en España a comienzos del siglo XIX: Martínez Marina." *Revista de Estudios Políticos* 81 (1955): 29–82.

Marías, Javier. *Understanding Spain.* Rio Piedras: U. of Puerto Rico, 1990.

Marinetti, F.T. "Manifesto of Futurist Dance." In *Selected Writings,* edited by R.W. Flint, 137–41. New York: Farrar, Straus & Giroux, 1972.

Martín de Pedro, Ezequiel. *Discurso leído en la universidad central en el acto solemne de recibir la investidura de doctor de la Facultad de Medicina—¿Cuáles son las ventajas prácticas de la escuela vitalista, sobre la escuela orgánica y anatómica?* Madrid: Imprenta de José M. Ducazal, 1865.

Martínez, Martín. *Anatomía completa del hombre.* Madrid: Miguel Francisco Rodríguez, 1745.

– *Juicio final de la astrología, en defensa del Teatro Crítico Universal, dividido en tres discursos.* Madrid: Diego López de Haro, 1727.

– *Medicina sceptica y cirugía moderna.* Vol 1. Madrid: Gerónimo Roxo, 1722.

– *Philosophia sceptica, extracto de la physica antigua y moderna.* Madrid: Francisco López, 1750.

Martínez Mata, Emilio. *Los 'sueños' de Diego de Torres Villarroel.* Salamanca: Universidad de Salamanca, 1990.

Martínez-Vidal, Àlvar. *El nuevo sol de la medicina en la ciudad de los reyes.* Zaragoza: Pórtico, 1990.

– *Neurociencias y revolución científica en España: la circulación neural.* Madrid: CSIC, 1989.

Martínez-Vidal, Àlvar, and José Pardo Tomás. "Las consultas y juntas de médicos como escenarios de controversia científica y práctica médica en la época de los novatores (1687–1725)." *Dynamis* 22 (2002): 303–25.

– "Un siglo de controversias: la medicina española de los novatores a la ilustración." In *La ilustración y las ciencias: para una historia de la objetividad,* edited by Josep Lluís Barona, Javier Moscoso, and Juan Pimentel, 107–35. Valencia: Universitat de València, 2003.

Mata y Fontanet, Pedro. *Compendio de toxicología general y particular.* 3rd edition. Madrid: Carlos Bailly-Baillere, 1857.

– *Doctrina médico filosófica española sostenida durante la gran discusión sobre Hipócrates y las escuelas hipocráticas.* Madrid: Carlos Bailly-Baillere, 1860.

– *Examen crítico de la homeopatía. Lecciones dadas en el ateneo científico y literario de Madrid.* Vol. 2. Madrid: Manini Hermanos, 1852.

– *Fotografías íntimas: Colección de poesías.* Madrid: Rojas, 1874.

– *Hipócrates y las escuelas hipocráticas.* Madrid: Manuel Rojas, 1859.

– *Tratado de la razón humana en sus estados intermedios.* Madrid: Carlos Bailly-Bailliere, 1864.

– *Tratado de Medicina y Cirugía Legal, Teoría y Práctica. Seguido de un compendio de Toxicología.* Vol. 1. 4th ed. Madrid: Carlos Bailly-Baillere, 1866.

Mayr, Ernst. "What Is the Meaning of 'Life'?" In *The Nature of Life: Classical and Contemporary Perspectives from Philosophy and Science,* edited by Mark A. Bedau and Carol E. Cleland, 88–101. Cambridge: Cambridge UP, 2010.

McClelland, Ivy L. *Diego de Torres Villarroel.* Boston: Twayne, 1976.

– *Ideological Hesitancy in Spain.* Liverpool: Liverpool UP, 1991.

McCulloch, John A. *The Dilemma of Modernity: Ramón Gómez de la Serna and the Spanish Modernist Novel.* New York: Peter Lang, 2007.

McFadden, JohnJoe, and Jim Ali-Khalili. *Life on the Edge: The Coming Age of Quantum Biology.* New York: Broadway, 2014.

Medical Press Circular. January to June 1872. London: 1872.

Meléndez Valdés, Juan. "Dedicatoria. A una señora." In *Poesías de Juan Meléndez Valdés.* Vol. 2, 7. Paris: Librería Hispano Americana, 1832.

– "Inmensidad de la Naturaleza, y bondad inefable de su Autor." In *Poesías de Juan Meléndez Valdés.* Vol. 4, 115–23. Paris: Librería Hispano Americana, 1832.

– "Orden del universo y cadena admirable de sus seres." In *Poesías de Juan Meléndez Valdés.* Vol. 4, 314–32. Paris: Librería Hispano Americana, 1832.

– "Vanidad de las quejas del hombre contra su hacedor." In *Poesías de Juan Meléndez Valdés.* Vol. 4, 66–72. Paris: Librería Hispano Americana, 1832.

Memorial literario, instructivo y curioso de la corte de Madrid. Mayo de 1786. Número XXIX. Tomo VIII. Madrid: Imprenta Real, 1786.

Menéndez y Pelayo, Marcelino. *Historia de los heterodoxos españoles.* Vol. 2. Madrid: CSIC, 1992.

Merleau-Ponty, Maurice. *Phenomenology of Perception.* Translated by Colin Smith. London: Routledge, 2002.

Miqueo, Consuelo. "Introducción y difusión del brusismo en España." In *Ciencia en expansión: Estudios sobre la difusión de las ideas científicas y médicas en España (siglos XVIII y XIX),* edited by Elvira Arquiola and José Martínez-Pérez, 161–80. Madrid: Editorial Complutense, 1995.

Mitchell, Robert. *Experimental Life: Romanticism in Romantic Science and Literature.* Baltimore: Johns Hopkins UP, 2013.

Molas Ribalta, Pedro. "El primer siglo XVIII." In Historia general de España y América. Vol. 10, *La España de las reformas,* 3–39. Madrid: Rialp, 1990.

– "Prólogo." In *La transición del siglo XVII al XVIII: Entre la decadencia y la reconstrucción,* edited by Molas Ribalta, 5–29. Madrid: Espasa-Caple, 1993.

Molina Martínez, José Luis. *Anticlericalismo y literatura en el siglo XIX.* Murcia: U. de Murcia, 1998.

Morales Moya, Antonio. "Jovellanos: Ilustración y liberalismo, 1759–1812." In *Homenaje a D. José Luis Comillas,* 31–58. Sevilla: Universidad de Sevilla, 2000.

Moreno, Luis Jiménez. "Azorín, pequeño filósofo vitalista." *Anales del seminario de historia de la filosofía* 15 (1998): 223–42.

– "El vitalismo científico y filosófico en el siglo XIX." *Antropológica* 1 (1973): 120–35.

– *Hombre, historia y cultura. Desde la ruptura innovadora de Nietzsche.* Madrid: Espasa Calpe, S.A., 1983.

– *Nietzsche: Antropología y nihilismo.* Valencia: Politénica, 2001.

– *Prácticas del saber en filósofos españoles: Gracián, Unamuno, Ortega y Gasset, E. d'Ors, Tierno Galván.* Barcelona: Anthropos, 1991.

– "Vitalismo estético en la nueva filosofía española de fin de siglo XIX." *Anuario Filosófico* 31, no. 1 (1998): 179–200.

Morris, Charles. "The Variability of Protoplasm." *The American Naturalist* 17 (1883): 926–31.

Mosácula Cabrera, Juan. *Elementos de fisiología especial o humana.* Madrid: Hijos de Catalina Piñuela, 1830.

Muñoz Utrilla, Raúl. "D. Juan de Cabriada y Borrás. Regidor perpetuo de la Villa de Ágreda, Médico Real e impulsor de la renovación científica en España." In *Ágreda: La villa de las tres culturas,* edited by Carlos de la Casa, 25–31. Soria: Imprenta Provincial de Soria, 2011.

Navajas Navarro, Gonzalo. *El paradigma de la enfermedad y la literatura en el siglo XX.* Valencia: PUV, 2013.

Navarro-Brotóns, Víctor. "Descartes y la introducción en España de la ciencia moderna." In *La filosofía de Descartes y la fundación del pensamiento moderno: Actas del XII Encuentro de la Sociedad Castellano-Leonesa de Filosofía (Salamanca, 13–16 de noviembre de 1996).* Salamanca: Sociedad Castellano-Leonesa de Filosofía, 1997.

– "Science and Enlightenment in Eighteenth-century Spain: The Contribution of the Jesuits before and after the Expulsion." In *The Jesuits II: Cultures, Sciences, and the Arts, 1540–1773,* edited by John W.O'Malley et al., 390–404. Toronto: Toronto UP, 2002.

Navarro-Brotóns, Víctor, and William Eamon. "Preface." In *Beyond the Black Legend: Spain and the Scientific Revolution,* edited by Víctor Navarro-Brotóns and William Eamon. Valencia: CSIC, 2007.

Navarro Domínguez, Eloy. *El intelectual adolescente: Ramón Gómez de la Serna (1905–1912).* Madrid: Biblioteca Nueva, 2003.

Nichols, Ashton. "The Loves of Plants and Animals: Romantic Science and the Pleasure of Nature." Romantic Circles Praxis Series. November 2001. https://www.rc.umd.edu/praxis (accessed 1 June 2015).

Nicolás, César. *Ramón y la greguería: morfología de un género nuevo.* Cáceres: Universidad de Extremadura, 1988.

Nieremberg, Juan Eusebio. *Obras cristianas.* Vol. 1. Sevilla: Lucas Martin, 1686.

Nieto y Serrano, Matías. "Discurso sobre Calderón de la Barca, considerado como filósofo y en relación a la medicina." In *Anales de la Real Academia Nacional de Medicina.* Vol. 3, 214–33. Madrid: Manuel Tello, 1881.

Nietzsche, Friedrich. *Beyond Good and Evil.* Edited by Rolf-Peter Hortsmann and Judith Norman. Cambridge: Cambridge UP, 2002.

– *Birth of Tragedy and The Case of Wagner.* Translated by Walter Kaufmann. New York: Random House, 1967.

– *The Complete Works of Friedrich Nietzsche.* Vol. 11: *Unpublished Writings from the Period of Unfashionable Observations.* Translated by Richard T. Gray. Stanford: Stanford UP, 1995.

– *Human, All Too Human: A Book for Free Spirits.* Translated by R.J. Hollingdale. Introduction Richard Schacht. Cambridge: Cambridge UP, 1996.

– *On the Genealogy of Morals and Ecce Homo.* Edited and Translated by Walter Kaufmann. New York: Random House, 1967.

– *Thus Spoke Zarathustra.* Translated by Graham Parkes. Oxford: Oxford UP, 2005.

– *Twilight of the Idols.* Translated by Richard Polt. Introduction Tracy Strong. Indiana: Hackett, 1997.

– *Will to Power.* Translated by Walter Kaufmann and R.J. Hollingdale. New York: Vintage, 1967.

Nordau, Max. *Degeneration.* New York: Appleton & Co., 1895.

Normandin, Sebastian, and Charles T. Wolfe. "Vitalism and the Scientific Image: An Introduction." In *Vitalism and the Scientific Image in Post-Enlightenment Life Science, 1800–2010,* edited by Sebastian Normandin and Charles T. Wolfe, 1–18. New York: Springer, 2013.

Nozick, Martin. "Introduction." In *Selected Works of Miguel de Unamuno.* Vol. 7: *Ficciones: Four Stories and a Play.* Translated by Anthony Kerrigan, xiii–xxix. Princeton UP, 1976.

Núñez Ruiz, Diego. *La mentalidad positiva en España: Desarrollo y crisis.* Madrid: Tucar, 1975.

Olson, Paul R. *The Great Chiasmus: Word and Flesh in the Novels of Unamuno.* West Lafayette: Purdue UP, 2003.

Olson, Richard G. *Science and Religion, 1450–1900: From Copernicus to Darwin.* Westport, CT: Greenwood, 2004.

Onians, Richard B. *The Origins of European Thought: About the Body, the Mind, the Soul, the World, Time, and Fate.* Cambridge: Cambridge UP, 1951.

Orringer, Nelson. "El Nietzsche de Baroja: filósofo-poeta modernista." *Anales del Semanario de Historia de la Filosofía* 25 (2008): 137–50.

Ortega Cantero, Nicolás. "Paisaje, historia e identidad nacional: La imagen moderna de la Cartuja del Paular, en el Valle de Lozoya." In *Historia, clima y paisaje: Estudios geográficos en memoria del profesor Antonio López Gómez,* 187–99. Valencia: Universidad de Valencia, 2004.

Ortega y Gasset, José. "El siglo XVIII, educador." *Obras Completas.* Vol. 2. Madrid: Revista de Occidente, 1966.

– *Obras Completas.* Vol. 5. Madrid: Revista de Occidente, 1970.

– "Thoughts on Pío Baroja." *Critical Inquiry* 1, no. 2 (1974): 415–46.

Otis, Laura. *Organic Memory: History and the Body in the Late Nineteenth and Early Twentieth Centuries.* Lincoln: U. of Nebraska P, 1994.

Packham, Catherine. *Eighteenth-century Vitalism: Bodies, Culture, Politics. New York*: Palgrave Macmillan, 2012.

Pagden, Anthony. "The Reception of the 'New Philosophy' in Eighteenth-century Spain." *Journal of the Warburg and Courtauld Institutes* 54 (1988): 126–40.

Pardo Tomás, José. *Ciencia y censura: La Inquisición Española y los libros científicos en los siglos XVI y XVII.* Madrid: CSIC, 1991.

– *El médico en la palestra: Diego Mateo Zapata (1664–1745) y la ciencia moderna en España.* Salamanca: Junta de Castilla y León, 2004.

Parkinson, Saz, and Carlos Roberto. *Positively Negative: Pío Baroja the Essayist.* Newark, DE: Juan de la Cuesta, 2010.

Paster, Gail Kern. "Nervous Tension: Networks of Blood and Spirit in the Early Modern Body." In *The Body in Parts: Fantasies of Corporeality in Early Modern Europe,* edited by David Hillman and Carla Mazzio, 107–25. New York: Routledge, 1997.

Patt, Beatrice P. *Pío Baroja.* New York: Twayne, 1971.

Payne, Stanley G. *A History of Fascism, 1914–1945.* Madison: U. of Wisconsin Press, 1995.

– *Spanish Catholocism: An Historical Overview.* Madison: U. of Wisconsin Press, 1984.

Paz, Octavio. *Children of the Mire: Modern Poetry from Romanticism to the Avant-Garde.* Translated by Rachel Phillips. Harvard: Harvard UP, 1991.

Peraita, Carmen. "Catalina Clara Ramírez de Guzmán: 'A una sangría del pie de una dama.'" In *Seis siglos de poesía española escrita por mujeres: Pautas poéticas y revisiones críticas,* edited by Dolores Romero López et al., 162–76. New York: Peter Lang, 2007.

Peraza, Martín. *Segundo tomo de sermones cuadragesimales, y de la resurrección.* Salamanca: Andres Renaut, 1604.

Perdiguero, Enrique. "Medicine in the Spanish Enlightenment." In *The Popularization of Medicine,* edited by Roy Porter, 160–93. New York: Routledge, 1992.

– "Popularizando la ciencia: el caso de la medicina doméstica en la España de la Ilustración." In *La ilustración y las ciencias: para una histórica de la objetividad,* edited by Josep Lluís Barona, Javier Moscoso, and Juan Pimentel, 155–78. Valencia: Universitat de València, 2003.

Pereyra, Miguel A. "Hubo una vez unos maestros ignorantes: Los maestros de primeras letras y el movimiento ilustrado de las academias." *Revista de educación* 1 (1988): 193–224.

Pérez López, Manuel María. "Para una revisión de Torres Villarroel." In *Revisión de Torres Villarroel,* edited by Manuel María Pérez López and Emilio Martínez Mata, 13–35. Salamanca: U. of Salamanca, 1998.

Pérez y López, Antonio Javier. *Principios del orden esencial de la naturaleza, establecidos por fundamento de la moral y política, y por prueba de la religión: Nuevo sistema filosófico.* Madrid: Imprenta Real, 1785.

Peset, José Luis. "Academias y ciencias en la Europa Ilustrada." *Península* (2003): 391–400.

– "Enlightenment and Renovation in the Spanish University." In *Universities and Science in the Early Modern Period,* edited by Mordechai Feingold and Victor Navarro-Brotóns, 231–9. Dordrecht: Springer, 2006.

Peset, José Luis, and Salvador Albiñana. *La ciencia en las universidades españolas.* Madrid: Akal, 1996.

Peset, Mariano, and José Luis Peset. "Las universidades españolas del siglo XIX y las ciencias." In *La ciencia en la España del siglo XIX*, edited by José María López Piñero, 17–49. Madrid: Marcial Pons, 1992.

Pick, Daniel. *Faces of Degeneration: A European Disorder, c.1848–c.1918*. Cambridge: Cambridge UP, 1989.

Pimentel, Juan. "The Iberian Vision: Science and Empire in the Framework of a Universal Monarchy, 1500–1800." *Osiris* 15 (2000): 17–30.

Piñal, Francisco A. *La biblioteca de Jovellanos (1778)*. Madrid: CSIC, 1984.

Piñera y Siles, Bartolomé. "Prólogo del traductor." In *Elementos de medicina práctica* by William Cullen, i–xii. Madrid: Benito Cano, 1799.

Piquer, Andrés. "Andrés Piquer y el hipocratismo en la España de la ilustración." In *Andrés Piquer: Las epidemias de Hipócrates con observaciones de los antiguos y modernos*, 9–37. Madrid: Ministerio de Sanidad y Consumo, 1987.

– *Discurso sobre el sistema del mecanismo*. Madrid: Joachin Ibarra, 1768.

– *Lógica Moderna o arte de hallar la verdad y perfeccionar la razón*. Valencia: Joseph García, 1747.

Piquer, José Antonio. *Sobre la nueva doctrina médico-fisiológica, y sobre los llamados impropiamente sistemas de medicina, en vista del Catecismo de Broussais, y de su Refutación y Vindicación publicadas en Madrid en los dos últimos años*. Madrid: Miguel de Burgos, 1827.

Plato. *The Republic and Other Works*. Translated by Benjamin Jowlett. New York: Anchor, 1973.

Ponce de León, José. *Phisiología chímica del cuerpo humano*. Vol. 2. Granada: Imprenta de las Heredera de Don Nicolás Moreno, 1804.

Popper, Karl. *Conjectures and Refutations*. London: Routledge, 1962.

Powers, John C. *Inventing Chemistry: Herman Boerhaave and the Reform of the Chemical Arts*. Chicago: U. of Chicago Press, 2012.

Predmore, R.L. "Flesh and Spirit in the Works of Unamuno." *PMLA* 70, no. 4 (1955): 587–605.

Preus, Anthony. *Historical Dictionary of Ancient Greek Philosophy*. New York: Rowan & Littlefield, 2015.

Priestly, Joseph. *Disquisitions concerning Matter and Spirit*. Vol. 1. Birmingham: J. Johnson, 1782.

Puertas, José Luis. "El doctor Pío Baroja (1872–1956)." *Ars Médica* 2 (2006): 198–215.

Pullman, Bernard, and Axel Reisinger. *The Atom in the History of Human Thought*. New York: Oxford UP, 2001.

Purrington, Robert D. *Physics in the Nineteenth Century*. Piscataway, NJ: Rutgers UP, 2006.

Quevedo, Francisco de. *Obras Completas*. Vol. 3, *Prosa*. Madrid: Aguilar, 1974.

Quinlan, Sean M. *The Great Nation in Decline: Sex, Modernity, and Health Crises in Revolutionary France, c. 1750–1850*. Burlington, VT: Ashgate, 2007.

Rabaté, Jean Claude, and Colette Rabaté. *Miguel de Unamuno: Una biografía*. Madrid: Taurus, 2009.

Rabinbach, Anson. *The Human Motor: Energy, Fatigue, and the Origins of Modernity*. Berkeley: U. of California Press, 1992.

Rama, Carlos M. *La crisis española del siglo XX*. Madrid: Fondo de Cultura Económica, 1976.

Ramos, Tomás. "La polémica hipocrática en la medicina española del siglo XIX." *Archivo iberoamericano de historia y de la medicina antropológica médica* 6 (1954): 115–61.

Ramos Gorostiza, José Luis. "Jovellanos y la naturaleza: economía, ciencia y sentimiento." *Scripta Nova* 11, no. 241 (June 15, 2007). http://www.raco.cat/index.php /ScriptaNova/article/view/71814 (accessed May 29, 2015).

Reill, Peter Hans. "The Legacy of the 'Scientific Revolution': Science and Enlightenment." In *The Cambridge History of Science*. Vol. 4, *Eighteenth-century Science*, edited by Roy Porter, 21–43. Cambridge: Cambridge UP, 2003.

– *Vitalizing Nature in the Enlightenment*. Berkeley: U. of California Press, 2005.

Richards, Robert J. *The Romantic Conception of Life: Science and Philosophy in the Age of Goethe*. Chicago: U. of Chicago Press, 2004.

Richerand, Anthelme. *Elements of Physiology*. Translated by Gilbert de Lys. London: R. Gilbert, 1819.

Riera Palmero, Juan. "El vitalismo y enfermedad." In *Historia de la enfermedad*, edited by A. Albarracín, 245–53. Madrid: EMA, 1987.

– "Los estudios en el Reino Unido de Ignacio María Ruiz de Luzuriaga (Documentos y epistolario, 1785–1787)." *Cuadernos de historia de la medicina española* 14 (1975): 269–301.

– "Los médicos y la medicina: Un capítulo de la obra del jesuita Vicente Requeno y Vives (1743–1811)." In *Vicente Requeno (1743–1811): Jesuita y restaurador del mundo grecolatino*, edited by Antonio Astorgano Abajo, 263–78. Zaragoza: Universidad de Zaragoza, 2012.

Riffaterre, Michel. *Fictional Truth*. Baltimore: Johns Hopkins UP, 1990.

Rivero Gómez, Miguel Ángel. "Cuaderno XXVI. Notas íntimas y reflexiones políticas del joven Unamuno. Un texto inédito." *Cuadernos de la Cátedra Miguel de Unamuno* 42 (2006): 189–221.

Roberts, Stephen G.H. *Miguel de Unamuno o la creación del intelectual moderno*. Salamanca: Universidad de Salamanca, 2007.

Rodríguez, Antonio José. *Medicina palpable, y escuela de la naturaleza donde se franquean importantes doctrinas, y seguras reglas para el más recto uso de la sangría, ajustadas a las inviolables leyes del movimiento con cuatro problemas físico-médicos y una disertación mecánico-médica*. Madrid: Imprenta Real, 1743.

Rodríguez Sánchez, Rafael. *La introducción de la medicina moderna en España: una imagen de nuestra renovación científica (1687–1727) desde la teoría de la ciencia de Thomas S. Kuhn.* Sevilla: Alfar, 2005.

Roe, Shirley A. "*Anatomia animata.* The Newtownian physiology of Albrecht von Haller." In *Transformation and Tradition in the Sciences: Essays in Honour of I. Bernard Cohen,* edited by Everett Mendelsohn, 273–300. Cambridge: Cambridge UP, 1983.

– *Matter, Life, and Generation: 18th Century Embryology and the Haller-Wolff Debate.* Cambridge: Cambridge UP, 1981.

Roger, Jacques. *Buffon.* Translated by Sarah Lucille Bonnefoi. Ithaca, NY: Cornell UP, 1989.

– *The Life Sciences in Eighteenth-century French Thought.* Edited by Keith R. Benson. Translated by Robert Ellrich. Stanford, Stanford University Press, 1998.

Rojas, Clemente, and Simón de Rubio. *Ensayo sobre las variedades de la vida común que vegetan en Andalucía.* Madrid: Villalpando, 1807.

Romeo, Lorenço. *Desengaño del abuso de la sangría y purga.* Tarragona: Gabriel Roberto, 1623.

Rousseau, George. "The Perpetual Crises of Modernism and the Traditions of Enlightenment Vitalism: With a note on Mikhail Bakhtin." In *The Crisis in Modernism,* edited by Frederick Burwick and Paul Douglass, 15–75. Cambridge: Cambridge UP, 1992.

– *On the Origins of Inequality.* Translated by G.D.H. Cole. New York: Cosimo, 2005.

Rousseau, Jean-Jacques. *The Major Political Writings of Jean-Jacques Rousseau.* Edited and Translated by John T. Scott. Chicago: U. of Chicago Press, 2012.

Rozemond, Marleen. *Descartes's Dualism.* Cambridge, MA: Harvard UP, 1998.

Rueda, Ana. "Jovellanos en sus escritos íntimos: El paisaje y la emoción estética de 'lo sublime.'" *Revista de literatura* 68 (2006): 489–502.

Ruiz-Manjón, Octavio. "Notas sobre Miguel de Unamuno en la crisis del reinado de Alfonso XIII." In *Miguel de Unamuno: Estudios sobre su obra II,* edited by Ana Chaguaceda Toledano, 277–86. Salamanca: Ediciones Universidad de Salamanca.

Rumeu de Armas, Antonio. *De arte y de historia.* Madrid: Real Academia de Historia, 2004.

Ruse, Michael. *Monad to Man: The Concept of Progress in Evolutionary Biology.* Harvard: Harvard UP, 2009.

Rütten, Thomas. "Hippocrates and the Construction of 'Progress' in Sixteenth- and Seventeenth-century Medicine." In *Reinventing Hippocrates,* edited by David Cantor, 37–58. Burlington, VT: Ashgate, 2002.

Sala Catalá, José. *Ideología y Ciencia Biológica en España entre 1860 y 1881: La difusión de un paradigma.* Madrid: CSIC, 1987.

Sánchez Alonso, J.B. "Jovellanos y la geología." *La Nueva España,* 14 October 1973.

– "Jovellanos visto por un geólogo." *La Nueva España,* 16 December 1973.

Sánchez-Blanco, Francisco. *La ilustración en España.* Madrid: Akal, 1997.

Sánchez Corredera, Silverio. *Jovellanos y el jovellanismo, una perspectiva filosófica (estudio histórico y filosófico sobre Jovellanos, en la perspectiva del Materialismo Filosófico, desde la ética, la política y la moral).* Biblioteca Filosofia en Español. Oviedo: Gustavo Bueno, 2004.

Sánchez Llama, Iñigo. *Galería de escritoras isabelinas: La prensa periódica entre 1833 y 1895.* Madrid: Cátedra, 2000.

Sánchez-Moscoso Hermida, Angustias. "¿Química o alquimia en la medicina de los novatores? (1675–1725)." In *Actas VIII Congreso de la Sociedad Española de la Historia de las Ciencias y las Técnicas,* edited by Luis Español, José Javier Escribano, and María Ángeles García, 757–76. Logroño: Universidad de la Rioja, 2004.

Santa Cruz, Ponce de. *De impedimentis magnorum auxiliorum in Morborum curatione.* Madrid: Imprenta Real, 1629.

Santander Rodríguez, Teresa. *Hipócrates en España (Siglo XVI).* Madrid: Dirección General de Archivos y Bibliotecas, 1971.

Santo-Tomás, Enrique García. *La musa refractada: literatura y óptica en la España del Barroco.* Madrid: Iberoamericana/Vervuert, 2014.

Sanz del Río, Julián. "Prólogo." In *Ideal de la humanidad para la vida, con introducción y comentarios* by Karl Christian Friedrich Kraus, xi–xxii. Translated by Julián Sanz del Río. Madrid: Galiano, 1860.

Sarreal, Julia J.S. *The Guaraní and Their Missions. A Socioeconomic History.* Stanford: Stanford UP, 2014.

Sarrión Mora, Adelina. *Médicos e Inquisición en el siglo XVII.* Cuenca: U. de Castilla la Mancha, 2006.

Sawday, Jonathan. *The Body Emblazoned. Dissection and the Human Body in Renaissance Culture.* New York: Routledge, 1995.

Saz-Orosco, Carlos. *Dios en Juan Ramón.* Madrid: Razón y fe, 1966.

Scheler, Max. "Lived Body, Environment, and Ego." In *The Philosophy of the Body: Rejections of Cartesian Dualism,* edited by Stuart F. Spicker, 159–83. Chicago: Quadrangle Books, 1970.

Schelling, Friederich Wilhelm Joseph. *System of Transcendental Idealism.* Translated by Peter Heath. Introduction by Michael Vater. Charlottesville: U. of Virgina Press, 1997.

Schickore, Jutta. *The Microscope and the Eye: A History of Reflections, 1740–1870.* Chicago: U. of Chicago Press, 2007.

Schopenhauer, Arthur. *The World as Will and Representation.* Vol. 1. Translated by E.F. Payne. New York: Dover, 1969.

Schouls, Peter A. *Descartes and the Enlightenment.* Montreal: McGill-Queen's UP, 1989.

Schrödinger, Erwin. *What Is Life? The Physical Aspect of the Living Cell, with Mind and Matter and Autobiographical Sketches.* Cambridge: Cambridge UP, 2012.

Sebold, Russell P. "El desencanto romántico de Jovellanos." In *Ensayos de meditación y crítica literaria,* 277–80. Salamanca: U. de Salamanca, 2004.

– *Trayectoria del romanticismo español: desde la ilustración hasta Bécquer.* Barcelona: Editorial Crítica, 1983.

Segel, Harold B. *Body Ascendant: Modernism and the Physical Imperative.* Baltimore: John Hopkins UP, 1998.

Seifert, Josef. *What Is Life? The Originality, Irreducibility, and Value of Life.* Amsterdam: Rodopi, 1984.

Shilling, Chris. *The Body and Social Theory.* London: Sage, 2003.

Simmel, Georg. *Georg Simmel on Individuality and Social Forms.* Edited and with an Introduction by Donald N. Levine. Chicago: Chicago UP, 1971.

Sinclair, Alison. "Authority of Authenticity? The Battle of the Cultures at the Millennial Crossroads." In *Spain's 1898 Crisis: Regenerationism, Modernism, Post-colonialism,* edited by Joseph Harrison and Alan Hoyle, 132–45. Manchester: Manchester UP, 2000.

– *Uncovering the Mind: Unamuno, the Unknown, and the Vicissitudes of Self.* Manchester: Manchester UP, 2001.

Skirry, Justin. *Descartes and the Metaphysics of Human Nature.* London: Continuum, 2005.

Slater, John. "Fables of Communication: The Rhetoric of Investigative Methodology in Golden Age Literature." In *Beyond the Black Legend: Spain and the Scientific Revolution,* edited by Victor Navarro-Brotóns and William Eamon, 209–20. Valencia: CSIC, 2007.

– "Rereading Cabriada's *Carta*: Alchemy and Rhetoric in Baroque Spain." *The Colorado Review of Hispanic Studies* 7 (2009): 67–80.

Smethurst, Paul. *Travel Writing and the Natural World, 1768–1840.* New York: Palgrave Macmillan, 2012.

Smith, C.U.M., Eugenio Frixione, Stanley Finger, and William Clower. *The Animal Spirit Doctrine and the Origins of Neurophysiology.* Oxford: Oxford UP, 2012.

Smith, Pamela, and Paula Findlen. "Commerce and the Representation of Nature in Art and Science." In *Merchants and Marvels: Commerce, Science, and Art in Early Modern Europe,* edited by Pamela Smith and Paula Findlen, 1–28. New York: Routledge, 2002.

Smith, Wesley D. *The Hippocratic Tradition.* Ithaca, NY: Cornell UP, 1979.

Sobejano, Gonzalo. *Nietzsche en España.* Madrid: Gredos, 1967.

– "Prólogo: El primer teatro de Ramón Gómez de la Serna." In *Ramón Gómez de la Serna. Obras completas.* Vol. 2, edited by Ioana Zlotescu, 13–41. Barcelona: Galaxia Gutenberg, 1996.

Soldevilla, Francisco Fabra. *Elogio histórico del Doctor en Medicina Don Ignacio María Ruiz de Luzuriaga.* Madrid: Leon Amarita, 1822.

Sotelo Vázquez, Adolfo. "Pío Baroja en 1901." *Bulletin Hispanique* 92, no. 2 (1990): 857–80.

Souto Rodríguez, José Manuel. *El siglo XVIII español: cultura, ciencia y filosofía.* Madrid: Mileto, 2004.

Spackman, Barbara. *Decadent Genealogies: The Rhetoric of Sickness from Baudelaire to D'Annunzio.* Ithaca, NY: Cornell UP, 1989.

Spinoza, Baruch. *Spinoza: Complete Works.* Translated by Samuel Shirley. Edited and with an Introduction by Michael L. Morgan. Indianapolis: Hackett Publishing Co., 2002.

Stafford, Barbara Maria. *Body Criticism: Imaging the Unseen in Enlightenment Art and Medicine.* Cambridge, MA: MIT Press, 1991.

Steedman, Carolyn. *Strange Dislocations. Childhood and the Idea of Human Interiority, 1780–1930.* Cambridge, MA: Harvard UP, 1995.

Steinke, Hubert. *Irritating Experiments: Haller's Concept and the European Controversy of Irritability and Sensibility, 1750–1790.* Amsterdam: Rodopi, 2005.

Stewart-Williams, Steve. *Darwin, God, and the Meaning of Life: How Evolutionary Theory Undermines Everything You Thought You Knew.* Cambridge: Cambridge UP, 2010.

Subirats, Eduardo. *La ilustración insuficiente.* Madrid: Taurus, 1984.

Sullivan, Richard Joseph. *A View of Nature, In Letters to a Traveller among the Alps, with Reflections on Atheistical Philosophy Now Exemplified in France.* Vol. 3. London: Becket & Pall Mall, 1794.

Tamayo, J.A. "Jovellanos y el romanticismo." *Sí* 3 (1944): 6.

Tanganelli, Paolo. "Del erostratismo al amor de Dios: en torno al avantexto de *Del sentimiento trágico de la vida.*" In *Miguel de Unamuno: Estudios sobre su obra II,* edited by Ana Chaguaceda Toledano, 175–94. Salamanca: Ediciones Universidad de Salamanca, 2003.

Templin, E.H. "Pío Baroja and Science." *Hispanic Review* 15, no. 1 (1947): 165–92.

Terrada Ferrandis, María Luz. *La anatomía microscópica en España: la doctrina de la fibra yla utilización del microscopio en España durante el Barroco y la Ilustración.* Salamanca: Universidad de Salamanca, 1969.

– "La teoría de la fibra y el tejido celular en la obra de Sebastián Miguel Guerrero (1774)." In *Actas del IV Congreso Español de Historia de la Medicina,* 197–9. Granada: SEHM, 1973.

Thacker, Eugene. *After Life.* Chicago: U. of Chicago Press, 2010.

Thomson, Ann. *Bodies of Thought: Science, Religion, and the Soul in the Early Enlightenment.* Oxford: Oxford UP, 2008.

Thorndike, Lynn. *Magic and Experimental Science – Part 4.* New York: Columbia UP, 1958.

Thorndike, Townsend. "A History of Bleeding and Leeching." *British Medical and Surgical Journal* 197, no. 12 (1927): 437–77.

Timmermans, Stefan. *Sudden Death and the Myth of CPR.* Philadelphia: Temple UP, 1999.

Tissot, Samuel Auguste. *Aviso a los literatos y personas sedentarias sobre su salud.* Zaragoza: Francisco Moreno, 1771.

Tixedas, Cristóbal. *Verdad defendida, y respuesta a Fileatro, a la carta medico chymica, que contra los Medicos de la Junta, de la Corte, y contra todos los Galenicos, le escriviò el Doctor Medico-Chymico D. Juan de Cabriada.* Barcelona: Antonio Ferrer, 1688.

Torrebadella-Flix, Xavier. "Del espectáculo acrobático a los primeros gimnasios modernos: una historia de las compañías gimnástico-acrobáticas en la primera mitad del siglo XIX en España." *Aloma* 31, no. 2 (2013): 67–84.

Torrente Ballester, Gonzalo. *Literatura española contemporánea.* Vol 1. Madrid: Guadarrama, 1969.

Torres Villarroel, Diego de. *Anatomía de todo lo visible, e invisible de ambas esferas.* Salamanca: Antonio Villarroel, 1738.

– *Entierro del juicio final y vivificación de la astrología.* In *Libro segundo en que se continúan las ideas extractadas de los pronósticos y dedicatorias que empiezan desde el año 1745 hasta el de 1753, y al final otros papeles sobre los mismos asuntos.* Vol. 9, 191–257. Madrid: Viuda de Ibarra, 1798.

– *Tratado de los temblores y otros movimientos de la tierra.* Madrid: Convento de la Merced, 1748.

– *Tratado físicos, médicos y morales, vida natural y católica.* Vol. 4. Madrid: Viuda de Ibarra, 1794.

– *Viaje fantástico.* Sevilla: López de Haro, 1725.

– *Vida y ascendencia de don Diego de Torres.* Barcelona: Linkgua, 2012.

Tuana, Nancy. "Preface." In *Feminism and Science,* edited by Nancy Tuana, vii–xi. Bloomington: Indiana UP, 1989.

Tubbs, Nigel. *Contradiction of Enlightenment: Hegel and the Broken Middle.* Aldershot: Ashgate, 1997.

Tuells, José. "The Unpublished Essay on Vaccines by María Ruiz de Luzuriaga (1763–1822)." *Dynamis* 35, no. 2 (2015): 459–80.

Tuells, José, J.L. Duro Torrijos, and I. Díaz-Delgado Peñas. "Anotaciones a la biografía de Ignacio María Ruiz de Luzuriaga (1763–1822): el inicio de la vacunación contra la viruela en España." *Vacunas* 13, no. 3 (2012): 128–32.

Tully, James. *Strange Multiplicity: Constitutionalism in an Age of Diversity.* Cambridge: Cambridge UP, 1995.

Unamuno, Miguel de. "¡Adentro!" In *Miguel de Unamuno. Obras Completas*. Vol. 8, *Ensayos*, edited by Ricardo Senabre, 312–20. Madrid: Fundación José Antonio de Castro, 2007.

– "Educación por la historia." In Miguel de Unamuno, *Ensayos II*, 1059–66. Madrid: Aguilar, 1945.

– *En torno al casticismo. Ensayos I*. Madrid: Residencia de Estudiantes, 1916.

– *Escritos bilbainos (1879–1894)*. Edited, with an introduction, by José Antonio Ereño Altuna and Ana Isasi Saseta. Bilbao: Ikur, 1999.

– *Escritos socialistas: Artículos inéditos sobre el socialismo, 1894–1922*. Edited by Pedro Ribas. Madrid: Ayuso, 1976.

– "Faith." In *Selected Works of Miguel de Unamuno*. Vol. 5, *The Agony of Christianity and Essays on Faith*, 148–64. Translated by Anthony Kerrigan. Princeton, NJ: Princeton UP, 1974.

– "Ideocracia." In *Miguel de Unamuno. Obras Completas*. Vol. 8, *Ensayos*, edited by Ricardo Senabre, 323–32. Madrid: Fundación José Antonio de Castro, 2007.

– "La regeneración del teatro español." In *Miguel de Unamuno. Obras Completas*, vol. 8, *Ensayos*, edited by Ricardo Senabre, 227–55. Madrid: Fundación José Antonio de Castro, 2007.

– "La vida es sueño: Reflexiones sobre la reflexión de España." In *Miguel de Unamuno, Obras Completas*. Vol. 8, *Ensayos*, edited by Ricardo Senabre, 301–9. Madrid: Fundación José Antonio de Castro, 2007.

– *Obras completas*. Vol 6. Barcelona: Vergara, 1968.

– *Our Lord Don Quijote: The Life of Don Quijote and Sancho, with Related Essays*. Translated by Anthony Kerrigan. Introduction Walter Starkie. Princeton, NJ: Princeton UP, 1967.

– *The Private World: Selections from the Diario íntimo and Selected Letters, 1890–1936*. Translated by Anthony Kerrigan, Allen Lacy, and Martin Nozick. Introduction by Allen Lacy. Princeton, NJ: Princeton UP, 1984.

– "Prólogo." In *Orígenes del conocimiento (El hambre)*, by Ramón Turró, 7–18. Madrid: Maroto, 1921.

– *Recuerdos e intimidades*. Prologue by Julián Marías. Madrid: Tebas, 1975.

– "Selected Letters, 1890–1936." *Selected Works of Miguel de Unamuno*. Vol. 2, *The Private World: Selections from the Diario Íntimo and Selected Letters 1890–1936*, 85–260. Translated by Anthony Kerrigan, Allen Lacy and Martin Nozick. Introduction Allen Lacy. Princeton, NJ: Princeton UP, 1974.

– "Socialismo." In *Unamuno socialista: Páginas inéditas de don Miguel*, by D. Gómez Molleda, 85–129. Madrid: Narcea, 1978.

– *The Tragic Sense of Life in Men and Nations: Selected Works of Miguel de Unamuno*. Vol. 4. Translated by Anthony Kerrigan. Introduction by Salvador de Madriaga. Princeton, NJ: Princeton UP, 1972.

Usandizaga, Manuel. *Los Ruiz de Luzuriaga: Eminentes médicos vascos "ilustrados."* Salamanca: U. de Salamanca, 1964.

Valdés y Valdés, Manuel Álvarez. *Jovellanos: vida y pensamiento.* Oviedo: Novel, 2012.

Valera, Manuel, and López Fernández, Carlos. "Giuseppe Cervi, Guillaume Jacobe y las relaciones entre la 'Regia sociedad de Medicina y demás Ciencias de Sevilla' y la 'Royal Society of London' en 1736." *Dynamis* 18 (1998): 377–426.

Vall, Xavier. "La ciència en la poesia catalana del segle XIX." *Caplletra* 39 (2005): 9–59.

Valverde, Nuria. "Small Parts: Crisóstomo Martínez (1638–1694), Bone Histology, and the Visual Making of Body Wholeness." *Isis* (2009): 505–36.

Van Baumer, Franklin Le. *Main Currents of Western Thought.* New Haven: Yale UP, 1978.

Van Berkel, Klaas. "Science in the Service of the Enlightenment, 1700–1795." In *A History of Science in the Netherlands: Survey, Themes, and Reference,* edited by Klass van Berkel, Albert van Helden, and Loewijk Palm, 68–94. Leiden: Brill, 1999.

Vázquez, Félix Bello. *Pío Baroja. El hombre y el filósofo.* Salamanca: Universidad de Salamanca, 1993.

Vega, Jesusa. *Ciencia, arte e ilusión en la España ilustrada.* Madrid: CSIC, 2010.

Vesalius. *On the Fabric of the Human Body, Books VI and VII.* Translated by William Frank Richardson and John Burd Carman. Novato: Norman Publishing, 2009.

Viguera, Baltasar de. *La fisiología de la mujer; o sea, historia analítica de su constitución física y moral, de sus atribuciones y fenómenos sexuales, y de todas sus enfermedades.* Vol. 3. Madrid: Ortega y compañía, 1827.

Vila, Anne C. *Enlightenment and Pathology: Sensibility in the Literature and Medicine of Eighteenth-century France.* Baltimore: John Hopkins UP, 1998.

Viñes, José Javier. *La sanidad española en el siglo XIX a través de la Junta Provincial De Sanidad de Navarra (1870–1902).* Navarra: Departamento de Salud, 2006.

Wall, Geoffrey. "Translator's Preface." In *A Theory of Literary Production,* by Pierre Macherey, xii–xiv. New York: Routledge, 1978.

Wallace, Alfred Russel. *Contributions to the Theory of Natural Selection: A Series of Essays.* London: Macmillan & Co., 1885.

Watson, James D., and Andrew Berry. *DNA: The Secret of Life.* New York: Random House, 2009.

Wayne, Randy O. *Plant Cell Biology: From Astronomy to Zoology.* London: Academic Press, 2009.

Weber, Max. *The Protestant Ethic and the Spirit of Capitalism.* Translated by Talcott Parsons. New York: Charles Scribner's Sons, 1958.

– "Science and the Disenchantment of the World." In *Conflict, Order, and Action: Readings in Sociology*, edited by Edward Ksenych and David Liu, 13–20. Toronto: Canadian Scholars' Press.

Wellek, René. *Concepts of Criticism.* New Haven: Yale UP, 1963.

Whitehead, Alfred North. *Science and the Modern World.* Cambridge: Cambridge UP, 2011.

Williams, Elizabeth Ann. *A Cultural History of Medical Vitalism in Enlightenment Montpellier.* Burlington, VT: Ashgate, 2003.

– "Hippocrates and the Montpellier Vitalists in the French Medical Enlightenment." In *Reinventing Hippocrates*, edited by David Cantor, 157–77. Burlington, VT: Ashgate, 2002.

– *The Physical and the Moral: Anthropology, Physiology, and Philosophical Medicine in France, 1750–1850.* Cambridge: Cambridge UP, 1994.

Willis, Martin. *Science and Literature.* New York: Palgrave, 2014.

Wilmshurst, Walter Leslie. *Christianity and Science: The Latest Phase.* Boston: R.G. Badger, 1909.

Wilson, Renate. *Pious Traders in Medicine. A German Pharmaceutical Network in Eighteenth-century North America.* University Park: Pennsylvania State UP, 2000.

Withers, Charles W.J. *Placing the Enlightenment: Thinking Geographically about the Age of Reason.* Chicago: U. of Chicago Press, 2007.

Wolfe, Charles T. "Empiricist Heresies in Early Modern Thought." In *The Body as Object and Instrument of Knowledge: Embodied Empiricism in Early Modern Science*, edited by Charles T. Wolfe and Ofer Gal, 333–44. New York: Springer.

Wolloch, Nathaniel. *History and Nature in the Enlightenment: Praise of the Mastery of Nautre in Eighteenth-Century Historical Literature.* New York: Routledge, 2016.

Woodward, Geoffrey. *Philip II.* New York: Routledge, 1992.

Wordsworth, William. *The Collected Poems of William Wordsworth.* Kent: Chatham, 1994.

Zabaleta, Juan. *Obras históricas, políticas, filosóficas y morales.* Barcelona: Texidò, 1704.

Zapata, Diego Mateo. *Verdadera apología en defensa de la medicina racional filosófica.* Madrid: Ferrando, 1691.

Zavala, Iris M. *Clandestinidad y libertinaje erudito en los albores del siglo XVIII.* Barcelona: Ariel, 1978.

– "Hacia un mejor conocimiento del siglo XVIII español." *Nueva Revista de Filología Hispánica* 20, no. 2 (1971): 341–60.

– *Historia de la literatura española.* Vol. 3, *Siglos XIX y XX.* Edited by J.M. Díez Borque. Madrid: Guadiana, 1974.

– *Románticos y socialistas: Prensa española del XIX.* Madrid: Siglo XXI, 1972.

Index

Page references in italics indicate a figure.